Remembering the Cold

Remembering the Cold War examines how, more than two decades since the collapse of the Soviet Union, Cold War legacies continue to play crucial roles in defining national identities and shaping international relations around the globe. Given the Cold War's blurred definition – it has neither a widely accepted commencement date nor unanimous conclusion – what is to be remembered? This book illustrates that there is, in fact, a huge body of 'remembrance', and that it is more pertinent to ask: what should be included and what can be overlooked?

Over five chapters, this richly illustrated volume considers case studies of Cold War remembering from different parts of the world, and engages with growing theorization in the field of memory studies, specifically in relation to war. David Lowe and Tony Joel afford careful consideration to agencies that identify with being 'victims' of the Cold War. In addition, the concept of arenas of articulation, which envelops the myriad spaces in which the remembering, commemorating, memorializing, and even revising of Cold War history take place, is given prominence.

David Lowe is Professor of History at the Alfred Deakin Research Institute, Deakin University, Australia. His research interests include the end of empires in Asia and the uses of history by politicians. He is the author/editor of seven books, including *Australian Between Empires* (2010) and *Menzies and the Great World Struggle* (1999).

Tony Joel is Lecturer in History at Deakin University, Australia. A former German Academic Exchange Service (DAAD) scholarship holder, his research interests include war memory and commemoration. Publications include *The Dresden Firebombing: Memory and the Politics of Commemorating Destruction* (2013).

Remembering the modern world
Series Editors: David Lowe and Tony Joel

The *Remembering the Modern World* series throws new light on the major themes in the field of history and memory in a global context. The series investigates relationships between state-centred practices and other forms of collective and individual memory; looks at the phenomenon of anniversaries and national days in the context of global and national identities; shows how some cities and sites play active roles in generating acts of remembrance and asks why some phenomena and events are remembered more widely and easily than others.

Remembering the Cold War
David Lowe and Tony Joel

Forthcoming titles in the series:

Remembering Genocide
Nigel Eltringham and Pam Maclean

Remembering the Great War
Bart Ziino

Remembering the Cold War

Global contest and national stories

David Lowe and Tony Joel

LONDON AND NEW YORK

First published 2013
by Routledge
2 Park Square, Milton Park, Abingdon, Oxon OX14 4RN

and by Routledge
711 Third Avenue, New York, NY 10017

Routledge is an imprint of the Taylor & Francis Group, an informa business

British Library Cataloguing in Publication Data
A catalogue record for this book is available from the British Library

Library of Congress Cataloging in Publication Data
Lowe, David, 1964-
Remembering the Cold War : global contest and national stories / David
Lowe and Tony Joel.
pages cm. – (Remembering the modern world)
Includes bibliographical references and index.
1. Cold War. 2. Cold War–Influence. 3. World politics–1945-1989.
I. Joel, Tony. II. Title: Remembering the Cold War.
D843.L616 2013
909.82'5–dc23
2013026371

ISBN: 978-0-415-66153-9 (hbk)
ISBN: 978-0-415-66154-6 (pbk)
ISBN: 978-1-315-85040-5 (ebk)

Typeset in Bembo
by Taylor & Francis Books

MIX
Paper from
responsible sources
FSC
www.fsc.org FSC® C013056

Printed and bound in Great Britain by
TJ International Ltd, Padstow, Cornwall

Contents

Illustrations

Series editors' foreword

Organized thematically, this ambitious new series takes a broad view of what constitutes remembering great historical events and phenomena in the late modern period (i.e. since 1789). Volumes in the series draw on such things as: ceremonies associated with anniversaries and national days; episodes of memorialization and commemoration including museum exhibitions; filmic representations and popular culture; public discourse and debate as shaped and reflected by speeches of political and civic leaders; and school curricula etc. *Remembering the Modern World* makes a fresh contribution to memory studies by placing much emphasis on narrative (with substantive introductory chapters addressing the main theoretical and methodological issues), and by drawing on the strengths of complementary disciplines including History, Cultural Heritage, Anthropology, Journalism Studies, Sociology, International Relations, and Law. To complement the text, wherever appropriate volumes are encouraged to make widespread use of maps, timelines, illustrations, and especially photographs taken by contributing authors during field research.

The series offers a comparative glance across the contemporary world in a manner that explores both the reach of globalization and the insistence of localizing forces. As for themes projected for examination throughout the series, these include *inter alia* war and peace, genocide, political and social emancipation, imperialism, decolonization, terrorism, sporting triumphs, tragedies, and rivalries, heroes and villains, political revolutions and constitutional crises, and feminism.

Each book in the series will start with an overview of the most significant theoretical and methodological approaches historians and other scholars have deployed in relation to the kind of material being explored within the volume. The aim is to sketch the theoretical and methodological landscape, enabling interested readers to follow key references to what has become a well-theorized field. The substantive chapters thereafter might be theoretically suggestive, but primarily focus on presenting narrative constructed around whatever case studies are being remembered.

Remembering the Modern World throws new light on key themes for students, scholars, and general readers of contemporary history. The series aims to: provide greater understanding of relationships between state-centred practices and other forms of shared or common memories; examine the phenomenon of anniversaries and national days in the contexts of global and national identities; explore the 'transition zones' between narrative histories and explorations of history's significance in contemporary societies; and ponder why some phenomena and events are remembered more widely and easily than others. In its ambitious geographical and topical reach, the series suggests connections and invites new research questions that inform further historical inquiry.

David Lowe
Tony Joel

Acknowledgements

Our first debt of gratitude is to Eve Setch, Senior Editor of History at Routledge, whose initial enthusiasm helped this series to take shape. Eve not only provided crucial support in commissioning the series, but also offered much creative input as the concept was first conceived and then developed. More recently, we would also like to thank Editorial Assistant Paul Brotherston for his interest, vigour, and forbearance in guiding this book through to its completion. And we are grateful to Production Editor Sarah Douglas and everyone else at Routledge involved in the production of this book.

For their support we thank the Contemporary Histories Research Group in the Alfred Deakin Research Institute, Deakin University, and the Menzies Centre for Australian Studies, King's College London. For much appreciated and ongoing collegiality at Deakin University we thank Rohan Bastin, Sarah Coates, Helen Gardner, Pam Maclean, Eric Meadows, Jon Ritchie, Mathew Turner, Chris Waters, Chad Whelan, and Bart Ziino. From elsewhere, we wish to thank Joan Beaumont, the Australian National University (ANU), Jost Dülffer, University of Cologne, Justinian Jampol and his helpful staff at the Wende Museum and Archive of the Cold War, Johannes Bach Rasmussen of the Baltic Initiative and Network, and David Reynolds, University of Cambridge.

We thank Zora Barisic, Xavier Fowler, and Ella Simson, promising History undergraduate students who made valuable early contributions to this project while undertaking internships at the Alfred Deakin Research Institute. We also thank Lisa Couacaud, Mark Humphries, and Murray Noonan for excellent research assistance. And in particular we thank Donna-Lee Frieze for her exceptional contribution to the research behind this book.

Those acknowledged above helped to make this book possible but, of course, the views that follow remain our own responsibility.

We also wish to express our gratitude to the following places for granting us permission to publish photographs of their collections: Memento Park, Statue Park Museum, Budapest, Hungary; the Museum of Communism, Prague, the Czech Republic; and the Wende Museum and Archive of the Cold War, Culver City, California, the United States.

Finally, our greatest debt of gratitude is owed to our respective families. For their unstinting love, encouragement, and understanding, our thanks to Andrea Shimmen and Ben and Tristan Lowe, and to Shan, Bethany, Chelsea, Sienna, and Lucas Joel.

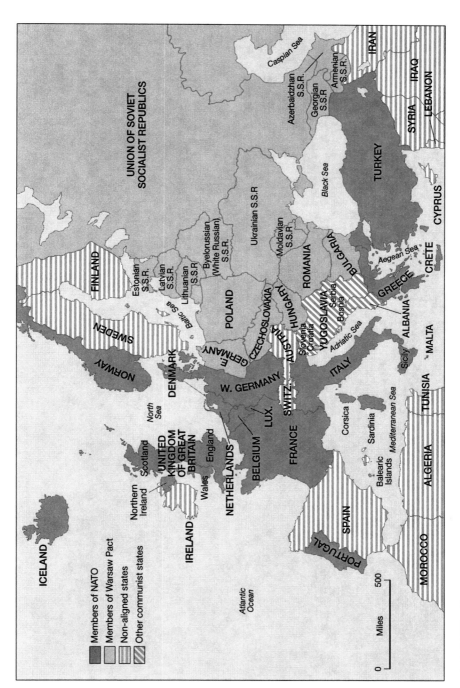

Map 1 Cold War Europe

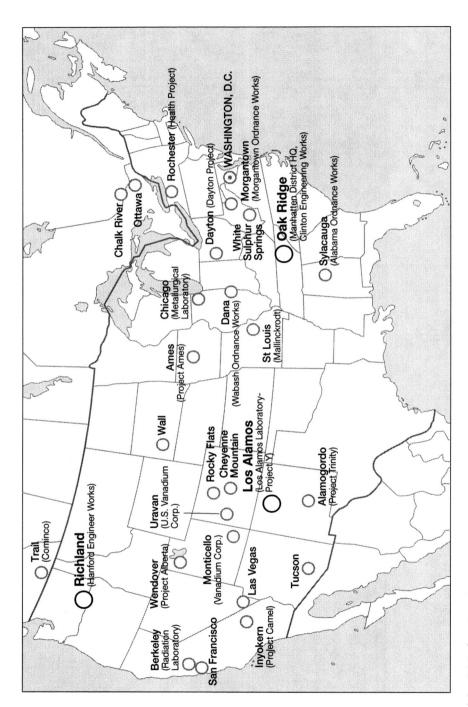

Map 2 Nuclear America

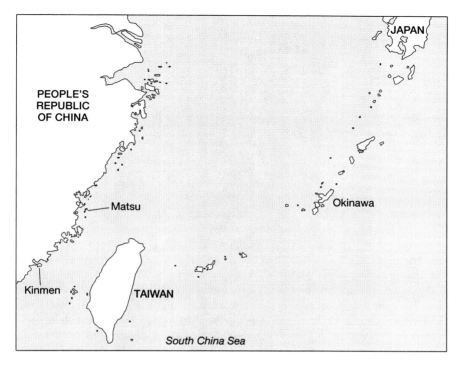

Map 3 Asia's Cold War Archipelago

Introduction

Tucked away in a niche at the north-east corner of the Reichstag in central Berlin, a red-brick section of wall stands in sharp contrast to the light sandstone colour of the German parliament building. If viewed from across the adjacent River Spree, the brick-wall segment appears inconsequential as it is dwarfed by Paul Wallot's impressive neo-baroque historical edifice. Upon closer inspection, however, it becomes evident that this peculiar piece of wall – consisting of 32 rows of bricks capped by a concrete plinth and standing at around 12 feet high – is deceptively significant in size. It is even greater in symbolism. What is it? When was it erected in this rather conspicuous location, and, moreover, why? On 17 June 2009, in a modest ceremony attended by Germany's chancellor Angela Merkel and president of the lower house (*Bundestag*) Norbert Lammert, the wall segment and an accompanying bilingual plaque was unveiled by Bronisław Komorowski. A trained historian and future president of Poland, Komorowski was acting in his then role as Speaker of the Polish parliament (*Sejm*) when gifting to the Federal Republic of Germany a piece of the Gdansk shipyard wall that Lech Wałęsa had scaled in August 1980 to organize the strike that led to the founding of the Solidarity movement (*Solidarność*). The brass plaque's German-Polish inscription reads: 'To commemorate the struggle of "Solidarity" for freedom and democracy and Poland's contribution to Germany's reunification and a politically united Europe'.[1] The ceremony's date was no coincidence: in an important pre-emptive step toward stabilizing Central Europe's political situation following the fall of the Berlin Wall, on 17 June 1991 Helmut Kohl and his Polish counterpart Jan Krzysztof Bielecki had signed the so-called 'Good Neighbourliness and Friendly Cooperation' treaty that subsequently served as a cornerstone of improved relations between these traditionally antagonistic nations.[2] Precisely eighteen years later, the binational ceremony promoted a clear message that remembering the past is an important aspect of forging a mutually prosperous present and future.

Lower down on the wall, a smaller sign, in German only, provides some clues about the possible inspiration, or motivation, behind the *Sejm* presenting a piece of Gdansk shipyard wall as a monument in a city where *the* Wall continues to cast a shadow long after most of it has been dismantled.

The wall section stands as a corporeal reminder of Solidarity's leading role in 'the beginning of the end' of communist rule in Eastern Europe.[3] By initiating the democratization process at home in Poland, furthermore, the Solidarity movement ultimately inspired the overcoming of Europe's division as symbolized by the fall of the Berlin Wall. In other words, by utilizing walls as a common denominator the *Sejm* drew a direct line between the tumultuous events that erupted in Gdansk at the start of the 1980s and the extraordinary scenes witnessed in Berlin at the end of the decade. It is, of course, a legitimate and worthwhile connection to make. Nonetheless, could a touch of envy be discerned here with Poles aggravated by their seminal role being overshadowed as Germany revelled in the central role – then and now – in celebrating the collapse of communism? Perhaps. It certainly was a stance Wałęsa himself adopted a few months later when *Der Spiegel* journalist Charles Hawkey travelled to Gdansk to interview him in the days leading up to the twentieth anniversary of the fall of the Berlin Wall.[4] Wałęsa counted among the long and distinguished list of former and current world leaders invited to the German capital to partake in official celebrations. Indeed, he was bestowed with the honour of pushing over the first of a thousand oversized plastic dominoes set out along a one-mile stretch where the Berlin Wall once stood near the Reichstag and Brandenburg Gate.[5] Schoolchildren had painted the 7.5 feet high dominoes – conceived as metaphorically representing both the Wall and the fall of communism – and the first one ceremoniously shoved by Wałęsa featured a Solidarity-inspired theme including the words: 'It began in Poland'.[6] Here, then, with the global media spotlight fixated on the festivities in Berlin, German organizers openly embraced the same message that the Polish parliament had been so keen to promote through the gifting of the shipyard wall segment as a Cold War monument five months earlier. Wałęsa, however, was not entirely satisfied. When asked by Hawkey whether he was excited about his involvement in the looming celebrations in Berlin, an ambivalent Wałęsa answered:

> The first wall to fall was pushed over in 1980 in the Polish shipyards. Later, other symbolic walls came down, and the Germans, of course, tore down the literal wall in Berlin. The fall of the Berlin Wall makes for nice pictures. But it all started in the shipyards.[7]

These events during 2009, marking the twentieth anniversary of the fall of the Berlin Wall, are emblematic of a wider tendency in recent years: around the world the Cold War now is increasingly being embraced as an aspect of contemporary history to be publicly remembered. And, as encapsulated by Wałęsa's words and actions, this trend often sees collaboration and disapproval go hand-in-hand. A little more than two decades on from the collapse of the Soviet Union in 1991, these public acts of remembering take several forms. In addition to ceremonies based around anniversaries of key events or historically-focused films and television series, for instance, recent

Figure 0.1 Section of Gdansk shipyard wall erected outside the Reichstag, Berlin, on 17 June 2009.

years also have seen a proliferation of permanent museums, temporary exhibits, tourist attractions, monuments, memorials, commemorative parks, and the preservation of historically relevant sites or relics, particularly throughout Europe, across North America, and in Asia.

Cultural heritage practitioners and archaeologists, to cite one theme, have been active in trying to assess what physical remnants of Cold War preparedness now warrant listing and preservation. In 2005, English Heritage produced a heavily illustrated glossy paperback that surveys monuments constructed in England between 1946 and 1989 relating to preparations for nuclear war. These hitherto 'largely unknown' physical manifestations of Cold War preparations, warns the blurb, are now 'disappearing fast, like medieval monasteries and bastioned forts before them – only with more limited scope for regeneration and reuse'.[8] The Cold War, then, is enfolded within a lineage of English history worth preserving. Similar initiatives have sprung up in continental Europe, too. Driven by longstanding campaigner Leo Schmidt, the Department of Architectural Conservation at the Brandenburg University of Technology in Cottbus has facilitated a number of projects examining Cold War heritage in Germany and across Europe.[9] More recently, the Baltic Initiative and Network has joined forces with the Archipelago Museum (Øhavsmuseet) on Langelands, Denmark. As part of a mission to strengthen mutual understanding and exchange of information on their nations' (shared and conflicting) contemporary histories, in 2011 this joint venture produced a *Travel Guide* that traces Cold War era military installations and towns, airbases, prisons, bunkers, execution sites and cemeteries, secret police offices, socialist architecture, sculptures, and historical museums located in eleven countries.[10] Elsewhere, North America boasts numerous and diverse public spaces dedicated to remembering the Cold War including: the Diefenbunker, a formerly secret underground bunker constructed to protect the Canadian government from nuclear attack that now houses the national Cold War museum in Carp, Ontario; the Wende Museum, a privately operated, self-styled 'hybrid organization' in California that complements its rich collection of Cold War artefacts with educational programmes, art exhibitions, and street performances; the Victims of Communism Memorial in Washington DC; and an ever-expanding constellation of former weapons testing locales, missile base stations, and other sites turning to tourism. Asia not only offers its own rich assortment of historical sites, museums, and memorials, but also can lay claim to some distinctive forms of publicly remembering the Cold War. Consider Japan, for instance, where the spectrum runs from Hiroshima, the city synonymous with the dawn of the nuclear age, to Okinawa, the so-called 'Cold War Island' where the past very much remains unresolved. All of the above places and themes, plus many more, are explored in greater detail throughout the following study.

We acknowledge that acts of remembering particular aspects of the Cold War naturally began during its long duration, and some of these practices have continued. We are nonetheless most interested in the new energy that has been generated since 1991, and in particular this study focuses on acts of public remembering that have emerged in recent years. There remains much research to be conducted in this field. Indeed, the following work represents the first book-length memory study dedicated to broad coverage of the Cold War. What factors originally inspired this project, and what key topics of inquiry propelled it forward? Ultimately, moreover, what are this study's main aims? These issues are addressed in more detail in Chapter 1. Here, then, it suffices to say that essentially we were roused by a curiosity to explore the manifold and often competing ways in which a worldwide struggle like the Cold War is remembered within more localized parameters – hence the book's subtitle 'Global Contest and National Stories'. From the outset, it was decided that a 'broad-brush' approach was required in order to paint as big a picture as possible. For reasons explained in Chapter 1, however, we restricted ourselves to North America, Europe, Asia, and Australia and consequently Latin/South America and Africa are not covered. Even so, more than a dozen nations feature at various stages throughout this work: Australia, Britain, Canada, China, the Czech Republic, Denmark, Germany, Hungary, Japan, Lithuania, Poland, Russia, Taiwan, the United States, and Vietnam. Investigating examples of Cold War remembrance from such a wide and diverse range of nations enables us to consider commonalities and dissimilarities evident around the globe. Key questions here include: how is the Cold War being remembered? When and where, by whom, and, of course, why do these practices occur? In what ways are they embraced or contested? Can any patterns be identified or, conversely, are there any discernible shifts in Cold War remembrance that can be noticed either according to location or over time? What political, social, cultural, and historical factors impact on any such patterns or topical variances and temporal shifts?

As the first offering in the new series *Remembering the Modern World*, furthermore, this book is tasked with an additional role: it carries a responsibility to help set the desired tone and style to be duplicated throughout ensuing volumes. By organizing volumes thematically, this series takes a broad view of what constitutes remembering great historical events and phenomena in the late modern period (since 1789). Volumes shall provide a comparative glance across the modern world in a manner that explores both the reach of globalization and the insistence of localizing forces. In *Remembering the Modern World*, individual works will draw on such vectors as: ceremonies associated with anniversaries and national days; episodes of memorialization and commemoration including museum exhibitions; filmic representations and popular culture; public discourse and debate as shaped and reflected by speeches from political and civic leaders; and school curricula etc. Rather than adopting a theory-laden approach, much emphasis is placed on presenting narrative-driven accounts (with substantive introductory chapters tracing the main theoretical and methodological contours). To complement the text, widespread use of maps, timelines, illustrations, and especially photographs taken during field research is encouraged. The series is aimed at undergraduate and postgraduate students as well as scholars, and besides History the series is expected to appeal to audiences in Anthropology, Communication Studies, Heritage Studies, International Relations, Regional Studies, Politics, and Sociology. It is anticipated, furthermore, that *Remembering the Modern World* will attract a wider readership including teachers, museum curators, heritage practitioners, journalists and the media industry, plus general readers interested in contemporary history.

Taking on board all these general aims, *Remembering the Cold War* is a narrative-driven exploratory account of how this global contest has been and is being remembered through the prism of localized or national stories. It features supplementary materials in the form of maps and an extensive collection of photographs taken during field research across three continents. Although produced by historians, this work is not exclusively aimed at historians; rather, it is intended for anyone with an interest in memory studies generally and the Cold War especially. Theoretical and methodological issues that have shaped this project are discussed separately from the main thematic chapters of the book. The idea here is that scholars and students wishing to engage with interpretive and conceptual matters can find such a discussion in Chapter 1. Alternatively, any readers who would prefer to avoid academic discourse and instead commence with the overall account of Cold War remembrance can skip straight to Chapter 2 entitled 'Nuclear World'. This first chapter is then followed by a further two thematic parts: Chapter 3 'Cities and Sites', and Chapter 4 'Defining Our Times'. An explanation of the decision-making process behind the choice of these themes and a synopsis of each of the three substantive chapters can be found at the end of Chapter 1. Approaching a quarter-century since the fall of the Wall and the dissolution of the Soviet Union between 1989 and 1991, we believe this book offers a timely overview of leading forms of public remembrance of the Cold War. Finally, one byproduct of grappling with events of such a contemporary nature is that often this book raises more questions than it can provide answers. Accordingly, rather than a standard conclusion that could pose an unwanted sense of closure, this study ends with a short chapter on 'Endings' and the interconnectedness between remembering and forgetting. It reflects on what has been covered throughout the preceding chapters and then considers what are some likely developments for Cold War memory and commemoration, before suggesting possible directions for future scholarship on this intriguing subject matter.

Notes

1 '*Zur Erinnerung an den Kampf der "Solidarność" für Freiheit und Demokratie und den Beitrag Polens zur Wiedervereinigung Deutschlands und für ein politisch geeintes Europa.*' This and all further translations are our own unless indicated otherwise.

2 Rosalia Romaniec, 'From Antagonists to Friends: 20 Years of the German-Polish Treaty', *Deutsche Welle (DW)*, 17 June 2011, www.dw.de/from-antagonists-to-friends-20-years-of-the-german-polish-treaty/a-15164723 (Last accessed June 2012). The date also links back to the major uprising that occurred in East Germany in 1953, which is popularly known in Germany as the *Aufstand des 17. Juni.*

3 '*Dieses Mauerstück von der Danziger Werft soll an den Anfang vom Ende der kommunistischen Regime in Osteuropa erinnern.*'

4 Charles Hawley, 'Spiegel Online Interview with Lech Walesa: "It's Good that Gorbachev was a Weak Politician"', *Spiegel Online International*, 6 November 2009, http://www.spiegel.de/international/europe/spiegel-online-interview-with-lech-walesa-it-s-good-that-gorbachev-was-a-weak-politician-a-659752.html (Last accessed November 2012).

5 'Toppling of Dominoes Marks Fall of Berlin Wall', *CBC News*, 9 November 2009, www.cbc.ca/news/world/story/2009/11/09/berlin-wall-celebrations.html (Last accessed June 2012).

6 Allan Hall, 'World Leaders Gather to See the Berlin Wall Topple again, 20 Years On', *Daily Mail Online*, 10 November 2009, www.dailymail.co.uk/news/article-1226507/20-years-Berlin-Wall-topples-again.html (Last accessed November 2012).

7 Hawley, 'Spiegel Interview with Lech Walesa'.

8 Wayne Cocroft, Roger Thomas, and P. Barnwell, *Cold War: Building for Nuclear Confrontation 1946–1989* (English Heritage, 2005).

9 For examples, see Alex Klausmeier and Leo Schmidt, *Wall Remnants – Wall Traces: The Comprehensive Guide to the Berlin Wall* (Berlin: Westkreuz-Verlag, 2004). Winfried Heinemann *et al.*, *Die Berliner Mauer – Vom Sperrwall zum*

Denkmal, ed. Deutsches Nationalkomitee für Denkmalschutz, vol. 76/1 (Bühl: KONKORDIA GmbH, 2009). See also Fleur Hutchings, 'Cold Europe: Discovering, Researching and Preserving European Cold War Heritage' (Cottbus: Department of Architectural Conservation at the Brandenburg University of Technology, February 2004).

10 Johannes Bach Rasmussen, *Travel Guide: Traces of the Cold War Period. The Countries around the Baltic Sea* (Copenhagen: Norden, 2010). The countries covered are Denmark, Estonia, Finland, Germany, Iceland, Latvia, Lithuania, Norway, Poland, Russia, and Sweden.

1 Conceptualizing Cold War remembrance

The Cold War shapes our memory of change and international relations in the second half of the twentieth century. Indeed, the politico-ideological lines that divided most of the postwar world into two polarized blocs were drawn so deeply that, more than two decades after the end of that era, Cold War legacies continue to play crucial roles in (re)defining national identities and (re)determining international relations around the globe. Owing to both its peculiar nature and lingering contemporaneity, the Cold War presents certain challenges that set it apart from other more popular or 'conventional' subjects for examining war memory and commemoration. Memory studies fixated on the First World War, for instance, can explore ways in which a single event lasting the comparatively short time frame of 1914–18 has been and continues to be remembered. Or studies of phenomena that tend to occur in isolated and typically unrelated cases – acts of genocide, leading examples of sporting triumphs and tragedies, or prominent episodes of terrorism etc. – readily lend themselves to collections of 'stand-alone' chapters linked by an overarching theme. By its very definition of being 'cold', however, in strict terms the imagined 'war' at the centre of this book – a major conflagration, most likely nuclear, between the opposing power blocs – never actually broke out. This means that, on the one hand, it has neither a universally accepted commencement date nor a unanimously acknowledged conclusion (beyond partial agreement that it spanned from the 1940s up to around the time of the fall of the Berlin Wall, collapse of eastern European communism, and dissolution of the erstwhile superpower the Soviet Union). Notwithstanding the heat surrounding several notable flashpoints, on the other hand, its failure ever to become truly 'hot' accounts for why the Cold War endured for more or less a half-century. Yet the *absence* of apocalyptic conflict presents something of an anomaly when it comes to *remembering* a 'war' that, in essence, failed to ever materialize beyond more localized wars and acts of violence. Put another way, if the Cold War is defined as a sustained period in which political and military tensions between the two superpower-led blocs always simmered but never reached boiling point, then what is there left to remember? Indeed, is it even possible to *remember* something that, viewed a particular way, never actually happened? As discussed in more detail below, at least one influential memory scholar has argued that the Cold War lends itself to very little – if any at all – memorialization and commemoration. Contrariwise, while acknowledging that to date it has remained a largely fallow field of war memory and commemoration, we argue that the Cold War promises to be increasingly rich terrain for memory scholars in future.[1] As a way of signalling wider interest in this emerging topic we offer the present study as the first book-length memory study dedicated to international coverage of Cold War remembrance.

No single volume, of course, could possibly cover the subject of Cold War memory and commemoration in its entirety. It would be folly to attempt such a task, which perhaps explains why existing memory studies have tended to home in on examining specific foci such as events, nations, or themes.[2] Whereas this book aims to survey how the Cold War has been and continues to be remembered in a wide range of temporal and topical settings, there are obvious limitations to what can and cannot be covered. Selectivity, then, needs to be recognized – indeed, embraced – as an obvious and unavoidably limiting starting point. What should be included in such a study and what can be overlooked? It is pertinent to add here, too, that historical amnesia – so often a highly politicized and state-sponsored endeavour – plays a crucial role in determining why and how certain episodes or experiences seem to more readily lend themselves to memory at the expense of other apparently less usable aspects of the past.[3] Accordingly, the following study is partially influenced by questions concerning why particular facets of the Cold War have emerged more prominently than other less covered themes.[4] Ultimately, though, it focuses on acts of remembering rather than spending too much time wondering about what may have been forgotten.

In addition to our scholarly, linguistic, and cultural limitations, three key issues underpinned the reasoning and decision-making behind what to include and exclude. First, what inspired this study? Second, what core questions drive this project? And, finally, what are its chief objectives? Beyond its close linkages to the wider series on *Remembering the Modern World*, this book was inspired by a curiosity to explore the manifold and often competing ways in which a worldwide struggle like the Cold War is remembered within more localized parameters – hence the book's subtitle 'Global Contest and National Stories'. From the outset, it was decided that a 'broad-brush' approach would be needed in order to paint as wide a picture as possible. Some basic questions that have fundamentally shaped this work include: how has the Cold War been remembered? When and where, by whom, and, of course, why has this taken place? How the recent past is told and who is doing the telling can be very instructive when it comes to matters such as cultivating 'collective identity', myth-making (or debunking), and nation (re)building exercises including the universal principle of national self-determination. Remembering is a fluid rather than static activity and so it is imperative to consider how and why some practices change or vanish altogether while others remain more or less the same, thus becoming entrenched as rites or traditions. What acts of Cold War remembrance have come and gone? What developments are unfolding now? What, most likely, looms on the horizon? Drawing on all these considerations, the following study is especially interested in probing the political, social, cultural, and historical factors that help to account for topical variances and temporal shifts in memorialization and commemoration of the Cold War around the world. Approaching a quarter-century since the end of the Cold War, this work's main objective is to offer a timely, narrative-driven exploratory account of how this global contest has been and is being remembered under the rubric of localized or national stories.

As a survey study, a good deal of this book is innovative synthesis that necessarily draws on other scholars' work – even if we regularly differ in our interpretations and conclusions. Whereas standing on the shoulders of others proved to be a favourable vantage point, by no means is it the only locality from which we obtained materials and insight. On the contrary, research conducted specifically for this project has accessed primary sources ranging from commission reports and political speeches through to recent textbooks for school children. Extensive field research was conducted in Britain, the Czech Republic, Denmark, Germany, Hungary, Japan, Lithuania, Poland, Russia, Taiwan, the United States, and Vietnam, with several interviews conducted with fellow academics, museologists, archaeologists, cultural heritage practitioners, and tour guides along the way.

The 'frozen bloc' as an idiot's tale?

In his thought-provoking introduction to the 2002 edited collection *Memory and Power in Post-War Europe: Studies in the Presence of the Past*, Jan-Werner Müller observed that, within the first decade of the post-Soviet new world order, a 'fiercely contested "New Cold War History"' already had emerged. Conversely, though, Müller then argued that no such similar memory work on the Cold War had started to develop:

> … it almost appears as if now for us the entire period had become a 'frozen bloc' between the end of the Second World War and the 'return of history', a meaningless distraction or even a communist tale told by an idiot. One reason might simply be that unlike 'hot wars', the Cold War does not lend itself to memorialisation and, at least in the West, to the tales of suffering and mourning which are familiar from the world wars. Moreover, since the Cold War often blurred the line between war and peace, it became very difficult to define the beginnings and endings of conflicts which are central to the emergence of topographical and temporal sites of memory.[5]

In Müller's defence, at the time he made these remarks the Cold War was hardly subject to serious scrutiny with the two world wars and the

Holocaust already dominating the 'memory boom's' morbid fixation on manmade death and destruction.[6] Nonetheless, Müller clearly could not foresee the Cold War becoming a popular topic for memory studies any time soon. In fact, he further mused: 'Whether or not this period, and its memories, can be "unfrozen" remains to be seen – it might take another generational interval of forty years.'[7] In other words, around the turn of the century it seemed plausible to a leading memory scholar like Müller that it may take until at least 2040 or thereabouts before the Cold War could or would lend itself to widespread public memory and com-memoration. A decade later, a number of important works already have dismantled the misguided notion that the Cold War supposedly was some kind of ahistorical 'frozen' void destined to remain unsuited to memor-ialization or remembrance until the era's participant-observer generations pass away. Even so, another key aim of this study is to provide further evidence that the Cold War has engendered dynamic and diverse memory cultures in virtually every corner of the globe that experienced this contest in a significant manner. Furthermore, as our coverage of the continuing mnemonic struggles in Central and Eastern Europe and East Asia indi-cates, for a whole slew of reasons the idea that the Cold War era was a 'meaningless distraction' or some idiot's tale is anathema to the countless individuals and groups actively engaged in bringing the past to life in the present.

The challenges of immediacy and lingering contemporaneity

Writing a book like this would be an ambitious undertaking at the best of times; tackling such a project a little more than two decades since the fall of the Berlin Wall posed some daunting challenges. Reflecting on his monu-mental synthesis *One World Divisible: A Global History since 1945*, Cambridge Professor of International History David Reynolds warns: 'Any con-temporary historian must accept the risk that he [*sic*] will soon be reading his [*sic*] book with a wry, toothless grin.'[8] Prior to commencing this study, we abandoned all grandiose visions of producing a, or perhaps even *the*, defini-tive account of Cold War remembrance. We are under no illusions that, as time passes, future studies – armed with both the benefits afforded by extra time and space plus the groundwork laid by earlier works including this one – will come to offer more developed interpretations. In other words, our time for wry, toothless grins surely awaits! From the outset we heeded Rey-nolds' sage advice and never aspired to reach the lofty heights of 'definitive-ness'.[9] Instead, we accepted that the enormity of the subject matter coupled with our own scholarly, linguistic, and cultural limitations meant that we should embrace the fact that this study, by necessity, has been shaped by our combined capabilities along with our individual and shared views on the subject. By extension, then, we also must acknowledge that our lived experiences as 'survivors' of the Cold War era have impacted on our approach to this study. Eric Hobsbawm, in his seminal work *The Age of Empire: 1875–1914*, warns:

> For all of us there is a twilight zone between history and memory; between the past as a generalized record which is open to relatively dispassionate inspection and the past as a remembered part of, or background to, one's own life ... The length of this zone may vary, and so will the obscurity and fuzziness that characterizes it. But there is always such a no-man's land of time. It is by far the hardest part of history for historians, or for anyone else, to grasp.[10]

For Hobsbawm, born in 1917, the age of empire he was writing about formed the earliest phase of his personal 'twilight zone'. For the present authors, born more or less a half-century after Hobsbawm, the Cold War dominates this obscure and fuzzy 'no-man's land' between history and memory. On the one hand, we were far from ever morphing into Cold War Warriors – in this respect, like most ordinary citizens living through this era we counted among the observers rather than participants and so this provides at least some level of personal detachment. And our antipodean upbringings meant that we were as removed from the northern reaches of US–Soviet sparring as was geographically possible. Again, this can help to engender a little 'outsider' detachment given that the Cold War, while undeniably global, was largely rooted in the northern hemisphere. On the other hand, however, there is no escaping the fact that the Australian society in which we grew up during the Cold War was steeped in a western-centric worldview that hinged on political discourse, education, news reports, films, and other cultural representations propagating 'us' as part of the 'virtuous West' and the Soviet bloc as both 'enemy and other'. Writing from the very southern part of mainland Australia, we were conscious that author Neville Shute and Hollywood director Stanley Kramer caused the imagined Cold War apocalypse to spread to Melbourne in the award-winning 1959 film *On the Beach*. This particular reference also serves as a reminder of the power of fiction to realize the worst fears of a Cold War generation. We do not adopt an ideological stance in relation to explaining the war, for interpreting how it came about and who was most responsible is not our main task. We do, however, take into account the recent Cold War histories – often informed by post-communist archival releases and supplanting outdated orthodox and revisionist interpretations with more nuanced and balanced post-revisionist accounts.

Hobsbawm, of course, is not alone in identifying the complex but undeniably close relationship or interconnectedness between (contemporary) history and memory. 'In virtually all acts of remembrance', proposes the doyen of war-related memory studies Jay Winter, 'history and memory are braided together in the public domain'.[11] Similarly, Emily Rosenberg, in her impressive study of Pearl Harbor as an icon of American memory, warns against treating (scholarly) history and (popular) memory as binary opposites and instead recommends handling them as 'blurred forms of representation'.[12] For the purposes of the present study, with its international focus on surveying Cold War remembrance, the equation is complicated further by the need to consider how both history and memory intersect the vexed issue of national identity and all its associated trappings including myth-making and the (re)drawing of borders. Specifically in the case of remembering the Second World War, according to Patrick Finney, history, memory, and identity typically have been treated as if they are 'indissolubly intertwined'.[13] And, as the following study makes clear, there seems very little reason to think that the same sentiment does not hold true for the Cold War, too. Adding another layer of interest and intrigue, furthermore, victimhood often serves as the glue that binds together the history–memory–identity nexus for Cold War commemorative politics.

In a far broader sense, a touchstone of the politics of war memory and commemoration is what Winter and Emmanuel Sivan describe as the 'vigorously contested' question of victimhood.[14] Once shunned as both a bitter reminder of past or continuing domination and a signal of historical or enduring inferiority, victimhood now has become a prized commodity. In war memory and commemoration, victim status is sought after, indeed fought over, by representatives of two kinds of groups. First, what we can label the 'customary' groups already are formed on national, ethnic, religious, or political lines and are defined by their shared historical experiences of trauma, loss, suffering, and subjugation. These 'customary' groups pre-dated, endured, and outlasted the conflict(s) in question as, for instance: entire nations (think, for example, of Poland's self-anointed title as Christ among nations); ethnic or 'racial' minorities (Armenians in the Ottoman Empire and Jews throughout Nazi-occupied Europe, or Palestinians since the birth of modern Israel, and the Cham people in Pol Pot's 'Democratic Kampuchea'); and members belonging to a religion (Bosniaks etc.). The second category consists of what we can describe as the 'created' groups who did not exist previously and instead emerged out of the conflict at hand, including: physically impaired and psychologically affected individuals (war veterans, the disabled, widows and widowers etc.); the politically trapped (annexed populations and newly subjugated peoples, or longtime supporters of overthrown ideologies and political systems); as well as the geographically dislocated (ranging from displaced persons and expellees through to citizens of divided nations or disintegrated states). All such 'customary' and 'created' groups, which range from localized minorities through to nation-states, have a vested interest in controlling how the past is rendered in the present – and not only because their future identity may depend on it. With colossal sums attached to restitution claims – either in the form of reparation payments as compensation for losses or, when possible, the restoration of property to its rightful owners – and enormous political clout (and moral weight) hinging on the recognition of having suffered past wrongdoing, there is much at stake.

Perhaps the most controversial yet effective case of victimhood concerning what Idith Zertal calls the 'politics of nationhood' involves Israel's cultivation of nationalized victim status facilitated by the omnipresent 'ghost of the Holocaust'.[15] It can be preferential, too, if notions of 'victimhood' can be substituted with the equally advantageous but more assertive-sounding term 'survivor'. Again, for several decades now the Holocaust has loomed large as the most prominent exemplar of survivor/victim status being appropriated as a contemporary political 'asset'.[16] Not even memories of the Nazis' state-sanctioned industrialized attempt to exterminate European Jewry, however, are beyond usurpation – hence the widely used quip that 'there's no business like Shoah business'. The following study reveals how, although it currently may not be nearly as developed as the claims attached to the Holocaust, the Cold War similarly has given rise to a burgeoning victim/survivor cult of politicized memory.

When it comes to national or ethnic disputes, furthermore, the end of the Cold War concurrently exposed old scars and opened up new wounds; in other words, by and large the 'end of history' failed to offer many of its victims or survivors a fresh start.[17] As Chapter 3 on 'Cities and Sites' illustrates, such developments have been especially pronounced in Eastern Europe. Indeed, within less than a decade following the Soviet Union's dissolution, it was estimated that more than 120 'minor' disputes had erupted along with at least a handful of genuine wars.[18] Another decade on, and many of these conflicts are unresolved with tensions remaining as high as ever. Again, such developments raise questions about the history–memory–identity nexus, for as Müller remarks: ' ... the question of memory is often at the heart of issues about national self-determination, arguably *the* most salient political issue in eastern Europe after the end of the Cold War [emphasis in original].'[19] Whereas this study is interested in cultural dimensions to remembering the Cold War, it would be foolish, of course, to understate the very deliberate function of politicking when the past is rendered in the present.

Framing the study of Cold War remembrance

So far, we have addressed some important factors that helped this project to find its early shape. On the one hand, these relate to decisions about selectivity owing to the subject's immense scope. On the other hand, all manner of challenges are posed by the Cold War's lingering contemporaneity. Having previously set out the basic parameters of what this study covers, before venturing any further now it is time to explain how we conceptualized our methodological and analytical framework and determined the book's structure. The following discussion also maps out our use of some key terms, including why certain terminology has been adopted over other phrasing.

Over the past three decades, memory has become an increasingly prolific and enriched subject of scholarly inquiry. Several other humanities disciplines have made important contributions and interdisciplinary projects often have produced pathbreaking works, but History undisputedly has led the charge.[20] Whereas this 'surfeit of memory' has left barely a historical stone unturned, war memory and commemoration has proven to be one of the most industrious and absorbing topics.[21] Actually, it is more accurate to stress that, to date, remembering 'hot' wars has been remarkably popular. It is not hard to understand why, given the longstanding widespread fascination with war as a subject of historical inquiry. War, furthermore, is a subject particularly conducive to representation and remembrance for a host of compelling reasons including: successions of important anniversaries marking a particular conflict's beginning and end plus all the key episodes in between; victors' proclivity to reminisce and rejoice; the vanquished seeking ways to come to terms with the past; the oppressed and victimized searching for recognition and restitution; and, of course, modern total war's unparalleled capacity to produce loss and suffering taps into the very heart of humankind's natural inclination to mourn. As the following pages demonstrate, however, all such factors are equally applicable to studies focusing on Cold War memory and commemoration, too. Similarly, remembering war – hot or cold – lends itself to political, cultural, and social inspection and introspection, as well as moral reckoning and philosophical reflection. In the public realm, war can be remembered through a myriad of filters, triggers, settings, and media including political discourse, academic and popular histories, education, memorialization (official or otherwise), anniversary celebrations, artistic expressions, and fictional or documentary filmic representations to name but a few. The veritable explosion of academic interest in war memory and commemoration naturally has generated a proliferation of theory-laden publications that offer extensive literature reviews and detailed discussions on the main theoretical and methodological issues concerning this subject area. Consequently, for the purposes of this chiefly narrative-driven study there is no need here to present anything more than an overview of some of the most influential works and most relevant themes. In briefly tracing the main methodological contours and mnemonic techniques employed when investigating war memory and commemoration, the following passages also explain why some possible approaches were rejected while others have been adopted as part of this study's conceptual framework.

With few notable exceptions, scholarly works engaging in war memory and commemoration typically investigate either the private or the public realm.[22] Admittedly, much important work remains to be done in documenting and analysing private memories of the Cold War, not least because there is no doubt that many personalized accounts shared by families sitting around kitchen tables or friends gathered behind closed doors bear little or no resemblance to 'official' state-driven metanarratives that permeate the public sphere. Even so, due to the vast scope of the topic at hand and in an endeavour to make this project manageable, one of the earliest decisions made in our selection process was to overlook private memories and instead exclusively focus on public forms of remembering. When speaking of the 'public' realm, we mean for this term to encompass any memory practices enacted openly (that is, anything clearly beyond whatever reasonably can be considered to fall within the private sphere) including: annual traditions and never-to-be-repeated events; popularized displays and solemn practices; carefully staged episodes and more organic developments; state-orchestrated or socially-engineered memorialization and commemoration; and acts ranging from localized occasions up to international extravaganzas.

In light of these manifold forms of public practice, moreover, it is vital to consider various approaches to studying war memory and commemoration. Here, the insightful work of T.G. Ashplant, Graham Dawson, and Michael Roper is especially helpful in identifying two main paradigms: first, what they label the 'state-centred' approach, which primarily fixates on political perspectives; and, second, what they define as the 'social-agency' approach, which is more concerned with the psychological dimensions.[23] The former, originally propelled by Benedict Anderson's *Imagined Communities* and Eric Hobsbawm's and Terence Ranger's *Invention of Tradition* (both published in 1983), essentially follows a top-down approach.[24] It stresses the nation-state's role in shaping the 'rituals of national identification [to bind ...] citizens into a collective national identity'.[25] The latter, which in many respects developed as a counter-perspective heavily influenced by Jay Winter, downplays state-centred politicization and instead concentrates on the various civil agencies engaged in the public expression of war memory and mourning. Eschewing a myopic 'either-or' outlook and instead embracing a more nuanced 'as-well-as' mentality, whenever relevant this study employs regular 'slippage' between the state-centred and the social-agency approaches to remembering the Cold War.

Our study acknowledges the dominance of two common renderings of the Cold War: first, the idea of the 'long peace', the notion of simmering tensions that never erupted into full-scale war; and, second, the fixedness of the end of the Cold War in 1991, with the collapse of the Soviet Union. It necessarily interrogates the relevance of each of these common renderings, however, in the context of remembering. Here, Heonik Kwon's imaginative bridge-building between ethnographic experiences in Korea and Vietnam and the scholarship of Cold War international history is instructive. Rather than as a fixed moment of empirical reality, Kwon sees the 'end' of the Cold War as an emerging 'proactive' aspect of contemporary history. Using the idea of its ongoing 'decomposition' as a means of understanding the diverse ways in which the Cold War still is coming to an end, Kwon argues:

> The decomposition of the cold war considers the end of the cold war as a participatory, ethnographic question rather than as a historical issue ... The decomposition of the cold war thus involves a two-pronged shift of perspective regarding cold war history: from a geopolitical history to a

social history, on the one hand, and from the exemplary central positioning of the cold war as imaginary or metaphoric war to a comparative position that privileges neither this peculiar history of war without warfare nor the peripheral 'unbridled reality' of state terror and violence, on the other.[26]

Even in very broad terms, without a determinedly ethnographic approach, the implications of seeing the end of the Cold War as an ongoing process made more explicable by social history and by eschewing a dominant definition but moving between global and local renderings of cold war, are liberating. This is especially the case for studies concerned with modern memory – such as this one – and we share Kwon's dissatisfaction with overly fixed depictions of the Cold War and its ending. One of our aims, then, is to add to the productive conversation he has started between differing forms of Cold War scholarship by detailing different acts of remembering.

There are numerous strategies available to scholars choosing to explore public war memory and commemoration spanning from the local to the global level. Some of the most popular and fruitful approaches include, for instance: thematic volumes;[27] interdisciplinary projects;[28] historiographical studies;[29] concentrating on a given period or a specific nation;[30] comparative analyses of similar case studies;[31] transnational investigations;[32] synthesizing multiple case studies into a master narrative;[33] compiling a loose collection of ostensibly unrelated accounts;[34] or interpreting the ongoing resonance of a particular – often catastrophic – event or episode.[35] Some studies ruminate upon the complex relationship between 'memory and national identity'.[36] Other works scrutinize how 'memory and memorials' are mobilized for nation-building or bonding exercises.[37] Commemorative politics is an especially popular topic.[38] So, too, is investigating our generation's 'museum-mania'.[39] Under this rubric, furthermore, the role of history exhibitions as controversial 'displays of power' designed to either forge, perpetuate, or discredit popularized myths is a highly engaging approach.[40] Additional approaches involve probing any of the seemingly endless stream of oral testimonies and interviews, newspapers and other contemporary accounts, archival documentation, literary, artistic, and filmic depictions, pop culture references, monuments and sculptures, architecture, war cemeteries and old battlegrounds, new or reignited controversies, war crimes trials, reparations claims, and other public spaces that spark interest and debate.

All such settings, combined with the bearers of memory responsible for their creation and carriage, represent what Ashplant, Dawson, and Roper have advanced as the two core elements underpinning the 'articulation of memory': *arenas* of articulation; and *agencies* of articulation. In this sense, of course, agency does not refer to Stalin and Truman or Reagan and Gorbachev, but rather all those carriers of memory engaged in remembering the Cold War.[41] The notion of agencies of articulation, then, straddles both 'official' (state-centred) and 'unofficial' (socially-based) carriers of memory – individuals or collectives – spanning from local forces through to transnational movements. This study features examples emblematic of all such levels of (usually competing, and often uneven) agencies involved in the articulation of Cold War memories. Two of the more obvious umbrella categories are the 'victors', meaning carriers of memory attached to the US-led capitalist western democracies, and the 'vanquished', namely agencies somehow still associated with Soviet-inspired communism. It is not all cut-and-dried, however, for even the 'vanquished' can spin positive Cold War memories by focusing on high-water marks such as Soviet achievements in space exploration. As raised earlier, furthermore, 'victims' is another prominent category of Cold War agencies of articulation. Chapters 3 and 4 ('Cities and Sites' and 'Defining Our Times' respectively) both address, for instance, some rather intriguing developments whereby formerly 'vanquished' nationalities have very deliberately (re)cast themselves in the role of 'victims'. Eastern Europeans led by Poles, Czechs, and Hungarians have robustly divorced themselves from their Warsaw Pact past and instead promote narratives in which they are hapless victims initially of Stalinist expansionism and tyranny followed by enduring and unwanted Russian repression. Not content with simply remembering their problematic past, these neo-Cold War Warriors prioritize national stories in which they effectively 'switch sides' and retrospectively denounce communism while embracing capitalism and democratic (read EU) ideals.

Moreover, the concept of arenas of articulation, which envelops the myriad public spaces in which the remembering, commemorating, memorializing, and even revising of Cold War history takes place, is given prominence in this book. Close parallels can be drawn between the Ashplant-Dawson-Roper model of arenas of articulation and the pioneering work of Pierre Nora. In the 1980s, the French scholar introduced the profoundly influential concept of 'sites of memory' (*lieux de mémoire*) to define all public realms where 'memory crystallizes and secretes itself'.[42] Arguing that there is no such thing as 'spontaneous memory' at a collective level, Nora suggests that we are compelled to 'deliberately create archives, maintain anniversaries, organize celebrations, pronounce eulogies [and promote our ...] most symbolic objects' as these realms or sites of memory.[43] How Nora's paradigmatic theory of purposely-cultivated *lieux de mémoire* along with the analogous concept of arenas of articulation espoused by Ashplant, Dawson, and Roper fundamentally shape this book is further detailed below in the discussion outlining its structure.

It is hard to think of a more contested concept within this entire field than the widely used and equally widely spurned term 'collective memory'. It does not help, of course, that the situation is complicated by the fact that so many works nonchalantly adopt this loaded term without any explanation whatever as to how it is actually being defined or employed. Be that as it may, and without getting too bogged down in debate, it should be acknowledged that arguments presented by both advocates and critics of the notion

of collective memory have demonstrated considerable strengths and weaknesses. Subscribers, for whom the Durkheimian sociologist Maurice
Halbwachs serves as a quasi-godfather of collective historical consciousness,
gravitate toward the influence of societal push and pull factors in studying
the continual formation and reformation of social memory.[44] Studies that
present this kind of wide-lens view can offer valuable insights into the ways
in which holistic forces simultaneously shape and reflect what Aleida
Assmann refers to as 'common historical memory'.[45] If left wholly
'unpacked', however, then such an approach can fall for the trap of failing to
consider how 'collectively constructed' acts of remembering may be coded,
decoded, and recoded in diverse and even opposing ways by various individuals partaking in public memory and commemoration.[46] Put another way,
the notion of 'collectiveness' can be considered problematic precisely
because it implies that a certain harmony, or perhaps even unanimity, has
been agreed upon.

Any supposed unity in or of remembering is a real sticking point for
critics of collective memory who argue that such a notion undervalues
divergence – or individuality – in interpretation. If a crowd of people engage
in or observe a public act of remembering the past – the unveiling of a local
memorial or the premiere of a film, for instance – does anyone process or
decode the occasion in precisely the same way as others around them? In
many cases, the short answer is surely not. For others, however, on some
levels perhaps there is a general sense of agreement about what meanings and
messages can and should be attached to any such public articulation of
memory. Here, though, a critic of collective memory such as Susan Sontag
would argue that what is happening is not some form of communal
'remembering' but rather an ideologically-driven and externally-enforced
'stipulating' of what stories about the past are important and thus should be
internalized and prioritized by individuals.[47] According to Sontag, collective
memory is an absurd notion since 'all memory is individual, unrepro-
ducible – it dies with each person'.[48] For two interrelated reasons, however,
Assmann rejects Sontag's viewpoint as incomplete: first, her talk of 'stipulating' focuses on the role of ideologically-inspired imagery in determining
what thoughts and feelings about a past event individuals should internalize
as the preferred metanarrative; and, second, Sontag fails to recognize that,
once individuals' memories are expressed publicly, they can become fused
through common language and this creates important new 'dimensions of
memory'.[49] Once fused together, argues Assmann, individuals' memories are
'no longer a purely exclusive and unalienable property'. Instead, they can be
'exchanged, shared, corroborated, confirmed, corrected, disputed – and, last
but not least, written down, which preserves them and makes them potentially accessible to those who do not live within spatial and temporal reach.'
For Assmann, then, it is crucial to think about the (intergenerational)
'externalization' of memory, too. On the one hand, there is a certain
reciprocity at play whereby individuals' memories of particular events they

actually observed or experienced simultaneously shape and reflect popularized verbal and non-verbal forms of remembering. Such exchanges can result
in shared approval or just as easily lead to disputes over interpretation and
meaning. On the other hand, anyone who shares a sense of belonging to an
ethnic group, society, or nation etc. that values certain texts or images as
'triggers' for recollecting a shared history can join in the act of 'remembering' events they never personally experienced.

Assmann mounts a persuasive argument that, either way, individuals are
receptive to 'shared material documents' in the form of texts and photographs or other images that serve as external triggers enabling them to share
in memories that are not merely personal constructs. It must be acknowledged, however, that not all individuals' memories are 'carried' or 'absorbed'
into the collective – competition over what is to be remembered and what is
to be discarded, of course, is one of the hallmarks of the politics of memory.
Still, we cannot forcefully and falsely separate individuals' memories from
the social, political, and cultural 'memory formats' they both mould and
mirror as if they are mutually exclusive entities.[50] Indeed, as Wulf
Kansteiner has warned there is a need to consider the interplay between the
individual and the collective when 'finding meaning in memory'.[51] Consequently, a strong if difficult to define relationship exists between collective
memory and collective identity, which is a theme that is implicitly touched
upon regularly throughout this book.[52]

If one adopts a rigid stance on the issue, it is hard to disagree with
Sontag's argument that collective memory belongs to 'the same family of
spurious notions as collective guilt'.[53] Critics are right to point out that all
memory belongs to the individual and therefore we cannot ever truly speak
of a collective memory being at play; as cultural anthropologists Eric Gable
and Richard Handler observe, strictly speaking it is an oxymoron for neither
a society nor a culture has the capacity to remember.[54] But such a literal
reading only serves to construct a straw-man argument. Sensible advocates
of collective memory use it as a metaphorical concept rather than literally,
and, as Müller points out, all serious memory scholars readily 'concede that
ultimately only individuals can remember'.[55] Even Halbwachs, who coined
the phrase 'collective memory' in the 1920s, never meant for it to imply that
any two people share exactly the same memories (though he was equally
quick to stress that if individual memory was not properly contextualized
within the wider social memory in which it occurred then it was more or less
'devoid of meaning').[56] Debating whether collective memory actually exists
in some kind of tangible form is a rather pointless exercise, then, because its
best advocates employ it more as a mnemonic trope than a concrete reality.
The term 'collective memory' should not be used to denote some supposed
communal state of mind or to imply that verbalized and non-verbalized acts
of societal remembrance are undisputed, unanimously accepted and supported episodes free of controversy. Rather, it is a fluid process constantly
subject to change and debate with contemporary intellectual discourse,

social trends, and political developments often the most influential factors. As a concept it is helpful for analysing all kinds of (contested) public articulation of memory. And the 'collective' agencies engaged in such acts may be as small as, say, a handful of committee members gathered at a local hall, as large and concentrated as an entire nation, or as vast yet scattered as a transnational movement. Equally, though, one must be mindful of the dangers attached to blanket 'big picture' approaches that overlook the finer details. If adopted as a figurative concept, collective memory can be an excellent tool for investigating war memory and commemoration – but only if the subject is examined through both a telescopic and microscopic lens.

In producing a survey study of public Cold War remembrance it would be not only nonsensical but, moreover, counterproductive to adopt Sontag's hardline stance that 'there is no such thing as collective memory'.[57] One would be left with the impossible task of trying to make sense of wading through how countless individual carriers of memory articulate the past. Indeed, by no means is this book primarily concerned with investigating examples of individuals practising public acts of Cold War memory and commemoration – or, put a shorthanded way, with 'individual memory'. Nonetheless, even though it far more closely aligns to what is covered in the following pages, we are not entirely comfortable with employing the term collective memory, either. During the research behind this book, particularly in the wake of multiple field trips conducted across three continents, what became increasingly palpable was the sense of ongoing conflict or contestation attached to and evident in state-centred and socially-based articulation of Cold War memory and commemoration. For us, then, it proved difficult to dispel connotations of harmony or consensus fomented by any talk of 'collectiveness' in remembering. Instead, we are drawn to the similar but subtler concepts of 'shared' and 'common' memory. The term 'shared memory' relates to a group or groups of individuals (and their ancestors) who experienced and now remember the *same* event, whereas 'common memory' denotes when otherwise unrelated groups (and even erstwhile opponents) join together in remembering *cognate* experiences.[58] For our purposes, prominent examples of shared and common memories of the Cold War include: Hungarian remembrance of the 1956 uprising; the universal fear of nuclear threat and Mutually Assured Destruction (MAD); or East and West Germans remembering decades of division. The German case is especially useful in illustrating how the terms shared or common memory can transcend borders and embrace variance in interpretation far more readily than talk of collective memory. For this reason, we decided that it is better to frame our analysis in terms of shared or common memories of the Cold War.

Any number of methodological approaches could be used effectively for surveying public acts of Cold War memory and commemoration. Setting up case studies, for instance, would provide an excellent framework for examining how the Cold War is remembered in various nations.[59] Likewise, a comparative analysis could identify commonalities and dissimilarities between, say, European and Asian trends in Cold War memory and commemoration, or how the two superpowers approach the subject, or 'official' (namely state-orchestrated) and 'unofficial' (that is, any socially-cultivated) acts of remembering. An episodic approach could unfold chronologically; along the way it could feature, for example, flashpoints including the Berlin Blockade and the Cuban Missile Crisis, war in Vietnam and Afghanistan, diplomatic and political standoffs like the boycotting of the Moscow and Los Angeles Olympic Games in 1980 and 1984 respectively, through to the dramatic turn of events during 1989–91 that culminated in the collapse of eastern European communism. Adopting a thematic approach enables all kinds of mnemonic vectors to be explored. A full-length study of Cold War museums and exhibitions, for example, would make an important contribution to our developing understanding of this sub-field of war memory and commemoration; so, too, could a book entirely based on cultural representations of the Cold War including filmic portrayals and literary works.[60] Political rhetoric is another theme that could easily occupy an entire book on remembering the Cold War, with speeches by politicians and civic leaders along with parliamentary acts and debates promising to be rich sources of material. There are now ample Cold War memorials scattered around the globe to warrant a lengthy study exclusively fixated on this theme, too. So the list goes on, and, with much Cold War memory work to be done in the coming years, all such approaches surely will be employed to good effect in future publications.

For a number of reasons we have adopted a thematic approach, but not one limited to a single topic or type of Cold War remembrance. Confining our investigation to museums and exhibitions only, or to cultural representations, or nothing other than political rhetoric, or memorials or any other lone theme simply would not facilitate the wide-ranging approach required for the kind of survey this work aims to present. Instead, this study is structured around four main themes of Cold War memory and commemoration: first, this chapter's conceptual sketch underpinning our approach; second, the nuclear threat that enveloped the globe following Hiroshima; third, cities and sites that have become topographical arenas for articulating memories of the Cold War; and, finally, ways in which the Cold War, as contemporary history that remains with us in the present, continues to help define our times through tales of espionage, recently opened museums, education curriculum, political policy, and even ghostly conversations. These themes are not designed as mutually exclusive 'silos' and there is plenty of overlap between the chapters.

Like any methodological or conceptual framework, there were pros and cons to weigh up before proceeding with such an ambitious multi-faceted approach. It meant obviously that none of the substantive themes could be covered in nearly as much detail as if they were the sole focus of our inquiry. And, as one very helpful colleague Günter Bischof forewarned early on, survey studies of such magnitude always face the danger of ending up 'a mile wide and an inch deep'. In other words, there is a risk that, in endeavouring to present such an extensive survey, we could spread ourselves too thinly with the end result being a rather shallow analysis of Cold War memory and commemoration. As the first book-length survey study of this subject, however, one of this project's most important tasks is to provide a template and set some parameters for how to treat Cold War remembrance; subsequent scholarship then can expand on themes raised here, providing more detailed analyses of individual trajectories or sites. On the positive side, furthermore, structuring the book around these themes enabled us to roam far and wide in the search for examples that encapsulate the diverse agencies and arenas of articulation involved in Cold War memory and commemoration. Indeed, more than a dozen countries spread across three continents feature prominently throughout this work. All three substantive chapters contain a good blend whereby coverage of the most obvious cases is complemented by telling some more obscure stories. And, in the spirit of the book's sub-title, our focus zooms in and out frequently so that national stories are contextualized within a broader metanarrative of the Cold War as a global contest. The idea is not to compile a random grab-bag of ostensibly unrelated cases just for the sake of variety, but rather to stitch together a rich tapestry that illustrates the complexities associated with remembering the Cold War in Europe, North America, and Asia. Our thematic approach also provides the additional bonus of enabling a transnational dimension at various stages of the investigation with Chapter 2 ('Nuclear World') and Chapter 4 ('Defining Our Times') especially conducive to analytical commentary that transcends national frameworks. Here it is important to emphasize that, although the nation-state remains a fulcrum of war memory and commemoration, in the twenty-first century globalized forces are becoming increasingly instrumental.

Why choose these themes over other seemingly endless possibilities? Admittedly, any number of topics could have been conceptualized for this kind of survey study and produced equally effective results. There is no real point, then, in trying to justify the exclusion of other feasible themes beyond stating that we experimented with several formats before concluding that the structure finally settled upon appears to best serve our stated objectives.[61] The first substantive theme, entitled 'Nuclear World', was an automatic inclusion for an investigation of Cold War memory and commemoration. As mentioned earlier, there is no universally accepted commencement date for the Cold War; we take Hiroshima as our starting point. The first of only two sites where an atomic bomb has been used for mass killing, Hiroshima quickly transformed into an international icon and rallying point for anti-nuclear activism. In the decades that followed, MAD – Mutually Assured Destruction – lay at the heart of the Cold War. An episode like the Cuban Missile Crisis of October 1962 is remembered for its lessons in crisis management as well as at more popular levels. And, while some Cold War nuclear launch and storage sites remain active, many other test sites and shelters/bunkers bear witness to more specific East–West fears of yesteryear. Test sites in the Australian desert, Nevada, and Kazakhstan, for instance, provoke particular forms of state-centred remembering as well as socially-based evaluations of their heritage potential. These contentious nuclear sites, furthermore, have become embroiled in attempts to seek compensation for exposure to radiation. In French Polynesia, the nuclear past has not been forgotten as indigenous groups campaign for the restoration of reefs and island habitats in the wake of tests. Elsewhere, Greenham Common – the site of women's protests against nuclear missiles in Britain – is remembered for the mobilization of gender fused with anti-nuclear protest. Since the world was spared a nuclear apocalypse, we also have been invited to blend memory and history with an imagined experience. On the one hand, governments and private entrepreneurs have converted former nuclear fallout shelters into tourist destinations particularly in the UK, Scandinavia, and surrounding Berlin, while IT developments mean that it is now possible to take a virtual tour of sites such as the Diefenbunker, Canada's national Cold War museum, from anywhere in the world. On the other hand, Hollywood has invited us to consider the end of the world in ways that recall or echo Cold War nuclear dread.

The second and largest substantive chapter, entitled 'Cities and Sites', was devised as the most straightforward way to canvass arenas of articulation of all shapes and sizes that serve as public places where the Cold War has been and continues to be remembered. Several cities and towns have had the Cold War woven into the fabric of their modern identities in such a way that makes it impossible for residents and visitors alike not to remember this era. Other cities, understandably, adopt a more selective approach to memory and commemoration because they are synonymous with specific Cold War episodes. Due to the Prague Spring and the Velvet Revolution, for instance, the Czech capital fixates on the events of 1968 and 1989, whereas the Hungarian Uprising of 1956 is the bedrock of remembering the Cold War in central Budapest. Hanoi draws on not only 1954 and the defeat of the French at Dien Bien Phu, but also the heavy American bombing campaign of December 1972 now celebrated among Vietnamese as the 'Dien Bien Phu in the Air'. Smaller and more isolated sites of memory proliferate wherever the Cold War made an impact, such as Vint Hill in Northern Virginia.

If any theme rivals the nuclear dimension as a leading paradigm – then and now – of the Cold War, the murky world of spies and espionage must come close. The world's most famous spy James Bond 007 may have moved with the times, replacing Dr No and ensuing Cold War-era villains obsessed with missiles and spacecraft with new-age nemeses who personify today's perceived threats. Nonetheless, spies and espionage remain synonymous with the Cold War and they proliferate in fiction and institutional memory. Accordingly, this topic features prominently in the third and final substantive chapter entitled 'Defining Our Times'. The spectacular success of Tomas Alfredson's recent filmic adaptation of John le Carré's 1974 novel *Tinker, Tailor, Soldier, Spy* gives some indication of how popular remembering Cold War espionage remains in the present day. Espionage was a prominent theme on both sides of the Atlantic, and remembering the American story perhaps is best exemplified by the remarkable scenes witnessed in the early Cold War years: J. Edgar Hoover's Federal Bureau of Investigation (FBI) and his pursuit of American 'subversives' plus trials of those who 'betrayed' such as Alger Hiss; and, naturally, the communist witchhunts of McCarthyism. And, in Australian shared memory, the Petrov Affair of 1954 remains one of the most vivid episodes of the Cold War down under. Beyond stories constructed around individuals or small groups, consideration also must be given to governmental organizations that acted as secret police and intelligence agencies during the Cold War. How are the (typically clandestine) roles played by the FBI, MI6, ASIO and others in the West remembered? What about the KGB and its eastern European counterparts? To cite just one example, remembering the dreaded *Stasi* is a painful and often politically uncomfortable process not only for former East German victims but, indeed, for reunified Germany *in toto*. In the case of Berlin, a very moving *Stasi* exhibit and documentation centre is only a short walk from Checkpoint Charlie, which, along with the Glienicke Bridge on the city's outskirts near Potsdam, lends itself to 'nicer' memories of Cold War spying and espionage such as prisoner exchanges.

As emphasized at the start of this chapter, investigating how the Cold War is appropriated for contemporary political purposes is one of the driving impulses behind this whole project. Along with spies and espionage, it is one of the main themes addressed in 'Defining Our Times'. It probes various settings in which articulating the Cold War as contemporary history continues to help shape the world in which we live. The chapter also offers an extended opportunity to revisit the interplay between history, memory, and nation-building or myth-making either 'from below' or through high politics. It also examines the instructional capabilities of the Cold War as a toolbox for experiments in public diplomacy or a source of analogies that might guide current decision-makers facing international crises. Educational texts are assessed to gauge how the Cold War is taught to younger generations. And, while not being truly historiographical, the chapter also teases out the role of historians in the construction of shared or common memories of the Cold War. How mass media, rapid advancements in information and communication technologies, and our generation's obsession with memory shape and reflect these developments in an increasingly globalized environment naturally must be given due consideration, too, in the context of what might be called 'Cold War tourism'.

'The power of memory as a historical concept,' according to Alon Confino and Peter Fritzsche, 'lies in its openness to questioning and renewal.'[62] Accordingly, rather than a standard conclusion that could pose an unwanted sense of finality or closure, this study ends with a short chapter that probes the concept of 'Endings' and the interconnection between memory and forgetting. It briefly reflects on what has been covered throughout the preceding chapters, and then considers the fascinating situations currently playing out in Berlin and Moscow before finishing with some suggestions about possible directions for future scholarship on this subject matter.

Notes

1 To cite a few recent exceptions, see Heonik Kwon, *The Other Cold War* (New York: Columbia University Press, 2010). Jon Wiener, *How We Forgot the Cold War: A Historical Journey Across America* (Berkeley: University of California Press, 2012). Igor Torbakov, 'History, Memory and National Identity: Understanding the Politics of History and Memory Wars in Post-Soviet Lands', *Demokratizatsiya: The Journal of Post-Soviet Democratization*, vol. 19, no. 3 (2011).

2 For examples, see above. Also, here it should be acknowledged that sport was a very prominent theme in the Cold War but it is not covered in the following study. The key reason for this decision is that it is anticipated that a later volume in this series will include detailed coverage of Cold War case studies as part of a wider study of 'remembering sporting triumphs, tragedies, and rivalries'.

3 From the context of nationhood, such an observation can be traced back to Ernest Renan, '"What is a Nation?" (lecture delivered at the Sorbonne on 11 March 1882)', in *Becoming National: A Reader*, eds Geoff Eley and Ronald Grigor Suny (New York: Oxford University Press, 1996).

4 For instance, we can juxtapose the Cuban Missile Crisis of October 1962 and the Sino-Indian border conflict that occurred at the same time (October–November 1962). In the English-speaking world, the former remains a, if not *the*, paradigmatic event of the Cold War whereas the latter has never received widespread attention.

5 Jan-Werner Müller, 'Introduction', in *Memory and Power in Post-War Europe: Studies in the Presence of the Past*, ed. Jan-Werner Müller (Cambridge: Cambridge University Press, 2002), p. 11.

6 To cite just one example relating to each event, see Jay Winter, *Sites of Memory, Sites of Mourning: The Great War in European Cultural History* (Cambridge: Cambridge University Press, 1996). Helmut Peitsch, Charles Burdett, and Claire Gorrara, eds, *European Memories of the Second World War* (New York/London: Berghahn Books, 1999). James E. Young, *The Texture of Memory: Holocaust Memorials and Meaning* (New Haven: Yale University Press, 1993).

7 Müller, 'Introduction', p. 12.

8 David Reynolds, *One World Divisible: A Global History since 1945* (London: Penguin Books, 2000), p. 2.

9 Ibid.

10 Eric Hobsbawm, *The Age of Empire: 1875–1914* (London: Abacus, 1994), p. 3.

11 Jay Winter, *Remembering War: The Great War between Memory and History in the Twentieth Century* (New Haven: Yale University Press, 2006), p. 6.

12 Emily Rosenberg, *A Date which will Live: Pearl Harbor in American Memory* (Durham & London: Duke University Press, 2003), p. 5.

13 Patrick Finney, *Remembering the Road to World War Two: International History, National Identity, Collective Memory* (Abingdon, Oxon: Routledge, 2011), p. 22.

14 Jay Winter and Emmanuel Sivan, 'Setting the Framework', in *War and Remembrance in the Twentieth Century*, eds Jay Winter and Emmanuel Sivan (Cambridge: Cambridge University Press, 1999), p. 18.
15 Idith Zertal, *Israel's Holocaust and the Politics of Nationhood* (Cambridge: Cambridge University Press, 2005). For other international perspectives, see also Peter Novick, *The Holocaust in American Life* (Boston: Houghton Mifflin, 1999). Norman Finkelstein, *The Holocaust Industry: Reflections on the Exploitation of Jewish Suffering* (London: Verso, 2000).
16 If victim status has become a contemporary political 'asset', then the obverse of the memory coin means that identifying a perpetrator is the necessary 'deficit' to balance the historical ledger. Here, owing to its Nazi past, Germany is the most obvious exemplar. For an excellent discussion about victimhood as an asset and perpetrator status as the deficit, see especially the thought-provoking epilogue 'Whose Holocaust? Whose History' in Charles S. Maier, *The Unmasterable Past: History, Holocaust, and German National Identity* (Cambridge, Mass.: Harvard University Press, 1988).
17 Francis Fukuyama, *The End of History and the Last Man* (London: Penguin Books, 1992).
18 T.G. Ashplant, Graham Dawson, and Michael Roper, 'The Politics of War Memory and Commemoration: Contexts, Structures and Dynamics', in *The Politics of War Memory and Commemoration*, eds. T.G. Ashplant, Graham Dawson, and Michael Roper (London: Routledge, 2000), p. 5.
19 Müller, 'Introduction', p. 9.
20 For examples of important works from non-historians, see Aleida Assmann, 'Re-Framing Memory. Between Individual and Collective Forms of Constructing the Past', in *Performing the Past: Memory, History, and Identity in Modern Europe*, eds Karin Tilmans, Frank Van Vree, and Jay M. Winter (Amsterdam: Amsterdam University Press, 2010). And Susan Sontag, *Regarding the Pain of Others* (New York: Farrar, Straus and Giroux, 2003). For an example of an influential interdisciplinary study, see Harald Welzer, Sabine Moller, and Karoline Tschuggnall, *'Opa war kein Nazi': Nationalsozialismus und Holocaust im Familiengedächtnis* (Frankfurt-am-Main: Fischer Verlag, 2002).
21 Charles S. Maier, 'A Surfeit of Memory? Reflections on History, Melancholy and Denial', *History and Memory*, vol. 5, no. 2 (1993).
22 For an excellent article that uses the case of Germany to demonstrate the virtues of considering the overlap between various strands of not only public and private but also intergenerational war memories, see Aleida Assmann, 'On the (In)compatibility of Guilt and Suffering in German Memory', *German Life and Letters*, vol. 59 (April 2006).
23 Ashplant, Dawson, and Roper, 'Contexts, Structures, Dynamics', pp. 7–12. They also outline a third paradigm, labelled the 'popular-memory' approach, which is not considered here. See pp. 12–14.
24 Benedict Anderson, *Imagined Communities* (London: Verso, 1983). Eric Hobsbawm and Terence Ranger, eds, *The Invention of Tradition* (New York: Cambridge University Press, 1983).
25 Ashplant, Dawson, and Roper, 'Contexts, Structures, Dynamics', p. 7.
26 Kwon, *The Other Cold War*, pp. 8–9.
27 Bill Niven, ed., *Germans as Victims* (New York: Palgrave Macmillan, 2006). Robert G. Moeller, *War Stories: The Search for a Usable Past in the Federal Republic of Germany* (Berkeley/Los Angeles: University of California Press, 2001). Chalmers Johnson, ed., *Okinawa: Cold War Island* (Cardiff, California: Japan Policy Research Institute, 1999).
28 Welzer, Moller, and Tschuggnall, *'Opa war kein Nazi'*. Martin Gegner and Bart Ziino, eds, *The Heritage of War*, Key Issues in Cultural Heritage (Abingdon, Oxon:

Routledge, 2012). Alon Confino and Peter Fritzsche, eds, *The Work of Memory: New Directions in the Study of German Society and Culture* (Urbana; Chicago: University of Illinois Press, 2002).
29 Finney, *Remembering the Road.*
30 Norbert Frei, *Adenauer's Germany and the Nazi Past: The Politics of Amnesty and Integration,* trans. Joel Golb (New York: Columbia University Press, 2002). Rosenberg, *A Date which will Live.* Jeffrey Herf, *Divided Memory: The Nazi Past in the Two Germanys* (Cambridge, Massachusetts: Harvard University Press, 1997).
31 Matthias Hass, *Gestaltetes Gedenken: Yad Vashem, das U.S. Holocaust Memorial Museum und die Stiftung Topographie des Terrors* (Frankfurt/New York: Campus, 2002). James E. Young, 'Holocaust Museums in Germany, Poland, Israel, and the United States', in *Contemporary Responses to the Holocaust,* eds Konrad Kwiet and Jürgen Matthäus (Westport: Praeger, 2004).
32 Aleida Assmann and Sebastian Conrad, eds, *Memory in a Global Age: Discourses, Practices and Trajectories* (Basingstoke, Hampshire: Palgrave Macmillan, 2010). Daniel Levy and Natan Sznaider, *The Holocaust and Memory in the Global Age,* trans. Assenka Oksiloff (Philadelphia: Temple University Press, 2006).
33 Rudy Koshar, *From Monuments to Traces: Artifacts of German Memory, 1870–1990* (Berkeley: University of California Press, 2000). Siobhan Kattago, *Ambiguous Memory: The Nazi Past and German National Identity* (Westport, Connecticut: Praeger, 2001).
34 Klaus Neumann, *Shifting Memories: The Nazi Past in the New Germany* (Ann Arbor: University of Michigan Press, 2003).
35 Peter Gray and Kendrick Oliver, eds, *The Memory of Catastrophe* (Manchester: Manchester University Press, 2004). Tony Joel, *The Dresden Firebombing: Memory and the Politics of Commemorating Destruction* (London: I.B.Tauris, 2013 in press).
36 John Gillis, ed., *Commemorations: The Politics of National Identity* (Princeton: University Press, 1994). Especially helpful is Gillis' introduction, 'Memory and Identity: The History of a Relationship'. See also Young, *The Texture of Memory.*
37 William Kidd and Brian Murdoch, eds, *Memory and Memorials: the Commemorative Century* (Aldershot: Ashgate, 2004).
38 T.G. Ashplant, Graham Dawson, and Michael Roper, eds, *The Politics of War Memory and Commemoration* (London: Routledge, 2000). Jost Dülffer, 'Erinnerungspolitik und Erinnerungskultur – Kein Ende der Geschichte', in *Eine Ausstellung und ihre Folgen: Zur Rezeption der Ausstellung 'Vernichtungskrieg. Verbrechen der Wehrmacht 1941 bis 1944',* ed. Hamburger Institut für Sozialforschung (Hamburg: HIS Verlagsges.mbH, 1999). Michael J. Hogan, 'The Enola Gay Controversy: History, Memory, and the Politics of Presentation', in *Hiroshima in History and Memory,* ed. Michael J. Hogan (New York: Cambridge University Press, 1999). Zertal, *Israel's Holocaust.*
39 Bettina Messias Carbonell, ed. *Museum Studies: An Anthology of Contexts* (Oxford: Blackwell Publishing, 2004). Young, 'Holocaust Museums'. Hass, *Gestaltetes Gedenken.* Kenneth Lunn and Martin Evans, *War and Memory in the Twentieth Century* (Oxford, UK: Berg, 1997).
40 Steven C. Dubin, *Displays of Power: Controversy in the American Museum from the Enola Gay to Sensation* (New York: University Press, 1999).
41 This is not to say that 'carriage' should be understood as a passive term. As Müller states, all 'carriers of memory are engaged in a constant process not just of remembering, but also of reshaping'. Müller, 'Introduction', p. 30.
42 Pierre Nora, 'Between Memory and History: Les Lieux de Mémoire', *Representations,* no. 26 (1989), p. 7.
43 Ibid. p. 12.
44 Maurice Halbwachs, *On Collective Memory,* trans. Lewis A. Coser (Chicago and London: The University of Chicago Press, 1992 [1925]).

45 Aleida Assmann, 'Europe: A Community of Memory? (Twentieth Annual Lecture of the GHI, 16 November 2006)', *GHI Bulletin*, no. 40 (Spring 2007), p. 12.
46 For the coding/decoding/recoding of sites of war memory and commemoration, see the work of urban sociologist Martin Gegner, 'War Monuments in East and West Berlin: Cold War Symbols or different Forms of Memorial?' in *The Heritage of War*, eds Martin Gegner and Bart Ziino (Abingdon, Oxon: Routledge, 2012).
47 Sontag, *Regarding the Pain of Others*, pp. 85–86. See also Assmann, 'Re-Framing Memory', p. 36.
48 Sontag, *Regarding the Pain of Others*, p. 86.
49 Assmann, 'Re-Framing Memory', p. 36.
50 For a discussion on individual, social, political, and cultural 'memory formats', see ibid. pp. 40–44.
51 Wulf Kansteiner, 'Finding Meaning in Memory: A Methodological Critique of Collective Memory Studies', *History and Theory*, no. 41 (May 2002), pp. 185–90.
52 Müller, 'Introduction', p. 21.
53 Sontag, *Regarding the Pain of Others*, p. 85.
54 Eric Gable and Richard Handler, 'Forget Culture, Remember Memory? (Keynote Address)' (paper presented at the Annual Meeting of the Southern Anthropological Society, Staunton, Virginia, 2008).
55 Müller, 'Introduction', p. 20.
56 See Kansteiner, 'Finding Meaning in Memory', p. 185.
57 Sontag, *Regarding the Pain of Others*, p. 85.
58 These concepts are developed in Ashplant, Dawson, and Roper, 'Contexts, Structures, Dynamics', pp. 18–19.
59 For two upcoming volumes in this series that adopt such an approach, see Nigel Eltringham and Pam Maclean, eds, *Remembering Genocide* and Bart Ziino, ed., *Remembering the Great War*.
60 For a recent film, see Toke Constantin Hebbeln, *Shores of Hope* (Germany 2012). For a recent fictional account from Australia set in the 1950s, see Judy Nunn, *Maralinga* (Sydney: William Heinemann, 2009).
61 Here, we would like to thank several anonymous reviewers for providing insightful feedback and suggestions during the preliminary stages of this project. We also wish to thank the following colleagues for similarly providing constructive criticism that helped to improve this study: Professor David Reynolds, Professor Jost Dülffer, Professor Carl Bridge, Johannes Bach Rasmussen, Assoc. Professor Christopher Waters, Dr Helen Gardner, Eric Meadows, Dr Joanna Cruickshank, Dr Murray Noonan, Dr Mark Humphries, Dr Don Gibb, and Dr Bart Ziino.
62 Alon Confino and Peter Fritzsche, 'Introduction: Noises of the Past', in *The Work of Memory: New Directions in the Study of German Society and Culture*, eds Alon Confino and Peter Fritzsche (Urbana, Chicago: University of Illinois Press, 2002), p. 3.

2 Nuclear world

By way of entering the world of remembering the Cold War, we should acknowledge the extraordinary double-event that frames most discussions of its beginnings: the dropping of atomic bombs on Hiroshima and Nagasaki. The two atomic bombs dropped on Japan in August 1945 form substantial architecture in most explorations of the start of the Cold War; and the image of the aftermath of an atomic bomb's explosion – the mushroom cloud – is one of the most reproduced symbols with reference to the Cold War. It acts as a visual mnemonic thread from 1945, through the peaks of tensions between East and West all of which carried the threat of cata-clysmic devastation wrought by atomic warfare, to the end of the Cold War. To the extent that it captures the incredibly high stakes during a period of protracted tension that resists easy summary, the mushroom cloud also has become the Cold War's greatest emblem. And, crucially, the connection between the mushroom cloud as apocalyptic portent and Hiroshima as reality also carries the trans-generational memory of human suffering in most dramatic forms. The images of horrific .burns, and of human-shaped shadows etched against the walls of buildings in Hiroshima by the heat blast of the bomb, are well known. If, as Jan Werner-Müller has suggested, (Eurocentric views of) the Cold War may lack for remembering on account of a lack of tales of suffering and mourning, then it effectively borrows on the extraordinary event of atomic-bomb suffering at the end of the Second World War.[1] Even if later narratives of bomb-related suffering relate to weapons testing and arise through accident or neglect, such is the power of Hiroshima in modern memory that the borrowing is near-automatic.

This is a realm in which commentators also have been effective agents of memory. Historians and journalists, for instance, have sustained memories of atomic bombs in debates over their first use. Even if they struggle to reach agreement on when the Cold War started, the atomic backdrop to the escalation of tensions between the Soviet Union on the one hand and the United States and its allies on the other, looms large for most. It not only frames debate about origins, but also is hotly contested and recur-ringly remembered. Both the Hiroshima reality and the gigantic nuclear threat thereafter serve to illustrate the problems in framing starting points for remembering the Cold War, thereby highlighting central questions: how do nationally-organized or appropriated acts of public remembering of the Cold War link to the more global and diffuse backdrop of the Cold War? And, especially in the case of the recent rush of remembering and memorialization barely 20 years since the collapse of the Soviet Union, what conceptual and historical architecture carries messages? To what extent do the contours of the Cold War fall away, so that remembering becomes more episodic and necessarily grounded in localized circumstances, including structured silences about others involved in a bigger conflict? Does this happen in order to fit the remembering into more easily processed war-like moments of struggle, in a manner consistent with two earlier world wars, or does it reflect an avoidance of explication based on ideological grounds?

Interest in the United States' reasons behind the dropping of the atomic bombs is piqued in secondary and higher education as well as among the general public to such a level that the decision-making remains one of those subjects of historical debate that easily crosses between academic and public curiosity. Consider this statement: the dropping of two atomic bombs on the Japanese cities of Hiroshima and Nagasaki, on 6 and 9 August 1945 respectively, ushered in the atomic age and hastened the end of the Second World War. At first glance, this description might seem balanced and uncontroversial. If we elaborate further, however, the tension between the 'ushering in' and 'hastening end' in this statement becomes clear. In overly-simple terms, the more the atomic bombs ended the maelstrom of death and destruction that was wrought by the Second World War, the more they can be considered a necessary evil; and the more they mark a new, atomic age, and a new preparedness to use weapons of mass destruction on civilian populations, the more fraught becomes their use. It is hard to explicate the circumstances of their use in 1945 without wading through controversy and competing interpretations, such is the ongoing inscription, debate, and re-inscription associated with remembering the events. Much of the strongest argument turns on Washington's thinking behind the decision to use the bombs and whether they were necessary to bring the war to an end. And some of the strongest emotion in explanations arises from the horrific images of those burnt in the blast and the resultant death toll – overwhelmingly civilian – of at least 200,000 Japanese and other nationalities (including conscripted Koreans). Those arguing that US president Harry S. Truman and his advisers were justified in wanting to use the weapons in order to avoid enormous anticipated casualties in an invasion of the Japanese home islands have benefited from archival releases over the last 20 years supporting their case, but the debate still rages.[2] Even to suggest that the dropping of the bombs 'hastened' the end of the war in the Pacific is not without argument, as, according to one recent account, the Soviet invasion of Manchuria between the dropping of the two bombs was the decisive factor in the Japanese surrender on 15 August.[3]

The growing tensions between the United States and the Soviet Union during 1944–45 feature somewhere in debates on the use of the bomb. In this sense, the mushroom cloud frames the descent of a wartime alliance into implacable, mutual hostility – a Cold War. Those historians who most directly bring this debate into Cold War origins argue that Truman was strongly motivated in deciding to drop the bombs by his desire to prevent the Soviets from playing a decisive role in the defeat of Japan and thereby gain geopolitical influence in East Asia.[4] While support for this particular argument has weakened somewhat in recent years, the significance of the bomb for US–Soviet relations is hard to ignore completely. And, whatever the relative weight given to the Soviet factor and the dropping of the bombs on Japan, it is hard to uncouple these two features in explanations of Japan's surrender.

At the same time, historians have become fond of disrupting conventional ideas about beginnings and endings of major world events such as the two world wars. For many, the atomic bomb conveniently straddles the end of the Second World War and start of the Cold War and is a more spectacular jumping point for Cold War exploration than alternative Cold War origins found in telegrams and diplomatic clashes.[5] Arguably, there also is a strong Japanese interest in positioning the dropping of the bomb on Hiroshima as the start of the nuclear age rather than as the end of the Second World War. By maximizing the event (and it should be noted that the dropping of the second bomb on Nagasaki is less-well publicly remembered), Japanese authorities assume some of the victimhood attached to the extremities of a war that was described as 'total' in nature; and, in association with victimhood and the sense of a new terror unleashed, perhaps can dwell less on Japanese wartime atrocities committed in the 1937–45 period. The Japanese experience was unique for reasons of their immediate and protracted suffering resulting from the atomic bombs and, as John Dower reminds us, for the US-enforced censorship in the aftermath that prevented them from publicly engaging with the meaning of what had happened. But a much broader international citizenry, according to Dower, shared the sense that 6–9 August 1945 represented a pivotal moment in modern history:

> For much of the world, the Holocaust in Europe and the nuclear genocide of Hiroshima/Nagasaki signified the closure of 'modernity' as it had been known and dreamed about until then and the advent of a new world of terrible and awesome potentialities.[6]

Remembering the bomb

Peace activists in Japan and heritage lobbyists in the United States, in different ways, have built bridges between the dropping of the atomic bombs in August 1945 and contemporary acts of remembering that necessarily incorporate the Cold War. Japan has a long lineage of remembering the bomb. In 1946, on the first anniversary of the dropping of the bomb, surviving citizens of Hiroshima held a Peace Restoration Festival, something that became an annual event, compelling officialdom into involvement. In the same year, American journalist John Hersey published his now-famous essay 'Hiroshima' in the *New Yorker*. Detailing the effects of the bomb on six survivors, it was quickly published (and repeatedly reprinted) in book form, and remains one of the most influential sources for those seeking to understand the bomb's impact.[7] In 1949, Hiroshima, led by Mayor Shinzo Hamai, confirmed its transition to a site of international remembrance by selecting a design for the Peace Memorial Park and having the Japanese parliament proclaiming it a 'City of Peace'. Importantly, in the planning between the city of Hiroshima and the Japanese state for a collective urban definition of survival, the city administration and the mayor gained, and have maintained, considerable influence over final decisions. Subsequent mayors of Hiroshima have been integral to the transformation of the Hiroshima Peace Memorial Museum from a site of memory that spoke mostly to survivors to an arena of articulation that anticipates high numbers of international visitors. And, from the late-1980s, the memorial museum located within the peace park has addressed contentious debates and incorporated prewar and postwar material relating to the story of the city.[8] The distinctive name given to Japanese survivors, the *hibakusha* (literally, explosion-affected people), has further enabled the carriage of memory from 1945 through to current times; so, too, has publication of their accounts of the aftermath of the atomic bombings, and the Japanese legal and policy provisions designed to assist the *hibakusha*.[9]

Today, the interpretive commentary in the Peace Memorial Museum centres the city of Hiroshima in a narrative that acknowledges its identity in the context of nineteenth- and twentieth-century Japanese industrialization and militarism. There is a vague symmetry about the contextual material either side of the pivotal moment of the bomb's detonation at 8.15 am on 6 August 1945, when 'the world entered the nuclear age'.[10] Japanese aggression in the 1930s and early-1940s is acknowledged, but balanced by the lead role played by Hiroshima authorities in peace and anti-nuclear movements after the war. The Cold War, then, is an important carrier of the 'nuclear age' in which postwar Hiroshima plays an important leadership role in the quest for peace. Extending this role, the mayors of Hiroshima and Nagasaki founded the Mayors for Peace group in 1982, a global network now involving over 5,600 cities in efforts to abolish nuclear weapons. And Hiroshima's current mayor Matsui Kazumi, whose father counts among the *hibakusha*, invoked the memory of August 1945 when lamenting the deadly consequences of the accident at Japan's Fukushima nuclear power plant following the tsunami in March 2011. In his Peace Declaration of 6 August 2012, Kazumi stated:

> Here in Hiroshima, we are keenly aware that the survivors of that catastrophe still suffer terribly, yet look forward to the future with hope.

We see their ordeal clearly superimposed on what we endured 67 years ago. I speak now to all in the stricken areas. Please hold fast to your hope for tomorrow. Your day will arrive, absolutely. Our hearts are with you.[11]

Such is the focus on peace efforts that, within a context of ongoing historical interpretation traversing and moving beyond the nuclear age, the Hiroshima Peace Memorial Museum seems to identify as a temple in a religion of peace.[12] In its display narratives, the Cold War enjoys particular references as well as serving as an omnipresent backdrop to the rise and rise of nuclear weapons. It features in explanation for why the bomb was dropped – the gigantic scale of the Manhattan Project and 'enormous expenditure' loom large, and, according to the exhibit text: 'The U.S. believed that if the atomic bomb could end the war, Soviet influence after the war would be restricted and domestically the tremendous cost of development would be justified.'[13] On another display narrating the treatment of scarred survivors, visitors learn of the fall-out that showered upon the Japanese fishing boat *Fukuryu-maru No. 5* near Bikini Atoll in March 1954, as a result of a US nuclear test. 'One of the crew members died later that autumn,' reads the caption, 'from symptoms similar to those common in Hiroshima and Nagasaki.'[14]

The Hiroshima Peace Memorial Museum attracts more than one million visitors a year. Its interpretations, complete with suggestions of victimhood, sacrifice (i.e. Hiroshima bearing the brunt of retribution for earlier conquests by Imperial Japan), and Cold War leadership in peace efforts, carry weight. Newer museums focused on the dropping of the atomic bombs have opened in Osaka, Kyoto, and Nagasaki, but it is Hiroshima's museum that draws on the Cold War's elevated threat of atomic warfare to highlight the city's leadership in peace arising from the ashes of August 1945. The Cold War swiftly becomes, after the end of the Second World War, the main vehicle for the 'nuclear age'. This age, of course, endures beyond 1989 with the continued presence of atomic weapons in volatile and potentially lethal ways, and, as mayor Matsui Kazumi argues, the reality of accidents at nuclear power plants.

However successful in building this story, the Hiroshima Peace Memorial Museum and city authorities have had to work hard to control the city's international symbolic status. Within Japan, there have been waves of recurrent political struggles between revisionists and 'rightists' over the relative standing of contested themes, such as the space accorded to Korean victims. The international struggle over where to keep the first atomic bomb in modern memory was highlighted in 1996 when Japanese delegates successfully argued to have the iconic Genbaku Dome (literally, the atomic bomb dome, now also called the Hiroshima Peace Memorial) inscribed on UNESCO's World Heritage List. The Genbaku Dome, part of the Hiroshima Peace Memorial Park in which the museum is located, is the skeletal remains of the building that prior to its destruction was the

Figure 2.1 Memorial Monument for Hiroshima, City of Peace (Memorial Cenotaph for the A-Bomb Victims), erected 6 August 1952. Accompanying text in multiple languages embedded into the ground in front of the monument states: LET ALL THE SOULS HERE REST IN PEACE FOR WE SHALL NOT REPEAT THE EVIL. This monument embodies the hope that Hiroshima, devastated on 6 August 1945 by the world's first atomic bombing, will stand forever as a city of peace. The stone chamber in the center contains the Register of Deceased A-bomb Victims. The inscription on the front panel offers a prayer for the peaceful repose of the victims and a pledge on behalf of all humanity never to repeat the evil of war. It expresses the spirit of Hiroshima—enduring grief, transcending hatred, pursuing harmony and prosperity for all, and yearning for genuine, lasting world peace.

Figure 2.2 Genbaku Dome, Hiroshima, in February 2013.

Hiroshima Prefectural Industrial Promotion Hall. It is close to the hypocentre of the bomb blast, being below the point of detonation some 600 metres above the ground.

In 1996, the UNESCO selection criterion used was such that the Dome needed to be deemed 'directly or tangibly associated with events or living traditions, with ideas, or with beliefs, with artistic and literary works of outstanding universal significance'.[15] American delegates argued against such inscription on the grounds that the dome did not have outstanding universal value as a symbol of peace but needed to be understood in the context of war – which was not a heritage priority. While US opposition was put forth without great enthusiasm, and reflected fears of a political backlash among US Army veterans more than an absolute rejection of the World Heritage argument, it also was consistent with the official US approach up to that time, of the bombs – plural – needing to be understood primarily as ending the war in the Pacific. The Chinese also expressed reservations, lest the listing detract from the huge suffering inflicted by the Japanese on other Asian peoples. But, in succeeding with the World Heritage listing, the Japanese took another step towards their articulation of Hiroshima as a symbol of peace and reconstruction, and a basis for their identification as victims of war. They did not seek to link Nagasaki to Hiroshima's heritage listing, for this would have reinforced the connection between the dropping of the first atomic bombs and the end of the war.[16]

At the height of the Cold War, both the United States and the Soviet Union engaged in public celebrations of the power of the atom (and even in Japan the enormity of the bomb's power underpinned a postwar vision for a nation of science).[17] From 1956 to 1989, a 'Pavilion for Atomic Energy' featured in Moscow's Exhibition of Achievements of the People's Economy (now called the All Russia Exhibition Centre, or VDNKh).[18] In the United States, 'atomic museums' sprang up around nuclear weapons complexes, emphasizing the triumphal nature of scientific breakthroughs, with appropriate photographs, artefacts, and other records. One of the best known, the American Museum of Atomic Energy, opened at Oak Ridge, Tennessee, in 1949 as the town itself opened to the public for the first time. Oak Ridge was a secret town (a heritage it still enjoys recalling) built as part of the Manhattan Project and, until 1949, known only by those outsiders who needed to know. The Manhattan Project was the massive research and development project involving Britain and Canada and led by the United States during the Second World War to build an atomic bomb. The three key sites in the United States were Oak Ridge (where enriched uranium was produced), Hanford, Washington DC (where plutonium was produced), and Los Alamos, New Mexico, which acted as the home of the main research and design laboratory. Scientists at Oak Ridge produced the uranium-235 that went into the bomb dropped on Hiroshima. Renamed the American Museum of Science and Energy in 1978, the museum's message has changed over time. Having initially embraced the widespread utopianism associated with the exciting powers of the atom – promising limitless, clean, and cheap forms of energy – the displays later changed in tone, in the eyes of critics, to nostalgia. In its early incarnation, tourists could literally buy into the excitement of scientific genius, modernization, and the power of the atom by purchasing small chunks of uranium as souvenirs. For a short time, at least, it seemed as though the atom would partly escape the shadow of Hiroshima.

But the atomic bomb quickly dominated how the Cold War took shape, because it sparked a very tangible and terrifying arms race. The Soviets had developed their own bomb by 1949; and both the Americans and Soviets built and successfully tested hydrogen bombs during 1952–55. These new weapons could be one thousand times more powerful than the bomb dropped on Hiroshima. While the two chief protagonists would be the main players in the race for bigger and better weapons, and improved and varied ways of delivering them, other nations that boasted atomic bombs were Britain (1952), France (1960), and China (1964). In the absence of any meaningful treaty or other mechanism controlling the development of atomic weapons, however, leaders in Moscow and Washington led the way in redefining security as superiority in nuclear capability. The quest to harness the atom for weapons first also ushered in a new era of atomic espionage (as discussed further in Chapter 4).

There were crisis moments when it seemed that atomic warfare might ensue. Early in 1951, as Chinese and North Korean troops overran most of

South Korea, some incautious remarks by US president Truman left his nervous British allies wondering if the bomb might be deployed. More than any other moment of the Cold War, though, it was thirteen days in October 1962 that seemed to have the world on the brink of nuclear war. When an American spy plane discovered that nuclear missiles were being installed in Cuba – less than 100 miles off the coast of Florida – US president John F. Kennedy responded with a naval blockade of the island. The backdrop to the showdown was a personal test of strength between Kennedy and Soviet premier Nikita Khrushchev, who had 'verballed' the younger American during their Vienna Summit in June 1961. In the wake of this, Kennedy made operational some nuclear missiles in Turkey, and stepped up harassing pressure on the Cuban communist leader and Soviet ally Fidel Castro. Khrushchev's reaction was to install air defence and nuclear missiles in Cuba. In a dramatic television broadcast, Kennedy told the American public about the Soviet missiles, his consequent 'quarantine' of the island and his readiness to treat any missile launched from Cuba at the United States as an attack by the Soviet Union requiring full retaliation. It was not clear which side would blink first. Soviet ships and a submarine virtually sailed up the US Navy's 'quarantine' line. An American U-2 spy plane was shot down while making one of the increased surveillance flights over Cuba. 'Nuclear catastrophe,' Soviet General and Army Chief of Operations Anatoly Gribkov later reflected, 'was hanging by a thread'. In the wake of Kennedy's television address, Americans prepared evacuation plans and those who had built fall-out shelters readied them. Had war broken out, the devastation would have been even worse for the Soviet Union. The US nuclear arsenal at the time was around 20 times the size of the Soviet one, and would have been delivered with greater accuracy. The crisis was finally defused when Khrushchev agreed to dismantle the missiles and return them to the Soviet Union in return for an American promise not to invade Cuba (and, as was subsequently revealed, to dismantle the missiles in Turkey). Given the huge stakes, it was clear to both leaders that the means of communications between Moscow and Washington needed reform, and a new direct hotline was installed between the Kremlin and the White House. They also collaborated on a partial nuclear test ban treaty (1963), sending nuclear weapons testing underground. The French did not sign on, nor would the soon-to-be-nuclear China.[19]

By the mid-1960s, Mutually Assured Destruction (better-known by its much-used and apposite acronym MAD) was the strategic doctrine providing rationale behind the nuclear arms race. It assumed the use of multiple and powerful nuclear weapons by both sides in the Cold War, resulting in reciprocal total annihilation. It also assumed that both sides had enough weapons to destroy each other, even in the event of a first-strike attack causing major destruction in the first to be hit. It assumed, moreover, a preparedness to use nuclear weapons on a scale resulting in utter devastation. The development in the 1960s of enhanced radiation weapons, neutron bombs, designed to maximize disabling and killing through pulses of high energy neutrons without extending the physical destruction of a blast range, elaborated on the possibilities being contemplated by military planners. And, although not built, the concept of a cobalt atomic bomb, mooted as early as 1950, became part of doomsday thinking. In theory, cobalt bombs would spread radioactive materials over much wider areas than conventional bombs. They constituted, at least in the minds of some, the ultimate retaliatory threat, potentially shrouding the world in inescapable radiation.

MAD, then, is one of the most shared memories associated with the Cold War and is easily tapped in remembrance, especially in association with events such as the Cuban Missile Crisis. Inviting contemplation of the nuclear arms race in any modern museum invokes, either explicitly or implicitly, the idea of the apocalypse: the two sides destroying each other and rendering the world uninhabitable. Here, remembering the Cold War generates distinctive versions of a powerful idea with a long lineage. The nuclear version of the end of the world as we know it takes particular forms, including the prospect of devastating climate change – a nuclear winter – resulting from the realization of MAD, but also can connect with astronomy, literature, and religion for older roots. As several commentators have pointed out, there also is a rich vein of twentieth-century art, literature, film, and various other forms of pop culture engaging with the idea of a modern apocalypse and its aftermath.[20] Similarly, MAD cannot be completely confined to the conventional periodization of the Cold War, because nuclear weapons have continued to loom large in international relations and security dilemmas beyond the early-1990s. Including non-deployed warheads and those awaiting dismantlement, in 2013 Russia and the United States each possess over 5,000 nuclear warheads.[21]

The Cold War arms race was as much about capability to deliver atomic weapons as it was about the weapons themselves. For this reason, Moscow's triumphant launch of the first satellite to orbit the earth, *Sputnik*, in 1957, humiliated Washington and sparked renewed spending on missile technology and weapons. As mentioned, the Soviets in fact were a long way from matching US atomic capabilities at that time and only caught up in numbers of intercontinental ballistic missiles (ICBMs) in the late-1960s. In 1969, the Soviets had 1,140 ICBMs to the Americans' 1,054; but the Soviets had less than one-third of the number of nuclear-capable bombers and submarine-launched ballistic missiles of the United States.[22] By this time, there was another possible way in which nuclear war could be triggered: as a clash between the Soviets and the Chinese following their acrimonious split, which itself derived partly from Moscow's concerns about the Chinese bomb. In 1969, a Soviet act of brinksmanship near the Chinese border in Mongolia led to sudden mobilization of the Red Army and the two communist nuclear powers faced off before they backed down. There followed a period of what became known as détente in the early-1970s when relations between the great powers either improved or settled into new, more stable patterns enabling US–Soviet agreement to limit the number of anti-ballistic missiles used to defend against incoming missiles (in an Anti-Ballistic Missile Treaty, 1972). Following the Soviet invasion of Afghanistan in December 1979 and the election of Ronald Reagan as US president the following year, however, a 'new cold war' and a renewed arms race commenced. This time, the focus was on Western Europe where new US intermediate range missiles began to be deployed from November 1983, and where anti-nuclear protest movements sprang up with renewed vigour. The focus also was in space, where president Reagan said his Strategic Defense Initiative (SDI) would build a special anti-missile shield comprising lasers and other devices, a project so ambitious it was quickly dubbed 'Star Wars'. The mid-1980s, then, was another period of high tension and nuclear-charged brinksmanship.[23] There soon followed a series of breakthroughs towards arms reduction. In 1987, the Intermediate-Range Nuclear Forces Treaty (INF) between the United States and the Soviet Union banned ground-launched and cruise missiles (with range up to 5,500 kilometres or some 3,400 miles), and provided for inspections by both sides to monitor adherence. Then, in 1991, in the wake of the collapse of communism in Europe, the Strategic Arms Reduction Treaty (START I) between the two superpowers stipulated that both the United States and the Soviet Union reduce their respective stocks of nuclear warheads to 6,000 each, across a range of delivery systems; in 1993, START II banned multiple independently targetable reentry vehicles. Although neither treaty is now in force, they signalled major brakes and reductions in an arms race that had dominated the Cold War.

Atomic themed museums in the United States now reflect both the utopianism of discovery and the sobriety of the arms race in their messages. Since the 1990s, at Oak Ridge the excitement of science remains. It is aimed particularly at children and school groups, but, as the renaming of the museum suggests, is now less exclusively anchored to the atom. The mission of the American Science and Energy Museum Foundation, chartered in 1996 as a non-profit organization, is for the museum to grow as 'a premier museum for educating the public in science, technology and history of the Manhattan Project'.[24] The nuclear identity of Oak Ridge still is captured in a blend of nostalgia for the special years of the 'secret town', and pride in helping to end the Second World War.[25] But the permanent exhibits mix the story of the town with nuclear-related careers at the still-operating Y-12 National Security Complex and the 'World of the Atom'; and they blend with displays relating to other sources of power and hands-on robotics and other science activities of colour and movement. Souvenirs available at the museum hark back to Einstein and the early atomic days of Oak Ridge, but the science kits are more solar- and weather-related, and there is a strong emphasis on classroom programmes across the spectrum of exciting science for juniors.[26]

Weapons production and testing

American atomic weapons testing from the 1950s through to the early-1990s is remembered publicly in museums, but with only muted references to the Soviet side of the nuclear arms race and the apocalyptic fears this inspired. The national pride in achievement derives more from scientific prowess and realizing hugely ambitious projects than from progress driven by external threat. In the United States, between 1951 and 1992 there were 928 declared tests conducted at the main test site in Nevada, 100 of which were above-ground explosions. Today, the National Atomic Testing Museum at Las Vegas is fulsome in recalling the history of Cold War atomic testing in the Nevada desert. The museum, however, is careful to keep the Cold War narrative in the background, and overseas events are marginalized. Designated a national museum in 2012, permanent exhibits there provide visitors with a blend of: information and displays about atomic testing in Nevada; a simulated bomb blast, including sudden blasts of air; the story of the atomic bomb's development; tracking and monitoring radiation; the technology and science of underground testing; and atomic culture, including civil defence preparations.[27] The museum works closely with schools, and in 2012 was involved in one of the more unusual exchange programmes: a group of local Las Vegas high school students travelled to East Kazakhstan, in the region near the Soviet nuclear test site of Semipalatinsk, where more than 600 tests (including more than 100 above-ground) took place between 1949 and 1989. Later, Kazakhstani students made the reciprocal trip to Las Vegas and swapped notes on living in the shadow of nuclear test grounds. It was a human face on the legacies of Soviet nuclear testing that has not featured either in the former Soviet Union or elsewhere.

A quiet transnationalism thus flavours some of the remembering attached to pioneering atomic science and the development of weapons. Probably the best-known example of atomic 'twinning' is between Los Alamos and the Russian closed city of Sarov, almost 500 kilometres east of Moscow, where the first Soviet atomic bomb was built.[28] Formerly called Arzamas-16, the city disappeared from Soviet maps in 1946 when the All Russian Scientific Research Institute of Experimental Physics was built there. During 1992–93, scientific exchange and high school pen-pal activity, both prompting reciprocal visits, brought the cities together, and the 'Sister-Cities' relationship was declared in May 1994.[29] Today, the city of Sarov has emerged on the other side of the Cold War: still trail-blazing in science, it is home to Russia's largest supercomputer and Europe's largest station for laser-induced thermo-nuclear fusion. Sarov remains 'closed', and foreigners thereby need special arrangements to visit. Upon gaining entry, they may visit the Museum of Nuclear Weapons now open, which boasts full-size casings of the first Soviet atomic bomb, their first (and the world's first) hydrogen bomb, and the so-called Tsar-Bomb – with a yield of 50 megatons, the biggest hydrogen bomb ever built.[30]

Another closed city producing nuclear weapons, Zarechny (formerly Penza-19), now hosts the Russian Nuclear Weapons Museum with a similar array of nuclear bombs, shells, and missile casings, with accompanying narratives about their development. While little detailed information on the consequences of Soviet testing has emerged, intrepid journalists visiting Semipalatinsk have found high levels of radiation, continuing high incidences of cancers, and official scrambling to cope with the health and economic consequences.[31] East Kazakhstan's testing area is hardly a tourist destination; and is more frequented by US-sponsored drones guarding against the removal of highly contaminated soil that might be used in a terrorist's 'dirty bomb'.

Chinese nuclear testing also attracts attention for its deadly legacies. Pointing to a cavalier approach to safety, one Japanese researcher suggests that the Chinese atomic testing programme at the Malan test site in Lop Nur, in the Xinjiang Uygur Autonomous Region, resulted in a likely death toll of more than 190,000 victims between 1964 and 1996. Using models to extrapolate from incomplete data, the same research suggests that up to 1.5 million people may be adversely affected.[32] Both the location of the 23 atmospheric tests and the medical data relating to numbers affected remain hard to corroborate. In 2012, however, the European Parliament heard evidence from experts and human rights groups and resolved to uncover further information and pursue the matter with Chinese authorities.[33] Unfazed, Beijing has recently been 'cleaning' the test area in order to add it to its list of 'Red Tourism' sites, significant for their role in communist Chinese history.[34] In 2006, an atomic-themed museum (closed to foreigners) already opened in the city of Mianyang, Sichuan, where the first Chinese bomb was made in 1964, and where weapons production and research continues.[35]

It is hard to predict how Chinese atomic tourism will fare. Despite the substantial investment and special effects, the National Atomic Testing Museum in Las Vegas attracts only modest numbers (although the number of alternative attractions in Las Vegas makes it a special case).[36] Arguably more enduring and more easily found (via the internet) are photographs of hotel-sponsored 'Miss Atomic Bomb' beauties and 'bomb-watch parties' showing citizens of Las Vegas watching post-test mushroom clouds over the rooftops of their city.[37] Such photographs, and artistic works on the same theme of atomic testing foregrounded by Las Vegas scenes, play prominent roles in the visual mnemonic thread of the mushroom cloud from Hiroshima to subsequent test explosions and the reminder of potential self-destruction that Cold War brinksmanship posed.[38]

Is it possible to remain nostalgic about atomic weapons development, especially when it was linked so closely to a Cold War arms race of frightening proportions? The answer at least partially appears to be 'yes', provided that the excessive utopianism accompanying early hopes for the powers of the atom, and the hugely destructive effects of weapons, both recede in public remembering. In the cases of Oak Ridge and Las Vegas, there are smoothing agents building bridges between potential controversy and the public desire to remember. Running through the museum is display information that one historian has called an 'alchemical narrative', inviting visitors to recall the transformational excitement of the powers of the atom. As the public learned about atomic energy in the late-1940s and 1950s, it assumed near magical qualities, with the invisible dangers of radiation even adding to a sense of mystery.[39] A celebration of scientists associated with atomic research, including the well-recognized Albert Einstein, builds a focus on pioneering achievement rather than its horrific consequences. And highlighting the sacrifices and achievements of those who lived through depression and then the Second World War before embarking on heroic postwar rebuilding taps into the discourse of the 'greatest generation', made popular by US writer Tom Brokaw.[40] The delineation of such a valorized generation eases places such as Los Alamos and Oak Ridge into a patriotic landscape, but does not take 'Atomic America' much beyond the end of the Second World War. In the jostling for memory 'space' in the minds of modern Americans, the Cold War lacks an alternative generation that is so easily recognized and worthy of embrace for its achievements.

There is an alternative hook for audiences in Las Vegas, which extends the narrative of fantasy associated with atomic power. Since March 2012, the National Atomic Testing Museum has embraced the mystery and mythology surrounding Area 51, the highly secret military base and testing facility in Southern Nevada that has spawned conspiracy theories and suggestions of work with UFOs and their inhabitants.[41] The base adjoins an area used for nuclear testing and its name, Area 51, is an Atomic Energy Commission designation. Area 51's association with the top-secret development of US reconnaissance aircraft, including the high-altitude U-2 spy-plane and fore-runners to the Lockheed SR-71 'Blackbird', is well-established. Popular culture sustains it, furthermore, as the site of extravagant imaginings. Hollywood's 1996 blockbuster *Independence Day*, for instance, sees the US military making use of alien technology in Area 51 to fight off alien invaders. Special lectures in the National Atomic Testing Museum's calendar for early 2013 included 'Hunting UFOs', 'The U2 and Area 51', and 'Inside Top Gun'. Veering towards the top secret reflects the long-standing pervasiveness of the US government in Nevada. Even in the 1990s, some 86 per cent of the state was federally owned or administered;[42] and the state therefore remains a rendezvous point for atomic imagination and conspiracy theories tapping a deep vein of suspicion toward Washington's hidden experiments. Similarly, as a tourist destination Los Alamos in New Mexico is sometimes bundled up in 'Top Secret' tours taking in the Bradbury Science Museum operated by the Los Alamos National Laboratory, the National Museum of Nuclear Science and History in Albuquerque, and the UFO Museum in Roswell.[43]

No amount of information in modern museums and official reports can disturb recourse to these tropes of mad scientists, over-eager generals, and governments anxious to experiment in unfettered and dangerous ways. And, given a new lease of (virtual) life by the internet, the pop culture deriving from atomic literature, official and fiction, music, movies, and comic strips, is eagerly consumed. Sources such as the US 'CONELRAD' website, since 1999 devoted to 'the pop culture fall out of living with the atomic bomb', invite visitors to recall the music, movies, TV sitcoms, civil defence materials, and personal reflections of especially the late-1940s and 1950s as a distinctive period overlooked in the rush to remember the 'sixties'.[44] With one eye on stirrings of memory, including museum exhibits, and the other eye on the generation for whom atomic pop culture was entwined with blossoming consumerism, such collections can become an elegy for modernism: good and mad consumerism, including atomic kitsch; the emergence of the nuclear family in the 1950s; frightening military preparations and operational plans; and new forms of living room entertainment. Appropriately, nostalgia for Cold War consumerism invites baby-boomer consumption of the past, too, with many opportunities to buy artefacts and music or TV and movie collections.

In more grounded forms, acts of public remembrance are emerging after the scheduled disestablishments of weapons sites and production in the 1990s. It was not only the immediacy of the Cold War's end that caused a pause before acts of public remembering unfolded, but the 1990s saw a rapid reduction of resources around the management of former defence sites. The Strategic Arms Reduction Treaty (START I) of 1991 committed the United States and the USSR then Russian Federation to substantial reduction of nuclear weapons and means of delivering them. Missile sites in the American Mid-West began to be dismantled with START I rendering a fraction available for tourist opportunities, or adding to what Edward Linenthal has called the 'martial landscape' sustaining American patriotism.[45] There was an understandable interlude between military dismantling and the proponents of remembering them gathering to lobby and work with different arms of government to secure resources for museums or memorialization. Then, the 9/11 attacks in 2001 prompted a surge in public recollection of previous crises, in particular ways. Politicians and the media drew lines between these sneak attacks and the best-known previous 'act of infamy', the Japanese attack on Pearl Harbor. As Emily Rosenberg writes, this popular connecting involved a sense of passing the baton from one generation to another:

> The Pearl Harbor story itself had taken shape within the conventions of earlier frontier legends of challenge and triumph. Now, Pearl Harbor could be to 9/11 what the Last Stand and the Alamo had been to Pearl Harbor: a widely recognized iconic tale of threat and harm that worked to rally patriotism, marshal manly values, and promise eventual and righteous triumph in a nervous nation.[46]

As is discussed further in Chapter 4, the Cold War re-emerged strongly in some of the post 9/11 public commentaries on lessons and modern history.

But the 9/11 attacks also complicated acts of remembering recent wars in the United States. The North American Aerospace Defense Command control centre, a bunker complex built inside Colorado's Cheyenne Mountain and operational from 1966, was suddenly closed to the public. This monumental feat of engineering – almost 5 acres of chambers and tunnels accommodating not only military command but also shops and other attributes of a small city dug out beneath 2,000 feet of granite – is one of the most elaborate and best-known Cold War redoubts. There were drastic upgrades of security attaching to weapons and materials sites that retained working roles. A tourists' bus tour of buildings at Oak Ridge, for example, was restricted to those with US citizenship and photographic proof of identity, thereby accentuating the already localized messages.[47]

Today, tourists can visit several decommissioned weapons silos, including the Minuteman Missile site in South Dakota, the Nike Missile site near San Francisco, and the Titan Missile Museum in Arizona. All of these places strive to recapture the high stakes and the international tension behind their former purposes. 'At the Titan Missile Museum, near Tucson, Arizona,' reads the museum's website:

> ... visitors journey through time to stand on the front line of the Cold War. This preserved Titan II missile site, officially known as complex 571–77, is all that remains of the 54 Titan II missile sites that were on alert across the United States from 1963 to 1987.[48]

The missiles were constantly ready for launch in retaliation to nuclear attack on the United States. To conjure the desert plain near Tucson, Arizona, as the front line of the Cold War is not a simple task, nor is conveying a sense of high alert across a span of 25 years. Yet as the Titan II was the largest of the US inter-continental missiles, able to deliver a nine-megaton nuclear warhead to targets over 6,000 miles away, the scale of the portent probably assists in making the invited imaginative leaps. Tours of the museum range from one to five hours, and novel experiences vary from sleeping overnight in the crew's subterranean quarters (they worked 24-hour shifts) to children becoming 'Junior Missileers' through games and other activities. But the size of the missile (more than 100 feet long), the power of its engines, the eight underground levels associated with its storage, and the security attaching to the day in the life of a crew member there – three blast doors with elaborate codes and two-person failsafe procedures needed before a missile could be launched – evoke the high stakes of a nuclear arms race more than latter-day spin-offs. Absent from the museum is information about the many accidents associated with Titan silos during the Cold War, due to their temperamental complexity and use of liquid fuel. The climax to the popular one-hour tour is the invitation for two tourists to sit in the launch control room and turn the two keys that make the console light up indicating the successful 'launch' of a missile.[49] The contrast between the child-friendly Titan Missile Museum and what one might find in the former eastern bloc is stark. There are poorly maintained museum-missile bases at Zeltini in Estonia (with an impressive bust of Lenin in front of one of the hangars), Plokstine in Lithuania, from where missiles were sent to Cuba in the lead-up to the Cuban Missile Crisis, and an abandoned site in Lambarte, Latvia. In the former Soviet Union, the adventurous tourist might explore derelict silos at several former bases, including Kingisepp, near St Petersburg, and Saryozek, Kazakhstan, the site of the first weapons destruction in 1988 in the wake of the INF Treaty.

One of the most recently opened American museums, the Rocky Flats Cold War Museum in Arvada, near Denver, Colorado, aspires to a nuclear form of remembering that is much less playful than its Titan counterpart. Rocky Flats was the site of a nuclear weapons production plant, secretly building 70,000 plutonium triggers for nuclear weapons between 1952 and 1989, after which it was decommissioned and the surrounding area 'remediated'. The mission of the new museum is ambitious: 'to document the historical, social, environmental, and scientific aspects of Rocky Flats, and to educate the public about Rocky Flats, the Cold War, and their legacies through preservation of key artifacts and development of interpretive and educational programs.'[50] Although not flagged directly in their website information, one of the major challenges for the museum will be to manage the struggle for the history of Rocky Flats. Fires at the plant in 1957 and 1969 resulted in radioactive materials being released into the air, and subsequent tests found elevated levels of plutonium in the area, including in the nearby City of Denver. From the 1970s, and prompted by news of these fires and of chemical leaks from containers, protestors began picketing the plant in growing numbers. In the late-1970s and 1980s, thousands of protestors spilled on to the rail tracks leading to the plant. Some were prosecuted as trespassers. The plant's closure in the wake of an FBI raid, in June 1989, for criminal breaches of environmental law, convinced many that the consequences of radioactive leaks will be with the community for untold years.[51] One of the major sources of information complementing museum exhibits is a collection of more than 200 oral histories of those who worked, lived near, or protested around the plant.[52] Interestingly, an online Rocky Flats Virtual Museum, predating the recent opening of the physical one, remains live and with dramatic impact focuses on the fire of 1969: 'On Sunday, May 11, 1969 – Mother's Day – a fire erupted in a bomb-manufacturing building containing more than 7,600 pounds of plutonium, enough for 1,000 nuclear bombs.' Web-pages, images, audio-visual material, and oral history unfold underneath headings such as: 'The Day We Almost Lost Denver'; 'Blue Flash of Death'; and 'Citizens Awaken'. The site builds a story of near disaster averted mostly by good luck, the persistence of poor safety and environmental practices at the plant in the wake of the accident, and the rising tide of protests aimed both at the production of weapons and at the poor practices of the plant. There also is a sub-plot of corporate greed.

In the aftermath of the 1957 fire, suggests the virtual museum site, Dow Chemical should have learned some lessons and implemented safety changes. 'Instead, Dow officials had made a series of short term decisions to speed production, reduce costs, and increase profits. By 1969 key production facilities at Rocky Flats had the jerry-rigged quality of a shade tree mechanics garage shop.'[53] It seems likely that the unknowns of possible health and environmental problems will ensure that debate over the legacies of Rocky Flats will persist.

Atomic-themed heritage and museum activity is costly, but this has not prevented its rise in the United States. In 2002, the Atomic Heritage Foundation, a non-profit organization, established itself in Washington DC with the mission to preserve and interpret the Manhattan Project and the legacies of the atomic age.[54] Supported by a Save America's Treasures grant, the foundation has successfully raised more funds and championed the creation of a Manhattan Project National Park.[55] In March 2013, three congressmen, following action already taken in the US Senate, introduced legislation to establish a Manhattan Project National Historical Park, comprising the three key sites Oak Ridge, Los Alamos, and Hanford. Although proponents of the park are optimistic that their dream will be realized, the park may not be inviting to all. Hanford and Los Alamos are admitting visitors already, as is the testing site in Nevada, but visitors are restricted to US citizens who must not carry phones or cameras. The current restrictions reflect dilapidation of buildings and low-level radiation sites to be avoided as well as security concerns. If the national park is approved by Congress (as is expected), the US National Park Service will spend US$21 million over five years to help restore and preserve crumbling buildings at the three sites.[56] Others, of course, will not welcome the Manhattan National Park on the grounds of its celebratory message. There has been something of a rehearsal of the debates likely to accompany the realization of the national park in the furore that erupted in the mid-1990s around the US Smithsonian Institution's brief display of the *Enola Gay*, the US B-29 Bomber that carried the 'Little Boy' atomic bomb to its detonation point over Hiroshima. In anticipation of the fiftieth anniversary of the Hiroshima bombing, the *Enola Gay* was displayed at the Smithsonian's National Air and Space Museum in Washington DC. Initially, the display was a multi-dimensional progressive narrative, with the *Enola Gay* as its centerpiece. It drew on a wide range of materials, including Japanese accounts, and an exhibition script that questioned whether the bomb was needed to end the war, querying the motives of those who decided on its use, and demonstrating a high level of sympathy for the Japanese killed by it. After an avalanche of protests from veterans groups as well as conservative commentators and politicians who argued that the exhibit dishonoured the memory of those US soldiers who had fought in the Pacific, Martin Harwit, the museum's director, was forced to resign and the full exhibit was abandoned (although the unscripted remains of the idea – a display of the forward fuselage of the *Enola Gay* – attracted millions).[57]

The Atomic Heritage Foundation is upbeat about having learned from these debates, and thus far has adopted a tone of pioneering efforts resulting in exciting and sobering changes for the world. The underlying idea of the United States as the engine room for breakthrough, transformative discovery, is likely to attract a broader base of support amidst any controversy. The Foundation envisages a Travelling Exhibit featuring the diversity of peoples involved in, and affected by, the Manhattan Project, sustained by a 'multiple voices' oral history base. It will doubtless find that no matter how 'balanced and comprehensive' an approach, there will be silences and omissions at key moments in interpretation that generate heat. Alexandra Levy, the Foundation's programme manager, provides an excellent illustration in her selective list of 'legacies' of the Manhattan project:

> Today, you can't pick up a newspaper without coming across a story that involves the legacy of the Manhattan Project. From North Korea and Iran's nuclear programs, to radiation treatment of various illnesses, to the Mars Rover's plutonium power, the legacy of the Manhattan Project continues to reverberate in today's world.[58]

Throughout this US activity, there is a mix of social agency as well as state involvement in remembering, and it is a productive blend. The pattern of funding for the Rocky Flats museum is similar to that of the Manhattan Project National Park. Those behind the Rocky Flats museum gathered momentum by drawing on state and private donations before securing a crucial federal grant in 2007. The Save America's Treasures organization supporting the Manhattan Project National Park is a public–private partnership. The American Science and Energy Museum is owned by the US Department of Energy (which contracts out management) and is supported by its Foundation, drawing on public, private, and volunteer support. The Minuteman site in South Dakota is maintained by the US National Park Service (NPS). And the Titan Museum in Arizona and the new Rocky Flats Cold War Museum are operated privately. In most cases there is room for volunteers to guide visitors and steer their engagement in particular directions. Indeed, another missile site, the SF-88 Nike Missile Site near San Francisco, the base for 280 anti-aircraft Nike missiles with nuclear warheads between 1953 and 1979, also is managed by the NPS, yet for its tour guides and ongoing restoration it remains dependent on volunteers.[59] The Nike missiles were sited in rings around major US cities and military installations in the 1950s as a 'last ditch' line of defence against Soviet bombers and later missiles that may have made it past long-range defence measures. The Californian-based Nike Historical Society grew out of the efforts to restore the SF-88 site, and it now promotes communication between Nike veterans and the preservation of memories from some 300 similar Nike missile sites that once operated in different parts of the United States.[60] Since the early-1990s, the NPS interpretive guidelines have emphasized the need for consideration of mainstream, radical, and revisionist histories, engagement with a wide range of professional historians and other interpreters, and the production of appropriate, high quality site-based and other educational materials. Sometimes this has been hard to implement in the face of growing volunteer enthusiasm for Cold War site restoration and remembering. One analysis found that dependence on volunteers for staffing at SF-88 (many of whom are base veterans) has fostered a narrative of heroic defence of the nation but with little complexity or perspectives from the other side of the Cold War.[61] The NPS website for the Minuteman site in South Dakota, on the other hand, links to oral histories and a scholarly and richly contextualized study of the 'missile plains', incorporating details of the Soviet strategies and missile capabilities, local protests against US missile bases, and the role of the US Air Force generally in South Dakota's modern history.[62]

Recently, historian Jon Wiener toured Cold War monuments, memorials, and museums across the United States. Wiener was looking for, but apparently found little evidence of, a heroic, triumphalist 'we won' discourse at work. The conservative interpretation of the Cold War, concludes Wiener, has failed to take hold with the American public. This is all the more notable when there is strong evidence that the public craves museums and engagement with the 'memory industry' in ever-expanding ways.[63] Wherever present, contends Wiener, connections between the military industrial complex and American 'victory' in the Cold War are mostly tentative and muted. At the Titan Missile Museum in Arizona, for example, he encountered a guide who at the end of the tour reflected on the vast enterprise of retaliatory capability: "'It was expensive, but I guess it worked.'"[64] Wiener's study perhaps is not sufficiently sympathetic to the unique challenges facing those involved in such museums. Rather than forgetting the Cold War, as his book title suggests, such comments reflect an understandable uncertainty about how to remember weapons sites effectively. In relation to the crews who manned the silos, it never will be easy to capture the human stories, on the one hand, of psychological stress attached to living in a state of alert and readiness to launch weapons of mass destruction, and, on the other hand, the sheer boredom of countless days and nights. But, as the substantial oral history collection at Rocky Flats suggests, there are plenty of human stories linked to research and the production of nuclear weapons. And, such is the need for volunteers, this is likely to continue to be a strong feature of how Cold War remembering takes shape around particular sites. The social history that commentators such as Heonik Kwon argue will inform another dimension of how we understand the Cold War has a strong base in nuclear facilities.[65] At its peak in the 1980s, the network of government-owned, contractor-operated factories, laboratories, and test sites in US nuclear weapons production employed around 100,000 people.[66] Adding others who were mobilized, including protestors, the numbers swell even further. And post-Cold War employment in nuclear-related industries remains significant, sometimes at the same sites where weapons were produced and including work on the decommissioning of weapons and the storage of waste. In contemporary Russia, approximately 250,000 people are employed in nuclear facilities.[67]

Others' backyards

Where it surfaces at all, atomic testing in others' backyards is remembered differently. In relation to nuclear testing by the United States (1946–62) and France (1968–96) in the South Pacific, the Cold War stands more as a backdrop to what is more commonly couched as advanced forms of colonialism in the Pacific. The local view, according to one analysis, takes the pattern of 'militarisation, environmental devastation, and the displacement of Indigenous or local peoples'.[68] Bikini Islanders, for example, remain excluded from the atoll where US hydrogen bomb testing occurred in the 1950s. Some locals moved back once the atoll was declared safe in the 1970s, before being relocated again in 1978 when tests showed excessive human exposure to radiation. In recent times, there has been little more human presence than locally-managed dive tours travelling among the wrecks of ships purposely sunk in testing – a reminder of the grand-scale exploration of the new bomb's capacities behind the testing more than 60 years ago. The other feature common to such groups (and consistent with the theme of colonial exploitation in need of redress) is the quest for compensation. This, and the related needs to establish the scale of injustice and the membership of those who might properly be called victims, drives public remembering in particular ways. The long-term impact of US testing in the Marshall Islands, for instance, is a recurring theme in relations with now-independent Marshall Islanders, due to the inadequacy of the fund established to compensate victims of the tests. In 1983, a formal agreement between Washington and the Marshall Islands provided US$150 million for damages caused by 67 tests conducted at Bikini and Enewatak atolls. The agreement provided for a Nuclear Claims Tribunal, using this money as the basis for a special fund to provide compensation for personal injuries and property damage. By the mid-2000s, it was clear that the funds provided were exhausted. The Tribunal had determined award sums that far exceeded those available, and had yet to process more claims.[69] Angry Marshall Islanders who point to unpaid awards and the persistence of cancers and other radiogenic diseases in the population periodically attract media attention, ensuring that US testing in the Marshalls is not easily forgotten. And the continued use of the Ronald Reagan Ballistic Missile Defense Test Site (the Reagan Test Site or RTS for short), which provides a Major Range Test Facility Base (MRTFB) for ballistic missile testing and space operations on Kwajalein Atoll and Wake Island, presents a resonant backdrop and continuing thread of the military/colonial story.[70]

French testing of nuclear weapons took place in Algeria, between 1960 and its independence in 1962, and then in French Polynesia in the South

Pacific at Mururoa and Fangataufa atolls. Algeria saw thirteen underground
and four atmospheric tests. There were 44 atmospheric tests at the South
Pacific atolls between 1966 and 1974, then 149 underground tests to 1996.
When French Polynesia elected anti-nuclear and pro-independence leader
Oscar Temaru in 2004, the related issues of clean-ups, monitoring, and
compensation suddenly gained public prominence.[71] Only in 2010 did a
French court acknowledge a link between the testing and health problems
for up to 150,000 servicemen and civilians; and only a handful of people
have been awarded compensation.[72] Organizations such as the Nuclear Free
and Independent Pacific Movement maintain efforts towards the identification of those affected by nuclear testing in the Pacific as victims warranting
further compensation. This group, as its name suggests, explicitly links the
struggle against colonialism with the imperial acts of nuclear testing across
the Pacific for the whole period of US and French testing between 1945 and
1992. They have declared 1 March to be an annual 'Nuclear Free Independent Pacific Day', marking, as it does, the first US thermo-nuclear test
'Castle Bravo' near Bikini Atoll in 1954.[73]

The Australian experience of atomic weapons testing, although very
different in its origins, is remembered mostly along familiar lines to the
Pacific cases. In a late and grandiose act of imperial condescension the
British, so the popularly-understood narrative unfolds, talked their way into
the Australian desert and remote north-western islands in the 1950s, where
they could be cavalier about the dangers of testing – especially as they
impacted on local Aboriginal groups. A Royal Commission report into the
Australian atomic tests, released in 1985, substantiated some of this story.
Following hearings that were held in open session, featuring 311 witnesses
and 210 written submissions, the report was sharply critical of the inadequacy of safety measures, and the consequent likely exposure of Australian
and British servicemen and Australian Aborigines to dangerous levels of
radiation. It was likely, concluded the report, that cancers occurred among
these groups that would not have occurred otherwise, and the Commission
also found that a UK-led clean up of affected areas in 1968 was inadequate.[74]
The carcinogenic legacies of over-eager testing were lessons drawn in detail,
even if some of the historical context was over-simplified by the Royal
Commission. (Separate from any sense of British loyalty, Australian prime
minister Robert Menzies and his colleagues had not only joined in the
utopianism associated with the unfolding powers of the atom – magnified by
discoveries of large Australian uranium reserves in the 1950s – but also
wanted to possess or have access to the bomb.)[75] Significantly, for those who
identify as victims, and importantly for ongoing public reminders of the
consequences of atomic testing, the first efforts to provide compensation
have not stopped the mustering of legal class actions. In 1993, the British
government provided AUS$30 million compensation towards a clean up,
but these efforts stopped in 1999 after an unexplained subterranean
explosion in a dumping area. Aboriginal custodians of the land around the

main desert test site at Maralinga have accepted the need to avoid certain areas in return for their control of the lands. Individuals identifying as victims of the tests continue to press claims for compensation, and contemporary debate over the siting of nuclear waste dumps in the Australian desert inevitably stirs memories of past injustices especially as affecting Aboriginal people.[76]

Four special features of remembering nuclear testing stand out. The first hinges on the presence of state-originating commissions and reports designed to assess connections between testing and subsequent health problems (in particular the incidence of thyroid cancer arising from possible exposure to unsafe levels of Iodine-131, commonly found in post-explosion radiation). The second concerns the tension between these state-driven historical narratives and the social agents, groups of servicemen, indigenous and local populations, and others who identify as victims and seek various forms of compensation or restitution. The third feature is the distrust between state and social agents that persists beyond attempts at redress. This results not only from the imprecision around cause and effect (partly arising from inadequate monitoring and less developed research capabilities in the 1950s and 1960s), but also it reflects an air of conspiracy that lingers with the secrecy that attached to the testing at the time and, in the eyes of some, carries over into official stories of what did and did not happen. In the ongoing contests between state authorities and aggrieved groups trying to confirm their victim status, the high degree of secrecy surrounding atomic testing complicates resolution and perpetuates popular views of cover-ups. For instance, although legislation in the United States in 1990 has provided for compensation for those affected by atomic tests in Nevada (nearly 100 above-ground tests and a dozen underground tests between 1951 and 1962), it has been hard to draw legal and moral boundaries around the grievances brought to hearings. A review in 1999 of a recent US National Cancer Institute report into possible cancer links arising from the Nevada testing found significant methodological difficulties in accurately assessing causation. The review also commented on the public consequences of the gaps in knowledge:

> Two legacies of the testing program and its aftermath are the considerable, and sometimes intense, distrust of the government as a source of information and advice, and the fact that a segment of the public is convinced the health impacts of exposure are significant and severe. These circumstances create significant challenges for DHHS [Department of Health and Human Services] in constructing a credible and effective public communication program.[77]

The fourth and final feature is the radicalizing impact on all of these by the Chernobyl reactor disaster in what was then the Ukrainian Soviet Socialist Republic. On 26 April 1986, the explosion at Chernobyl's Reactor

Number Four sent more radioactive material into the air than had resulted from the atomic bombings of Hiroshima and Nagasaki combined. In addition to the 31 people killed at the time or in the immediate aftermath, probably tens of thousands of people have suffered adverse health impacts resulting from the radioactive cloud that spread west and northwards over Europe. The highest doses of contamination were suffered by the local Ukrainian and Belorussian populations, who also endured psychological and other illnesses resulting from mass evacuations and relocations following the accident.[78] The dramatic increase in short-term birth defects and the longer-term incidence of thyroid cancers among children exposed to radiation after the Chernobyl accident provided strong evidence for the connection between radiation exposure, Iodine-131, and thyroid cancer. The images of blighted children were and are especially powerful, but the causation on ghastly display from Chernobyl does not necessarily help possible victims strengthen claims relating to older incidences of radiation exposure.

The Cold War, typically defined as a simmering contest between Washington and Moscow that never turned into nuclear war, sits at times in stark contrast to the real bodily and psychological damage inflicted over a period that also outlives the nuclear consequences of a contest between superpowers. When Hiroshima's mayor Matsui Kazumi linked his sympathy for victims of the Fukushima nuclear power plant with the memory of 6 August 1945, he used an atomically appropriate metaphor that resonates with other victims of atomic weapons production. Survivors of testing continue to surface in the media and press claims for compensation partly because their stories form part of a military-imperial era, generally accompanied by iconic photographs of mushroom clouds. They are 'superimposed' on popular, common memories of the arrival of the nuclear age.

Protesting the bomb

The anti-nuclear movement was borne along by the Cold War arms race and the threatening symbol of the bomb. The detailed history of its best-known and most enduring organization, the Campaign for Nuclear Disarmament (CND) in Britain, is told elsewhere.[79] There were peaks of CND activity, first from its formation in 1957 to 1963 and then again in the 1980s, which today are remembered in published works including participant and oral histories. In Europe and the United States there was a similar pattern in anti-nuclear protests, with climax moments such as when one million people rallied in New York's Central Park in June 1982. Anti-nuclear groups in the United States, while very active in different parts of the country, remained more localized than in the UK until the mid-1970s, when their coalition took shape at the national level. Commemoration of such movements has proven difficult through the lack of consensus on their effectiveness. The decline of the anti-nuclear protest movement since the 1980s might be construed generously as being a victim of its own success, but the connection between mass protest and arms reductions in the late-1980s to early-1990s is debated. The post-1991 accumulation of nuclear weapons, moreover, has not been matched with a resurgence of protest.[80] Remembering protests outside the academy and the realm of memoir, then, takes varied and often subdued forms.

Those who organized to protest the bomb tend to be remembered less by physical monuments and more by social histories, collections of testimonies for use by researchers, and in panels or sections of museums recalling their peak moments. One of the most celebrated and continuous acts of protest took the form of women protesting the presence of nuclear weapons at the US Air Force Base at Greenham Common in Berkshire, England. Women-led protests at the base had occurred first in 1962, but it was twenty years later, with the imminent arrival of US cruise missiles, that the protests took on new proportions. Kate Hudson, the CND's current general secretary, recalls travelling there from London in December 1982 and joining hands with other women surrounding the perimeter fence. Hudson was one of around 30,000 participants that day, by which time a women's peace camp occupied the nearby common. Despite forcible eviction in 1984, protestors returned and maintained a vigil, with recurrent acts of fence-removal and base invasion. The Greenham Common Women's Peace Camp hit news headlines repeatedly with protestors' determination to compromise the military base's operation. After breaking into the base on New Year's Day in 1983, for instance, 44 women were arrested for dancing on top of the missile silos. This predominantly women's protest at Greenham Common inspired similar protests at other air force bases, and became a beacon for activist feminism as well as the anti-nuclear movement, a dual symbolism that also shapes its remembering. Although the last missiles were removed from the camp in 1991, a small group remained in protest at the British adoption of Trident nuclear missiles (submarine-launched ballistic missiles) and in an ultimately successful effort to establish a memorial on the site. Hudson's reflections, on the twenty-fifth anniversary of her journey to Greenham Common, include recalling the women's solidarity and defiance, and declaring them agents of change:

> Such was the spirit of the Greenham women, which continues to inspire peace activists around the world. The missiles were finally removed in 1991, under the terms of the Intermediate-range Nuclear Forces Treaty, a major disarmament treaty signed in 1987, by Reagan and Gorbachev. There can be little doubt that the extent of popular opposition to the new missiles helped shape their decision to stake steps towards nuclear disarmament.[81]

The Greenham Common Women's Peace Camp has acquired several meanings in its remembering.[82] It has the standing of a Cold War mobilization of incipient 'people power' that should be recalled in general histories and museum displays recalling the period.[83] As the women took a decision to rule that only women could live at the camp, it stands as an example of effective political and social mobilization of women in the late phase of second wave feminism. And, as illustrated in Hudson's reflections, the feminist dimension is a point proudly recalled by the anti-nuclear protest movement as something that made a difference (however contested this might be). The result is that Greenham Common's remembering takes several overlapping forms. Although the numbers involved point to the forging of common memories in the remembering of Greenham Common and other acts of protest, and the women were successful in gaining their physical memorial, it is somewhat compromised as an iconic site inspiring a sense of pilgrimage. This partly owes to the industrial park that now occupies much of the area, effectively overwriting earlier meanings invested in the landscape, and partly reflects the construction of monuments in other locations. One such memorial is actually in Cardiff, Wales, marking the location from which 36 members of the Welsh group 'Women for Life on Earth' walked to the air base in late August 1981, thereby counting among the first protestors at the site following the announcement that cruise missiles would be located there.[84] In July 2003, a bronze statue commemorating the 1981 trek was erected in the main foyer of Cardiff City Hall. The statue, raised by public subscription, is of a life-size young woman carrying a child who is holding a dove in its outstretched hand. The woman has chains around her waist, recalling the action of Greenham protestors who sometimes chained themselves to perimeter fencing around the air base. The nearby plaque's caption reads (in Welsh and English): 'Her soul ignited goodness on our nuclear land; The burning bush of her sacrifice and faith will never be extinguished.'[85] While evocative, the statute seems to speak to those who already know about the 1981 walk and subsequent protest and camp for there is no explicit mention of Greenham Common.

At the former Greenham base, the women secured a fountain monument in a memorial garden dedicated in 2002 to the memory of Helen Thomas, a Welsh protestor accidentally killed on the road to the base in 1989. A circular structure, the fountain is inscribed with the words: 'You can't kill the spirit: Women's peace camp 1981–2000'. The garden also features seven boulders brought from Wales and a sculpture of an eternal red flame. A local school later added a collage monument, featuring symbols of peace and nature on one side, with letters spelling out 'Greenham Common' and photographs of the land's contested use on the other. It stands near the airfield's old control tower. Since September 2012, it has competed for attention with three memorial stones remembering 49 US airmen who died in accidents at the earlier incarnation of the US base in 1944. The splintering of physical commemoration, however, has not stopped Greenham Common from occupying spaces in museums, inspiring collective oral histories, and inviting moments of recollection around anniversaries.[86] In the English-speaking world, it remains one of the best-known, and most easily recalled, protest movements against the bomb.

Elsewhere in the UK, London hosts a number of open spaces and monuments with links to the anti-nuclear movement. The Greater London Council led by socialist Ken Livingstone in the 1980s created a number of peace parks, some including commissioned peace statues and monuments, in the open spaces and squares of London. Although they spoke to a cause that predated the Cold War, these initiatives, combined with Livingstone's declaration that London was a 'nuclear-free zone', also took place in a more immediate context. While not all of them have weathered time and local politics, some parks and memorials still testify to the burst of activity in the 1980s.[87]

In the United States, women also played a prominent role in protesting nuclear weapons through the 'Women Strike for Peace' group. Founded in 1961, it brought 50,000 women onto the streets of US cities protesting nuclear weapons in November that year. The group has endured, having played prominent roles in subsequent broader-based protests against US involvement in Vietnam, in other wars, and against nuclear weapons. Its earliest action perhaps is less well remembered because it just predated second wave feminism, drawing on more traditional images of motherhood and the dangers of radioactive material in mother's milk and cow's milk. President Kennedy and his wife Jacqueline both acknowledged the significance of the group's demands in 1961.[88] In addition to groups, individual stories of women protesting or affected by nuclear weapons have attracted publishers' and media attention. Kristen Iverson, a resident and former worker of the plant at Rocky Flats, Colorado, has launched a successful publishing/speaking career on the back of her memoir mixing the misfortunes of her 'company town' family with the consequences of living in the nuclear shadow of the weapons plant.[89] Attracting media attention is a fundamental requirement for successful protest, so it is not surprising that those who have dedicated much of their life to campaigning against nuclear weapons include some who also have become well-known: examples include Dr Helen Caldicott, whose work straddles Australia and the United States, and who is a well-published author on the need to rid the world of nuclear weapons and power stations; and the late Coretta Scott King, the prominent civil and human rights activist, wife and then widow of Martin Luther King, and also one of the early sources of energy behind the 'Women Strike for Peace' movement. At the broader level of social history, the trend towards collection of oral histories around nuclear activities now closed down, including the above-mentioned Rocky Flats archive, gathers a range of reflections from opposition or suspicions through to strong endorsement of weapons testing and production. These collections, growing in the United States and Britain in particular, are likely to feed further studies of citizen unrest and/or consent in relation to nuclear industries.

In the former Soviet Union, whereas prominent dissenters such as 'scientist and father' of the Soviet hydrogen bomb Andrei Sakharov made their concerns widely known, it took Chernobyl for a broader-based opposition to nuclear power and weapons to develop. Much earlier, protesting the bomb in the 1950s was akin to a 'Gulag wish', and it proved similarly formidable to take a stand in the following quarter-century. The disastrous accident at the Chernobyl reactor in Ukraine in 1986 was of such magnitude that it broke Moscow's capacity to limit dissent as well as any hopes of containing the resultant fallout (a situation further amplified by the accident's timing coinciding with Gorbachev's policy of *glasnost* or 'openness'). Chernobyl did more than anything else to make Soviet leaders halt plans for the building of more nuclear power plants. The crippling costs of encasing the stricken plant in concrete, relocating thousands of people, and attempting various forms of clean-up and monitoring came at a time when the Soviet economy already was in crisis. On a smaller scale, there was a parallel development in weapons testing. In the face of Chernobyl (and as a demonstration of their separate authority), the Soviet military then embarked on a new series of weapons tests at Semipalatinsk between 1987 and 1989. On 12 February 1989, gas from an underground test escaped from what was becoming a highly cracked ground surface and it covered a military base some 75 miles away at Chagan. Although the ensuing Kazakhstan–Moscow crisis talks resulted in a series of statements designed to reassure the local population before ploughing on with testing, public opposition mobilized into mass protests. Partly inspired by a passionate televised speech by local poet Olzhas Suleimenov, a coalition of social, religious, and humanitarian groups took the form of the 'Nevada-Semipalatinsk' anti-nuclear movement – just as the walls and borders starting tumbling in Eastern Europe. In August 1991, following the dissolution of the Soviet Union, the new president of Kazakhstan closed the testing area.[90]

In the Pacific, protesting against French weapons testing resulted in an act of state reprisal that is well remembered by both the non-government organization and country affected. In the early-1980s, the environmental organization Greenpeace protested French testing in the South Pacific with such effectiveness that their flagship vessel, *Rainbow Warrior*, was blown up in Auckland Harbour, New Zealand, on 10 July 1985. One crewman died in the attack. New Zealand police arrested two of the French agents involved before they could escape the country, and by September that year the French government had admitted that their intelligence service had carried out the bombing. The subsequent legal action and sentencing in Auckland was rejected by the French government and UN mediation helped broker a settlement including compensation and the removal of the two agents to a French Pacific atoll where they were exiled for three years. The New Zealanders were unhappy with both the nature of the French apology and their secret relaxation of exile to fly the two agents home within two years. More than twenty-five years later, the *Rainbow Warrior* affair has become a signal moment in New Zealand foreign policy. It is understood less through the lens of victimhood – after an act of state terrorism inflicted on home waters – and more as a turning point in

New Zealanders striking out independently and successfully in foreign affairs. In the aftermath of the incident, New Zealand received little support from its nuclear-equipped allies Britain and the United States in their negotiations with the French. The whole affair accelerated momentum towards the 1987 declaration of New Zealand as a Nuclear Free Zone, which meant no more nuclear weapons in New Zealand waters. As the Americans insisted on not declaring whether nuclear-capable warships were carrying atomic weapons, this effectively excluded them, which, in turn, led to Washington suspending its obligations under the Australia New Zealand United States (ANZUS) Security Treaty of 1951 – until then, a foundation stone of postwar New Zealand foreign policy. Subsequently, however, these actions have become a source of pride as world events and opinion have strengthened the anti-nuclear position. As one commentator reflected in 2010:

> The result was a more independent New Zealand foreign policy, with an increasing focus on working with United Nations. This new necessity for self-reliance gave New Zealand the drive it needed for the anti-nuclear battle and to demonstrate to countries such as France, the United States and the United Kingdom that the colonial era was indeed over.[91]

The incident generated several memoirs and other books, and a television movie screened in 1993.[92] Greenpeace, too, carries the memory in maintaining the *Rainbow Warrior* name into later flagships. The movement also recalls anniversaries of the *Rainbow Warrior* bombing, and leverages the moral outrage for other anti-nuclear causes in the Pacific such as the ongoing hardships of the Marshall Islanders.[93] The same is true for the Nuclear Free and Independent Pacific Movement.

Atomic culture

Atomic weapons production and testing was one of the most secretive dimensions of the Cold War, and their remembering taps a vein of popular, often fictional, images of scientific and military hubris and eccentricity. As described above, remembering 'atomic culture' can take the form of quirky nostalgia. It also can be recalled in contemporary echoes of popular culture revitalizing Cold War era tropes, found in the fiction, cartoons, and movies of the 1950s and 1960s, of Armageddon, irresponsible government and corporate experimentation, espionage, and hubris-fuelled self-destruction. In Nevada, Area 51 caters for the heady blend of science fiction meeting popular culture. Some of the popular US comic strip series of the 1950s and 1960s engaged with the power of the atom, as did Japanese manga cartoons. Those characters who endured or were recycled in the aftermath of the Cold War include the remarkable Astro Boy, first penned by Japanese manga cartoonist Tezuka Osamu in 1951, and known briefly as Ambassador Atom.[94] The nuclear-powered robotic Astro Boy not only propelled himself at enormous velocity and bristled with hip-attached machine guns, but also enjoyed super-heightened senses including being able to tell good from evil. He often saved Japan from atomic bombs, but never was triumphalist about the powers of modern science, and he elicited apologies from most of the evil-doers he brought to justice. As historian Marc Steinberg has pointed out, Astro Boy also helped usher in a new era of character merchandising, featuring stickers in particular.[95] While reflecting contemporary Japanese concerns, the character of Astro Boy became well-known overseas and remains iconic of Cold War Japan. Moving image depictions include the Astro Boy television series, screened not only in Japan but adapted for US and other English-speaking audiences from the 1960s to the 1980s. More recently, this has been followed by a full-length movie in 2009.

In 1954, filmmaker Ishirō Honda brought to life Godzilla – the mutant creature spawned in radiation following a nuclear explosion – for Japanese cinemas. A dinosaur-like creature that emerged from under the sea, Godzilla inspired a new wave of science fiction on the big screen featuring mutant and deadly creatures resulting from nuclear explosions or accidents. Latter-day watchers of zombie movies that feature mutated survivors of global catastrophe might not be conscious of the Cold War and Godzilla-like echoes, for the forms taken since 1954 are themselves much transformed. Honda's original *Godzilla* film ushered in one of the most enduring paradigms of the genre, inspiring cinematic remakes to the extent that it is the world's longest-running film franchise. Screened in the wake of the radioactive dusting of the Japanese fishing boat *Lucky Dragon 5* as a result of the US test in the Marshall Islands, the original film had notable anti-nuclear and anti-American tones. These elements were excised in a Hollywood adaptation in 1956 that proved popular with monster-craving audiences, and the Godzilla phenomenon was established in America. Many Japanese Godzilla films later, several Hollywood versions (including a new one to be released in 2014), and a steady flow of video games, the irradiated monster is very much a part of popular culture in ways that connect with, but also exceed the boundaries of, the Cold War. Among other features, commentators point to the more humane and caring forms of science that recur in the Japanese scientists featured in several Godzilla movies, standing in contrast to the inhumanity of the atomic bombs.[96]

Some of the most powerful television and film focused on nuclear weapons emerged in the 1980s, at least partly inspired by the new arms race in Europe. In Britain, a number of documentaries explored the consequences of a bomb dropped on a population centre. In 1985, the BBC showed Peter Watkins' docu-drama film *The War Game*. This devastatingly realist depiction of events that followed an imagined nuclear missile detonated on Rochester was so disturbing that it was banned for two decades after its making in 1965. In the same year, the critically acclaimed BBC serial thriller

Edge of Darkness took viewers into a murky and murderous world of state-corporate secret weapons production and experimentation on their home soil. Raymond Briggs, best-known for his cartoon and animation of *The Snowman*, usually broadcast at Christmas, also is well-remembered for *When the Wind Blows*, his nuclear war tale published in 1982.[97] Briggs's affectionate portrayal of an elderly couple in the English countryside struggling to comprehend first the prospect and then the dreadful reality of a nuclear missile attack indeed might be more easily recalled than government civil defence booklets such as *Protect and Survive*.[98] Briggs's loving couple highlights the obscene gulf between nuclear war and their nostalgic memories of sheltering and surviving bombing in the Second World War, and between rudimentary home preparations and the horrible spread of death following a nuclear bomb blast. In the United States, the ABC's television blockbuster *The Day After* also focused on the aftermath of a major nuclear exchange, including detonations on and around Kansas City. More than 100 million viewers watched its first broadcast and US president Ronald Reagan was deeply affected by it. Such screenings told of the *Zeitgeist* of the 1980s, and, thanks to Hollywood's love of remaking what proved successful, they also carried into artistic forms beyond the Cold War's end. *Edge of Darkness* was remade into a film starring Mel Gibson in 2010; *Red Dawn*, a 1984 movie in which the Soviets and their Cuban and Nicaraguan allies invade the United States only to meet dogged resistance from high school students, was remade for 2012 release but now with North Koreans as the invaders. Similarly, the 1959 classic *On the Beach*, about the end of the world as radiation clouds drift towards Australia – the last remaining inhabitable place on earth – enjoyed a remake in 2000.

Fiction connects occasionally with well-known Cold War icons. Some of the most important command bunkers may have transformed into tourist destinations or shifted to non-active status, but they reverberate in popular film and fiction. The NORAD part of the military complex built in Cheyenne Mountain was effectively moved in 2008 (still leaving a thriving underground community of military, security, and intelligence tenants). Yet it lives on in all its real and imagined glory in Hollywood hit outs such as: Stanley Kubrick's famous dark satire *Dr Strangelove or How I Learned to Stop Worrying and Love the Bomb* (1964), in which the war-room resembles Cheyenne Mountain's command room; and *War Games* (1983), in which a teenager hacks into the centre's main computer, threatening to unleash war on the world.

And satirical allusions to civil defence measures of the Cold War recur in popular culture and public language as the days of such instructions and exercises recede. Nostalgia and activism led to the classic US Civil Defense film *Duck and Cover* (1951), instructing millions of school children during the 1950s in how to shelter from a nuclear attack, being selected for the 2004 National Film Registry of 'culturally, historically and aesthetically significant' motion pictures.[99] (As if in anticipation, a year earlier comedians and the media had delighted in the idea of 'duct and cover' – the US Department of Homeland Security's recommendation that, in preparation for a potential terrorist alert, New Yorkers should buy duct tape with which to seal doors against possible biological or chemical attack.)[100] While some of the satire might seem lighthearted, cultural commentators point out that Hollywood's Cold War ventures of the 1990s (such as *Matinee* from 1993 and *Blast from the Past* from 1999) carried renewed longings for old-fashioned values with part-nostalgic, part-critical perspectives on shelter training and building in the 1950s and 1960s. Some of the post-9/11 US television serials returned to this era but carried darker references to Cold War alarms and shelters, providing something of a safety valve for suppressed fears about the present.[101] In Britain, remembering civil defence measures seems to be an even keener pursuit at collector level, notable perhaps for its lineage with, and radical departures from, the popularized stoicism of the population sheltering from bombing during the Second World War. The work of enthusiasts exploring all things underground in Britain – *Subterranea Britannica* – ensures regular updates, and sometimes considerable engineering detail, on the shelters marking the British landscape.[102]

Bunkerland

In Moscow's Tagansky District, a former air command bunker lies deep under a hollow house, with fake but realistic windows and trimmings dating from the secrecy with which it was built. Today, as a Cold War Museum called Bunker-42, it attracts tourists willing to pay the steep $40 entrance fee. In a capital of decidedly little reference to the Cold War, the museum seems to relish the challenge of catering for tourists looking beyond Red Square and the formidable ramparts of the Kremlin for traces of the forty-year struggle against the West. Bunker-42 offers everything a modern-day Cold War tourist could want. The most conventional experience is a tour of a huge bunker complex, complete with air command control centre, wherein, like in Arizona, the visitor can be part of a two-person team dispatching nuclear weapons to their targets (in this case, dispatching long-range bombers bearing atomic bombs). Completed in 1956, the complex housed between 100 and 600 workers for most of its operational days. It was built by engineers who constructed the nearby metro tunnel and who disguised their comings and goings by using doors between the bunker and the metro. As a consequence, the bunker complex features thick, train tunnel-like steel plating, ribs, and rivets, plus some rooms of impressive size. It was, according to a guide, a very active place during the Cuban Missile Crisis of 1962, but its utility in other Cold War crises is oblique. Today's visitor can see seminar and conference rooms as well as a karaoke room, all for hire, and contemplate weddings and parties in the bunker restaurant. The list of possibilities includes children's parties wherein kids can battle zombie survivors of a nuclear holocaust; and longer hire for team-building events.[103]

Even without considering the more innovative work/recreational possibilities, there is minimal narrative in Bunker-42 and maximum appeal to the novelty of the underground experience – if gas masks, capes, samples of 1960s communications equipment, and air command maps will not stir the tourist, then the chance to wield a Kalashnikov AK-47 assault rifle might do the trick. The feel is consistent with a Moscow blend of forgetting the Cold War as a determining narrative while embracing its more thrilling and sinister by-products.[104] Tourists searching for acts of Cold War remembrance in Moscow can run from Bunker-42 to Stalin's own bunker, or they might visit the (only partly Soviet focused) Museum of Torture on the popular walking strip, the Arbat, or, when it was open, the KGB Museum in the Lubyanka prison, where the emphasis was on spies' gadgets and trophies taken from captured American spies. Then again, they might choose to strap in and fly a Cold War era MIG-29 jet fighter over Moscow.

Bunker-42 is one of the more extravagant versions of the tourist attraction, growing steadily, of nuclear bunkers that formerly served as command posts for governments or command personnel of armed forces. These are not restricted to the United States and former Soviet Union. A less flashy example lies roughly 50 miles east of Riga, Latvia, underneath the Ligatne Rehabilitation Centre. Designed to shelter the Latvian Communist Party leadership in the event of nuclear war, the bunker became operational in 1982. As befitting a complex designed to host 250 people for up to three

Figure 2.3 Entrance to Bunker-42, Moscow, November 2012.

months, its steel and concreted protection, communications gear, storage and provision for electricity, water, and air are the main features beyond some typical Soviet paraphernalia. The bunker was decommissioned in 2003, and guided tours now run by appointment. In this newer bunker, it is the connection to Moscow as well as the implications of planning survival in a world destroyed by atomic bombs that invites the visitor's imagination. In the Ligatne Bunker hotline phones going direct to the Kremlin, along with Soviet-style canteen food, are reminders of both the rule of communist parties in the Baltic States and their subservience to Moscow.[105] In a country that lost around 20 per cent of its population through Soviet occupation in 1940, and then saw one-tenth of its rural population deported by the Soviets on one day in March 1949, popular resentment at the consequences of Soviet occupation is strong. Identity and memory politics is further complicated by a large ethnic Russian community, including descendants of émigrés from the time of the Bolshevik Revolution. Not surprisingly, then, the Ligatne Bunker is not asked to carry heavy historical interpretation, but rather serves as a strange 'window' on the Cold War and its strategic consequences.[106]

Elsewhere in Northern Europe, on the outskirts of Copenhagen, the Ejby Bunker, a former Danish air command facility, opened to visitors in 2012. Now overgrown with ivy, its thick concrete exterior is nestled into the ramparts of an old mound fortress system built in the 1890s. This makes for easy integration with the history of Copenhagen, and it has been worked into school excursion programmes. Ejby was operated by the Danish Air Force between 1954 and 1971, before being used for storage and then decommissioned in 2005. Inside, minimal furnishings and textual interpretation help build an atmosphere of quiet watchfulness, with some of the illumination coming from the green dials of radar screens making imaginary sweeps of the air. In the middle of the control room, a large battlefield screen invites visitors (and especially children, one presumes) to grab controls and dispatch aircraft to 'Stop the Third World War'. Footage of Danish newsreaders reporting the events of October 1962, as the situation in Cuba unfolded, add to the recreation of drama; and other documentary film reminds visitors of the power of atomic bombs.[107] In the case of Denmark, the Ejby Bunker helps tell the tale of the country's emergence from neutrality in international relations to alliance with the West in the Cold War. Denmark became a member of NATO in 1949, enhanced its national service and civil defence preparedness, and, by virtue of its potential to lock in the Soviet Baltic Fleet, became a potential target in Cold War confrontations. More than other bunkers elsewhere, the recent opening of the Ejby Bunker is part of a broader Danish engagement with Cold War history. Revelations that successive Danish governments behaved contrary to public position and allowed their American allies to store nuclear weapons at Thule Air Base on Greenland, coupled with government-sponsored research into national security policy, intelligence, and espionage, have spurred new waves of historical inquiry and museum activity in recent years.[108] Among these developments, the Danish Agency for Culture features 25 designated 'Cold War Hot Spots', including bunkers, radar stations, and airstrips, as available to the public. Director of the agency, Anne Mette Rahbaek, comments that the Cold War is an essential source for understanding Danish society after the Second World War:

> This is the same period in which Denmark begins to forge the welfare state. The two parallel developments each left their mark, which we would like to make visible. It is also extremely important for young people to understand that the world is changeable and that these changes can affect Denmark.[109]

The idea of a bunker as a museum of larger narrative-bearing mission arguably has the fullest expression in Canada, where the 'Diefenbunker' also serves as Canada's Cold War Museum. Located on the edge of Ottawa, the Diefenbunker is a play on the name of the Canadian prime minister John Diefenbaker (1957–63), who ordered the bunker's construction in 1959. Until its decommissioning in 1994, the bunker was maintained by Canada's Department of National Defence as the Central Emergency Government Headquarters in the event of nuclear attack. The four levels and more than 9,500 square feet of floor space included a small hospital, a bank vault to

Figure 2.4 Entrance to the Ejby Bunker, Copenhagen, November 2012.

protect Canada's gold reserve from irradiation, the Prime Minister's Room and War Cabinet Room, secure communications equipment, and a radio studio. The bunker could have held more than 500 people for 30 days. As a site of memory, the Diefenbunker started slowly with local volunteers seizing a chance to draw it into the community's tourism. It has gathered profile as a not-for-profit charitable museum and now claims to average around 25,000 visitors a year. Consistent with the order of words in its title, the Cold War narrative history in international context plays a significant secondary role in the bunker's Canadian-centric presentation. As with other bunkers, there is strong engagement with younger visitors, explicit links offered with junior and higher schools' curricula, interactive games and availability for party hire, and special provision for summer camps on such themes as code making and breaking, spies at work, and the science behind spying. One of the differentiating features is a requiem room towards the end of the bunker tour, inviting quiet contemplation and honouring those killed in the atomic bombing of Hiroshima and Nagasaki.[110]

The largest British Cold War bunker complex is the Burlington Bunker, a 35-acre small 'town' built in the early-1950s underneath Corsham, Wiltshire. The scale that emerges from diagrams and video footage shot inside is striking. Battery-powered buggies motored along the more than 50 miles of roads, named first, second, and third avenue, etc. As well as providing a headquarters for an emergency government, the complex could have accommodated more than 4,000 people for three months and featured correspondingly huge water provision (an underground lake), recycling, and elaborate communications equipment. The complex was completed in 1961 and remained operational until 1991, before being decommissioned (and the 50 staff dedicated to its maintenance redeployed) and, in 2004, finally declassified as a secret institution. In November 2009, BBC television was able to tour the complex as a prelude to the Ministry of Defence's putting it up for sale. The news story emphasized not only the size of the complex but the contrast between preparations and what actually happened, or did not happen, inside Burlington. Viewers were pointed to rows of stools and bakelite telephones still in their plastic wrapping, and industrial kitchen ovens and boilers never once used.[111] At the time of writing, the bunker, much viewed on news services and on various websites but open only to those making a purchase bid, still awaits its buyer.

Another British government regional command bunker at Kelvedon Hatch, in Essex east of London, is more accessible. The Kelvedon Hatch Bunker has been open to tourists after it was decommissioned in 1992 and sold back to the family who originally owned the land. Built in 1952–53, initially as part of an upgrade of Royal Air Force Fighter Command preparations, it also became an emergency Regional Government Headquarters, from which a surviving government could try to govern in the wake of nuclear war. Like other larger bunkers it has extensive shelter and self-containment capability and considerable communications equipment including a BBC studio.

There was storage and space on three levels for up to 600 government personnel. Today, Kelvedon Hatch is marketed as a 'Top Secret' Nuclear Bunker (including, somewhat ironically, the road signposts leading to it), and its testimony to the Cold War is somewhat compromised by its private ownership. The organization and upkeep of displays is very tired and occasionally misplaced (a dummy of former prime minister Margaret Thatcher, for instance, sits next to communications equipment dating from the 1960s), and the bunker jostles with youth-focused outside activities such as quad bikes, paintball, and rope courses. The self-guided audio tour aims at the younger visitor, and the owners encourage party hire for those aged under 12 or over 40.[112] The greatest sense of dread emerging from Kelvedon Hatch emanates from television screens replaying two films: *The Hole in the Ground*, a 1962 dramatization of how the UK Warning and Monitoring Organisation (UKWMO) would monitor radiation levels in different parts of the country, thus enabling civilians to be told when it was safe to emerge from sheltered areas; and the British documentary *1983: The Brink of Apocalypse*. This latter production tells how Able Archer, an annual NATO military exercise in November 1983, had almost sparked a Soviet reaction on the assumption that they were really about to be attacked with nuclear weapons. This near-disastrous episode, as depicted by the documentary, reflected the heightened state of East–West tensions in the wake of other developments in the early-1980s including most notably: president Reagan's March 1983 announcement of his 'Star Wars' missile defence system; the so-called KAL007 incident of September 1983, which entailed the Soviet shooting down of a Korean airliner that had strayed into Soviet airspace; and the imminent deployment in NATO countries of new US Pershing II missiles that were capable of reaching Moscow in eight minutes. Soviet levels of panic also reflected the decrepitude of their warning systems and their conviction that Reagan was bent on war. *1983: The Brink of Apocalypse* was screened for the first time on television in 2008 to 1.2 million viewers.[113] It tells a dramatic story of how the popularly shared worst fears could have been realized: Armageddon resulting from brinksmanship and stretched nerves, a series of accidents, and entrenched misperceptions.[114]

In 1992, the *Washington Post* broke the news of an elaborate government bunker built in the late-1950s at the Greenbrier Hotel, the venerable luxury resort in White Sulphur Springs, West Virginia. Around five hours south of Washington DC, the Greenbrier Bunker was intended to shelter the US Congress and some aides. The five-star hotel, well-known on Capitol Hill, benefited from the government's construction of a new wing, in return for the addition of an elaborate shelter to be included beneath it. The Greenbrier Bunker was finished just in time for the Cuban Missile Crisis in 1962, and this was the only time it went on full alert. After more than 30 years of secretive updates and maintenance since then, the bunker opened to hotel guests in 1995 and to other tourists two years later. This is a bunker of grand proportions, featuring smaller versions of the House and Senate

Chambers, both capable of seating every member of Congress. There is a television studio, too, and a formidable amount of other communications equipment as well as dormitory sleeping quarters and a 'pathological waste incinerator' for disposal of the dead.[115] Greenbrier draws interest from both historical and contemporary speculations. It provides tourist-friendly evidence of a Cold War era characterized by the threat of nuclear war, and it feeds imaginations about other bunker systems awaiting possible use today. While other American bunker complexes are publicly known, including Raven Rock Mountain Complex, Pennsylvania, the Cheyenne Mountain Complex, and Mount Weather, Virginia, secrecy surrounds their use, and Greenbrier is one of the few places that the American public can visit.

Elsewhere, elaborate preparations for civil defence in times of nuclear/ chemical/bacteriological attack have left their mark. The Dutch invite tourists into a major Civil Defence crisis response bunker in the town of Rijswijk. The bunker sits in a public park alongside German bunkers dating from the Second World War. It has been restored with care, and adorned with 1960s glasses, maps, telephones, and other equipment by the Dutch Civil Defence Authority (*Bescherming Bevolking*).[116] More ambitiously, the Swedish government tried to provide shelter on a mass scale. During the 1950s, the citizens of Stockholm had the option of heading to huge underground shelters, including a central complex built into the side of a hill. There were three such shelters in the Stockholm region, each capable of protecting around 20,000 people and 500 cars in large galleries, each protected by thick slab doors that would slide from recesses to cover the openings, and with decontamination and sanitary facilities. All of Sweden's major towns and cities had extensive bunker systems. While they are used for mundane but practical purposes such as car parks (the role of the best-known in Katarinavägen in central Stockholm), today they retain a capacity to fulfil their civil defence role. Such is the continuity and normalization of mass-scale shelters in Sweden, however, that they may loom larger to non-residents remembering the heightened nuclear threat of the Cold War. Civil Defence shelters also were built elsewhere, including in United States towns and cities in the 1960s, primarily as sealable parts of public buildings offering shelter against fall-out rather than as protection against bomb blasts, but these were retired quietly in the 1970s and early-1980s. As they were unremarkable parts of buildings or tunnels, they held little intrinsic architectural interest, and they are recalled only through printed Community Shelter Plans or images of supply kits for the two-week stay envisaged for sheltering residents.[117] Although encouraged to build fall-out shelters, relatively few citizens did so, and those who did later tended to either convert them into storage spaces of some form or dismantle them.

Given the practice of selling some of the former bunkers from the mid-1990s as they were decommissioned, it is not surprising that secretive uses for bunkers cause them to surface publicly in the media. In March 2013, for instance, what has been described as the largest cyber-attack in the history of the internet was traced to the Dutch company Cyberbunker, which, as its name suggests, is based inside an old bunker near the town of Kloetinge. The bunker was completed in 1955 as a command post that could survive a nuclear attack, and, after 40 years of Cold War service, was sold in 1996. One of Stockholm's shelters, the Pionen White Mountain Bunker, has become a high-security ISP data centre. The Pionen site suddenly enjoyed the international limelight in 2010 when its hosting of the Wikileaks head-quarters became known.

The Cold War has left its mark on landscapes in less celebrated ways. There remains a huge number of unremarkable monitoring stations with basic bunkers spread throughout parts of Europe. In Britain, for example, more than 1,500 Royal Observer Corps bunkers were built, of which some 800 survived a rationalization in 1968. The bunkers generally were designed to hold three observers who would monitor the aftermath of a nuclear attack. Private sales of such bunkers in the new century have occasionally attracted media attention: 'There's no gas or electricity but locations are lovely' was how one newspaper summed up the advertising of thirteen such posts across northern England. Having originally been bought by a telecom company in the early-1990s, the sites were advertised for sale again – on eBay – in 2003, and attracted strong interest according to a pleased real estate agent: 'They've been snapped up by investors, Cold War enthusiasts and walkers, birdwatchers, and people who just wanted a cheap holiday home. The locations were perfect for bunkhouse accommodation.'[118] Witty newspaper sub-editors clearly welcome such sales, too: 'One careful owner wanted for H-Bomb bolt-hole (would suit a nuclear family)' rejoiced one regional newspaper in relation to the sale of a large munitions bunker at Dean's Hill, Wiltshire, in Britain.[119] Several Royal Observer Corps bunkers are open to tourists, and English Heritage opened an even larger former regional headquarters of the Observer Corps in the northern city of York as a tourist attraction in 2006.

All of these bunkers embrace a sense of anachronism as part of their appeal. They stand today as elaborate evidence of fears about something that never happened; but they also testify to the scale of the imagined threat and the extraordinary planning behind providing for the worst. Importantly, they open a door for curious publics to peer into governments' top-secret planning and defence assumptions – a door that is typically kept closed, leaving novelists and filmmakers to flesh out imagined realms. The passing of more than 50 years since official bunker building was at its peak around 1960 means that archival releases also can play a role in recreating the details of emergency planning. In 2011, the British public learned that 'orangeade' was the code word that would have alerted the Burlington Bunker to immi-nent nuclear attack at the time of the Cuban Missile Crisis.[120] Bunker tourism has evolved in fitful ways in different countries but, where money can support restoration and management, there has been steady expansion in what a curious public might see. This pattern of niche tourism with incremental growth is likely to throw open more bunker doors, but keeping them open may present challenges. As an example, the former East German Navy's big command and communications bunker in the forest near the town of Tessin opened in 2011 after being sealed for nearly 20 years, but is dependent on the enthusiasm of its private owner for its viability.

Bunker tourism, of course, relates to those Cold War bunkers that have been restored and maintained for that purpose. Enthusiasts who have documented the larger number have shown how many still await their post-Cold War fate, and that the layers of reinforced concrete that might protect inhabitants from a nuclear blast still decay, as do their interiors.[121] Explaining his suggestion that the Cold War might be best thought of as 'decomposing' rather than ending, Heonik Kwon pointed to empirical forms of decomposition in the form of human remains from battles in Korea and Vietnam. Given the state of many Cold War bunkers, they might well be added to the story of Cold War decomposition.

Notes

1 Müller, 'Introduction', p. 11.
2 There is a huge literature on this question. Some of the most recent accounts, revealing differing interpretations, are: Gar Alperovitz, *The Decision to Use the Atomic Bomb and the Architecture of an American Myth* (New York: Alfred A. Knopf, 1995). Richard B. Frank, *Downfall: The End of the Imperial Japanese Empire* (New York: Penguin, 1999). And Herbert Bix, *Hirohito and the Making of Modern Japan* (New York: HarperCollins, 2000). For a polemic, written by a veteran who later became an internationally renowned scholar, see Paul Fussell, 'Thank God for the Atom Bomb', *The Guardian*, 5 February 1989.
3 Tsuyoshi Hasegawa, *Racing the Enemy: Stalin, Truman and the Surrender of Japan* (Cambridge, Massachusetts: The Belknap Press of Harvard University Press, 2006).
4 A good historiographical essay, capturing important work up to the early 2000s, including a burgeoning 'middle ground' in the arguments between traditionalists (arguing that Truman was primarily motivated by a desire to end the war as soon as possible in order to avoid high casualties that would accompany the invasion of the Japanese home islands) and revisionists (arguing that Truman was motivated primarily by a desire to marginalize Soviet influence in postwar Japan) is J. Samuel Walker, 'Recent Literature on Truman's Atomic Bomb Decision: The Search for Middle Ground', *Diplomatic History*, vol. 29, no. 2 (2005).
5 One of the strongest examples is Alperovitz, *The Decision*.
6 John W. Dower, *Ways of Forgetting, Ways of Remembering: Japan in the Modern World* (New York: The New Press, 2012), p. 138.
7 John Hersey, *Hiroshima* (Harmondsworth, Middlesex: Penguin, 1946).
8 Stephanie Schäfer, 'The Hiroshima Peace Memorial Museum and its Exhibition', in *The Power of Memory in Modern Japan*, eds Wolfgang Schwentker and Sven Saaler (Folkestone: Global Oriental, 2008).
9 For example, see 25 personal accounts in *Hibakusha: Survivors of Hiroshima and Nagasaki*, trans. Gaynor Sekimori (Tokyo: Kōsei Publishing Company, 1986). And Michihiko Hachiya, *Hiroshima Diary: The Journal of a Japanese Physician, August 6 – September 30, 1945*, trans. Warner Wells (Chapel Hill: University of North Carolina Press, 1995).

10 'Hiroshima Peace Memorial Museum: Exhibit Text' (Accessed February 2013).
11 Kazumi Matsui, 'Hiroshima Peace Declaration', (6 August 2012). Copy in possession of the authors.
12 Daniel Seltz, 'Remembering the War and the Atomic Bombs: New Museums, New Approaches', *Radical History Review*, vol. 72 (1999).
13 'Hiroshima Peace Memorial Museum: Exhibit Text.'
14 Ibid.
15 'Hiroshima Peace Memorial (Genbaku Dome)', UNESCO *World Heritage List*, http://whc.unesco.org/en/list/775 (Last accessed December 2012).
16 World Heritage Committee, 'UNESCO World Heritage Convention concerning the Protection of the World Cultural and Natural Heritage, World Heritage Committe Report, Twentieth Session, Merida, Mexico, 2–7 December 1996, Annex V: Statements by China and the United States of America during the Inscription of the Hiroshima Peace Memorial (Genbaku Dome)', UNESCO, 1996, http://whc.unesco.org/archive/repco96x.htm#annex5 (Last accessed February 2012). Olwen Beazley, 'A Paradox of Peace: The Hiroshima Peace Memorial (Genbaku Dome) as World Heritage', in *Fearsome Heritage: Diverse Legacies of the Cold War*, eds A.J. Schofield and Wayne Cocroft (Walnut Creek: Left Coast Press, 2009), pp. 33–34.
17 Dower, *Ways of Forgetting*, pp. 141–44.
18 Sonja D. Schmid, 'Celebrating Tomorrow Today: The Peaceful Atom on Display in the Soviet Union', *Social Studies of Science*, vol. 36, no. 3 (June 2006). Also, for a new study of two atomic cities – Richland (where the Hanford plant was closed) in the United States, and Ozersk (the Maiak plant) in Russia – see Kate Brown, *Plutopia: Nuclear Families, Atomic Cities, and the Great Soviet and American Plutonium Disasters* (New York: Oxford University Press, 2013).
19 There is a substantial literature on the Cuban Missile Crisis, and also many related collections of documents. See, for examples, two books by Sheldon M. Stern, the first of which contains transcripts of White House conversations at the time of the crisis, and the second is an exploration of the remembering and mythologizing around this event. Sheldon M. Stern, *The Week the World Stood Still: Inside the Secret Cuban Missile Crisis* (Stanford, California: Stanford University Press, 2005). And Sheldon M. Stern, *The Cuban Missile Crisis in American Memory: Myths versus Reality* (Stanford, California: Stanford University Press, 2012).
20 See, for examples, Abbas Amanat and Magnus T. Bernhardsson, eds, *Imagining the End: Visions of Apocalypse from the Ancient Middle East to Modern America* (London: I.B.Tauris, 2001). And Adam Parfrey, ed., *Apocalypse Culture II* (Los Angeles: Feral House, 2000).
21 These figures derive from records reproduced in Daryl Kimball and Tom Collina, 'Nuclear Weapons: Who Has What at a Glance', *Arms Control Association*, April 2013, www.armscontrol.org/factsheets/Nuclearweaponswhohaswhat (Last accessed May 2013).
22 Reynolds, *One World Divisible*, p. 325.
23 This includes a Soviet Fighter shooting down a Korean passenger airliner that had strayed into Soviet airspace in September 1983, and Moscow's near-overreaction to a realistic NATO exercise, Able Archer, in Europe two months later.
24 See the website: AMSE, *American Museum of Science & Energy (AMSE)*, http://amse.org/sponsorship/amse-foundation/ (Last accessed March 2013).
25 Lindsey A. Freeman, 'Happy Memories under the Mushroom Cloud: Utopia and Memory in Oak Ridge, Tennessee', in *Memory and the Future: Transnational Politics, Ethics and Society*, eds Yifat Gutman, Adam D. Brown, and Amy Sodao (London: Palgrave Macmillan, 2010).
26 As indicated on the museum's website: *AMSE*.

27 National Atomic Testing Museum, *National Atomic Testing Museum* www.national atomictestingmuseum.org/exhibit-featured.aspx (Last accessed August 2012).

28 Of the closed cities, ten were known as 'Atomgrads' for their identification with work on nuclear research and weaponry.

29 There are other atomic-themed sister cities, such as Russia's Obinsk with Oak Ridge in the United States.

30 While the Museum does not seem to have its own website, photographs of its galleries are at: 'Sarov's Museum of Nuclear Weapons', *RIA Novosti*, http://en. rian.ru/photolents/20130131/179143978_1/Sarovs-Museum-of-Nuclear-Weapons. html (Last accessed March 2013).

31 Jerome Taylor, 'The World's Worst Radiation Hotspot', *The Independent*, 10 September 2009, www.independent.co.uk/news/world/europe/the-worlds-worst-radiation-hotspot-1784502.html (Last accessed November 2012).

32 See especially, Zeeya Merali, 'Did China's Nuclear Tests Kill Thousands and Doom Future Generations?', *Scientific American*, 8 July 2009, www.scientificamer-ican.com/article.cfm?id=did-chinas-nuclear-tests (Last accessed November 2012). And Jun Takada, *Chinese Nuclear Tests* (Tokyo: Iryo Kagakusha, 2009).

33 There were 23 atmospheric and 23 underground tests conducted during the period. The European Parliament considered the issue in March 2012. See NTDTV, 'European Parliament Assessing the Impact of Nuclear Testing in Xinjiang', *YouTube*, www.youtube.com/watch?v=uPGcpXLydYk (Last accessed January 2013).

34 See 'Atomic Bomb Site Open to Tourists', *China Journeys*, 16 October 2012, http://china-journeys.com/travel-updates/atomic-bomb-site-open-to-tourists.html (Last accessed April 2013).

35 As described in Liu Xiangrui and Huang Zhiling, 'City Bases Smart Success on Legacy', *China Daily*, 1 March 2012, www.chinadaily.com.cn/bizchina/innovative/ 2012–03/01/content_14740592.htm (Last accessed April 2013).

36 In 2012, Jon Wiener reported visitor numbers at 50,000 per year. See Wiener, *How We Forgot*, p. 124.

37 See Jennifer Whitehair, 'Flashback Friday: When the Atom was King', *Vegas.com*, 7 August 2009, http://blog.vegas.com/more-las-vegas-news/flashback-friday-when-the-atom-was-king-2633/ (Last accessed April 2013).

38 See, for example, Doug Waterfield, 'The Doomtown Series', *DougWaterfield.com*, http://dougwaterfield.com/portfolio/doomtown (Last accessed March 2013).

39 See Robert A. Jacobs, *The Dragon's Tail: Americans Face the Atomic Age* (Amherst: University of Massachusetts Press, 2010).

40 Tom Brokaw, *The Greatest Generation* (New York: Random House, 1998).

41 See National Atomic Testing Museum, 'Exhibit – Area 51,' *National Atomic Testing Museum*, www.nationalatomictestingmuseum.org/exhibit-area51.aspx (Last accessed October 2012).

42 Reynolds, *One World Divisible*, p. 167.

43 See, for instance: 'UFO Tours – From Roswell to Area 51 and Beyond: Southwest UFO Discovery Tour', *Alpventures*, www.alpventures.com/topsecret/ TS_southwest_ufo_discovery_tour_PART1.html (Last accessed March 2013).

44 See the website Conelrad, *Conelrad*, http://conelrad.com/index.php (Last accessed November 2012).

45 Edward Tabor Linenthal, *Sacred Ground: Americans and their Battlefields* (Urbana: University of Illinois Press, 1993).

46 Rosenberg, *A Date which will Live*, p. 175.

47 Arthur Molella, 'Exhibiting Atomic Culture: The View from Oak Ridge', *History and Technology*, vol. 19, no. 3 (2003).

48 'Welcome to the Titan Missile Museum: A Rare Journey into Cold War History', *Titan Missile Museum*, www.titanmissilemuseum.org (Last accessed April 2013).

49 This summary draws on the museum's website, and two published accounts by commentators: Wiener, *How We Forgot*, pp. 227–40. And Liz Coffey, 'Titan Missile Museum: Authenticate!' *Conelrad*, December 2003, www.conelrad.com/groundzero/index.php?zero=01 (Last accessed March 2013).

50 Quote taken from 'Mission Statement', *The Rocky Flats Cold War Museum*, www.rockyflatscoldwarmuseum.org/mission.html (Last accessed March 2013).

51 For a powerful personal account of growing up in Rocky Flats and working at the weapons plant, see Kristen Iversen, *Full Body Burden: Growing Up in the Nuclear Shadow of Rocky Flats* (New York: Crown Publishing, 2012).

52 Available through the website of the Boulder Public Library, 'Maria Rogers Oral History Program', *Boulder Public Library*, http://oralhistory.boulderlibrary.org (Last accessed January 2013).

53 It is not surprising that the Rocky Flats Virtual Museum has a strong safety-environmental message, as it is sponsored by the Center for Environmental Journalism at the University of Colorado at Boulder. See '1969 Fire Exhibit', *Rocky Flats Virtual Museum*, www.colorado.edu/journalism/cej/exhibit/index.html (Last accessed February 2013).

54 'Our Mission', *Atomic Heritage Foundation*, www.atomicheritage.org/index.php/about/about-us.html (Last accessed March 2013).

55 The Foundation's work is well-captured in a book edited by its president, Cynthia Kelly, ed., *Remembering the Manhattan Project: Perspectives on the Making of the Atomic Bomb and its Legacy* (River Edge, New Jersey: World Scientific Publishing, 2005).

56 Sarah Reardon, 'Manhattan Project National Park Plan raises Questions', *New Scientist*, 9 August 2012, www.newscientist.com/article/dn22157-manhattan-project-national-park-plan-raises-questions.html?page=1#.UdZHLxYwaqA (Last accessed March 2013).

57 The details of this episode, and the broader context of the 'culture war' in which the controversy erupted, can be found in numerous works elsewhere. One good introduction is Richard H. Kohn, 'History and Culture Wars: The Case of the Smithsonian Institution's Enola Gay Exhibition', *Journal of American History*, vol. 82, no. 3 (December 1995). For another excellent analysis, see Hogan, 'The Enola Gay Controversy'.

58 Alexandra Levy, 'The Manhattan Project: Interpreting Controversial History', *National Trust for Historic Preservation: Preservation Leadership Forum*, 15 May 2013, http://blog.preservationleadershipforum.org/2013/05/15/manhattan-project-interpreting/#.UZP5D7Xvtys (Last accessed May 2013).

59 'Nike Missile Site', *National Park Service: Golden Gate National Recreation Area*, www.nps.gov/goga/nike-missile-site.htm (Last accessed March 2013).

60 *NikeMissile.org*, http://nikemissile.org (Last accessed March 2013).

61 Greg Shine, 'Presenting History at SF-88: An Exploration and Critical Analysis of the Role of Memory in Cold War Historical Interpretation at the Golden Gate National Recreation Area's Nike Missile Site SF-88', *NikeMissile.org*, 1998, http://nikemissile.org/ColdWar/GregShine/shine.shtml (Last accessed December 2012).

62 Mead & Hunt Inc. *et al.*, 'The Missile Plains: Frontline of America's Cold War (Historic Resource Study of Minuteman Missile National Historic Site, South Dakota, Prepared for United States Department of the Interior, National Park Service, Midwest Regional Office)', *National Park Service*, 2003, www.nps.gov/mimi/historyculture/upload/MIMI%20HRS%202006.pdf (Last accessed March 2013).

63 Wiener, *How We Forgot*.

64 Ibid. p. 237.

65 Kwon, *The Other Cold War*.

66 Bryan C. Taylor, 'Revis(it)ing Nuclear History: Narrative Conflict at the Bradbury Science Museum', *Studies in Cultures, Organizations and Societies*, vol. 3, no. 1 (1997).

67 The State Atomic Energy Corporation (ROSATOM), 'About Nuclear Industry', ROSATOM, www.rosatom.ru/en/about/nuclear_industry/ (Last accessed March 2013).

68 Anita Smith, 'Colonialism and the Bomb in the Pacific', in *Fearsome Heritage: Diverse Legacies of the Cold War*, eds John Schofield and Wayne Cocroft (Walnut Creek, California: Left Coat Press, 2009), p. 52.

69 As recounted by the Nuclear Claims Tribunal: Republic of the Marshall Islands, 'Welcome to the Marshall Islands Nuclear Claims Tribunal', *Nuclear Claims Tribunal*, http://nuclearclaimstribunal.com (Last accessed March 2013).

70 Philip A. Okney, 'Legacies and Perils from the Perspective of the Republic of the Marshall Islands Nuclear Claims Tribunal', in *The Oceans in the Nuclear Age: Legacies and Risks*, eds David D. Caron and Harry N. Scheiber (Leiden: Martinus Nijhoff, 2010).

71 Laurence Cordonnery, 'The Legacy of French Nuclear Testing in the Pacific', ibid. pp. 69–78.

72 *Le Monde*, 10 June 2010.

73 Roy H. Smith, *The Nuclear Free and Independent Pacific Movement after Muroroa* (London: I.B.Tauris, 1997). Nic Maclellan, 'The Nuclear Age in the Pacific Islands', *The Contemporary Pacific*, vol. 17, no. 2 (2005), p. 368. Ohnie, 'Nuclear Free Independent Pacific', *Moana Nui*, 19 February 2013, http://mnaa-ca.org/nuclear-free-independent-pacific/ (Last accessed March 2013).

74 Royal Commission into British Nuclear Tests in Australia, 'The Report of the Royal Commission into British Nuclear Tests in Australia, Volume I', *Australian Government, Department of Resources, Energy and Tourism*, 1985, www.ret.gov.au/resources/radioactive_waste/documents/royal%20commission%20into%20british%20nuclear%20tests%20in%20australia%20vol%201.pdf (Last accessed November 2012).

75 Wayne Reynolds, *Australia's Bid for the Bomb* (Melbourne: Melbourne University Press, 2000).

76 See, for example, Jim Green, 'Dumping on Traditional Owners: The Ugly Face of Australian Racism', *ABC: The Drum*, 29 March 2012, www.abc.net.au/unleashed/3919296.html (Last accessed February 2013).

77 Institute of Medicine and National Research Council, 'Exposure of the American People to Iodine-131 from Nevada Nuclear-Bomb Tests: Review of the National Cancer Institute Report and Public Health Implications', *National Center for Biotechnology Information (NCBI)*, 1999, www.ncbi.nlm.nih.gov/books/NBK100842/ (Last accessed April 2013), p. 8.

78 This summary is drawn from reports around the twenty-fifth anniversary of the accident, accessible from World Health Organization (WHO), 'Ionizing Radiation: Health Effects of the Chernobyl Accident', *World Health Organization*, April 2011, www.who.int/ionizing_radiation/chernobyl/en/ (Last accessed November 2012).

79 See Lawrence S. Wittner, *The Struggle against the Bomb*, 3 vols, vol. 1. *One World or None: A History of the World Nuclear Disarmament Movement through 1953* (Stanford: Stanford University Press, 1993). Lawrence S. Wittner, *The Struggle against the Bomb*, 3 vols, vol. 2. *Resisting the Bomb: A History of the World Nuclear Disarmament Movement, 1954–70* (Stanford: Stanford University Press, 1997). Lawrence S. Wittner, *The Struggle against the Bomb*, 3 vols, vol. 3. *Toward Nuclear Abolition: A History of the World Nuclear Disarmament Movement, 1971 to the Present* (Stanford: Stanford University Press, 2003). And Lawrence S. Wittner, *Working for Peace and Justice: Memoirs of an Activist Intellectual* (Knoxville: University of Tennessee Press, 2012). Also Jennifer Smith, ed., *The Antinuclear Movement* (San Diego: Greenhaven Press, 2002). And Christian Peterson, *Ronald Reagan and Antinuclear Movements in the United States and Western Europe* (Lewiston, New York: Edwin Mellen Press, 2003).

80 See, for reflective commentary on the rise and fall of the anti-nuclear movement, Jonathan Schell, 'The Spirit of June 12', *The Nation*, 14 June 2007, www.thenation. com/article/spirit-june-12#axzz2YFIGyR1t (Last accessed October 2012).

81 Kate Hudson, 'Remembering Greenham Common', *The New Statesman*, 10 December 2007, www.newstatesman.com/archive/2013/04/remembering-greenham-common (Last accessed April 2013).

82 For the movement's own webpage dedicated to the era, see Sarah Hipperson, 'Greenham Common Women's Peace Camp, 1981–2000', *Greenham Common Women's Peace Camp*, www.greenhamwpc.org.uk (Last accessed December 2012).

83 For example, see the online descriptions by the Imperial War Museum, 'Greenham Common: The Women's Peace Camp 1981–2000', *Imperial War Museum*, http://archive.iwm.org.uk/upload/package/22/greenham/index.htm (Last accessed January 2013). And the National Cold War Exhibition, 'Greenham Common', *RAF Museum Cosford: National Cold War Exhibition*, www.nationalcoldwarexhibition. org/learn/social-economic-issues/greenham-common.cfm (Last accessed November 2012).

84 The group included four babies and six men.

85 For a description and photographs accessible online, see Toban Black, 'Glimpsing a History of Anti-Nuclear Activism', *Waging NonViolence: People-Powered News & Analysis*, 13 September 2009, http://wagingnonviolence.org/feature/glimpsing-a-history-of-anti-nuclear-activism/ (Last accessed December 2012).

86 For a museum example of oral history involving a protestor, see Sarah Gudgin (Interviewer) and Sue Sanders (Interviewee), 'Extract from Interview with Sue Sanders', *Museum of London*, 2009, www.museumoflondon.org.uk/Collections-Research/Collections-online/object.aspx?objectID=object-800279& start = 5& rows = 1 (Last accessed March 2013). And for a scholarly example, see Sam Carroll, '"I was Arrested at Greenham in 1962": Investigating the Oral Narratives of Women in the Committee of 100', *Oral History*, vol. 32, no. 1 (2004).

87 For an overview of the Council's activities, see Paul Gough, 'The Greater London Council: Selected Peace Sites', *Vortex*, www.vortex.uwe.ac.uk/places_of_peace/ sites.htm (Last accessed November 2012).

88 Amy Swerdlow, *Women Strike for Peace: Traditional Motherhood and Radical Politics in the 1960s* (Chicago: University of Chicago Press, 1993).

89 Iversen, *Full Body Burden*.

90 As summarized by Dinara Sagatova, 'Semipalatinsk Polygon: A Nuclear Test Site', *Semipalatinsk Polygon*, www.dinarasagatova.com/polygon/ (Last accessed January 2013).

91 James Veitch, 'A Sordid Act: The Rainbow Warrior Incident', *New Zealand International Review*, vol. 35, no. 4 (July 2010), p. 9.

92 For an early account written by someone on board the ship, see Dave Robie, *Eyes of Fire: The Last Voyage of the Rainbow Warrior* (Auckland: Lindon, 1986). Robie's book was republished by South Pacific Books on occasion of the bombing's twentieth anniversary in 2005. See also Michael King, *Death of the Rainbow Warrior* (Harmondsworth: Penguin, 1986). And for a filmic depiction, see Michael Tuchner, *The Sinking of the Rainbow Warrior* (1992).

93 For a recollection on occasion of the twenty-fifth anniversary of the bombing, see J. McKeati, 'Remember the Rainbow Warrior and the Marshall Islands', *Greenpeace*, 9 July 2010, www.greenpeace.org/international/en/news/Blogs/nuclear-reaction/remember-the-rainbow-warrior-and-the-marshall/blog/12910/ (Last accessed October 2012).

94 See Ferenc M. Szasz and Issei Takechi, 'Atomic Heroes and Atomic Monsters: American and Japanese Cartoonists Confront the Onset of the Nuclear Age, 1945–80', *The Historian*, vol. 69, no. 4 (Winter 2007).

95 Marc Steinberg, 'Anytime, Anywhere: Tetsuwan Atomu Stickers and the Emergence of Character Merchandizing', *Theory, Culture & Society*, vol. 26, no. 2–3 (March/May 2009).
96 See the essays in William M. Tsutsui and Machiko Ito, eds, *In Godzilla's Footsteps: Japanese Pop Culture Icons on the Global Stage* (New York: Palgrave Macmillan, 2006).
97 Raymond Briggs, *When the Wind Blows* (London: Hamish Hamilton, 1982).
98 Central Office of Information (for the Home Office), *Protect and Survive* (London: Her Majesty's Stationery Office, 1976; repr., 1980). Accessible online at: www. atomica.co.uk/main.htm (Accessed December 2012).
99 In 1955, the US Federal Civil Defense Administration aimed civil defence films at half a billion viewers. Melvin E. Matthews Jr, *Duck and Cover: Civil Defense Images in Film and Television from the Cold War to 9/11* (Jefferson, North Virginia: McFarland and Co., 2012), p. 7.
100 *Courier Mail*, 15 February 2003.
101 Matthews Jr., *Duck and Cover*, pp. 180–82, 196–98.
102 The emphasis on sheltering in the home rather than in communal shelters was very different from popularly distributed photographs of Londoners sheltering during the Blitz. For an online archive, see George Coney, 'Protect and Survive: An Archive of UK Civil Defence Material', *Atomica*, 2002, www.atomica.co.uk (Last accessed January 2013). See also Nick Catford, *Subterranean Britain: Cold War Bunkers* (London: Folly Books, 2010). And the website *Subterranea Britannica*, www.subbrit.org.uk (Last accessed October 2012).
103 'Bunker-42 on Taganka', *Bunker-42*, http://bunker42.nichost.ru (Last accessed April 2013).
104 This analysis draws on author David Lowe's visit to Bunker-42 in November 2012.
105 'Secret Nuclear Bunker, Ligatne', *The Baltic Initiative and Network*, http://coldwarsites.net/country/latvia/secret-nuclear-bunker-ligatne (Last accessed April 2013).
106 Vieda Skultáns, *The Testimony of Lives: Narrative and Memory in Post-Soviet Latvia* (London: Routledge, 1998), p. x. Those who resisted the Soviets in the early 1940s included a number of Latvians who collaborated with Nazi authorities in the murder of Jews and local resistance, thereby adding to the complications of identifying and commemorating heroism in modern Latvia. See Ed Vulliamy, 'David Cameron's Rightwing "Allies" March in Riga to Commemorate the SS: Row over SS Veterans' Parade in Latvia puts the Spotlight on Tory Links to Eastern Europe's Far Right Nazi Sympathisers', *The Guardian*, 14 March 2010, www.guardian.co.uk/world/2010/mar/14/latvia-divided-communists-nazis (Last accessed March 2013).
107 Based on author David Lowe's visit to the Ejby Bunker in November 2012. Also 'The Ejby Bunker, Copenhagen', *The Baltic Initiative and Network*, http://coldwarsites.net/country/denmark/the-ejby-bunker-copenhagen (Last accessed March 2013).
108 Danish Institute for International Studies, 'Denmark During the Cold War: Highlights of the DIIS Report, National Security Policy and the International Environment 1945–91' (30 June 2005). Accessible online at: www.diis.dk/sw26673.asp.
109 As quoted by Danish Agency for Culture, 'Danish Cold War Hot Spots Open to the Public', *Danish Agency for Culture*, 28 February 2013, www.kulturstyrelsen. dk/english/news/danish-cold-war-hot-spots-open-to-the-public/#.UdfxrxYwaqC (Last accessed May 2013). Furthermore, the Royal Danish Arsenal Museum in Copenhagen, the *Tøjhusmuseet*, also plans a permanent exhibition on the Cold War.

110 Summary drawn from the downloadable audiovisual guide accessible online at 'Diefenbunker', *Diefenbunker: Canada's Cold War Museum/Musée canadien de la Guerre froide*, www.diefenbunker.ca/en_index.shtml (Last accessed May 2013).

111 See the news story accessible online at BBC News, 'BBC News: Secret Underground City For Sale', *YouTube*, www.youtube.com/watch?v=V-bYGlijhIU (Last accessed November 2012).

112 J.A. Parrish, 'The Kelvedon Hatch Secret Nuclear Bunker: The Biggest and Deepest Cold War Bunker Open to the Public in Southeast England', *The Kelvedon Hatch Secret Nuclear Bunker*, www.secretnuclearbunker.com (Last accessed January 2013).

113 Viewer numbers reported in *The Guardian* newspaper, 8 January 2008.

114 *1983: The Brink of Apocalypse* (Channel 4, 2007). Arnav Manchanda, 'When Truth is Stranger than Fiction: The Able Archer Incident', *Cold War History*, vol. 9, no. 1 (2009). Vojtech Mastny, 'How Able was "Able Archer"? Nuclear Trigger and Intelligence in Perspective', *Journal of Cold War Studies*, vol. 11, no. 1 (2009).

115 The Greenbrier Hotel website now features bunker tours: 'Bunker History', *The Greenbrier: America's Resort*, www.greenbrier.com/Activities/The-Bunker/Bunker-History.aspx (Last accessed February 2013).

116 City of Rijswijk Public Information Department, *Rijswijk Travel Planner* (Rijswijk: September 2009), p. 52.

117 There is a privately sponsored virtual museum at Eric Green, 'Civil Defense Museum', *Civil Defense Museum*, www.civildefensemuseum.com/index.html (Last accessed April 2013).

118 'British Buyers Snap Up Bunkers', *Toronto Star*, 12 July 2003.

119 *Western Daily Press* (Bristol), 12 July 2005.

120 As reported by Neil Tweedie, '1961: Codeword to Enter Secret Bunker at the End of the World', *The Telegraph*, 30 December 2011, www.telegraph.co.uk/news/uknews/defence/8978410/1961-files-codeword-to-enter-secret-bunker-at-the-end-of-the-world.html (Last accessed March 2013).

121 For the larger bunkers and some of the smaller British ones, see Nick McCamley, *Cold War Secret Nuclear Bunkers: The Passive Defence of the Western World* (London: Pen & Sword, 2007).

3 Cities and sites

To survey many and varied topographical sites of memory that serve as very public places where the Cold War has been and continues to be remembered, this chapter is built around eight case studies. It commences in the Lithuanian capital Vilnius, where victimization is a cornerstone of the politics of the past. It then sweeps across Eastern Europe, exploring how the Cold War is commemorated publicly in Prague, Budapest, and Warsaw – all capitals of former Warsaw Pact nations that followed very similar westward orbits into the NATO/EU constellation following the collapse of communism. Whereas all these eastern European examples experienced notable Cold War 'flashpoints' in their own unique ways, Hanoi is examined as a city in which the era is remembered for having been truly 'hot'. The Vietnamese case also differs inasmuch as it offers a national story in which the East emerged victorious over the West. Next, two initiatives based in Washington DC and nearby Vint Hill, in Northern Virginia, are scrutinized as long-running yet ultimately floundering attempts to memorialize the Cold War through the prism of American-led western triumphalism. Here, chronic problems faced when trying to raise public support and private funding over the past two decades indicate that, even in and around the nation's capital, Cold War warriors experience difficulties in drumming up support for memorializing the United States' 'victory against evil communism'. And, finally, the chapter finishes with a detailed exploration of a privately operated Cold War museum based in California. Growing out of remarkably organic beginnings, it has become an unbridled success story that demonstrates the potential for increasingly innovative approaches to remembering the Cold War in the twenty-first century. Coverage of all eight case studies that feature in this chapter is heavily based on recent field research.

The tides of Vilnius

The Lithuanian capital faces more challenges than most in exhibiting and articulating shared and common memories from the Cold War period. Drivers include the volatility in the composition of Vilnius' population (including much that pre-dates the Cold War era), the multiple and competing claims to victim status, and hesitancy about what these demands imply by way of actions against perpetrators. Vilnius has long hosted communities of different ethnicity and has repeatedly changed hands in modern European power struggles. As part of the Russian Empire, the city weathered first Napoleon's advance into Russia followed by his retreat, then blossomed in the second half of the nineteenth century, driven by a dominant Jewish population and culture (which had led to Napoleon dubbing the city the 'Jerusalem of the North').[1] While trying to claim autonomy in the first decades of the twentieth century, Vilnius instead was passed back and forth between warring nations like a slippery football. Between 1915 and 1920, during and after the First World War, it was taken over successively by the Germans (who named it Wilna), then local Poles (who called it Wilno), the Bolsheviks, again the Poles, and then again the Bolsheviks (or the new Soviet Union), before becoming the subject of a long and unresolved struggle between Poland and Lithuania. During the interwar years, in fact, ethnic Poles made up most of the population of Vilnius, and Jews were the second largest recorded category. As part of the Nazi–Soviet Pact, upon the outbreak of the Second World War in September 1939 the city was occupied by Soviet forces and temporarily incorporated into the Byelorussian Soviet Socialist Republic. The following month, Stalin transferred Vilnius to Lithuania, heralding a process of establishing Vilnius as the capital, repopulating the city with ethnic Lithuanians, and encouraging discrimination against ethnic Poles and Jews. In June 1940, the Soviets reoccupied Vilnius as part of Stalin's annexation of Lithuania, before the *Wehrmacht* captured the region following the launch of Operation Barbarossa in June 1941. Nazi Germany controlled the city for three years up to July 1944, during which time Jews were first ghettoized and then exterminated (with only a fraction of the city's prewar Jewish population of some 200,000 surviving the Holocaust). During the Nazi occupation, large numbers of ethnic Poles and other groups designated as politico-ideological or racial enemies were persecuted, too. Soviet forces took Vilnius again in 1944, and the city became part of the Lithuanian Soviet Socialist Republic. The new regime implemented wide-reaching reprisals against resisters, including torture and execution by the Soviet secret police – first the People's Commissariat of Internal Affairs (*Narodny Komissariat Vnutrennikh Del*, NKVD), then the Committee for State Security (*Komitet gosudarstvennoy bezopasnosti*, KGB) – and deportations to forced labour camps in the Gulag archipelago. It also oversaw deportations and repatriations effecting a 'Lithuanization' of the formerly Polish-Jewish Vilnius. In the decade 1944–54, the Soviet authorities helped refashion Vilnius into a determinedly Lithuanian capital. In addition to emptying the city of ethnic Poles, they resurrected old Lithuanian hero figures, 'discovered' pioneering revolutionary workers, elevated the nation-making role of the Second World War, and repressed recent memories of the Polish and Jewish past in Vilnius. Immigrants from Russia and other Soviet republics made up a significant Russian minority. The city was engineered as a centre of Lithuanian culture and scholarship and also as a modern city that met the needs of the new 'Soviet citizen'.[2] In return, Vilnius remained under Soviet control until August 1991 when Moscow recognized Lithuania's independence.

Decades of Soviet rule in Lithuania kept out not only capitalist ways but also the spreading awareness, debate, and legal actions over the Holocaust. Because the crimes of occupier violence were so great and so close together – there were only eight days in June 1941 separating the Soviet deportations of thousands to Gulag camps in Siberia and Kazakhstan and the German invasion of the Soviet Union that quickly led to German-Lithuanian collaborator massacres of Jews – the newly independent country has struggled to separate its acknowledgement of one atrocity without complicating its relationship with the other. To compound the problem, the Nazi occupation was sandwiched between two Soviet occupations – first in the early phase of the Second World War, and second a much longer period from 1944 to 1990.

The Museum of Genocide Victims highlights some of these unresolved tensions. It is located on the renowned *Gedimino prospektas* (Gediminas Avenue) near the edge of the central business district in a building that once housed the headquarters of the Gestapo and then the KGB. Created in 1992, and in 1997 put under the authority of the Genocide and Resistance Research Centre of Lithuania, the title of the museum can mislead. In its narrowest sense, the term 'genocide' as defined by the United Nations Convention on the Prevention and Punishment of the Crime of Genocide (1948) refers to 'acts committed with the intent to destroy, in whole or in part, a national, ethnic, racial or religious group'.[3] The term's use (and over-use) is widely contested, but notwithstanding historical revisionists there is universal acceptance around its accuracy in relation to the Holocaust. The Museum of Genocide has only one small chamber relating to the murder of Lithuanian Jews. The great impetus for the museum's creation came from former freedom fighters, prisoners, and deportees under Soviet rule, their fresh and raw grievances leading to both the controversial title and an early concentration on the crimes of that period. The heart of the museum is in the 1940s and 1950s, as it was in this period that the 50 basement cells were the most busy, and incarceration there typically led to torture and/or execution. Some of the torture methods included various forms of deprivation, beatings, and isolation on a tiny 'standing stone' surrounded by freezing water or ice. In the chilling 'execution room', visitors watch on a television screen a short re-enactment of the preferred mode of killing: the prisoner was brought into the room by officers either side of him, and upon entering the room was shot in the back of the head by another officer standing behind the door. There is a chute used to remove the bodies to a courtyard from where they were taken away and buried secretly. According to the museum's official guidebook, more than 1,000 people were killed here between 1944 and the early 1960s.[4] The museum and its printed guide give special prominence to the estimated 50,000 partisans who resisted the second Soviet occupation from 1944 to 1953, before being killed or captured.[5] The other theme relating to communist brutality also focuses on the mid-1940s to mid-1950s, when thousands of former leaders, supposed enemies, and non-complying farmers were sent to Soviet prisons or hard labour camps. In conditions of little food, rampant disease, and either freezing or boiling temperatures, more than 20,000 died in the Gulag system and prisons spread across the Arctic regions, Kazakhstan, Tadzhikistan, and elsewhere. Letters, photographs, personal effects, and details of transport and life in the camps feature in one section of the museum. From 1956, in the wake of Stalin's death and Khrushchev's denunciation of his excesses, there began waves of releases of deportees, but many of these had to remain in exile or were unable to register for work in their former home. Under these circumstances, around 50,000 released Lithuanians did not return.[6]

The Museum of Genocide Victims is grimly connected to a mansion on the other side of the central part of Vilnius. The early-nineteenth-century manor house of Tuskulėnai on the bank of the River Neris is a monument to classical architecture, but its grounds also were the secret burial site for 724 victims of the executions carried out in the former KGB building – now the Museum of Genocide Victims – between 1944 and 1947. The victims' remains were uncovered during archaeological digs in the mid-1990s, and in November 2004 were reburied in a chapel and columbarium of what is now

Figure 3.1 Museum of Genocide Victims. Vilnius, November 2012.

Tuskulėnai Peace Park, under the governance of the Genocide and Resistance Research Centre.[7] An exhibition in the basement of one of the buildings, the White Manor House, relates the ways in which capital sentences were decreed and carried out during Soviet occupation, includes personal effects of some of those executed, and pays special tribute to leading religious figures, especially Bishop V. Borisevicius who hid Jews during the Nazi occupation and then continued to practise his faith under the communists. The bishop was sentenced to death in 1946, and died in prison in 1963.[8] A vexed problem, and one that symbolizes the devilish complexity of remembering across multiple forms of terror and different groups of victims and perpetrators, is that some of the unidentified human remains at Tuskulėnai appear to be those of Jews and of their German persecutors, intermingled in ways that resist identification.

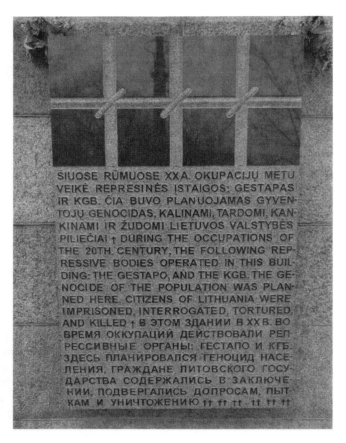

Figure 3.2 Plaque on the external wall of the Museum of Genocide Victims. Vilnius, November 2012.

There is both continuity and overlap between the Museum of Genocide Victims and the Tuskulėnai Peace Park in the displays and textual information. Excursions of school children count among the regular visitors to both sites. The Tuskulėnai Peace Park offers large conference space where students can display and discuss projects relating to the museums, or even compile photo-diaries of trips that some make to Lithuanian pockets of Siberia, tracing the routes of deportation and talking to those (and the descendants of those) who stayed there as well as those who were able to return.

Although anchored in the horrors of the 1940s and 1950s, the Museum of Genocide Victims relates the whole story of occupation up to independence in 1991. It is less fulsome about the growth of the security state in ways, typical of other communist regimes, which inducted local citizens as integral to surveillance and control. After the Soviets suppressed the freedom fighters in the mid-1950s, protest was led by the Catholic Church, challenging the arrest and ill-treatment of religious figures in particular. In the 1970s, human rights and nationalist groups came to the fore. As democratization grew in the Soviet Union in the mid-1980s, Vilnius became the focal point for popular Lithuanian protests at Soviet rule. One of the most spectacular demonstrations against Soviet domination was a coordinated human chain of around two million people joining together across the three Baltic States of Latvia, Lithuania, and Estonia on 23 August 1989. On 11 March 1990, the

Figure 3.3 Entrance to Tuskulėnai Chapel and Columbarium. Vilnius, November 2012.

Supreme Council of the Lithuanian Soviet Socialist Republic, fortified by the recent election of Popular Front members (*Sąjūdis*, founded in May 1988), declared the restoration of Lithuanian independence through the reestablishment of the independent Republic of Lithuania, first adopted on 16 February 1918. In other words, the Supreme Council declared that it was reestablishing the independent state that had existed between the two world wars, and had endured legally despite Soviet occupation. The Soviet Army attempted to reverse this move, with considerable support from local Russians and pro-Soviet elements, which by this time had broken away from Moscow. The newly declared independent government responded by calling people into the streets to protect important buildings. Soviet troops killed thirteen people (and one died of heart-attack) and injured many others outside the State Radio and Television Building on 13 January 1991; and they surrounded the Lithuanian Parliament Building on Gediminas Avenue, but there they were stopped by a ring of around 100,000 human defenders and concrete barricades protecting the Supreme Council. Much of the drama was captured on videotape by protestor and former partisan Albinas Kentra. His footage of defiant Lithuanians singing national songs, building barricades, waving flags, and arguing with nervous Soviet soldiers travelled quickly around the world via several news services. Soviet troops did not try to blast their way through, and withdrew instead. Today, part of the concrete wall hastily built by those protecting their leaders remains outside the parliament, glass-encased, to commemorate the successful resistance. Several crosses stand in the front of the TV tower, marking the location where the thirteen protestors died, and a small museum inside the building tells the story of the event.

Soviet forces did not leave immediately after the events of January 1991, but Lithuania's restored independence was secured. In the familiar acts of statue and monument removal and destruction that followed, four prominent statues from 1952, of socialist realist style, remained. They adorn the 'Green Bridge' in the middle of Vilnius. The original bridge was destroyed by the Germans in the Second World War but rebuilt by Soviet engineers and named after the Soviet general Ivan Chernyakhovsky. After independence in 1990, the bridge returned to its former name but the statues remained. Although they generated, and continue to generate, opposition and calls for their removal, they are protected 'as an object of cultural heritage'.[9] These relics and several Soviet-era buildings, including the famous Neringa Restaurant (built in 1959 and still boasting murals and paintings with familiar Soviet motifs), have weathered the tide of change and have been embraced as part of a post-communist architectural synthesis.

Lithuania and its capital Vilnius have been to the fore in ongoing efforts to recall the crimes of both Nazi and Soviet occupiers. In 1998, president Valdas Adamkus set up an International Commission for the Evaluation of the Crimes of the Nazi and Soviet Occupation Regimes in Lithuania. The purpose of the commission was to establish the veracity of crimes of both

Figures 3.4 and 3.5 Lithuanian parliament, with anti-Soviet memorial. And the Green Bridge, with Soviet-era statues. Vilnius, November 2012.

occupation regimes, and take measures to commemorate victims and educate the public. While comparable commissions in Central Europe placed
more emphasis on the legacies of communism, Lithuania's version tried to
establish stronger appreciation of the Holocaust. Eleven years later, a
European Parliament resolution 'On European Conscience and Totalitarianism' required members to recognize the crimes of former communist
regimes, condemn and commemorate as appropriate, and incorporate lessons about communism in school texts. This was followed by a similar
'Vilnius Declaration' in 2009, condemning all forms of glorification of totalitarian regimes. The declaration invites academics and opinion leaders to
contemplate more collaborative and consensual history on the central theme
of totalitarian crimes. In October 2011, under the Polish EU presidency, a
Platform of European Memory and Conscience was set up to coordinate
research and awareness and educational programmes on the crimes committed under European totalitarianism.[10] The platform's activities are discussed further in Chapter 4.

Among Lithuania's observed and official holidays are: 13 January, a day of
remembering the victims of the events of January 1991; 16 February, the day
of restoration of the State of Lithuania in 1918; 11 March, the day it was
restored again, from the Soviet Union, in 1990; and 14 June, the anniversary
of the first act in the great exile of Lithuanians to Siberia and elsewhere by
the Soviets in 1940. By ethnicity, modern Vilnius comprises an overwhelming majority of Lithuanians but also significant minorities of ethnic
Poles and Russians.[11] Such is the unfinished business relating to the killing
and deportations of the 1940s and early-1950s in Lithuania that this is where
the greatest state and non-government work is focused. Logically, the
objectives of the important Genocide and Resistance Research Centre of
Lithuania are:

> ... to establish historical truth and justice; to investigate the physical and
> spiritual genocide of Lithuanians carried out by the occupying regimes
> between 1939 and 1990; and the resistance to the regimes; to immorta-
> lise the memory of the freedom fighters and the genocide victims; and
> initiate the juridical evaluation of the aftermath of the occupying
> regimes.[12]

Thus, the Cold War cannot be rendered especially significant. While new
information emerges and gestures towards reconciliation are made, both are
fraught with difficulties. In 1991, for example, in the rush to rehabilitate
around 50,000 locals who had been convicted for crimes against the Soviets,
some who accepted the amnesty were shown to have taken part in the killing
of local Jews.[13] More recently, the Genocide and Resistance Research Centre
has released archives documenting KGB activities in Vilnius in the years
leading up to 1990, and in the process identifying more than 200 Lithuanians
who were KGB reservists ready to be called up to the cause if needed. Some

prominent reservists already had been identified to the detriment of their careers.[14] The complexity and enormity of violence perpetrated on residents of Vilnius is starting to gain prominence outside the region, thanks to widely-read works such as Timothy Snyder's *Bloodlands*, which encompasses the area of Lithuania, Latvia, Estonia, and Poland that saw the worst violence and bloodshed in Europe's violent twentieth century.[15] While the term 'Cold War' might not loom large, the Soviet occupations do. The second wartime occupation from 1944 begins an awful story that not only denies the Second World War special significance (for 1945 hardly was a moment of 'liberation'), but also confines to a distant background the great power struggle associated with the Cold War.

Kitsch and confrontation in Prague

The self-anointed 'historical pearl of Europe' whose foundations as the Bohemian capital can be traced back to the local castle's construction from the ninth century, Prague enjoys a rich and storied past as one of the continent's oldest and largest cities.[16] It even boasts an imperial dimension of truly continental significance, having first served as the seat of the Holy Roman Empire during the reign of King Charles IV (1346–78). While its political, cultural, and commercial importance may be traced back several centuries, Prague's recent history is dominated by its role as Czechoslovakia's capital during the Cold War. Following February 1948, when the Communist Party of Czechoslovakia (*Komunistická strana Československa*, KSČ) seized control in a *coup d'état*, Prague functioned as the seat of government and party headquarters for over four decades while the nation – willingly or otherwise – remained firmly entrenched in the Soviet sphere. In the history of the Cold War, the city is equally synonymous with two events: the Prague Spring of 1968, when Czechoslovakia's brief flirtation with democratic reforms was crushed by Warsaw Pact military intervention at Moscow's behest; and the Velvet Revolution of 1989, so-named due to the overwhelmingly peaceful nature of the abrupt end to communist rule.

The Prague Spring is publicly remembered within the city, as evidenced by the case of national hero Jan Palach (1948–69) whose sacrifice in protest against the Soviet-led invasion to crush Alexander Dubček's attempted reforms is memorialized in several ways. Five months after Warsaw Pact tanks rolled into Prague, Palach, a university student, self-immolated in front of the National Museum at the top end of Wenceslas Square. The site is now marked with a large, stylized bronze cross that is embedded into the pavement and simply known as the Jan Palach Memorial.[17] A commemorative plaque has been erected on the Faculty of Arts building of Charles University, which features a relief based on Palach's death mask as well as the date of his act: 16.1.1969. Between this building and the nearby River Vltava, a public square formerly named in honour of Red Army soldiers was renamed Jan Palach Square during the Velvet Revolution on

20 December 1989 (in fact, remembering Palach through the naming of streets, squares, schools, and other public places is a trend not only carried across the rest of the Czech Republic but also internationally).[18] Like the case of Hiroshima (discussed in Chapter 2), the Palach story effectively taps into both sacrifice and victimization and thereby it readily lends itself to public commemoration of the events of 1968, which hold great historical significance but ultimately ended in violently repressed failure.[19] Even so, the euphoria witnessed in 1989 means that the Velvet Revolution avails itself to more triumphant shared public memories of the Cold War era in Prague. Indeed, even after the state peacefully splintered into the Czech Republic and the Slovak Republic in 1992, the developments of late '89 remain a cause for national celebration. The following pages reveal how examples of publicly remembering the Velvet Revolution range from solemn ceremonies conducted annually at a prominent site of memory through to commercially sponsored artwork paraded around as a travelling exhibition. Furthermore, although '68 and '89 represent high-water marks, an American bagel mogul has discovered that in Prague there remains scope for wider remembrance of the more mundane Czechoslovakian experiences during the Cold War.

With their Polish, Hungarian, and East German comrades setting the pace in 1989, Czechoslovakians were relatively late to join in the public shows of passive resistance against communist rule. When they did stir, Václav Havel (1936–2011), the prominent playwright and longtime dissident, emerged as the popular figurehead of opposition to the state. Historian and political writer Timothy Garton Ash, who had first met Havel upon his release from prison earlier in the decade, travelled to Prague again in late 1989 and, seeking out another interview, found Havel holding court in his favourite basement pub. In his moving obituary for the Czech national hero in 2011, Garton Ash recalled that 22 years earlier he had quipped to Havel that what took 10 years to achieve in Poland, and 10 months in Hungary, and 10 weeks in East Germany, perhaps would be achieved in just 10 days in Czechoslovakia.[20] In the event Garton Ash's off-the-cuff remark was not too far off the mark, for Havel – a creative writer and political activist who had emerged as his nation's revolutionary leader largely through happenstance – would become the new post-communist president of Czechoslovakia within weeks.[21] The so-called Velvet Revolution was, indeed, remarkably swift and as its popular (western) name suggests it was overwhelmingly peaceful, too; nonetheless, it did not pass without some notable incidents in which demonstrators and state authorities clashed.[22] Indeed, violent scenes witnessed on 17 November 1989, when riot police forcibly dispersed a large gathering of mostly students, provided the initial impetus for what transpired during the next six revolutionary weeks.

Independent student leaders joined forces with representatives of the Socialist Union of Youth (*Socialistický svaz mládeže*, SSM), the KSČ's youth wing, to organize a march through central Prague in observance of the International Day of Students on 17 November 1989.[23] Though a transnational phenomenon, the day held special significance for Czechs generally and Prague students especially. It marked the fiftieth anniversary of when Nazi occupying forces had retaliated to protests by Czech students in the capital by raiding Charles University, executing nine students without trial, sending some 1,200 further students to concentration camps, and closing down all universities and colleges across the Protectorate of Bohemia and Moravia. After first being observed by the International Students' Council in London in 1941, a tradition formed in which this date was used to celebrate student activism.[24] In 1989, SSM members' involvement in the planning (coupled with the occasion's anti-fascist origins) meant that the KSČ sanctioned it as an official peace march. Around 10,000 students had first congregated in the afternoon and initially the commemorative practices went according to script, with participants tracing the route taken by the funeral procession for Jan Opletal (1915–39), one of the Czech students murdered by the Nazis a half-century earlier.[25] By the early evening, however, the crowd's numbers had swelled closer to 15,000 people and feelings of resentment and frustration at life under communist rule were palpable. It was only a week after the fall of the Berlin Wall, and disgruntled Czecho-slovakian students sensed the moment had arrived to publicly challenge the KSČ's authority: could the outcome of '68 be turned upside down in '89?

Just hours earlier, news reports from the state-controlled Czechoslovak Radio suggested that everything was in order. But then came the first signal across the airwaves that perhaps something extraordinary was happening: 'Reports are coming in that certain people are attempting to abuse this solemn occasion for anti-socialist provocations.'[26] The 'certain people' alluded to by the newsreader, as David Vaughan wryly observes, 'were in fact many thousands of students, who had continued their peaceful march into the centre of Prague'.[27] What had commenced as a state-endorsed peaceful march to observe the anniversary of brutal acts perpetrated by a totalitarian regime against Czech students in the past, suddenly transformed into a demonstration of passive resistance by Czech students against another oppressive government in the present. And history repeated itself with student demonstrators violently attacked again – this time by their own authorities. Carrying flags and makeshift banners, protestors called for democratic reforms as they embarked from the Czech national cemetery located inside the Vyšehrad Citadel and snaked their way along the River Vltava and through Prague's streets toward Wenceslas Square. Students were joined en route by other dissatisfied citizens, most notably gaining support from actors and other stage workers when passing the National Theatre. They never reached the nearby Wenceslas Square, however, after riot police blocked their path in one of the city's main thoroughfares *Národní třída* (National Avenue).[28] Exit routes were cordoned off, momentarily creating a tense impasse. Some unarmed demonstrators attempted to defuse the situation by placing a row of candles on the ground parallel to the barricade line and then approaching police to offer them flowers. But violent scenes erupted in *Národní třída* as police used nightsticks to beat the students. Some 150–200 demonstrators were injured before the crowd was allowed to disperse. Ludvík Zifčák, an undercover agent who apparently fainted amid the commotion, was carried away by police officers.[29] That evening, a rumour spread like wildfire across Prague that the body carried away by police was a student who had been beaten to death. That it was not true mattered little, for such 'news' had the immediate effect of mobilizing far wider support. Students and theatre workers called for strikes, and by the following day some trade unions already were backing the movement. The Civic Forum was established and hundreds of thousands of Czechoslovakians took to the streets of not only Prague but also Bratislava and other cities. The entire Presidium resigned on 24 November 1989, and within a fortnight of the student demonstrations of 17 November communist rule in Czechoslovakia collapsed (making Garton Ash's '10 days' quip to Havel seem even more prescient).

The Velvet Revolution, then, commenced with some minor bloodshed (but no fatalities) on 17 November 1989. Although it may be with a liberal dose of hyperbole that Czechs refer to this event as the *masakr* (Massacre), its significance as a, if not *the*, trigger for the swift downfall of communist rule in Czechoslovakia cannot be overstated. Accordingly, this date is a Czech national holiday marking the Day of Struggle for Freedom and Democracy; and 16 *Národní třída* has become enshrined not simply as the site of the 'massacre' but rather in a more encompassing manner as Prague's foremost arena of articulation for publicly remembering the Velvet Revolution *in toto*. A remarkably modest approach to marking this site, however, has been adopted. There is no great monument constructed to commemorate the event. Instead, a small austere memorial has been erected on the wall inside a pedestrian arcade that runs underneath a dilapidated eighteenth-century neoclassical building once known as the Schirdingovský Palace.[30] Because it is not visible from the street, visitors must either know the memorial's precise location or stumble across it by chance when passing through the nondescript arcade. Commonly known as the Velvet Revolution Memorial, it consists of a bronze plaque featuring no written details other than: 17.11.1989. Above the date, a series of eight life-sized hands hold up outstretched fingers: two hands hold out all five digits with palms facing outward to mimic the gesture Czech demonstrators made toward riot police to emphasize that they were unarmed and seeking nonviolent change; the remaining six replicate the ubiquitous 'V' sign that protestors made during the revolution to signify both peace and, moreover, victory. A gridded plinth runs underneath the hands and the date to hold candles and flowers left by passers-by, a regular occurrence throughout the year. Each November, furthermore, hundreds of candles adorn the footpath in front of the memorial. They are placed there mostly by ordinary citizens, but only after leading Czech politicians and other public figures have laid wreaths and lit candles to officially commemorate the anniversary of the student demonstration. In

Figures 3.6 and 3.7 The Schirdingovský Palace under which runs the pedestrian arcade featuring the Velvet Revolution Memorial. And the memorial surrounded by floral arrangements and candles days after the anniversary. Prague, November 2011.

Figure 3.8 The Velvet Revolution Memorial adorned with decorations days after the anniversary of the student demonstration, November 2011.

2011, for instance, the speaker of the Chamber of Deputies of the Czech parliament Miroslava Němcová and Prague's mayor Bohuslav Svoboda flanked the Czech president Václav Klaus and prime minister Petr Nečas. Former president Havel was a notable absentee on this occasion, however, for unlike previous years the national hero of 1989 failed to attend the annual ceremony owing to his ailing health (Havel would pass away four weeks later).

Ordinarily the Velvet Revolution Memorial at 16 *Národní třída* is as revered as it is unassuming. In November 2009, however, it was temporarily subjected to unofficial modification. Roman Týc, a native of Prague and guerilla-style street artist renowned for making unauthorized alterations to public spaces, embellished the memorial in order to challenge what he perceived as a common misconception that the Velvet Revolution gives his fellow Czechs cause for national celebration. Týc added another date and set of hands on either side of the memorial's relief. He replicated the measurements, material, and style so accurately that, far from appearing as obvious vandalism, Týc's recoding of the memorial gave the impression of being an officially sanctioned amendment. Unsuspecting passers-by thus could be forgiven for thinking that the memorial had been updated for the twentieth anniversary of the student demonstration. But what, then, would they have made of the new – and very confrontational – message attached to the memorial? For on the left Týc had added the date 17.11.1939 accompanied by eight hands giving the Nazi salute, and on the right-hand side the contemporary date 17.11.2009 was complemented by eight hands raising the middle finger to signify the universally recognized non-verbal insult meaning 'fuck you'.[31] In doing so, Týc's provocative intervention, which he entitled 'Nothing to Celebrate' ('*Není co slavit*'), expressed a twofold criticism: first, Czechs had meekly raised their hands under Nazi occupation and continued to be servile; and, second, two decades later the triumphs of 1989 now seemed hollow because everyday life for most Czech citizens was a pale imitation of what was envisaged amid the euphoria of overthrowing communism.[32] On both accounts, argued Týc, his fellow Czechs had no real cause to celebrate. It was a message that struck a chord with at least some of his compatriots, for two years later – when Němcová, Svoboda, Klaus, and Nečas attended the annual ceremony in 2011 – some 2,000 disenchanted Czechs gathered in nearby Wenceslas Square to express their anger at the government's austerity measures as well as general frustration at the state of affairs after 22 years of democracy.[33] Apparently many older Czechs in particular had become so disillusioned that they increasingly felt pangs of nostalgia for the old communist system, not least because they believed it had always offered retirees a more certain future compared to 'being a slave to capitalism'.[34] As for Týc's temporary recoding of the Velvet Revolution Memorial in November 2009, it serves as an instructive paradigm of how sometimes even the most venerated sites of memory can be appropriated to articulate very different – indeed, polar opposite – messages.

Besides the 'V' finger salute, the most memorable mass-scale action by demonstrators during the Velvet Revolution was the symbolic jingling of keys. Meant as a signification of freedom, it simultaneously conveyed both anticipation and closure: on the one hand, rattling keys indicated that hitherto impenetrable doors were about to be opened; on the other hand, it also offered a thinly veiled hint to communists that the time had come to lock up and leave. Two decades on, both Czechs and Slovaks remembered the end of their Cold War through the prism of keys. To mark the twentieth anniversary of the start of the revolution, Mincovňa Kremnica, the Slovakian mint, issued a specially commissioned €2 coin featuring a stylized set of keys that combine to form the outline of a bell (in reference to the ringing of church bells that, along with the honking of car horns, soon had added to the jingling of keys to produce a cacophony of sound heard across revolutionary Czechoslovakia).[35] Bordering the keys in an arc, the coin's legend features the date 17 November and the all-capitalized words *SLOBODA* (FREEDOM) and *DEMOKRACIA* (DEMOCRACY) as well as the years 1989–2009. If the Slovakian 'key coin' affirmed democracy both literally, through its inscription, and allegorically, owing to it being Eurozone currency, then another key-inspired enterprise in the Czech Republic largely gained its impetus from capitalism. In March 2010, at Franz Kafka Square in central Prague, influential Czech artist Jiří David unveiled his 20-feet high 'Key Sculpture' (*Klíčová socha*).[36] Its name is not a reference to the sculpture taking the shape of a giant key; rather, David used approximately 85,000 recycled keys to vertically construct the word *REVOLUCE* – the Czech term for revolution. The seven letters are in different fonts that draw inspiration from common products in Czechoslovakia during the Cold War era: the R is taken from the initial letter of the KSČ's official daily newspaper *Rudé právo* (translated as either the *Red Right* or *Red Law*); the E is from the socialist-era toilet paper; the V comes from what was a ubiquitous brand of cotton wool; the O from Pedro chewing gum first made popular during Gustav Husák's rule; the L from the cartoon *Mr. Egg* television commercials; the U from Tuzex vouchers used for imported goods; the C from a travel agency's logo; and finally, located at the bottom and thus crushed by the sculpture's weight, a second E that is taken from Czechoslovakian communist ID cards.[37] David's installation was made possible due to nationwide support from international mobile operator Vodafone, who organized the world's largest key collection that resulted in 85,741 keys being deposited in Vodafone shops across the Czech Republic.[38] After its unveiling, the *REVOLUCE* installation toured the nation as an outdoor exhibition for several months before returning to Prague for indefinite showing. Whereas the circumstances surrounding David's very public project stood in stark contrast to the clandestine work undertaken by Týc, the two artists seemed to share in similar inspirations behind their inventiveness. As Týc had wanted to challenge his fellow Czechs to question what the Velvet Revolution truly meant for them twenty years later, David explained:

> This object represents a personal polemic on the development of the Czech Republic. It certainly isn't a tribute but, on the contrary, a critical work. The installation expresses the ambivalence that I feel when I think about today's society and politics.[39]

While local artists recently may have taken provocative or even polemical approaches to publicly remembering the Cold War as a way to comment on what they perceive as ills of contemporary Czech society, the organizers responsible for Prague's novel Museum of Communism have adopted a markedly different approach. The museum's website expressly states, for instance, that its exhibitions, artefacts, and historical documents should not be appropriated as 'a filter for contemporary political issues in the Czech Republic'.[40] The identity of the man behind the museum's establishment perhaps gives the best clues as to why there is an explicit desire to keep out of domestic political issues. Glenn Spicker, a native of Connecticut who undertook his postgraduate studies in Soviet foreign policy at the University of Essex, was in his mid-twenties when in the wake of communism he decided to relocate to Prague in the early-1990s to explore new business opportunities and opened up a bar. Owing to his next venture, Spicker

Figure 3.9 The Museum of Communism, signposted (with a Russian Matryoshka doll
        brandishing razor-shape teeth) outside the building it shares with a casino
        and a McDonald's store. Prague, November 2011.

became known as the city's 'Bagel King' after he introduced this food to
Prague in 1996 through the establishment of his Bohemia Bagel franchise.
The entrepreneurial American then employed the services of Jan Kaplan, a
London-based Czech émigré filmmaker and exhibition curator, as Spicker
turned his attention to collecting communist-era artefacts with a view to
creating a museum. On 26 December 2001, Spicker opened the House of
Communism in a most conspicuous site on two accounts: first, it is located
only a short walk around the corner from the bottom end of Wenceslas
Square in *Na příkopě*, one of the busiest and most fashionable streets in the
capital's *Nové Město* (or New Town) district; and second, moreover, it is
perched above a McDonald's store and also shares its premises with another
icon of western capitalism – a casino that offers customers a choice between
slot machines, American roulette, and stud poker.

Figure 3.10 Mock communist-era workshop, the Museum of Communism. Prague, November 2011.

Conceptually, the Museum of Communism is divided into three vectors as encapsulated by its motto: 'Communism – the Dream, the Reality, the Nightmare'. According to Kaplan, this effectively sets up the museum as 'a tragedy in three acts'.[41] Its elaborate layout, which sprawls across more than 4,000 square feet of floor space, exhibits a rich blend of rare and common artefacts that portray various aspects of Czechoslovakian life from 1948–89. Themes covered include, *inter alia*, politics, economics, education, sport, the arts, the armed forces, propaganda and censorship, rural life, and Stalinist tyranny. In between extensive collections of socialist-era paintings and busts of Marx, Lenin, Stalin, and local party leaders, countless authentic pieces are utilized in a series of permanent displays depicting 'typical' scenes such as: a rudimentary factory workshop where basic tools sit atop benches with socialist posters adorning the walls; a classroom in which rows of crude wooden desks face toward a chalkboard with a lesson scrawled out in Russian; a farm scene featuring primitive hand tools; a grocery store with

Figures 3.11 and 3.12 Display devoted to technological advances during the Cold War, and chronic food shortages under communism. Prague, November 2011.

scarcely-stocked shelves; and an interrogation room of the dreaded StB –
Czechoslovakia's state security service. The museum also includes a small
theatre in which a very sobering documentary film (mostly centred on scenes
from '68 and '89) is played on permanent loop. Another section, entitled
'Cult of Personality', critically documents the public adulation lavished on
Czechoslovakian presidents and other leading communist figures. Finally,
the museum concludes with a section that, by name at least, apparently is
dedicated to the Velvet Revolution. It represents, however, a rather peculiar
end to the tour because a large mock-up of the Berlin Wall dominates this
space. Why visitors are suddenly transported from Cold War-era Prague to
divided Berlin is unexplained. Moreover, for a museum that boasts an
impressive collection of authentic artefacts it is a strange decision to
conclude with what can only be described as an amateurish – indeed,
kitschy – imitation of the Berlin Wall.

Figure 3.13 Mock Berlin Wall, Museum of Communism. Prague, November 2011.

Before exiting, visitors can browse a small gift-shop where some vintage memorabilia and (mostly Czech-language) books can be purchased alongside a large range of novelty souvenirs including t-shirts, posters, and postcards. Perhaps the best known of these images (because the museum uses it for promotional work including its advertising posters found all over Prague) features a menacing-looking Russian Matryoshka doll brandishing razor-sharp, vampiric teeth. Other products mock either Marxist/Leninist doctrine or really existing socialism by overlaying socialist artwork with facetious slogans or comments. An image of Lenin striking an imposing stance, for instance, is accompanied by the text: 'We're above McDonald's. Across from Bennetton. Viva la imperialism!' A socialist realist image of a man carrying a sledgehammer and a woman holding a loaf of bread features the remark: 'Sometimes there was no toilet paper in the shops. Luckily there was not much food either.' Similarly, combining Czechoslovakian shops' reputation for a scarcity of products and second wave feminism, a photograph of six smiling women from the 1960s, in which the front woman is wearing socialist-style work overalls and a snood, runs with the caption: 'Like their sisters in the West they would've burnt their bras, if there were any in the shops.' And Régis Bossu's iconic shot of the 'fraternal kiss' shared by Soviet leader Leonid Brezhnev and his East German counterpart Erich Honecker in 1979 is overlaid with the text: 'If he slipped you the tongue you knew you were going places.' Wherever remembrance of the Cold War in Prague leads in the future, it is sure to remain fixated on '68 and '89.

From the bleak to the bizarre in Budapest

It was not until 1873, during Emperor Franz Joseph's reign over the Dual Monarchy (1867–1918), that the three historically separate towns of Buda, which had developed into a prosperous trading and commercial hub sprawled along the west bank of the Danube, and Pest, a splendid royal seat located on the opposite side of the river, and Óbuda (literally Old Buda) officially merged to form the Hungarian capital Budapest. Traces of human settlement in this area of the Carpathian Basin, however, can be traced back as far as the Stone Age. And, like its Bohemian counterpart Prague, from the medieval period through to the modern era the primate city of the Magyar people has boasted an international reputation as one of the great historical epicentres of Middle Europe. The two cities' experiences of the Second World War differed markedly; whereas Prague endured brutal Nazi occupation, Budapest remained one of Berlin's staunchest allies until early 1944 when Hitler was forced to occupy Hungary to shore up Axis support in the face of an imminent invasion of Magyar territory by the advancing Red Army. In some important respects, though, their postwar fates were strikingly similar. Irrespective of whether locals liked it or not, during the early onset of the Cold War both cities found themselves firmly entrenched within Stalin's sphere of influence. As Winston Churchill described in his 'Sinews of Peace' address in Fulton, Missouri, in March 1946, an Iron Curtain had descended across the continent:

> Behind that line lie all the capitals of the ancient states of Central and Eastern Europe. Warsaw, Berlin, Prague, Vienna, Budapest, Belgrade, Bucharest and Sofia, all these famous cities and the populations around them lie in what I must call the Soviet sphere, and all are subject, in one form or another, not only to Soviet influence but to a very high and, in some cases, increasing measure of control from Moscow.[42]

Despite Soviet military occupation, attempts were made to develop Hungarian politics into a multiparty democracy. By 1949, however, Moscow's increasing intervention in domestic affairs facilitated 'from above' the establishment of the People's Republic of Hungary as a Marxist-Leninist single-party state under Mátyás Rákosi's authoritarian leadership. Running from 23 October to 10 November 1956, the Hungarian Uprising erupted as a spontaneous nationwide revolt against Rákosi's ruling communist government and its Soviet masters. The short-lived mass rising of East Berliners on 17 June 1953 notwithstanding, the events in Hungary during late 1956 marked the first major challenge to Moscow's control of Eastern Europe since the war's end. The uprising caused a fall of government, effecting a change of leadership as János Kádár was installed with Soviet support. Nonetheless, like the Prague Spring twelve years later, the Hungarian Uprising ended in failure after Soviet military intervention had brutally crushed the revolt (and the hardliner Kádár would remain Hungarian leader until his retirement in 1988). And, in a similar vein to the Czech case discussed above, the revolutionary scenes witnessed during late '56 remain synonymous with Hungary's Cold War history.[43] Yet, unlike the events of '68, which have become somewhat overshadowed by the developments of '89, when it comes to remembering the Cold War in Budapest the Hungarian Uprising serves as the undisputed focal point. Here, then, it is appropriate to start by examining four discrete but complementary forms of public memorialization that occupy prominent spaces within close proximity to the Hungarian Parliament Building. The importance of these four sites of memory came under threat in 2006, when Hungary's incumbent socialist government poured enormous resources into a new monument constructed near the Heroes' Square on the edge of the expansive, picturesque, and popular *Városliget* (or 'City Park') gardens to mark the fiftieth anniversary of the 1956 uprising. This massive and abstract monument, however, not only proved to be divisive from the outset but also it ultimately has failed to attract the same attention still afforded to the four pre-existing forms of memorialization located near the parliament.[44] Gazing a little outside the rubric of 1956, furthermore, there are other sites of Cold War memory in and around Budapest that also warrant consideration. Two very different examples are covered in detail below: the House of Terror museum housed in a former interrogation building located on Budapest's grandest thoroughfare; and, in an obscure location in the XXII. District on the capital's outskirts, the bizarre Memento Park that is home to an assortment of Cold War-era sculptures collected after the collapse of communism.

Commencing with peaceful student demonstrations in the capital that soon developed into a far wider protest, the Hungarian Uprising culminated in nationwide armed fighting. The national parliament, located on Lajos Kossuth Square overlooking the Danube in central Budapest, was the scene of the most prominent and perhaps heaviest hostilities during the three-week revolt. Accordingly, the public space around the Hungarian Parliament Building serves as the city's foremost arena of articulation for remembering the tumultuous events of 1956. Here, in close proximity to each other, four separate forms of memorialization promote public remembrance of the uprising in diverse ways: following the end of the Cold War two national monuments have been constructed on the Lajos Kossuth Square; historical remnants of the fighting have been not only preserved but also embellished within the façade of a ministry building located directly opposite the square; and another memorial has been erected diagonally across from parliament in Martyrs' Square.

In 1996, the incumbent Hungarian president Árpád Göncz, who decades earlier had been sentenced to life imprisonment for his involvement in the uprising but was released in 1963, commissioned the internationally renowned and multi-award winning artist and native Budapestian Mariá Lugossy to create a new national monument.[45] Her work, which was unveiled immediately outside the entrance to parliament, is visually simple yet striking: a tall rectangular slab of polished black granite features a roughened, undulating top that is lit up by an eternal flame flickering in honour of the uprising's tens of thousands of victims. Engraved on the front side of the monument facing toward the parliament, the year 1956 sits underneath a stylized 'Kossuth' coat of arms. Variations of pan-Magyar heraldry have contained similar elements and colour schemes for many centuries. A common version, known as the Kossuth coat of arms, adopts a dexter of eight alternating red and silver horizontal stripes (the so-called Árád Stripes, which are named after Hungary's founding dynasty and date from at least the thirteenth century) and a sinister that features a Byzantine-inspired silver double cross on a red background above three green hills. Hungarian revolutionaries had adopted the Kossuth escutcheon as a unifying nationalist symbol when fighting against their state authorities and Soviet invaders. For her monument, Lugossy used the unofficial and simplified version – or what often is referred to as the 'Republican' variant of the Kossuth coat of arms – that does not include the royal crown. The monument serves as a focal point of annual commemorative practices, such as on the eve of the anniversary of the uprising's starting date when peaceful marchers gather around and use its eternal flame to light candles and torches before parading through nearby streets. And each year the monument's eternal flame is turned up higher than usual from 23 October to 10 November.

Although revolutionaries adopted the Kossuth coat of arms during their fight against state guards and Soviet forces, when it comes to remembering the Cold War in Budapest the escutcheon's significance pales in comparison to another nationalist symbol from the uprising of 1956: the (modified) Hungarian flag. Except for a brief deviation when the short-lived Hungarian Soviet Republic had employed an all-red flag in 1919, since the establishment of the Dual Monarchy in 1867 the Hungarian flag was based on a horizontal tricolour design. Furthermore, the red, white, and green bands typically were complemented by the national coat of arms. In 1949, however, the communist government kept the tricolour design but introduced a new socialist-styled insignia as the flag's centrepiece. Deriving its name from Hungary's incumbent communist ruler, this so-called Rákosi badge, which mirrored

Figure 3.14 Mariá Lugossy's 1956 memorial in front of the Hungarian parliament. Budapest, November 2011.

the state emblem of the Soviet Union by featuring ears of wheat, a red star, and a hammer, proved immensely unpopular among Hungarian citizens. During the uprising, freedom fighters modified the national flag by cutting out this circular badge to be left with only the red, white, and green tricolour design. As captured most famously in a black-and-white photograph taken in the *Corvin köz* (or Corvin Passage) – a small circuitous street in central Budapest where some of the fiercest clashes occurred – the doctored flag with a hole cut into its centre became *the* iconic image of the revolution. When thousands of Hungarians gather on the Lajos Kossuth Square annually to commemorate 23 October – the date that was officially made the national Remembrance Day following the collapse of communism and proclamation of independence in 1989 – massive vertical tricolour flags with holes symbolically cut out of their centre are unfurled against the façade of the adjacent Hungarian Parliament Building.[46] On a more permanent basis, and only a short distance from Lugossy's granite monument with the eternal flame, a replica 'hole' flag remains on perpetual display. The flag is hoisted above an allegoric grave that was unveiled in October 1991 to commemorate Hungarian citizens killed when the crowd of demonstrators was fired upon at the Lajos Kossuth Square on 25 October 1956. The grave's inscription makes no reference whatever to the role of Soviet invaders, and instead focuses on the role of Hungary's own secret police the State Protection Authority (*Államvédelmi Hatóság*, ÁVH).[47] In November 2011, an unofficial plastic sign erected adjacent to the symbolic grave and 'hole' flag presented a broader narrative of how one group interpreted the site's functionality for public remembrance. The bilingual sign, attributed to the obscure 'World Council of the Hungarians of 1956', stated in less-than-perfect English:

> This Hungarian flag has a hole in it because on October 23, 1956 the revolutionists, those Hungarian who revolted against the Soviet Union, tore out of it the foreign coat of arms that symbolized the power of the Soviet Union and Communism. Since then this flag has symbolized the freedom of the Hungarian nation.
>
> This memorial is a symbolic grave. Here, on this square, several hundreds of people fell dead onto the ground due to the killer blow of a firing squad on October 25, 1956. Honour and remembranche to the victims!

The sign then concluded by quoting – again in poor English – a phrase well known among Hungarians that was first penned in 1967 by the prolific émigré writer and journalist Sándor Márai, who fled his homeland in the late-1940s and established a new life in the United States:

> The system of communism has failed in every sense. However itt will be very hard to get rid of communists, for there is nobody as dangerous as the usurper of a failed system, who abandons the system but quards his loot, and power-position.[48]

Figure 3.15 Hungarian flag with symbolic hole cut out of the centre, on permanent
display in front of the parliament building. Budapest, November 2011.

On Thursday 25 October 1956, ÁVH guards, supported by Soviet tanks,
were deployed to quash the rising demonstrations around the parliament.
In order to disperse the large crowd gathered on the Lajos Kossuth
Square, the ÁVH opened fire in an indiscriminate fashion. It is estimated
that several hundreds were killed, and nearby buildings were sprayed with
bullets.[49] Similar to the case of the RAF Church of St Clement Danes in
the Strand, London, which still carries pockmarks that have been preserved as corporeal reminders of the Battle of Britain, the façade of the
building that now houses Hungary's Ministry of Agriculture and Rural
Development features dozens of holes created by machine-gun fire.
Indeed, to make the effect even more pronounced, the holes are capped
with large round metal plugs that protrude from the building's surface. A
small commemorative plaque marks the date and states that the survivors
remember the victims of 'Bloody Thursday'.[50] The embellishment of

Figure 3.16 The allegoric grave at the base of the flag pole in front of the parliament. Budapest, November 2011.

these bullet holes is an example of utilizing historical remnants to engender shared national memories.

As far as agency is concerned, it is the collective rather than particular individuals who encapsulate the Hungarian Uprising. This approach, for instance, was both shaped by and reflected in the choice made by *Time* when the 'Hungarian freedom fighter' was honoured as its 1956 'Man of the Year'.[51] As made clear by Boris Chaliapin's artistic impression for the cover of the 7 January 1957 edition, the weekly news magazine was collectively celebrating the actions of all demonstrators involved in the revolt. In the foreground of Chaliapin's scene, a man holding a PPSh-41 submachine gun in his bandaged hand looks ahead with a steely gaze; he is flanked by a teenage boy and an adult woman – both armed – who also stare ahead determinedly. A large Hungarian flag with the Rákosi badge cut from its centre flies between the three freedom fighters and a backdrop of damaged

Figure 3.17 Plugged bullet holes from the 1956 uprising, in government building opposite parliament. Budapest, November 2011.

buildings. The most notable exception to this trend toward the collective is Imre Nagy, who, although he was not one of the uprising's initiators, soon came to be fêted as the unofficial figurehead of the Hungarian fight against Soviet domination. Nagy was a devoted communist who, following Rákosi's sudden demise and due to popular demand, temporarily assumed leadership of the government during the revolt. Years earlier, however, Nagy the 'reformer' had fallen out of favour with Moscow and so once the uprising was crushed he immediately lost his newfound position. In fact, Nagy was clandestinely abducted, put on trial for treason, and summarily executed. His body was dumped in a prison grave and for three decades Hungarians were not permitted to publicly commemorate their former leader. Emboldened by the spreading influence of Soviet leader Mikhail Gorbachev's *glasnost*, by 1989 some of Nagy's strongest admirers successfully agitated for the ruling communist government to accept – or at least no longer block – his public rehabilitation. In June 1989, on the thirty-first anniversary of his execution, Nagy's body was exhumed and in a solemn ceremony attended by thousands he was finally given a 'hero's burial'.[52] Following the end of the Cold War, a large memorial dedicated to both Nagy and the national Remembrance Day of 23 October was constructed in Martyrs' Square. Created by Hungary's leading contemporary sculptor Imre Varga, it depicts a pensive-looking Nagy standing alone in the middle of a bridge – presumably meant as a mediating symbol of negotiation and compromise. It is immediately evident that Nagy is looking directly at the Hungarian Parliament Building. What is initially much less obvious but perhaps far more telling is the fact that the monument's location means that, by gazing toward the house of the national assembly, Nagy has his back turned to the nearby US Embassy. Speaking to locals, whether it was by accident or design apparently it is considered very fitting because Hungarians felt abandoned by Washington both at the end of the Second World War and then again at the time of the 1956 uprising when Nagy resigned from the Warsaw Pact and hoped for NATO support in breaking away from Moscow's clutches. In any case, once this effect is pointed out, the posturing of the lone figure Nagy begs considerable reflection and leaves a lasting impression.

In 1987, UNESCO inscribed Budapest, and in particular its Banks of the Danube and its Buda Castle Quarter, onto the World Heritage List.[53] In 2002, UNESCO's World Heritage Committee approved an expansion of this listing (on cultural grounds) specifically to incorporate the capital's 'stately promenade' *Andrássy út*.[54] Owing to its neo-Renaissance apartments, theatres, fine cafés, and boutique shops, this spacious tree-lined avenue boasts a reputation as one of the world's leading thoroughfares. Located at 60 *Andrássy út*, however, one of the avenue's many impressive façades cloaks a building with an unusually dark past. During the Second World War, Ferenc Szálasi's fascist Arrow Cross movement used the building as its headquarters. The Arrow Cross carried out widespread torture of 'suspicious' Hungarian citizens in the basement of this building Szálasi dubbed the 'House of Loyalty'.[55] Immediately after the war's end, Hungarian communists, supported by the Red Army, seized possession of Arrow Cross headquarters. During the early Cold War era, 60 *Andrássy út* continued to be one of Hungary's most feared locations because the building then housed the secret state police (including the ÁVH following its two predecessor bodies). Interrogations, psychological and physical torture, and subsequent killings reached even higher levels. In February 2002, the building was reopened as a museum and documentation centre aptly called the House of Terror (*Terror Háza*). Effectively adopting the state-of-the-art approach so popular among twenty-first-century museums and documentation centres, the House of Terror exhibits its historical artefacts in combination with visually impressive displays such as lightbox panels, interactive screens, information walls, and special temporary exhibitions. It has been remodelled in such a way that the building at 60 *Andrássy út* now serves a twofold purpose: its history demands that visitors remember Hungary's victims of both fascism and communism in the twentieth century; and, in a wider sense, its post-Cold War contemporary functionality means that the House of Terror celebrates the eventual triumph of democracy over both right and left totalitarianism as trumpeted in the museum's guidebook:

By its conversion into a museum it does not merely contain an exhibition dedicated to the victims' memory; its appearance too conjures up the atmosphere of the place. For too long, for too many decades we have passed by this building with downcast eyes, with hurried steps, knowing, sensing that its walls were hiding monstrous crimes, a sea of suffering. 60 Andrássy Road has become a shrine, an homage to the victims. 60 Andrássy Road is the effigy of terror, the victims' memorial. The House of Terror Museum is proof that the sacrifice for freedom is not futile. Those who fought for freedom and independence defeated the dictatorships.[56]

The House of Terror's multi-level exhibition unfolds chronologically, and after commencing with the Arrow Cross horrors during the Second World War visitors soon encounter the 'Changeroom' where the focus shifts to the Cold War era. Stalin is quoted as reportedly having declared in 1946: 'Hungary must be punished in an exemplary fashion'.[57] A large hallway entitled 'The Fifties' is introduced as covering 'the darkest period of communism in Hungary'.[58] Smaller rooms are devoted to themes such as:

Figure 3.18 The House of Terror. The stencilled lettering in the building's awning casts a shadow of the word 'TERROR' as well as the Arrow Cross insignia and the communist star. (Also notice the segment of Berlin Wall in between the trees in the median strip.) Budapest, November 2011.

daily life in communist Hungary; the ubiquitously feared role of Soviet advisors (and Hungarian informants); resistance movements; torture chambers; and compulsory deliveries of produce to meet fixed state quotas. Another main hall focuses on the role of the secret state police, which commences with a kind of wall-of-shame featuring photographs of ÁVH chiefs of staff. Working from photographs and recollections, the office of ÁVH boss Gábor Péter has been recreated. In a display room called 'Travesty of Justice' the floors, benches, and a judge's chair are covered with copies of documents from the former Bureau of History. Similarly, the room's walls are lined with folders from political trials, indictments, sentences, appeals, and records of investigations from 1945–56. A monitor on the back wall shows a lengthy 1958 propaganda film made to condemn Imre Nagy as a traitor. The propaganda theme continues in the smaller adjacent room dedicated to 'Propaganda and Daily Life'. Religion is covered, too, in a large hall before visitors descend to the building's dank basement level where victims were interrogated and tortured at the hands of first Arrow Cross and later ÁVH agents.

The basement of 60 *Andrássy út* is reconstructed as a subterranean prison. Its former interrogation rooms, punishment cells, and execution site all are restored, which recreates the haunting atmosphere of yesteryear. Further along, in a room devoted to the (off-site) theme of 'Internment', a mining car full of large rocks is displayed. The ÁVH dispatched political prisoners to its camps near Recsk, Kistarcsa, Tiszalök, and Kazincbarcika, and here interviews with former internees run as short film clips. Some historical relics including an old automatic rifle, a Molotov cocktail, and a damaged bike are showcased in the long hall dedicated to '1956', which not only documents the uprising but also serves as 'a memorial to the fallen heroes'.[59] In the 'Reprisals' room, six replica execution scaffolds serve as haunting reminders of the communist regime's victims whose names are called out over a speaker system. Some 200,000 Hungarians fled their homeland after the 1956 revolution, and their plight is remembered in the 'Emigration' display. This small room's walls are covered by postcards sent from all over the world back to family members and loved ones who had remained behind in Hungary. Towards the end of the tour, a large, dimly lit room is populated with nothing other than tall, thin metal crosses. Entitled the 'Hall of Tears', its walls carry the names of all known political victims executed in Hungary between 1945 and 1967. Operating as the antithesis to the 'Hall of Tears', the stairway leading back to the ground level features portraits of dozens of state-based victimizers. Entitled the 'Perpetrators' Wall', it contains a mixture of Arrow Cross and communist leaders along with members and officeholders of numerous state organizations including the secret state police, chief prosecutors, Ministers of Justice, and presidents of the Supreme Court. Separating these two spaces dedicated to remembering victims or victimizers, a small room is simply titled 'Farewell'. Monitors show moving images of, *inter alia*, mass demonstrations in 1989, Imre Nagy's re-burial, the last Soviet troops leaving Hungary in June 1991, and, finally, the House of Terror's opening ceremony in February 2002. Speaking on that occasion, Viktor Orbán, in his first stint as Hungarian prime minister (1998–2002), perhaps best encapsulated how the House of Terror attempts to present a clear demarcation line between 'then and now' while simultaneously never losing sight of what caused so many Hungarians to suffer during the Cold War:

> We now lock fear and hatred behind bars, because we do not want them to have a place in our future lives. We shall lock them behind bars, but shall not forget them.[60]

It is hard to imagine how the sombre, indeed chilling, mood that envelops Budapest's House of Terror could be more different to the novel and at times even kitschy atmosphere surrounding Prague's Museum of Communism. But that is not to say, however, that Hungary's capital has not developed its own unique way to remember the 'spectres of communism' in a more unorthodox – indeed, eccentric – setting: Memento Park (*Szoborpark Múzeum*). Conceptualized by architect Ákos Előd in response to a nationwide competition and subsequently opened in June 1993 – a date chosen to mark the second anniversary of the Red Army's retreat from Hungarian

Figure 3.19 Portraits of victims under communism attached outside the House of Terror. Budapest, November 2011.

soil – it is a theme park designed to remember the Cold War era mostly through contemporary socialist-style monuments. Despite being located on a somewhat remote and hard-to-access site in the XXII. District on the out-skirts of Budapest, over the past two decades Memento Park has developed into one of the city's best-known and most popular tourist attractions among both Hungarians and foreigners alike.[61] It consists of three discrete sites of memory: an exhibition and education hall called the Northern Bar-rack; a full-scale replication of Budapest's infamous former monument destroyed by revolutionaries in 1956 that subsequently came to be cele-brated as the Tribune and Stalin's Boots; and the main attraction, an open-air museum commonly known as the Statue Park.

Housed inside an imitation of an old military barrack, Memento Park's exhibition and education hall primarily documents the 1956 uprising and the political developments experienced in 1989–91. By editing a series of instructional films the Kádár regime's Ministry of Interior Affairs produced to train its secret agents between 1958 and 1988, director Gábor Zsigmond created *The Life of an Agent* (2004), a four-part montage covering the themes: how to hide bugs; an introduction to house-searches; recruitment methods; and effective networking. Shown on perpetual loop in the barrack (and sold as a DVD in the park's Red Star Gift Shop), Zsigmond's film offers a dis-turbing depiction of how the state spied on virtually every aspect of daily life in communist Hungary – especially when concerning anyone suspected of flirting with western influences. The message conveyed by the film in particular and the barrack in general complements the commemorative politics that envelops both the Lajos Kossuth Square and the House of Terror: trapped behind Stalin's 'Iron Curtain' and consequently robbed of self-determination following the Second World War, Hungarians were an oppressed people trapped in the communist bloc. Remembering the Cold War period through such a lens means that, instead of belonging to the vanquished, Hungarians can be counted among the victimized.

Immediately adjacent to the barrack, another arena of articulation – com-monly known as the Tribune and Stalin's Boots – builds an extra layer on top of the 'Hungarians as Cold War victims' narrative. It simultaneously serves not only as a reminder of Stalinist tyranny but also of Hungarian fight and national pride. In 1949, a competition was held in Budapest to design a 'monumental gift' to Stalin as part of his seventieth birthday celebrations being staged across the Soviet bloc.[62] In December 1951, sculptor Sándor Mikus' winning design was unveiled near the Heroes' Square in the *Vár-osliget* gardens (on the exact site that would be used for the monument con-structed for the uprising's fiftieth anniversary in 2006, as discussed above). Known at the time as the Stalin Monument, it towered an imposing 80 feet skyward: a 26-feet high bronze statue of Stalin stood atop a large limestone base, which, in turn, rose out of a large tribune decorated with some three dozen life-sized working-class comrades – soldiers, workers, and mothers with children – depicted in a socialist realist high relief. Over the next five years, it was the scene of regular public demonstrations where party leaders addressed crowds from the tribune beneath the commanding figure of Stalin. Not surprisingly, then, the monument was one of the first things attacked by anti-communist demonstrators once the uprising commenced. The colossal Stalin statue was lassoed with steel ropes and blowtorches were used to cut through the legs just below knee-height. At around 9:30pm on 23 October 1956, Stalin toppled to the ground in Budapest. All that was left standing above the tribune were his large bronze boots, in which a Hungarian flag – sans the Rákosi badge – was placed.[63] The remaining bulk of the statue was dragged through Budapest streets before being dismantled by demonstrators for souvenirs. Unlike other Soviet monuments in Budapest desecrated during the uprising, in the midst of Khrushchev's destalinization the former tyrant never returned to his tribune, which, instead, underwent periodic remodeling over the decades until it was dismantled after 1989. Stalin's boots, meanwhile, always remained both a source of jokes among locals and an iconic image of the uprising. A full-scale model has been constructed at Memento Park. While it gives a sense of the original monument's gargantuan size, it makes no effort to be a faithful reenactment because the tribune is built out of concrete and bricks (and the high relief is missing, too). The presence of the Tribune and Stalin's Boots, however, is an

Figure 3.20 The (unfinished) full-scale model of the 'Tribune and Stalin's Boots' at Memento Park. Budapest, November 2011.

unmistakable attempt to link Memento Park to Hungary's ubiquitous, paradigmatic memory of the Cold War: 1956.

A far more diffuse outlook is adopted within Memento Park's main attraction, which its architect Előd conceptualized as the obscure-sounding 'One Sentence about Tyranny Statue Park' (popularly known as simply the Statue Park). Some of the most memorable scenes following the collapse of eastern European communism involve the toppling of public statues, particularly effigies of Stalin and Lenin but also other leading political figures. In Hungary, where literally thousands of statues and monuments had been erected during the previous half-century, public discourse in the early-1990s soon turned to the question: what could be done with these seemingly omnipresent corporeal reminders of a period of contemporary history dominated by a failed, oppressive system that was largely considered to have been enforced upon Hungary against the will of its people? Calls for them all to be demolished were rejected out of hand, and it was decided to relocate them in local museums and collections nationwide wherever possible, or otherwise place them in storage. Furthermore, the Budapest City Council announced a competition. All of the capital's District mayors joined forces with local cultural experts to select 42 of the nation's most emblematic and impressive socialist monuments, which were to be gathered and then put on permanent public display. Both the location and the layout of this collection were to be determined by the competition winner, with Előd's idea of an open-air museum built on the Tétényi moors on Budapest's outskirts the accepted submission. According to Előd, the guiding principle for his design was to capture the overarching paradoxical nature of these monuments in the past and present:

> I had to recognise that I needed to summarise the individual thought-provoking elements of a historical series of paradoxes into one conceptual thought process. Paradox, because these statues are both the reminders of an anti-democratic society and at the same time pieces of our history; paradox, because they are symbols of authority and at the same time works of art; and finally, paradox, because despite the fact that they were without doubt originally set up for the purpose of propaganda, in assigning them a new location, I deemed it important to avoid the possibility that they would become anti-propaganda, which would have been no more than a continuation of dictatorship mentality.[64]

The front entrance to the Statue Park, a high red brick neoclassical wall, sets the scene for what is concealed behind it by incorporating two monuments that provide some ideological and historical background: a 14-feet high granite statue of Karl Marx and Friedrich Engels sculpted by György Segesdi in 1971, which originally was located adjacent to party headquarters in central Budapest, now occupies an arched alcove on one side of the gate; a matching niche on the other side features Pál Pátzay's 13-feet high bronze

Figure 3.21 Front entrance to Memento Park, featuring statues of Lenin (l) and Marx
          and Engels (r). Budapest, November 2011.

statue of Lenin that had been erected at Budapest's Parade Square in 1965,
where the ideologue symbolically looked upon mass political rallies and
military parades. Inside the park, the monuments are presented in three
sections: first, the 'Endless Parade of Liberation Monuments'; second,
the 'Unending Parade of Workers' Movement Personalities'; and, finally, the
'Unending Parade of Workers' Movement Concepts and Events'.

   The 'Endless Parade of Liberation Monuments' consists of a series of ten
monuments – among them statues, friezes, and assorted styles of reliefs –
spaced around two linked circular paths that make a figure of eight shape.
The two common themes among these monuments are honouring Red
Army soldiers as heroes and thanking the Soviet Union as the liberator
responsible for Hungary's freedom. Ranging in size and crafted variously
from bronze, limestone, or granite, they date from as early as 1947 and as
late as 1975, an indication of how prevalent the 'Soviets as liberators' paradigm remained throughout the decades. Several contain inscriptions in
Hungarian and Russian that speak of the 'eternal glory' or 'eternal praise'
that the Soviets deserved for liberating Hungary and thus facilitating its
'freedom and peace'.[65] The most imposing statue among this set is Zsigmond
Strobl Kisfaludy's 20-feet high bronze statue entitled 'Liberating Soviet
Soldier'. It was commissioned in 1947 as part of a major Soviet memorial
erected in the citadel atop Gellért Hill, one of Budapest's most elevated

Figure 3.22 'Liberating Soviet Soldier' now at Memento Park. Budapest, November 2011.

spots, making it visible from virtually every part of the city. With a PPSh-41 submachine gun draped across his chest, the Red Army private soldier holds up a large hammer-and-sickle flag in his right hand. The version now in Statue Park is not the original dating from 1947, however, because it was destroyed during the Hungarian Uprising and so it is the replacement that the Soviets ordered in 1958.

Statue Park's middle section, entitled the 'Unending Parade of Workers' Movement Personalities', comprises sixteen monuments also placed around two linked circular paths. They are mostly statues or reliefs of individual figures. Memorials dedicated to individual Hungarian personalities range from rank-and-file party members Jósef Kalamár (1895–1956), János Asztalos (1918–56), and Róbert Kreutz (1923–44), all of whom were fêted as martyrs who gave their lives fighting for the communist cause, through to prominent functionaries including Ferenc Münnich (1886–1967), the hardline Minister of the Interior and Defence who played a key role in crushing the 1956 uprising, and the former trade union leader and one-time deputy prime minister Árpád Szakasits (1888–1965).[66] From an international perspective, in addition to two more Lenin monuments another personality individually memorialized is Georgi Dimitrov, Bulgaria's first postwar communist leader (1946–49) who earlier had been put on trial in Leipzig after the Nazis accused him of complicity in the Reichstag fire. Like Lenin, in fact, Dimitrov features twice in this section of the park: a modest bronze bust gifted to the Hungarian capital by its Bulgarian counterpart Sofia in 1954; and a large bronze statue crafted by Valentin Sztarcsev in 1983, likewise a gift to Budapest from Sofia. Both monuments had been located in what was then known as Dimitrov Square (nowadays known as *Fővám tér*, meaning the Main Customs Square) in Budapest's V. District.

Whereas most of the monuments dedicated to workers' movement personalities are either reliefs or statues that feature an individual, the Béla Kun Memorial stands out as particularly striking because the key figure Kun is accompanied by a mob. The revolutionary leader of the ill-fated Hungarian Soviet Republic in 1919, Kun (1886–1938) fled to the Soviet Union where he was later purged during Stalin's Great Terror in the late-1930s.[67] Following Nikita Khrushchev's policy of destalinization, Hungarian communists posthumously rehabilitated Kun as a national hero. To commemorate the

Figure 3.23 The main memorial dedicated to Béla Kun now at Memento Park. Budapest, November 2011.

centennial of his birth year, in 1986 a memorial was unveiled in the *Vérmező* public park in Budapest's I. District. Cast in chrome, bronze, and red copper typical of socialist realism, the memorial depicts Kun elevated on a platform in the background and waving his hat as a commanding gesture to the crowd below him that collectively thrusts forward in a dynamic manner. Upon closer inspection, the mob consists of an assortment of characters who represent developments in 1918–19: bringing up the rear, a bourgeois couple – he dressed in a trench coat and wearing a fedora, she in a long dress and holding a parasol – represents the so-called Aster Revolution; directly beneath Kun, a clutch of working-class demonstrators builds momentum; and, leading the charge, troops of the Hungarian Red Army rush forward with bayonets raised. The troops were employed effectively to crush counter-revolutionaries during Hungary's Red Terror, but also failed to repel the advancing Romanian forces and defeat in this conflict led to the short-lived soviet republic's downfall in August 1919. The artist commissioned to render the Béla Kun Memorial was Imre Varga, who, as discussed above, later would be entrusted with the task of creating the bridge memorial in Martyrs' Square dedicated to Imre Nagy and Hungary's national Remembrance Day of 23 October. Varga, born in 1923, enjoyed a long and distinguished career as one of his nation's pre-eminent artists during the communist era. As a nonagenarian, he has continued to be productive well into the twenty-first century. Straddling either side of 1989, then, Varga's work stands as a testament that public remembrance of the Cold War typically is a fluid process that is shaped by and reflects contemporary politics.

The third and final section of the Statue Park features thirteen monuments that, again, are spaced around a figure of eight path. The pieces selected for this part of the park encapsulate the public memorialization of 'Workers' Movement Concepts and Events' that proliferated in Cold War Hungary. A pattern similar to the park's first two sections is followed, whereby some memorials that date from the Cold War era but represent earlier episodes or developments are mixed among other works that were commissioned to capture contemporary events. Makrisz Agamemnon's 1968 monument, for instance, features three life-sized bronze guards saluting next to a limestone tablet with an inscription honouring Hungarians who fought in the Spanish International Brigade between 1936–39. A smaller bronze wall plaque from 1973 memorialized the ongoing service of the Workers' Militia, which was an armed brigade of volunteers established to protect party powers following the 1956 uprising. An example of socialist gigantism, the Republic of Councils Monument is easily the park's largest statue. Cast in bronze by István Kiss in 1969, this work was unveiled in central Budapest to commemorate the fiftieth anniversary of when Hungary had become – albeit fleetingly – the world's second communist state (only preceded by the Soviet Union). Kiss' massive sculpture, in fact, is based on the famous poster art 'To arms, to arms!' ('*Fegyverbe, fegyverbe!*'), produced by one of Hungary's leading avant-gardists Róbert Berény in 1919 to drum up support for the revolution. The

Figure 3.24 Cold War-era memorialization of Hungarians who fought in the International Brigade during the Spanish Civil War in the 1930s, now at Memento Park. Budapest, November 2011.

Berény/Kiss figure is a robust man who appears to be shouting as he takes a giant stride forward, waving in his left hand a large red flag while his extended right arm cocks back a clenched fist ready to strike out against any opposition. During the communist era, locals mockingly referred to this statue as the 'cloakroom attendant' (as though he is chasing after someone who has left behind their scarf). Despite, or perhaps because of, such popular contempt, the statue serves as an important reminder of how Hungarian leaders during the Cold War era reached back to 1919 to reinforce the notion that communism was not a 'foreign' politico-ideological system now being enforced upon Magyars by Moscow, but rather it had strong national roots.

It surely is no coincidence, then, that at Memento Park – which is designed to remember the Cold War era primarily through showcasing examples of its contemporary public memorialization – roughly one-third of the monuments are dedicated to personalities or events that predate the

Figure 3.25 The gigantic 'Republic of Councils Monument' now at Memento Park. Budapest, November 2011.

Second World War and Hungary's subsequent realignment with communism. It is not because Előd was inspired to extend back beyond the 1940s and document the nation's longer revolutionary lineage. Rather, it is a consequence of how Hungarian leaders during the Cold War very deliberately sought to remember the actions of their revolutionary predecessors in the wake of the First World War and dissolution of the Dual Monarchy as much as they celebrated their own achievements (and those of Soviet liberators). In any case, it means that this peculiar collection of monuments displayed on the city's outskirts is enveloped by a remarkably different atmosphere to other forms of public Cold War remembrance in central Budapest. Whereas there is no doubt that Memento Park evokes very different feelings among curious yet detached western tourists compared to Hungarians and other eastern Europeans who lived through communism, it is equally true that for all visitors it offers a unique experience that represents a most remarkable departure from the usual arenas of articulation.

Stalin's 'gift' and Wałęsa unveils 'the Gipper' in Warsaw

For all the talk of establishing a new European order 'without frontiers' in the immediate wake of the collapse of communism, only three states – Austria, Finland, and Sweden, all of whom officially had been neutral during the Cold War – were granted admittance to the European Union (EU) during the 1990s.[68] Indeed, it was not until the middle of the following decade that eastward expansion into the former communist bloc commenced. On 1 May 2004, Poland, Hungary, and the Czech Republic were among eight central and eastern European countries invited to join the EU.[69] It was the latest date in a line of momentous postwar developments shared by Poles, Hungarians, and Czechs. On 14 May 1955, Poland, Hungary, and Czechoslovakia were founding members of the Warsaw Treaty Organization of Friendship, Cooperation, and Mutual Assistance (or Warsaw Pact). Despite its ambiguous name, the Pact fundamentally was a military alliance the Soviet Union coordinated as a counterbalance to the western bloc's establishment of the North Atlantic Treaty Organization (NATO) during the early Cold War period.[70] And in between 1955 and 2004, after the Warsaw Pact's dissolution earlier in the decade Poland, Hungary, and the Czech Republic all joined NATO together on 12 March 1999.[71] On a basic level, then, the three nations have shared similar paths before and after 1989. The troika's parallel democratizing process that has resulted in them collectively moving westward into the NATO/EU orbit, furthermore, is a clear indication that, like Hungarians and Czechs, Poles have very deliberately set about disassociating their national master narrative from the overarching Cold War history of their former Soviet masters. Here, again, victimization is a convenient (and legitimate) theme whereby the prevailing interpretation of contemporary history commences with postwar Stalinist tyranny followed by a half-century of oppressive and unwanted communist rule imposed by Moscow and overseen by local stooges. From this perspective, by casting themselves as victims of the Cold War non-Soviets from the former communist sphere enter a kind of grey-zone in which they fall somewhere between the victors and the vanquished. And, to reinforce this message of 'in-betweenness', examples of internal resistance against external (i.e. Soviet) domination help to create further distance away from what US president Ronald Reagan infamously dubbed the 'Evil Empire' during a public address in March 1983.[72] Yet, whereas the national frameworks are comparable, the three capitals differ markedly when it comes to publicly remembering the Cold War.

Poland's capital may have lent its name to the communist bloc's most important and binding military pact (signed inside its presidential palace in 1955), but Warsaw did not witness any scenes analogous to the events in Budapest in 1956 or Prague in 1968. Indeed, quite unwittingly this point is made unmistakably clear to visitors of the city's Museum of Independence (*Muzeum Niepodległości*), which only can be described as barren.[73] Instead, other Polish cities are better remembered as places where the most decisive acts of resistance occurred. This is particularly true in the north, where mass demonstrations against massive increases in the prices of basic foodstuffs erupted in December 1970 around Gdańsk and Gdynia and spread to Elbląg, Słupsk, Tczew, and Szczecin.[74] As the introductory pages of this book make clear, moreover, around the world Gdańsk is the Polish city synonymous with the national struggle against communist rule after the Solidarity movement was forged in its Vladimir Lenin Shipyard in 1980. It would be misleading, however, to suggest that no momentous Cold War developments whatever took place in the Polish capital beyond 1955 and the signing of the Warsaw Pact. The papal visit of Pope John Paul II (born Karol Wojtyła) to his homeland in June 1979 is widely considered one of the most crucial 'turning points' that led to the eventual downfall of communism throughout Eastern Europe a decade later.[75] The first of several trips back to his native Poland, it was dominated by the pope's public appearances in Warsaw attended by hundreds of thousands of his fellow Poles. As reflected in the title of the 2010 film produced by the former Speaker of the US House of Representatives and 2012 Republican presidential hopeful Newt Gingrich and his wife Callista (for whom he converted to Catholicism in 2009), the pope's 1979 visit is widely remembered as 'nine days that changed the world'.[76] Nonetheless, unlike the respective Czech and Hungarian cases of Prague and Budapest covered already, or Germany's quintessential Cold War city Berlin discussed at the end of this book, public remembrance of the Cold War is not really a prevailing theme in Warsaw. While there are assorted sites of memory scattered across the city, arguably the two most noteworthy are polar opposites: a gaudy skyscraper, which has dominated Warsaw's skyline for more than a half-century, colloquially known as Stalin's 'gift'; and a modest monument to Ronald Reagan unveiled opposite the US Embassy in late 2011. Whereas the monumental building continues to serve as an unavoidable reminder of the early phase of the Cold War, building the monument was an act designed to celebrate the end of the era.

Speaking about Warsaw to a group of his officers on 17 October 1944, SS chief Heinrich Himmler declared: 'The city must completely disappear from the surface of the earth and serve only as a transport station for the Wehrmacht. No stone can remain standing. Every building is to be razed to its foundation.'[77] By this time, in fact, much of Poland's capital already had been destroyed during the Warsaw Uprising, which lasted two months from the beginning of August to the start of October. Before retreating in January 1945, the German forces carried out Himmler's orders and demolished whatever had survived the uprising. At the war's end, Warsaw literally was razed to the ground. Postwar reconstruction progressed steadily, but a shortage of funds and materials coupled with a reduction in the working-age population after five years of total war and brutal – indeed, genocidal – occupation meant that nothing overly ambitious was attempted. Consequently, when some 3,500 workers from the Soviet Union were sent to

Warsaw to construct a building as a gift from the Soviet people to their Polish comrades, the resultant 42-storey skyscraper towered above every-thing else even more so than would usually have been the case.[78] Built between 1952 and 1955, this classic example of socialist gigantism was offi-cially unveiled as the Josef Stalin Palace of Culture and Science. Owing to destalinization, the personal dedication soon vanished and for more than a half-century its official name has been the shortened Palace of Culture and Science (*Pałac Kultury i Nauki*, or PKiN). But the die was cast. Although technically a gift from the people of the Soviet Union to Poland, from the outset the building was made synonymous with Stalin and his cult of per-sonality. During construction, for instance, Soviet workers draped a large banner across the building's exterior with the words 'Glory to the Great Stalin' in Cyrillic lettering.[79] Stalin's death in March 1953, in the middle of the project, only served to strengthen the link between the 'Great Friend of Poland' and the building destined to carry his name.[80]

Despite the name-change in the wake of destalinization, among Varsovians the PKiN continued to be known colloquially as Stalin's 'gift'. And, over-whelmingly, it is an unwanted and ridiculed legacy of the Cold War. Indeed, an enduring local joke runs: 'Why is the PKiN's live-in caretaker the luckiest inhabitant of Warsaw? Because they are the only Varsovian whose view is not ruined by it!' Tourists are told that the centrally located landmark building is now there for the benefit of visitors rather than locals, for if they get lost it can be seen from virtually every part of the city. Some Varsovians with much darker senses of humour might even lament that it was built a decade too late, and calls for it to be demolished have been commonplace over the decades. All such appeals have amounted to naught, but habitual underutilization of its more than 3,200 rooms (covering an overall area in excess of 1.2 million square feet) means that Stalin's 'gift' has remained an idiomatic white elephant. Unlike purpose-built memorials or museums, the Palace of Culture and Science is not explicitly meant to facilitate Cold War remembrance; implicitly, however, this effect is inescapable. Over time the building has evolved into a paradox, with its functionality coming to repre-sent precisely the opposite message it was originally conceptualized to promote: a colossal gift from Moscow supposed to simultaneously showcase socialist architecture, embody communism's prosperity, and honour Stalin, it is mostly detested by the people of Warsaw as an ugly lingering reminder of Stalinist oppression and the decades of hardship Poles were forced to endure.

It is far too early to tell what longer-term role it will occupy among Warsaw's Cold War commemorative landscape, but the monument recently dedicated to Reagan clearly is aimed at the 'other' tale to be told about Poland's Cold War experience – its eventual freedom. Unveiled in a very public ceremony attended by several former and current Polish and American state dignitaries, the monument actually came about through the initiative of a private consortium of Polish business leaders fronted by

Figure 3.26 Stalin's 'gift': the Palace of Culture and Science. Warsaw, November 2011.

Janusz Dorosiewicz.[81] Interviewed by the BBC at the time of publicly launching the fundraising campaign in September 2006 (two years after Reagan's death), Dorosiewicz stated that the planned monument would be 'a way for his legacy to live on', further adding: 'Reagan was the person who defeated the communists and opened the way for freedom in Poland.'[82] Whereas westerners universally hold Mikhail Gorbachev in high regard, among former eastern bloc countries his role in ending the Cold War can tend to be overshadowed by memories of four decades of Moscow domination; his US counterpart Reagan, conversely, is widely celebrated in the former Soviet satellite states. Accordingly, the consortium wished to erect an 11.5-feet high stone and bronze statue of the 40th president of the United States – whose role in a 1940 film acquired him the endearing nickname of 'the Gipper' for the remainder of his life – as a way of posthumously thanking Reagan for his pivotal role in ending communist rule in Poland specifically and Eastern Europe more broadly. Dorosiewicz initially estimated that the project would cost approximately €140,000 and further anticipated that, by drawing on not only Poland's native population but also North Americans of Polish heritage, the necessary funding would be secured quickly enough to unveil the monument on 4 July 2007 – the next US Independence Day.[83] Such an ambitious timeframe proved unrealistic, however, not least because obtaining permission for a privately funded monument to be erected in such a prized public space was slowed by bureaucratic red tape.[84] Undeterred, Dorosiewicz and his associates stayed the course. They established the Ronald Reagan Foundation in Poland, and eventually the monument was ready to be unveiled in line with a more personal milestone: 2011 – the centennial of Reagan's birth year.

On a cold but clear day on 21 November 2011, a crowd – diminutive if measured by size, but imposing if measured by status – gathered at a public park opposite the US Embassy located on one of Warsaw's main thoroughfares, the leafy *Aleje Ujazdowskie*. Polish dignitaries in attendance included the foreign minister Radosław Sikorski, Warsaw's mayor Hanna Gronkiewicz-Waltz, and Tadeusz Mazowiecki, a key Solidarity figure who in 1989 became Poland's first non-communist prime minister after the Second World War. Three US senators who travelled to Poland specifically for this event accompanied the ambassador Lee Feinstein. Serving as a backdrop, a large temporary screen displayed a montage of Reagan's public life in office, including a photograph of him walking alongside Pope John Paul II. Before national hero Lech Wałęsa addressed the crowd and performed the official unveiling, to commence the ceremony statements from incumbent US president Barack Obama and Reagan's widow Nancy were read out. 'The location of this monument,' suggested Obama, 'is a fitting reminder of the close ties between the American and Polish people, and a tribute to the strong support the United States gave Poland during its long struggle to free itself from communist rule.'[85] Saying that such recognition for his accomplishments touched her, Nancy Reagan reflected:

> My husband always felt a strong bond with the people of Poland who longed for freedom. I remember the Christmas in 1981 [after martial law had been declared] when we placed candles in our White House windows, in honour of Solidarity, as [Reagan] was determined that America would do everything it could to advance liberty.[86]

Also reflecting on the past, Wałęsa said that only the generation who experienced these events first-hand can understand how at the time 'what happened seemed impossible or unthinkable'.[87] Three decades earlier, he pointed out, there had been over 200,000 Soviet soldiers stationed in Poland and more than a million across Eastern Europe, equipped with nuclear weapons. For this reason, argued Wałęsa, effecting major change – that is, the complete removal of communism – did not seem possible without triggering a nuclear conflict. In a remarkable show of modesty whereby he described himself as simply 'a participant' in the events that unfolded throughout Eastern Europe during the 1980s, the former Solidarity leader exclaimed that it was 'inconceivable' to think that 'today's Poland, Europe and world could look the same without president Reagan'.[88] Wałęsa also singled out for special commendation former British prime minister Margaret Thatcher, François Mitterrand, the ex-president of France, and the Polish-born Pope John Paul II – but, pointedly, not Gorbachev – for having played vital roles, too.[89] 'Let us bow before Ronald Reagan,' he then told the crowd, 'for the fact that our generation was able to bring an end to the great divisions and conflicts of the world.'[90] Wałęsa unveiled sculptor Władysław Dudek's monument, which consists of a bronze statue of Reagan standing behind a stylized podium crafted out of granite. It depicts Reagan during arguably his most famous public address, delivered in front of Berlin's Brandenburg Gate on 12 June 1987, when he demanded: 'Mr Gorbachev, tear down this wall!' Using an image that links Reagan to the Berlin Wall is a most intriguing choice for a monument in Warsaw. Two years prior to unveiling this monument, Wałęsa, as discussed in this book's opening pages, had been decidedly ambivalent about the extravagant celebrations marking the twentieth anniversary of the fall of the Wall. One wonders, then, how he reacted upon discovering what form Dudek's statue had taken. Irrespective of any personal feelings he may have had about this matter, Wałęsa's speech made it unequivocally clear that he holds 'the Gipper' in the highest esteem, whereas the same apparently cannot be said about what he thinks of Gorbachev whom he has described as a 'weak politician'.[91]

The monument unveiled in Warsaw was not an isolated case of memorializing Reagan in Eastern Europe during the centennial of his birth year. In developments that link Poles with Czechs and Hungarians in their common memories of the Cold War, earlier in 2011 a similar statue was erected in Budapest and in Prague a street was renamed in his honour. On 29 June, former secretary of state Condoleezza Rice acted as Nancy Reagan's emissary when a 7-feet high bronze statue of the 40th US president was unveiled in Budapest's Liberty Square.[92] With hundreds of Budapestians gathered in the square adjacent to the US Embassy, Viktor Orbán (during his second stint as Hungary's prime minister, 2010–) pronounced the kinds of sentiments that Wałęsa would echo five months later:

> Today, we are erecting here a statue to the man, to the leader, who changed, who renewed, this world and created in it a new world for us in Central Europe – a man who believed in freedom, who believed in the moral strength of freed people and that walls that stand in the way of freedom can be brought down.[93]

And it was not hollow rhetoric only produced by high politics. Kornelia Budai, a local septuagenarian who witnessed the deaths of several friends

Figure 3.27 Reagan monument a week after its unveiling. Warsaw, November 2011.

during the Hungarian Uprising and lived under communism most of her life, attended the unveiling to pay her respects to a foreign leader whom she described as 'a symbol of freedom for the peoples of Eastern Europe'.[94] In a similar vein Orbán's deputy prime minister Zsolt Semjén further added that, while strong differences of opinion naturally existed among former Soviet satellite states, 'when it comes to respecting the legacy of Ronald Reagan, we are indeed united'.[95] Two days later, on 1 July, Rice again represented the United States when she attended a ceremony in Prague to rename the street in front of the US ambassador's residence in Reagan's honour (renamed *Ulice Ronalda Reagana*).[96] Norman Eisen, the US ambassador to the Czech Republic, told the American and Czech guests in attendance that it was a 'truly fitting commemoration to the man who in so many ways lay the groundwork for our strong partnership today'.[97] The ceremony coincided with a two-day international conference conducted by the Czech Republic's Ministry of Foreign Affairs, entitled 'Ronald Reagan: Inspired Freedom'.[98]

The memorializing of Reagan in Poland, Hungary, and the Czech Republic in 2011, including the comments made by American and local representatives alike during the ceremonies, is emblematic of the wider politics of the Cold War past in these former Warsaw Pact nations. Remembering through the rubric of being a loyal Soviet satellite not only would necessitate a need to confront serious historical failings, but also, moreover, would serve as a reminder that their current embrace of democracy still is incipient. It suits the Americans, too, of course, for it portrays Washington – led by 'the Gipper' – as having served as the inspirational bastion of freedom and, as the eventual 'victor' in the Cold War, the liberator of oppressed peoples throughout Eastern Europe.

The empire bites flak: Hanoi

Although Vietnam's capital may not rank among the world's largest megacities or urban agglomerations (indeed, it belongs to the select list of capitals that are not their nation's most populous city), Hanoi has a well-earned reputation for being one of the busiest places on earth. In and around its Old Quarter, Hanoi is a pulsating throng of human movement and over the past few decades its scooter-dominated traffic has become the stuff of legend. Day or night, it can prove difficult to find a quiet place anywhere in Hanoi. In a fascinating development, the only time we experienced any relative calmness during four days spent in Hanoi as part of a field research trip in early 2013 was on a Saturday morning visit to the Ho Chi Minh Trail Museum. Discounting our taxi driver (who raced through the exhibits in less than 20 minutes and then spent the remaining time waiting in his vehicle), we did not encounter any other visitors while wandering through the museum for three hours. Admittedly, for some inexplicable reason it has been created a little off the beaten track and, perched out on the southwestern outskirts of the city heading toward Hoa Binh, the museum is not in the most convenient location for Hanoians or tourists to access. Presumably this at least partially explains why the general consensus among tourist guidebooks, online reviews, and local information bureau staff is that only 'war buffs' or returning 'vets' should bother to attempt a visit. It is a shame, however, that the Ho Chi Minh Trail Museum remains one of Hanoi's lesser known and least frequented public exhibitions because it presents an informative account of one of the most recognized features of the Vietnam War.

Its odd location notwithstanding, the museum clearly was designed for not only Vietnamese but also English-speaking (namely American) visitors. Most of the signage includes English translations. The museum, furthermore, has adopted the name first popularized by the Americans – Ho Chi Minh Trail – rather than the title Vietnamese typically use for the trail – Truong Son – which derives from the local name for the main mountain range through which the vast network of tracks passed. (On the English signage, however, there are numerous references to the 'Truong Son heroic soldiers' who worked along the trail during the war.) Outside of the museum's three-level building there is an impressive collection of vehicles linked to the trail during the war: Russian- and Chinese-built tractors and trucks gifted to the communist forces in North Vietnam for maintaining or expanding the trail and transporting goods down to the south; Soviet military vehicles including an armoured car and an anti-magnetic bomb car; a US Army jeep that was captured as 'war booty'; and even a Japanese-made Hino truck apparently gifted to Truong Son soldiers for use along the trail by Fidel Castro's Cuban government in 1973. Inside, the museum is densely populated with photographic exhibits interspersed among a rich collection of war artefacts: on the one hand, Vietnamese tools and equipment (some primitive, others slightly more advanced) stand as testament to communist ingenuity, engineering, and determination; on the other hand, more captured 'war booty' that simultaneously betrays how American forces may have been equipped with far more advanced weaponry and aids but nonetheless still were horribly outfought and defeated. Moral questions are raised almost immediately, too, for one of the first displays awaiting visitors as they enter from the front foyer is an imposing Agent Orange exhibit. Photo-boards depicting badly burned or deformed victims – many of whom are children – sit either side of authentic phosphorus grenades, incendiary grenades, and large canisters of fuels and chemicals used to concoct Agent Orange. Further display rooms are full of shrapnel bombs, machine guns, infra-red reconnaissance systems, fragments of destroyed US aircrafts, parachutes and ejector seats of American pilots shot down, mortar bombs, Hungarian-made communication switchboards from communist headquarters, flags, and other military paraphernalia. An auditorium upstairs features a sizeable diorama of the Ho Chi Minh Trail. As the room's lights dim, a recorded oration covers the trail's history chronologically as various tracks running down from the north toward Saigon via Cambodian and Laotian territory are lit up with hundreds of little LEDs. At the rear of the museum, a lush garden surrounds a large memorial dedicated in reverence and worship to the Truong Son heroic officers and soldiers who worked along the trail – of whom 19,387 were killed and a further 32,047 were wounded between 1959 and 1975.

The Ho Chi Minh Trail Museum forms part of what feels like an autoschediastic approach to remembering the Cold War from a very hot national perspective in the capital Hanoi. The state-centred cult of personality around Ho – revered as the revolutionary who led the Vietnamese people in their struggle to freedom against imperialist foreign powers – remains as strong as ever. His mausoleum arguably is the city's most visited site, and the adjacent Ho Chi Minh Museum (not to be confused with the aforementioned museum based on the trail that also bears his name) is a main attraction, too.[99] Beyond Ho, some of Hanoi's historically significant constructions now serve as sites of memory. The rickety old Long Bien Bridge, constructed by Parisian engineers during French imperial rule from 1899 to 1902, remained Hanoi's chief transportation route over the Red River.

Figure 3.28 The memorial dedicated to Truong Son heroic officers and soldiers located in garden outside the Ho Chi Minh Trail Museum. Hanoi, February 2013.

Consequently, this long cantilever bridge was doubly important because it linked the capital with the major port city of Haiphong. And it was for these reasons that the Long Bien Bridge was a chief target of American bombers throughout the war. Although it was frequently knocked out of service, invariably the bridge would be repaired again and again. The continual defence and mending of the bridge became a source of national pride during the war, and so decades later it continues to be looked on fondly as an icon of triumph. Memories attached to Hoa Lo Prison – better known as the infamous 'Hanoi Hilton' – are not so pleasant. Originally built by the French as a colonial prison to house mainly Indochinese political prisoners, the front entrance still bears the euphemistic name *Maison Centrale* (literally Central House, a generic title for French prisons in the nineteenth century). Following France's defeat in 1954, the prison was temporarily closed down before being utilized to incarcerate and interrogate captured US military personnel from 1964 onwards. It was during this period that the prison received the ironic nickname 'Hanoi Hilton' from American inmates owing to the abhorrent conditions. To accommodate urban development in the heart of Hanoi, most of Hoa Lo Prison was demolished during the 1990s. But a small section near the former entrance has been preserved as a museum. It documents both the earlier phase in which the French treated Vietnamese male and female inmates inhumanely (including one of the original guillotines on display) as well as the later phase when American POWs (including the future US presidential candidate John McCain, whose flight suit is on display) were held there. The commingling of the French colonial and American imperial phases of Vietnam's twentieth-century history at the Hoa Lo Prison museum also can be discerned from other sites of memory in and around Hanoi. These range from socialist realist memorials one can periodically stumble across in some of the streets and parks scattered over the city, through to the Vietnam Military History Museum located on a prime site in the heart of the capital.

It is most appropriate that the Vietnam Military History Museum is located in Dien Bien Phu Street, so-named in dedication to the climactic battle that signalled the defeat of colonial French forces. Immediately after

Figure 3.29 Front entrance to the Hoa Lo Prison ('Hanoi Hilton') museum. Hanoi, February 2013.

victory was secured at Dien Bien Phu in May 1954, moves were afoot to establish a national military museum. On 22 December 1959 – the fifteenth anniversary of the founding of the Vietnam People's Army – what originally was called the Army Museum opened.[100] It underwent a name change in 2002, becoming the Vietnam Military History Museum. Although it enjoys the privileged status of counting among Vietnam's seven national museums, it nonetheless suffers from a similar problem faced by a Cold War museum located near Los Angeles that was created by an individual Californian (discussed in detail later): an abundance of artefacts combined with a chronic shortage of space means that only around 4,000 objects from the overall collection of some 160,000 items are displayed at any one time.[101] Indeed, some of the storage yards adjacent to the museum's display buildings are so full of captured or decommissioned military vehicles and large weaponry that at first glance it appears to be a contemporary military base. Even so, the museum is not restricted to modern times. Rather, it traces Vietnamese military history over the course of several millennia, with artefacts on display ranging from spearheads dating from 2,500 to 3,000 years ago through to objects from the twentieth century. One of its most notable aspects is that, whether by design or out of necessity (owing to empty coffers), it is a museum that heavily relies on the authenticity of its rich collection of artefacts to tell the narrative. Unlike so many post-modern museums around the world, here there are no flashy lightbox panels, or interactive touchscreens, or dynamic wall panels seemingly fitted as much for their aesthetic impact as for the information they provide. Instead, besides a few dioramas and some photo-boards, modest signage is the order of the day as the focus is placed on all manner of weapons ranging from primitive spears, wooden clubs, and spike pits, to flying bombs, grenade launchers, and flame-throwers, through to the outside collections of air ordnance, helicopters, tanks, and a MIG-21 fighter jet. Perhaps the most impressive feature among the outdoor collection is a large sculpture formed by a montage of pieces taken from enemy aircraft destroyed in the Dien Bien Phu campaign against the French and then the air war against the Americans from 1965 to 1973.

The museum successfully contextualizes the nation's late-nineteenth- and early-twentieth-century struggles for independence within a longer history of military conflict. The contemporary national master narrative is told through a prism of socialist determination triumphing over imperialist/capitalist might. In this story, victory came about through the combination of Ho's dynamic leadership and the unbreakable spirit of the Vietnamese people. What is unmistakable, again, is the deliberate fusion of colonial French and imperialist Americans into an amorphous enemy. There are nonetheless several distinguishing features, of course, and just as Dien Bien Phu symbolizes the conflict against the French, the American War is epitomized by the iconography of the B-52 bomber.[102] And this is where a recent special exhibition by the Vietnam Military History Museum creates an extraordinary link. From 18–29 December 1972, the United States unleashed Operation

Linebacker II (also unofficially known as the 'December Raids' or the 'Christmas Bombings' due to the timing), one of the fiercest bombing assaults of the war in which Hanoi and Haiphong were hit with 'maximum effort' by B-52 bombers. Despite wreaking untold destruction north of the DMZ, the operation was cancelled after eleven days and within a month the Paris Peace Accords (signed on 27 January 1973) signalled the end of direct American military involvement in Vietnam. In the Vietnamese national story, then, this campaign is interpreted as a, if not *the*, decisive victory against the United States. To mark its fortieth anniversary, in 2012 the Vietnam Military History Museum curated a special exhibition for which the Americans' heavy bombing campaign was given the stunning title of the 'Dien Bien Phu in the Air' ('*Điện Biên Phủ trên không*'). An introductory sign at the exhibition's entrance states (in broken English translation):

Figure 3.30 One of the posters erected around Huu Tiep Lake in late 2012 to mark the 40th anniversary of the 'Dien Bien Phu in the Air.' Hanoi, February 2013.

End of December 1972, US Army used a large of B-52 strategic bombers to open a raid on Hanoi, Haiphong and other neighbor places. By bombs, the US army wanted to being Hanoi back to the 'Stone Age', with the plot to divide Vietnam country in long-term.

With a will 'determine to fight, determine to win', the people and army of North Vietnam have fought and won, making a 'Dien Bien Phu in the air', along with other victories in the South Vietnam had forced US government to sign the Paris Agreement, ending the war and restoring peace in Vietnam. This important victory of Vietnam was a good condition to liberate the South, reunify nation.

On the 40th anniversary of victory 'Dien Bien Phu in the air' (12/1972 – 12/2012), the Vietnam Military History Museum opens the exhibition 'Hanoi – Dien Bien Phu in the air'.

This special exhibition featured approximately 300 photographs, propaganda posters, and artefacts, with the iconic shape of the B-52 casting its shadow in virtually every corner. Photographs range from a B-52 on a tarmac waiting to be equipped with its extraordinary load of air ordnance, to dropping dozens of bombs mid-air, through to mutilated child victims of bombing raids. Posters (including some commissioned especially for the fortieth anniversary) depict heroic soldiers celebrating the destruction of

Figure 3.31 Remnants of the B-52 bomber shot down over Hanoi in December 1972, and since then left in Huu Tiep Lake. Hanoi, February 2013.

the heavy bombers, which scream through the air ablaze as the Long Bien Bridge remains intact in the background. Strategically placed at the end of the main corridor that dissects the exhibition, the most eye-catching item is a large, distorted piece of the engine from a B-52 bomber that was shot down over Hanoi on 27 December 1972 by the 72nd Missile Battalion of the 285th Regiment of the North Vietnamese air force and ground defence. As the centrepiece of the 'Dien Bien Phu in the Air' exhibition curated by a national museum, this artefact temporarily served as a cornerstone of state-centred articulation of war memory and commemoration. It is, then, part of a case study made particularly interesting due to the French–American nexus symbolized by the linkage between Dien Bien Phu and the B-52. But a far longer and even more fascinating history can be told about the plane wreckage from which this piece of engine was salvaged. The bomber shot down by the 72nd Missile Battalion on 27 December 1972 landed in Huu Tiep Lake in central Hanoi. Its name notwithstanding, by any measurement it is not an actual lake but rather a pond hidden away amongst residential quarters (it is so small and secluded, in fact, not even local taxi drivers seem to be able to locate it without stopping for directions on multiple occasions). To this day, part of the wreckage protrudes out of the water in what is a most remarkable example of organic war remembrance. Usually, a small plaque mounted on a stylized marble monument simply denotes that Huu Tiep Lake contains the 'historical vestiges' of a B-52 bomber. The message was embellished considerably as part of the fortieth anniversary commemorations of the 'Dien Bien Phu in the Air', with around a dozen large brightly coloured prints erected around the pond's perimeter. In similar designs to the posters on display at the national military museum's exhibition, these posters celebrate Vietnam's victory, independence, and (re)unification through the shape of blazing B-52s spiralling toward earth.

In Hanoi, the nation's very 'hot' but ultimately liberating experience during the Cold War understandably consumes public remembrance of the period. As a corollary, the American enemy is cast in the dual role of the villain and the vanquished. It is a very different story in Washington, where a foundation of Cold War warriors simultaneously peddles US triumphalism and projects communism as the epitome of evil.

A Washington monument: remembering victims or rejoicing in victory?

The intersection of Massachusetts Avenue and New Jersey Avenue in Northwest, Washington DC, is approximately a one-hour walk from the city centre. Circumscribed by busy streets and drab buildings, at first glance it appears to be a rather strange site to erect a national memorial to remember international victims of communism. After all, the nation's capital is awash with monuments in prime locations. It soon becomes clear, however, that it is actually a very strategic location for the national 'Victims of Communism Memorial'. As one circles around the monument, from a particular vantage point the splendid and unmistakable white dome of the United States Capitol – the meeting place of Congress, the legis-lature of the US federal government – suddenly looms large on the horizon. When framed by such a backdrop, the monument begs the question: is it a memorial to victims or the apparent victors? For, even though it is presented as honouring more than 100 million worldwide victims of communism past and present, it was incontrovertibly conceived to remember the Cold War.[103]

In July and October 1991 (that is, prior to the Soviet Union's official disintegration), concurrent resolutions were introduced to the House of Representatives and the Senate calling for congressional approval to:

> ... construct an International Memorial to the Victims of Communism
> at an appropriate location within the boundaries of the District of
> Columbia and for the appointment of a commission to oversee the
> design, construction and all other pertinent details of the memorial:
> *Provided*, That all costs associated for land acquisition, design, construc-
> tion and maintenance shall be obtained through private sources
> [emphasis in original].[104]

In December 1993, an Act of Congress was unanimously passed and signed by Democratic president Bill Clinton authorizing by Public Law the con-struction of such an anti-communist memorial in the nation's capital in accordance with the above resolutions' guidelines. More than a decade passed before Republican president George W. Bush finally unveiled the resultant monument in June 2007. And the end product bears no resem-blance to the extravagant designs originally proposed. Despite bilateral support, the project evidently did not go according to plan. What happened along the way?

In accordance with the Act, the National Captive Nations Committee (NCNC), an anti-communism lobby created in 1959 under Dwight Eisen-hower's presidency, was tasked with the responsibility of establishing an independent organization to raise funds and oversee the project. Although Congress had stipulated that no government funding would be forthcoming, from its inception the Victims of Communism Memorial Foundation devised ambitious plans. The proposed centrepiece was a museum (possibly including an education and research centre) to be housed in one of Washington's historic landmark buildings, the old General Post Office (also known as the Tariff Commission Building), at a projected cost of US$ 100 million.[105] Had this museum ever materialized, a 'Hall of Infamy' featuring displays such as a segment of the Berlin Wall, a reconstruction of a Gulag camp, and a boat used by Vietnamese refugees would have run parallel to a 'Hall of Heroes' containing statues of celebrated anti-communist figures including former US president Reagan and Russian nuclear physicist-turned-dissident Andrei Sakharov. Despite the memorial's name placing emphasis on remembering victims, the proposed juxtaposition of communist infamy and anti-communist heroism is indicative of how an overarching theme of 'good overcoming evil' underpinned this project as it took shape in the early-1990s. Indeed, Stephen F. Cohen, one of the United States' leading scholars of Russian Studies, observed at the time that memorializing anti-communism on such a grand scale in the immediate wake of the collapse of eastern European communism smacked of 'the triumphalist victory of cold-war warriors'.[106]

The Victims of Communism Memorial Foundation anticipated that the museum's doors would open by December 2000. In the period 1993–99, however, less than half a million dollars – in other words, less than 0.5 per cent of the target figure – had been raised.[107] Toward the end of the

Figure 3.32 The Victims of Communism Memorial, with the dome of the United States Capitol in the background. Washington, February 2013.

decade, the Act needed renewal and, moreover, the project required serious revision. As reality sunk in, the Foundation acknowledged that it was not simply a matter of scaling down its talk of a grandiose US $100 million complex but rather: 'Plans to build a "bricks and mortar" museum had to be put off as attention was placed solely on the construction of a $1 million monument.'[108] Put another way, irrespective of bilateral backing the proposed national anti-communist memorial shrunk from being a multi-faceted museum and research centre housed in a historic landmark building to become a smallish monument perched on an unused piece of land in the middle of a busy intersection (albeit with a highly symbolic vista).

From the beginning it was decided that a statue of the 'Goddess of Democracy' would serve as the memorial museum's centrepiece.[109] It was to be a replica of the impromptu statue that Chinese students had erected in Beijing's Tiananmen Square during the mass demonstrations conducted in 1989, which in turn apparently had been inspired by the Statue of Liberty. The foundation's board of directors thereby decided on the 'Goddess of Democracy' because of her dual symbolism: on the one hand, she is a reminder of ongoing oppression in the world's most populated nation; on the other hand, she encapsulates 'man's indomitable desire to be free'.[110] When the museum concept diminished into a single monument, the logical conclusion was for the Victims of Communism Memorial to take the form of a statue of the Goddess. It is a 10-feet high bronze statue that stands atop a cylindrical granite podium into which two messages are inscribed. On the front it states: 'To the more than one hundred million victims of communism and to those who love liberty'. Drawing on the NCNC's half-century mission, the rear dedication reads: 'To the freedom and independence of all captive nations and peoples'. The podium's two inscriptions implicitly present mixed messages: is the monument's fundamental purpose to remember the 100 million victims apparently claimed by communism throughout the twentieth century, or is it primarily aimed at promoting the ongoing fight against leftist authoritarianism around the globe? Perhaps a hint can be found in the accompanying information panel, which contains photographs of twentieth-century 'communist perpetrators', victims, and freedom fighters from across Europe, South America, and Asia as well as some complementary text – mostly in past tense – that states:

> The Victims of Communism Memorial enshrines the more than 100 million men, women, and children struck down by 20th century totalitarian communist regimes.
>
> Communist leaders attracted countless millions throughout the world with their 'big lie' promises of a classless, egalitarian society free of poverty and oppression. But in fact communist dictators wielded centralized authority and employed brutal measures to crush all those who rebelled against the suppression of their freedoms.

Imprisonment and executions were used with devastating effect as were deportation, famine, and forced labor. Millions of innocents died in Russia, Central and Eastern Europe, Asia, Africa, the Caribbean, and Latin America. Memories of their sacrifice endure in the hearts and minds of families and friends.

The memorial offers no image of repression or despair. Rather, it features a universally recognized symbol of hope inspired by the 'Goddess of Democracy' statue erected by Chinese students in Tiananmen Square in 1989. Like the Statue of Liberty, the memorial reminds us of the power of freedom to combat and ultimately overcome tyranny.

If there is any lingering doubt over whether this monument should be viewed primarily as the product of Cold War commemorative politics (as opposed to being a memorial against communism more generally), its unveiling ceremony puts the case to rest. The date selected for the occasion, 12 June 2007, was the twentieth anniversary of Reagan's 'Tear down this wall!' speech in Berlin. The Victims of Communism Memorial Foundation's honorary chairman George W. Bush, whose father George H.W. Bush was Reagan's vice-president and successor, accepted the invitation to perform the unveiling. In a 12-minute speech, the 43rd president of the United States covered a range of topics.[111] Yet, the triumph of faithful Americans over the godless 'Evil Empire' in the Cold War was a dominant theme. Consider, for instance, the following passages:

> ... here in the company of men and women who resisted evil and helped bring down an empire, I proudly accept the Victims of Communism Memorial on behalf of the American people. [Applause.]
>
> ... Some of Communism's victims are well-known. They include a Swedish diplomat named Raoul Wallenberg, who saved 100,000 Jews from the Nazis, only to be arrested on Stalin's orders and sent to Moscow's Lubyanka Prison, where he disappeared without a trace. They include a Polish priest named Father Popieluszko, who made his Warsaw church a sanctuary for the Solidarity underground, and was kidnapped, and beaten, and drowned in the Vistula by the secret police.
>
> The sacrifices of these individuals haunt history – and behind them are millions more who were killed in anonymity by Communism's brutal hand. They include innocent Ukrainians starved to death in Stalin's Great Famine; or Russians killed in Stalin's purges; Lithuanians and Latvians and Estonians loaded onto cattle cars and deported to Arctic death camps of Soviet Communism ... East Germans shot attempting to scale the Berlin Wall in order to make it to freedom; Poles massacred in the Katyn Forest.
>
> We dedicate this memorial because we have an obligation to future generations to record the crimes of the 20th century and ensure they're never repeated. In this hallowed place we recall the great lessons of

the Cold War: that freedom is precious and cannot be taken for granted; that evil is real and must be confronted; and that given the chance, men commanded by harsh and hateful ideologies will commit unspeakable crimes and take the lives of millions.

Bush, furthermore, did not miss the opportunity to harness the politics of the past and link these 'great lessons of the Cold War' to his ongoing War on Terror:

> It's important that we recall these lessons because the evil and hatred that inspired the death of tens of millions of people in the 20th century is still at work in the world. We saw its face on September the 11th, 2001. Like the Communists, the terrorists and radicals who attacked our nation are followers of a murderous ideology that despises freedom, crushes all dissent, has expansionist ambitions and pursues totalitarian aims. Like the Communists, our new enemies believe the innocent can be murdered to serve a radical vision. Like the Communists, our new enemies are dismissive of free peoples, claiming that those of us who live in liberty are weak and lack the resolve to defend our free way of life. And like the Communists, the followers of violent Islamic radicalism are doomed to fail. [Applause.] By remaining steadfast in freedom's cause, we will ensure that a future American President does not have to stand in a place like this and dedicate a memorial to the millions killed by the radicals and extremists of the 21st century.

Predictably, not only the memorial but also Bush's involvement in its unveiling ceremony provoked Sino-Russian criticism at the highest levels. According to a *Chicago Tribune* report, because the statue evokes the Tiananmen Square incident the Chinese Embassy immediately complained that the memorial was 'an attempt to defame China'.[112] A day after the ceremony, moreover, a spokesperson for China's Foreign Ministry released a statement via the ministry's website in which Bush was accused of trying to reignite an ideological battle: 'Some political forces in the United States, driven by a Cold War mentality and by political imperatives, are provoking confrontation between ideologies and social systems.'[113] A week later, Russian leader Vladimir Putin was quoted in the *Washington Post* as effectively arguing that the United States' nuclear attacks on Japan and later mass-bombings and use of chemical weapons on Vietnam were demonstrably worse than Stalin's purges.[114] Despite, or perhaps because of, Bush highlighting in his speech the plight of Ukrainians during Stalin's Great Famine, the memorial even met with a backlash in the Crimea, too.[115] In August 2007, one of Russia's largest state-owned news agencies *RIA Novosti* reported that, as a riposte to the anti-communist memorial in Washington (and another anti-Soviet one in Kiev), Ukraine's communist party had opened a 'makeshift museum to victims of U.S. imperialism in the central square of Simferopol'.[116] The exhibition displayed photographs, maps, and other documentation recording shameful episodes in domestic US history involving massacres of Native Americans, slavery, and institutional racism (including lynching), as well as US military interventions in foreign countries ranging from Vietnam through to Iraq and Afghanistan. This argument that American imperialism's history makes for at least as if not more grim reading than communism's track record in the twentieth century was recently revisited by Andrei P. Tsygankov, a Russian-born professor of International Relations and Comparative Politics based at San Francisco State University. Noting that Bush had taken 'a page from the Cold War' when referring to 100 million innocent victims of communism worldwide during his speech at the unveiling ceremony, Tsygankov added that the president 'failed to even mention victims of imperial wars conducted on behalf of the "free world"'.[117]

The memorial has attracted its share of supporters, too, of course. Representatives from the Czech and Hungarian parliaments along with various ambassadors attended the unveiling ceremony in 2007. And 'leaders of more than a dozen nations', according to the organization behind the project, 'have since visited the memorial to pay their respects and lay memorial wreaths'.[118] And, given the coverage of Cold War remembrance in Prague, Budapest, and Warsaw earlier in this section, it is fascinating to note that the Victims of Communism Memorial Foundation's international advisory council includes among its current or former members Václav Havel, Árpád Göncz, and Lech Wałęsa.[119] Havel (2003) and Wałęsa (2006) along with Viktor Orbán (2002) and Pope John Paul II (2005), furthermore, are recipients of the Truman-Reagan Medal of Freedom, which the Foundation struck and has awarded annually since 1999 to individuals or institutions who 'have demonstrated a life-long commitment to freedom and democracy and opposition to communism and all other forms of tyranny'.[120]

A decade-long chronic failure to attract private funding resulted in the understated 'Goddess of Democracy' monument replacing an elaborate 'bricks-and-mortar' museum located in Washington. Not to be denied completely, however, the Victims of Communism Memorial Foundation turned its attention to constructing a 'virtual museum' through the development of an interactive website.[121] Launched in June 2009, the Foundation's exclusively online Global Museum on Communism is self-styled as 'an international portal created to honor the more than 100 million victims of communist tyranny'.[122] Again, however, there is a conflation between remembering victims and rejoicing in victory because the Foundation claims to honour the victims' memory through its stated mission to educate 'the public about communism's crimes against humanity and the heroes who successfully resisted it'.[123] Indeed, educating the general public is a paramount concern for a Foundation that speaks of an alleged 'great moral failing that so many do not know the extent of Communism's atrocities'. Part of its approach, then, is to offer an online 'Quiz on Communism', and judging by the multiple-choice questions the Foundation evidently is convinced that it is not only a case of remembering versus forgetting but rather learning about this topic for the first time: Who became leader of the Soviet Union in 1924? (Stalin, Lenin, Gorbachev, Putin, or Trotsky); Who wrote the *Communist Manifesto*? (Lenin, Stalin, Marx and Engels, Dan Brown, or Chairman Mao); How many people have been killed by Communist regimes? (2 million, 30 million, 50 million, 5 million, or 100 million); and what country did the Soviet Union invade in 1979? (Estonia, Poland, Afghanistan, Syria, or Georgia).[124]

Visually striking and media-rich, the Global Museum on Communism features an extensive suite of 'exhibits' – the term employed for the website's various sections. Besides 15 'National Exhibits' (dedicated to Bulgaria, China, Cuba, Czechoslovakia, Estonia, Germany, Hungary, Latvia, Lithuania, Poland, Romania, the Soviet Union, Tibet, Ukraine, and Vietnam, with North Korea soon to be added at the time of writing), the virtual museum is based around five 'Main Exhibits'. One is an interactive timeline of key dates involving communism running from 1848 to the present, another features an interactive map with brief descriptions for countries or regions around the world that have experienced communist rule, and a third theme centres on a 3D virtual Gulag camp. The final two Main Exhibits clearly were inspired by the original plans for a bricks-and-mortar museum. First, the 'Gallery of Heroes' showcases 'the brave men and women who suffered as political prisoners, raised the banner of liberty as dissidents, and lived as everyday citizens under oppressive communist regimes'.[125] Second, the 'Hall of Infamy' features images of communist 'tyrants and mass murderers who caused untold suffering around the world'.[126]

According to its mission statement, the virtual museum is an integral component of the Foundation's three-pronged 'long-term action plan designed to memorialize, educate and document the grim legacy of global communism'.[127] The first phase, entitled 'Memorializing the Victims', eventually was accomplished with the erection of the anti-communist monument in Washington. Phase Two, aimed at 'Educating the Public', is serviced by the interactive website.[128] And hope springs eternal in these Cold War warriors, for the Foundation's third and final phase, entitled 'Documenting the Evidence', only will be realized through the construction of an actual bricks-and-mortar United States Museum on Communism in Washington DC. If it ever comes to fruition, the Foundation envisages that:

> This institution will collect, warehouse, and permanently display the evidence and artifacts of the communist system and its many crimes against humanity. Notably, the museum will also bring to light the vast number of heroes and champions who successfully opposed and triumphed over the tyranny of communism, serving as an inspiration to future generations.[129]

The father's son, and a ghost of an institution: the case of Vint Hill

What happens when the son of an iconic Cold War figure identifies an abandoned military base in rural Virginia as the ideal site for remembering the Cold War? The answer is the enigmatic Cold War Museum based in Vint Hill. Whereas the motivations behind the two ventures differ considerably in important ways, there nonetheless are some intriguing parallels to be drawn between how this case has developed and the events surrounding the Washington story discussed directly above.

Vint Hill, a small settlement in Fauquier County, Northern Virginia, is somehow both in the middle of nowhere and yet also within very close proximity to the nation's capital. Presumably, its remote-yet-close location is the reason why it held such appeal as a prime intelligence and communications centre during the twentieth century: on the one hand, it was sufficiently isolated not to draw any attention to what transpired in the region; on the other hand, it was geographically convenient to various departmental headquarters based in and around the greater Washington area. Vint Hill Farms Station (VHFS), a nondescript military installation sprawled across approximately 700 acres, was first established in 1942 when it served as an army base specializing in cryptography, intelligence gathering, and general 'eavesdropping on enemy communications for thousands of miles in all directions' during the Second World War.[130] Unlike numerous other similar bases that were closed down following the war, VHFS remained open and some 2,600 staff – many of whom were skilled intercept operators – carried on working. Their task, according to bestselling author and expert on US intelligence agencies James Bamford, was 'to handle the transition from hot war to cold war'.[131] Throughout four decades, VHFS then played an integral role in American signals intelligence and the development of electronic warfare as part of the nation's preparations against possible nuclear attack. Once the Cold War ended, however, Vint Hill's usefulness had seemingly run its course. As early as 1993, the site was placed on the Base Realignment and Closure (BRAC) list and subsequently underwent significant shrinkage in activities.[132] Before the end of the decade, furthermore, federal policymakers designated VHFS for complete dismantling as part of a nationwide Base Closure strategy. A military installation that was spawned by hot war and then thrived due to cold war suddenly was deemed redundant. As army and state security personnel along with those connected to them packed up and moved away from Vint Hill, besides some fledgling local industry all that was left behind is a closed rural community in which gun shops and churches seem to proliferate. Indeed, for at least one unsuspecting 'outsider' visiting for the first time, the peculiar atmosphere enveloping this township ironically conjured up memories of the satirical 'Kill a Commie for Christ' slogan that dates from the Vietnam War protests of the late-1960s.[133]

Just as Vint Hill effectively collapsed due to the end of the Cold War, recent developments suggest that the town's future prosperity could be tied to revisiting this very theme that produced its golden years. Stephen Fuller, a professor of Public Policy and Regional Development at George Mason University in nearby Fairfax County, Virginia, is a recognized expert in the field of urban and regional economic development. Fuller was commissioned by Virginia to report on how Defense Department expenditure impacts on the state's economy.[134] Among other findings, he has been quoted as predicting that 'a Cold War Museum located in Northern Virginia would draw over 300,000 visitors per year'. Fuller's claim is now highlighted on the website attached to a museum on the Cold War under development – in Vint Hill.[135] And one of the two driving forces behind this initiative is Francis Gary Powers Jr, the son and namesake of a Central Intelligence Agency (CIA) reconnaissance pilot who became a western Cold War icon after being shot down while invading Soviet airspace during the infamous U-2 spy plane incident of 1960.[136] As early as 1996, in fact, Powers Jr and his associate John C. Welch founded the Cold War Museum in order to 'preserve Cold War history and honor Cold War veterans'.[137] For more than a decade, however, it remained little more than a travelling exhibit based around historical artefacts mostly connected to the U-2 incident.[138] In other words, the plurality in the message was rather misleading because the exhibit was really attuned to promoting remembrance of a singular Cold War event and, moreover, honouring an individual Cold War veteran.[139] Anyhow, this mobile Cold War Museum was displayed at more than a dozen locations across the United States (typically at military museums and, owing to the espionage and flying aspects of the U-2 incident, at security/ intelligence centres and aviation museums in particular). The exhibit also travelled to Europe where it appeared in Norway and Berlin.[140] There was a longer-term strategy behind it, for Powers Jr and Welch apparently organized the mobile museum 'as a catalyst for the creation of a permanent Cold War Museum'.[141] By 'permanent' they meant an actual bricks-and-mortar museum, but the same basic challenge that confronted the Victims of Communism Memorial Foundation in nearby Washington also occurred in Northern Virginia: how, and from where, would the private funding required for such a project be collected? As a kind of bridging exercise – again, as in the Washington case – Powers Jr and Welch created a 'virtual museum'. By initially constructing the Cold War Museum as a website, the internet could be utilized to help the wider project build early momentum and raise its profile, which in turn could attract much-needed funding for the ultimate goal of an actual museum. Intriguingly, whereas the bricks-and-mortar version of the museum has been developing in Vint Hill since 2009, originally it was not the preferred location.

In 2002, the *Washington Post* reported that Powers Jr was negotiating with local officials to establish a Cold War museum in the Northern Virginian town of Lorton, Fairfax County, where some two dozen Nike anti-aircraft missiles had protected the nearby Baltimore–Washington metropolitan area during the Cold War.[142] Interviewed on-site in Lorton, Powers Jr beamed at the time: 'This is just a perfect spot for our museum'.[143] He envisioned that the former base's administrative buildings could be utilized to house thematic displays tracing the Cold War chronologically decade-by-decade from the 1940s to the 1980s. To add even more authenticity to the museum, the former missile silos were to be included as part of the permanent exhibition and tour. Plans included archives and a research library so that the museum could function as a specialized Cold War education and research centre, too. Acknowledging that various other groups across the United States were similarly attempting to preserve Cold War artefacts and promote Cold War history among the public, Powers Jr stated that his ambitious project was 'looking to be the umbrella for these groups, to promote education about the Cold War and preservation of these materials'. Claiming that his itemized collection of individual Cold War artefacts already counted 'in the millions', Powers Jr confidently predicted that the museum would open within two years of being granted approval. Preliminary support received from Lorton community leaders through to both branches of the state legislative body the Virginia General Assembly provided some encouraging signs – but there was a catch: neither state nor county coffers could contribute to the project. Like the Washington project, then, whatever transpired in Northern Virginia had to be a privately funded enterprise. And, just as had been the case with the Victims of Communism Memorial Foundation's experience, attracting funding and securing a site proved far more difficult than Powers Jr and his affiliates had anticipated. Nonetheless, over the coming years negotiations with Lorton representatives progressed promisingly enough for Powers Jr to contact the American Institute for History Education (AIHE) in November 2007 to announce that the Cold War Museum (that is, the travelling exhibit and accompanying website) was moving 'closer to a permanent residence' at the former Nike missile base. 'Please help spread the word about the Museum,' concluded the short promotional blurb to the AIHE, imploring history educators that 'together we can make this vision a reality.'[144] In April 2009, however, it was announced that Fairfax County officials and Powers Jr had ceased all negotiations because sufficient funding could not be raised.[145] 'The bottom line is we did not generate enough pledges or money,' admitted Powers Jr., whose concluding remark sounded like he had conceded defeat on the idea: 'I don't know that it would be worth it to reapply.'

By mid-2009, then, it appeared that this Cold War venture in Northern Virginia was destined to follow a similar path to the anti-communist project in Washington: the former would be limited to a touring exhibition and a 'virtual museum' (i.e. website) just as the latter was restricted to a monument and a 'virtual museum', with a bricks-and-mortar museum proving elusive in both cases. (By this time, Powers Jr also had turned his attention to offering his services as an 'expert public speaker regarding the Cold War, U-2 incident and the need to preserve Cold War history', as well as running the 'original spy tour of Washington' from his home near Richmond, Virginia.)[146] For each enterprise, more or less a decade of seeking to establish an actual concrete site had ended in frustration. In December 2009, however, suddenly it was announced that the Cold War Museum 'had found a physical home' after a lease was signed with the Vint Hill Economic Development Authority (EDA) that owns the land of the former VHFS communications centre.[147] By attracting major companies to relocate to the area through the provision of tax revenues, the Vint Hill EDA's vision is to redevelop the former base into a 'vibrant, mixed-use community [that] offers the opportunity to live, work and shop in a beautifully planned and landscaped park'.[148] Although future urban development and commercial investment naturally underpins the Vint Hill EDA's agenda, its chairman Edwin Broaddus acknowledged the land's heritage and historical significance is worth remembering:

> We are pleased to offer The Cold War Museum a home. It is highly appropriate for the museum to locate at Vint Hill, the former Vint Hill Farms Station used during the Cold War, by the National Security Agency, the Central Intelligence Agency, and the US Army to safeguard the United States against a surprise nuclear attack.[149]

Consistent with his earlier claim that a permanent museum could be established within two years of securing a home, in the December 2009 announcement Powers Jr declared that the Cold War Museum in Vint Hill would open its doors to the public in 2011. He also added, perhaps ominously, that the Museum was:

> ... currently looking for volunteers and other interested parties to assist with the work that needs to be done. Most importantly, now that we have a physical location, we are looking for individuals that [sic] would like to make a year-end tax deductible donation that will help facilitate our ongoing efforts to educate future generations and preserve Cold War history.[150]

The Cold War Museum in Vint Hill opened its doors in November 2011. Funding, however, clearly is an ongoing issue that threatens to derail this case of Cold War remembrance before it even gets fully established. In its current underwhelming form the museum is the incarnation of despair. Judging by general enquiries, even though it is only an hour's drive away Vint Hill appears virtually unknown among the Washington public. The town's apparent anonymity outside of Northern Virginia is only one of the reasons why it is hard to envisage this floundering project ever attracting more than a fraction of the hundreds of thousands of visitors that Stephen Fuller apparently predicted would annually flock to a Cold War museum in

Figure 3.33 The Covert Café. Vint Hill, March 2013.

the region. When Donna-Lee Frieze, an Australian colleague temporarily based in the United States, made repeated phone calls and emails attempting to tee-up a guided tour and interview of the museum on our behalf in February 2013, all her efforts went unanswered. When Frieze went ahead with a scheduled trip to Vint Hill the following month anyhow, a most peculiar day unfolded.

The visit started off promisingly enough, with the museum well sign-posted. A large roadside sign indicates that Vint Hill's Cold War Museum is situated among the eclectic mix of a music school, a shoe repair factory, a winery, and a café as well as a Christian school (the Providence Christian Academy) and a Christian worship centre (the Hope Christian Fellowship). It represents an odd assortment, of course, but the latter two reinforce the feeling that, although Northern Virginia may fall just outside the Bible Belt, Christianity is the cornerstone of the Vint Hill community. Implicitly, then, the museum's location evokes the idea that in this part of the world at least the Cold War can be remembered – nay, celebrated – as a battle in which godfearing Americans triumphed over godless Soviets. Down the road two old signs are erected on a post in front of a building. The top one is an old West German federal border police (*Bundesgrenzschutz*) warning sign to stop before overstepping the East German border (*Halt! Zonengrenze*). Below it, an old US Army sign, which is a scaled down replication of the one made most famous at Checkpoint Charlie in Berlin, cautions oncoming traffic in

English, Russian, French, and German: 'You are leaving the American sector'. The building directly behind the signs is not the actual museum but rather a shop with the catchy but kitschy name The Covert Café. It is not clear whether any irony is intended in the café's name, but with a silhouette of an undercover spy figure appearing inside the 'o' in Covert on the signage it appears that the café is attached to the museum somehow. When Frieze entered the café to enquire about Vint Hill in general and the Cold War Museum in particular, the woman serving behind the counter initially claimed that she knew nothing about it. Then, casting a suspicious gaze over this outsider, the shopkeeper asked Frieze where she was from. Not convinced by the answer, she retorted: 'You don't sound Australian.' When asked once more about the museum's location, the woman said abruptly 'It's not open' before retreating to the back of the shop. Bemused but undeterred, Frieze wandered outside and found the museum located directly behind the café. Although it was the middle of the day, it was indeed closed. There is a collection of further kitschy Cold War signage scattered around the building, and a notice on the door states that the museum is open by appointment only. (Frieze's additional messages also went unanswered.) Peering through a window, a couple of old space uniforms were on display in a dusty environment that appears as though it does not see much traffic.

Figure 3.34 The Cold War Museum, located in a barn and open by appointment only. Vint Hill, March 2013.

From a religious perspective, Vint Hill may not be the most appropriate place to cite the old proverb: 'If the mountain will not come to Muhammad then Muhammad must go to the mountain'. Regarding the Cold War Museum, however, perhaps it offers a most valuable lesson. That is, establishing a permanent home in a small, relatively unknown community off the beaten track evidently has not worked anywhere near as successfully as anticipated. If Powers Jr wishes to continue promoting Cold War remembrance and education – essentially through the prism of his father's U-2 incident – then maybe he is better off reverting back to a travelling exhibit (complemented by a 'virtual museum' on the internet). For, as it stands at the time of writing, despite best intentions and dedication to the cause stretching back more or less two decades, the Victims of Communism Memorial in Washington and the Cold War Museum in Vint Hill remain little more than ghost institutions whose existence mostly belongs to websites. A very different story has been unfolding on the other side of the United States, where a Cold War museum in California is moving from strength to strength.

Remembering Cold War 'otherness' in California: the Wende Museum

There scarcely could be a greater contrast between, on the one hand, the two cases from Washington and Northern Virginia covered above, and, on the other hand, the history behind a Cold War museum based in Culver City, California. For the two enterprises based over near the Atlantic, very deliberate approaches underpinned by long-term planning were the order of the day. Developing a virtual (online) presence was viewed as a way to raise profile and build momentum towards the ultimate goal of a permanent bricks-and-mortar museum. The Washington case, moreover, has even enjoyed congressional backing. Both the Victims of Communism Memorial Foundation based in the nation's capital and Francis Gary Powers Jr along with his affiliates now based around Vint Hill have stayed the course over more or less two decades and have produced (limited) material outcomes to complement their respective 'virtual museums'. Ultimately, though, any firm but fair judgement probably would determine that, to this point in time at least, both of these efforts to remember the Cold War have been failures. An actual museum remains the stated goal in Washington, but even if one ever materializes it surely will not resemble anything like the US$ 100 million pipedream originally conceived. And it is hard to imagine Vint Hill ever becoming a mecca for Cold War buffs, history teachers looking for interesting and informative excursions, or anyone else for that matter. Over on the Pacific coast, meanwhile, the Wende Museum and Archive of the Cold War (typically shortened to the Wende Museum) recently celebrated a most successful first decade in operation by securing a move to a much larger and more prominent site.[151] Intriguingly, in two respects this Cold

War museum's establishment was drenched in serendipity. First, the collection of artefacts around which it initially was based largely came about through happenstance and without any inkling that a museum would follow. Second, the Wende Museum has benefited enormously from its founder and director being in the fortuitous position of having ongoing access to an invitation-only source of ostensibly endless funding. The somewhat incidental nature behind the museum's creation coupled with its subsequent ability to tap a rich vein of funding are hallmarks that help to set apart this Californian success story from the floundering Washington and Northern Virginian cases previously examined.[152]

During the mid-1990s, Justinian Jampol, then a twenty-something Californian native with a mixture of Swiss-German, Polish, and Jewish ancestry who was based at Oxford for postgraduate studies, seized the historical moment unfolding around him. Jampol became an amateur – but increasingly avid and astute – collector of artefacts relating to everyday life under eastern European communism during the Cold War era. Initially, Jampol cut his teeth on the flea markets of Berlin where not only 'Ossis' (East Germans) but also many others from the former eastern bloc sought to make money while jettisoning unwanted personal belongings dating from the communist past in the pursuit of what they perceived to be superior, more appealing mass-consumer products of capitalism. Whereas these sellers from the former communist world immersed themselves in the hitherto unobtainable material culture that emblematized the 'otherness' of the West, conversely the American Jampol became obsessed with the 'otherness' represented by everyday objects from life under communism. As his collection kept expanding, established museums rejected overtures to display any of the objects. Jampol, however, had no pre-conceived ideas of creating his own museum and so the artefacts simply piled up in storage without any concrete plans in place for them ever to see the light of day. Essentially, Jampol's motivation was to purchase as many objects as possible before the material culture of communism was lost to history. As he reflected later, time was of the essence because all manner of materials were disappearing rapidly: 'Historical landmarks were being torn down, statues vandalized, consumer products discarded, film and photographs left to deteriorate and archives actively destroyed.'[153] Most of the pieces Jampol purchased early on related to the former German Democratic Republic (*Deutsche Demokratische Republik*, DDR), but support from German institutions was not forthcoming. (Even several years after Jampol had successfully established the museum in California, in fact, reactions to his mission remained rather dismissive – bordering on contemptuous – among some quarters in Germany similarly engaged in documenting the DDR era.)[154] Jampol shipped his collection back home to the Golden State where, even though his project was yet to be defined, his compiling of Cold War artefacts met with widespread interest among his fellow Californians.

Discussions with Peter Baldwin, an acclaimed professor of Modern European History and Jampol's erstwhile mentor during his undergraduate years at UCLA, were particularly influential for both short- and longer-term developments. Most immediately, reconnecting with Baldwin impacted on Jampol's decision to establish a Cold War museum in the County of Los Angeles. As evidenced by the Washington and Northern Virginian stories, however, without considerable funding such ventures simply do not eventuate. To accumulate such an impressive collection of Cold War artefacts emanating from Eastern Europe, Jampol already had invested a small fortune (reported to be around US$ 300,000) courtesy of a six-figure inheritance from his grandfather. But ongoing costs involved in the running of such a museum are even more consequential, of course, and so identifying suitable funding sources was the paramount concern in order for the project to materialize. And this is where Baldwin's influence again proved crucial. Along with his wife Lisbet Rausing, a notable historian of science and philanthropic heiress of the multi-billion-dollar Tetra Pak food packaging company, Baldwin is a co-founder of the grant-making fund Arcadia.[155] Established in 2001, the London-based fund's 'key mission is to protect endangered culture and nature'. To this end, as of January 2013 Arcadia had awarded in excess of US$ 234 million on projects relating to *inter alia* 'near extinct languages, rare historical archives and museum quality artefacts, and the protection of ecosystems and environments threatened with extinction'.[156] Besides being co-founders, Rausing and Baldwin also form Arcadia's two-person Donor Board. Baldwin, furthermore, serves as chair of not only the Donor Board but also the fund's Advisory Board. The decision-making over future funding occurs when the Donor Board and the Advisory Board meet annually. And applications for funding are by invitation only. In summary, then, Baldwin may not quite enjoy a monopoly over the distribution of Arcadia's funds but the likelihood of success must be high whenever he personally invites someone to apply. Whereas the entrepreneurial Jampol has secured competitive funding from a variety of avenues, the ongoing financial support from Arcadia has proven instrumental in enabling the Wende Museum to thrive since it opened its doors in 2002.[157] Initial funding helped the project to get off the ground, followed by a further US$ 991,500 grant from Arcadia to expand the collection, fund extra archivist help to maintain it, acquire additional storage space, and create a central database.[158] In 2004, Arcadia bestowed the Wende Museum with yet another grant of US$ 2.9 million. A fourth grant, of US$ 5 million spread over five years (2012–16), will cover running costs and the acquisition of new artefacts from all former Warsaw Pact nations. Arcadia summarizes this grant as its continuing support for the Wende Museum's 'bid to create the world's best collection of Cold War artefacts'.[159]

Aided by close to US$ 10 million in Arcadia grants and boasting in excess of 100,000 individual items, the Wende Museum is perhaps the most impressive collection of Cold War artefacts on public display anywhere in the world. Yet it is not a Cold War museum in the broadest sense of the term in the same way that, say, the National Cold War Exhibition at the RAF Museum in Cosford can lay claim (for details on the Cosford exhibit, see Chapter 4).[160] Seen in this light, Jampol's *sui generis* creation is best described not so much as a Cold War museum but rather as a museum of Cold War material culture. Its exclusively eastern-centric focus, furthermore, means that it is even more accurately characterized as a museum of communist bloc material culture dating from the Cold War era. It cannot possibly recapture what it was like for East Germans and other eastern Europeans to live under communism. But creating some kind of Rankean reproduction of 'how life essentially was behind the Iron Curtain' never has been Jampol's intention. Rather, he is more interested in preserving politico-cultural artefacts and documentary materials to aid scholarly investigation, while also gathering more personal objects and testimonies as a way of capturing an essence of 'the lived experience beneath the ideological battles and geopolitical struggles of the Cold War'.[161] The Wende Museum, which opens its collection to researchers, educators, students, lifelong learners, artists, journalists, and the general public, is a self-styled 'hybrid organization' that concurrently acts as 'an archive of material culture' while operating as an educational institution 'fusing interdisciplinary scholarship with its programs'. The project's far-reaching dual aims are succinctly encapsulated in its motto: 'Preserving the Past; Informing the Present'. A mission to document Eastern Europe and the Soviet Union during the Cold War drives the entire enterprise – encompassing the archives, permanent and temporary exhibitions, and educational programmes – in order to 'inform and inspire a broad understanding of the period and its enduring legacy'. Accordingly, the museum lends itself to the cultivation of both shared and common memories of the Cold War, and in particular its rich collection fixates on what Germans refer to as *Alltagsgeschichte* or the history of everyday life.[162] The fascination with communist-related artefacts is most intriguing, furthermore, because it means that the Wende Museum inadvertently reflects a Cold War mindset as the project is premised on the notion of the 'other'. In other words, it is the product of an American's obsession with documenting how communists lived during the Cold War through the prism of everyday items such as food, work, furniture, clothing, literature and so on.

The museum's name was purposefully chosen to reflect the past, present, and future. The *Wende* is the German term used to describe the 'turn' of events in 1989 that culminated in the fall of the Berlin Wall and collapse of eastern European communism. On the one hand, then, naming the museum after the *Wende* betrays the project's origins and Jampol's initial fascination with artefacts from the former DDR. On the other hand, this 'turning point' in contemporary history ushered in a new European – indeed, world – order and so its profound socio-political implications continue to be felt. For this reason, according to Jampol, the term *Wende* is 'an ideal name for a museum devoted to the Cold War-era and its present and future ramifications'.[163] Notwithstanding the museum's German-inspired name or the fact that DDR-related objects still dominate the museum's collection, over the past decade a concerted effort has been made to gather a more rounded selection of items from across the entire former Warsaw Pact region. Jampol used to tour Eastern Europe personally in the hunt for material culture ranging from expensive, rare objects purchased from governments through to trivial everyday items salvaged from rubbish piles. He now employs a team of scouts to locate potential artefacts on his behalf. Their acquisition of new pieces outpaces the museum's capacity to receive and catalogue them to such an extent that a climate-controlled intermediary storage facility had to be obtained in Berlin.

Apparently one of the most frequently asked questions Jampol hears is why such a museum, which focuses on eastern European experiences of

Figure 3.35 Segment of the Berlin Wall outside the Wende Museum. Culver City, March 2013.

the Cold War era, is located in California. The blunt answer may be that, as a native Angeleno, Jampol simply chose his hometown area. He nonetheless mounts a persuasive argument that the distance acts as a topographical virtue rather than a vice:

> Examining the history of Eastern Europe and the Soviet Union can be fraught with political and personal bias, and the complex, often contradictory stories that underlie the Museum's artifacts may provoke uncomfortable questions. The Museum's location in Los Angeles provides independence and critical distance from current political debates in Europe, and also facilitates the questioning of preconceived ideas about our past and present. Moreover, the Museum's physical remoteness from Central and Eastern Europe has enabled it to attract significant artifacts and collections that might otherwise have been destroyed as a result of emotional and political reactions.[164]

The Wende Museum is located in a nondescript business estate in Culver City, a smallish town in the County of Los Angeles best known for its longstanding connection to the film industry. Its premises are divided between a small museum space and a larger archival space. The former comprises three small display rooms, another room used for temporary exhibits, plus a small auditorium upstairs (fitted out with authentic East German seating). The latter, which is included as part of guided tours, is significantly larger and serves as a kind of storage area or warehouse. (Indeed, Jampol estimates that only 2 per cent of the collection can be displayed at any one time.)[165] Walls in the display rooms are adorned by communist-era paintings acquired from across Eastern Europe. A feature wall has dozens of framed commemorative plates inscribed in various languages including German, Russian, Czech, Romanian, Polish, and Bulgarian. Busts of Lenin and other communist figures abound. In recent years, Hungary has emerged as a particularly fruitful source of items. Over seventy artworks found in the basement of former secret state police headquarters, for instance, were purchased from the Hungarian government. Whereas most of these works will remain in storage due to space restrictions, one Hungarian piece already displayed in the museum is particularly eye-catching. The Wende Museum has purchased a small bronze model that dates from 1969 when sculptor István Kiss fashioned it in preparation for his mammoth Republic of Councils Monument (a.k.a. the 'cloakroom attendant'), which, as discussed earlier in this chapter, now can be found on the outskirts of Budapest at Memento Park.[166]

Whereas most museums and galleries keep their archives hidden away from the public, the opposite is the case with the Wende Museum where the archival space adjacent to the exhibition area is a feature of guided tours. Perhaps this decision was born out of necessity, owing to the limited display space. It is an inspired decision in any case, because it creates seamlessness

Figure 3.36 István Kiss' model for his Republic of Councils Monument, on display in the Wende Museum, Culver City. (Courtesy of Coleman-Rayner/Glen McCurtayne)

between the narrative told through the limited number of feature items showcased in the exhibits and the deeper impression made by the sheer volume of artefacts stockpiled out the back. Indeed, funders have requested that one-third of their financial support is devoted to new acquisitions and so on any given day truckloads of artefacts arrive and pour into the warehouse part of the museum. There are rows of literally tens of thousands of print materials, including some 8,000 books along with even more journals, brochures, programmes, magazines, restaurant menus, propaganda posters, and confidential files that avoided shredding. Shelving is stacked high with seemingly endless banners, pennants, fabric swatches, and over 5,000 flags. Hundreds of uniforms hang next to further shelves containing boxes of countless lapel pins, around 2,000 commemorative plates, and dozens of busts and sculptures periodically rotated through the display spaces. Hundreds of steel canisters are piled up in which film reels sit, still waiting to be catalogued. Items in lesser volume range from examples of distinctive communist bloc furniture, to official gold-rimmed fine china dinner sets from the government of the former DDR, through to listening devices used by secret police. Indeed, a tour through the archival space of the Wende Museum confronts visitors with a case of Cold War remembrance overload. And beyond all of this material culture, arguably the most impressive aspect of the museum's collection is its eleven full slabs of the Berlin Wall – comprising the largest authentic section anywhere in the world outside of the city in question (discussed further below).

Figure 3.37 Shelves of publications and documents in the Wende Museum's storage area, underneath a large authentic sign of the state emblem of the former DDR. Culver City, March 2013.

When interviewed in early 2013, Jampol stressed that, a little over a decade since its creation, the museum continues to be an intellectual pursuit and not 'just' a hobby. If there is any sense of satisfaction in what has been accomplished to date, then it is overshadowed by his infectious enthusiasm and energy toward what can be achieved in the future. Although Jampol began collecting military materials and he has a personal interest in political iconography (his PhD dissertation is entitled 'Swords, Doves, and Flags: Appropriation of Political Symbols in the GDR, 1949–89'), there is an insistence on the museum remaining focused on how and what people remember rather than the remembering that is manufactured *through* political symbolism. Evidently it is an approach that strikes a chord with the general public, with the museum's attendance figures steadily increasing. It is only open to the public on Fridays, but organized tours can be arranged on other

Figure 3.38 Shelves of film reels waiting to be catalogued in the Wende Museum's storage area. Culver City, 2013. (Courtesy of The Wende Museum and Archive of the Cold War)

days. School groups in particular are visiting in increased numbers. The educational programmes are considered an essential element of the museum's overall mission. Interestingly, Jampol and his staff do not view themselves and their programmes as academic but definitely intellectual in nature. The Wende Museum also actively pursues special visits by political figures, council representatives, and diplomats based in the local area. Recently it has hosted visitors from Romanian, German, and British consulates, too. When asked whether any politicians have sought to (mis)appropriate the museum as part of the politics of the past, staff members reacted in a surprised manner and replied that they do not believe this has ever occurred.

Collaboration is projected to become an increasingly important part of the Wende Museum's schema for remembering the Cold War. Educational programmes are run in conjunction with art institutions and universities. Donna Stein, the museum's associate director, and Cristina Cuevas-Wolf, the manager of collection development, are quick to stress that there is no interest in collaborating with right-wing institutions, but also point out that successful exhibitions have been conducted at the Ronald Reagan Presidential Foundation and Library, located nearby at Simi Valley in the Greater Los Angeles Area. When questioned about the Victims of Communism Memorial Foundation in Washington and the Cold War Museum in Vint Hill, Stein and Cuevas-Wolf stated that they are aware of the former (noting that it only has a virtual existence) but had never even heard of the latter venture. Joint exhibitions have been conducted with the International Spy Museum in Washington. A three-day scholarly conference on everyday German material culture during the Cold War was co-sponsored with the German Historical Institute also located in the nation's capital. And in 2009–10, the Wende Museum sent an exhibition entitled 'Art and the Cold War: German Positions 1949–98' first to the *Germanisches Nationalmuseum* in Nuremberg followed by the German Historical Museum (*Deutsches Historisches Museum*, DHM) in Berlin. The few examples cited here provide evidence that the Wende Museum's diverse collaborative endeavours stretch far and wide. From a more local perspective, ongoing linkages with the Los Angeles County Museum of Art (LACMA) have proved especially fruitful for the Wende Museum's deliberate fusion of art and history. One such project with LACMA was a 2009 exhibition entitled 'Art of Two Germanys/Cold War Cultures'.

Collaborative projects enable the Wende Museum to expand its role in remembering the Cold War, but much of its impetus still comes from 'in-house' activities including seminars, forums, film screenings, book launches, and other special events conducted within its own confined space. A month-long multi-faceted media and public art initiative, which culminated in a street exhibition staged in Central Los Angeles to mark the twentieth anniversary of the fall of the Berlin Wall in 2009, is both the museum's most spectacular effort and its proudest accomplishment to date. Simply entitled 'The Wall Project', it revolved around the temporary construction of two walls in Wilshire Boulevard. Stretching almost 40-feet long, the 'Wall Along Wilshire' consisted of ten original segments of the Berlin Wall transported

Figure 3.39 Busts in the Wende Museum's storage area. Culver City, 2013. (Courtesy of Coleman-Rayner/Glen McCurtayne)

Figures 3.40 and 3.41 Surveillance equipment from communist secret services, and Lenin on display in the Wende Museum, Culver City, 2013. (Courtesy of Coleman-Rayner/Glen McCurtayne, and The Wende Museum and Archive of the Cold War)

to California especially for this installation. One wall segment already had been painted by the well-known local contemporary street artist Bimer before it left Berlin, but the others were painted once relocated to Los Angeles. Local artists – some renowned, others emerging – were commissioned for most of the remaining segments. The French-born muralist Thierry Noir, who, as a longtime resident of (West) Berlin had been one of the first artists to decorate the Wall during the early-1980s, was commissioned to paint the final segment (which now greets visitors to the museum; see Figure 3.35). As an extension of 'The Wall Project', the Wende Museum arranged for Noir to stay in Los Angeles for a month courtesy of an artist residency programme funded by the city's Department of Cultural Affairs. At the same time, a 60-feet long faux wall was constructed off-site and the Wende Museum invited an 'eclectic group' of professional artists, graphic designers, illustrators, fresco painters, graffiti artists, and students to paint it before its installation as the so-called 'Wall Across Wilshire.' Temporarily dissecting the boulevard on the evening of 8 November 2009, this wall came crashing down in celebration of the twentieth anniversary of the iconic scenes witnessed in Berlin during the *Wende*. An estimated crowd of 1,000 onlookers gathered in Wilshire Boulevard to watch this spectacle, which attracted international media interest. This kind of event represents what Jampol envisages for the museum's future: using the past to reflect on the

Figure 3.42 The longest stretch of the Berlin Wall outside Germany, on display in California. (Courtesy of The Wende Museum and Archive of the Cold War)

present, engaging with people on the street, fusing together art, performance, and visual expression as a way of exploring history in a non-didactic way.

Growing out of somewhat adventitious origins, over the past decade the Wende Museum has become an unqualified success story. In 2014, it will move away from its cramped premises in the hidden business park to a much larger site (almost an acre) with a busy street front in Culver City. The extra space not only will enable the museum to showcase far more of its collection, but also a special sculpture garden has been designed in which all the segments of the Berlin Wall can be on permanent display. The new location belongs to the Culver City Council, which in 2012 unanimously voted to lease the property to the Wende Museum for 75 years at the nominal rate of US\$ 1 per annum. Jampol may be long gone before this lease expires, but the city council has given a resounding vote of confidence that his ever-expanding collection of artefacts will continue to play a prominent role in fostering shared and common memories of the Cold War in California for generations to come.

Notes

1 See VilNews, 'Napoleon Named Vilnius "Jerusalem of the North"', *VilNews: The Voice of International Lithuania*, 9 January 2011, http://vilnews.com/2011-01-napoleon-named-vilnius-'jerusalem-of-the-north' (Last accessed January 2013).

2 Theodore R. Weeks, 'Remembering and Forgetting: Creating a Soviet Lithuanian Capital, Vilnius 1944–49', *Journal of Baltic Studies*, vol. 39, no. 4 (2008). Živilė Mikailienė, 'Soviet Vilnius: Ideology and the Formation of Identity,' *Lithuanian Historical Studies*, vol. 15 (2010).

3 For a verbatim transcript, see 'Convention on the Prevention and Punishment of the Crime of Genocide,' *United Nations*, 9 December 1948, www.un.org/millennium/law/iv-1.htm (Last accessed December 2012). For an excellent introductory summary and a note in the procedural history from the world's leading legal scholar on genocide, see William A. Schabas, 'Convention on the Prevention and Punishment of the Crime of Genocide: Introduction, Procedural History, Documents, and Status', *United Nations: Audiovisual Library of International Law*, http://untreaty.un.org/cod/avl/ha/cppcg/cppcg.html (Last accessed December 2012).

4 Genocide and Resistance Research Centre of Lithuania, *The Museum of Genocide Victims: A Guide to the Exhibitions* (Vilnius), pp. 17–19. Analysis also based on museum visit by David Lowe in November 2012.

5 Ibid. pp. 32–49.

6 Ibid. pp. 58–66.

7 'The Memorial Complex of the Tuskulėnai Peace Park', *Genocide and Resistance Research Centre of Lithuania*, www.genocid.lt/tuskulenai/en/ (Last accessed March 2013).

8 Genocide and Resistance Research Centre of Lithuania, *The Secrets of Tuskulėnai Manor (Guide Pamphlet)* (Vilnius). Also based on David Lowe's visit to the Peace Park in November 2012.

9 Quotation taken from the plaque on the Green Bridge, Vilnius.

10 Torbakov, 'History, Memory and National Identity', p. 211.

11 'Census 2011 (Data from Population and Housing)', *Statistics Lithuania: Official Statistics Portal*, 2011, http://osp.stat.gov.lt/en/2011-m.-surasymas (Last accessed December 2012).

12 'An Outline of the History of the Genocide and Resistance Research Centre of Lithuania', *Genocide and Resistance Research Centre of Lithuania*, www.genocid.lt/centras/en/ (Last accessed December 2012).

13 Violeta Davoliūtė, 'The Prague Declaration of 2008 and its Repercussions in Lithuania: Historical Justice and Reconciliation', *Lituanus: Lithuanian Quarterly Journal of Arts and Sciences*, vol. 57, no. 3 (2011).

14 As reported by Liudas Dapkus, 'Lithuanian Archive Releases KGB Collaborator Names', *The Seattle Times*, 22 February 2012, http://seattletimes.com/html/nation world/2017567459_apeulithuaniakgb.html (Last accessed January 2013).

15 Timothy Snyder, *Bloodlands: Europe between Hitler and Stalin* (New York: Basic Books, 2010).

16 Prague Information Service, 'About Prague', *PragueWelcome: Prague's Official Tourist Portal*, www.praguewelcome.cz/en/visit/ (Last accessed January 2013).

17 The memorial also is dedicated to Jan Zajíc, another Czech student who self-immolated in political protest in Wenceslas Square a month after Palach.

18 For details, see Petr Blažek, 'Memorial Places', *Jan Palach: Charles University Multimedia Project*, www.janpalach.cz/en/default/mista-pameti (Last accessed January 2013).

19 The television mini-series 'Burning Bush' by the Polish director Agnieszka Holland, which is based around Palach and 1968, premiered in 2013. See Polskie Radio, 'Agnieszka Holland's Czech "Human Torch" Movie to Premiere in Prague', *Polskie Radio*, 22 January 2013, www.thenews.pl/1/11/Artykul/124864, Agnieszka-Hollands-Czech-human-torch-movie-to-premiere-in-Prague (Last accessed January 2013). Also of note is the divisive Memorial to the Victims of Communism, erected in the Lesser Town district of Prague in 2002. See Alena Škodová, 'Memorial to the Victims of Communism Unveiled in Prague', *Radio Praha*, 23 May 2002, www.radio.cz/en/section/curraffrs/memorial-to-the-victims-of-communism-unveiled-in-prague (Last accessed October 2012). A year later, this memorial was damaged by explosives. See Rob Cameron, 'Prague Monument to Communist Victims Damaged in Explosion', *Radio Praha*, 11 November 2003, www.radio.cz/en/section/curraffrs/prague-monument-to-communist-victims-damaged-in-explosion (Last accessed October 2012).

20 Timothy Garton Ash, 'Václav Havel: Director of a Play that changed History', *The Guardian*, 19 December 2011, www.guardian.co.uk/commentisfree/2011/dec/18/vaclav-havel-changed-history1 (Last accessed October 2012).

21 Havel served as the ninth and last president of Czechoslovakia (in office from 29 December 1989 to 20 July 1992), and the inaugural president of the Czech Republic (in office from 2 February 1993 to 2 February 2003).

22 What unfolded was not completely bloodless. Indeed, according to Radio Prague many Czechs do not like the term 'Velvet Revolution' and instead prefer to call what happened the 'November Events' (*listopadové události*) or even just 'November' (*listopad*) in shortened form. See Radio Prague, 'The "Velvet Revolution"', *Radio Prague's 'History Online' Virtual Exhibit*, http://archiv.radio.cz/history/history15.html (Last accessed October 2012).

23 The Organising Bureau of European School Student Unions (OBESSU) and the European Students' Union (ESU), '17 November: International Day of Students', *17 NOV: International Day of Students*, http://17thofnovember-internationaldayofstudents.webstarts.com (Last accessed October 2012).

24 The tradition remains, although some nations/universities have moved toward adopting the date as a non-political occasion to celebrate the multiculturalism of their student bodies.

25 David Vaughan, 'The Revolution Begins', *Radio Praha*, 11 August 2012, www.radio.cz/en/section/archives/the-revolution-begins-1 (Last accessed October 2012).

26 Quoted in ibid.

154   *Cities and sites*

27 Ibid.
28 Jan Richter, 'Národni třída: Prominent Prague Boulevard that has Witnessed History', *Radio Praha*, 17 November 2010, www.radio.cz/en/section/special/narodni-trida-prominent-prague-boulevard-that-has-witnessed-history (Last accessed October 2012).
29 The Institute for the Study of Totalitarian Regimes, 'Personnel File of Lt. Ludvík Zifčák: Career of the "Dead Student"', *The Institute for the Study of Totalitarian Regimes (Ústav pro studium totalitních režimů)*, www.ustrcr.cz/en/personnel-file-ludvik-zifcak (Last accessed October 2012).
30 The building is now known as the Kaňkův House after its architect F.M. Kaňkovi.
31 Roman Týc, 'Galerie', *romantyc*, http://romantyc.info/galerie/ (Last accessed February 2013). For English-language press coverage, see presseurop, 'Giving the Velvet Revolution the Finger', *presseurop*, 23 November 2009, www.presseurop.eu/en/content/news-brief/142411-giving-velvet-revolution-finger (Last accessed February 2013). For the original Czech article (with images), see Radek Wohlmuth, 'Památník 17. listopadu na Národní třídě hajluje a fuckuje', *Týden*, 22 November 2009, www.tyden.cz/rubriky/kultura/vytvarne-umeni/pamatnik-17-listopadu-na-narodni-tride-hajluje-a-fuckuje_149002.html (Last accessed February 2013).
32 presseurop, 'Giving the Velvet Revolution the Finger'. And Wohlmuth, 'Památník'.
33 Reuters, 'Czechs Protest against Austerity Plans', *Reuters*, 17 November 2011, www.reuters.com/article/2011/11/17/czech-protests-idUSL5E7MH3A620111117 (Last accessed February 2013).
34 Jana Kajnarová quoted in Sarah Karacs, 'The Velvet Revolution: Czech Students Look Back at What Their Forebears Started', *Spiegel Online International*, 20 November 2009, www.spiegel.de/international/spiegel/the-velvet-revolution-czech-students-look-back-at-what-their-forebears-started-a-661999.html (Last accessed January 2013).
35 The Euro Information Website, 'Slovenská republika: 2 Euro Commemorative Design 2009', *The Euro Information Website*, www.ibiblio.org/theeuro/InformationWebsite.htm?http://www.ibiblio.org/theeuro/forum/viewtopic.php?f=81&t=535&p = 1977 (Last accessed November 2012).
36 Jiří David, *Klíčová socha*, www.klicovasocha.cz (Last accessed April 2013).
37 See ibid. Also Martin Kacvinský, 'Brno – Key Sculpture – Jiri David (CZ), 2010', *360 Cities*, www.360cities.net/image/key-sculpture-revoluce#-12.65,0.00,110.0 (Last accessed April 2013).
38 See Vodafone, 'Press Release: People responded to Vodafone's Appeal by collecting over 85 Thousand Keys', *Vodafone: Czech Republic*, December 2009, www.vodafone.cz/en/about-vodafone/press-releases/message-detail/people-responded-to-vodafones-appeal-by-1/ (Last accessed April 2013). And Vodafone, 'Press Release: The Public Unveiling of Jiří David's Key Sculpture will take place on the 9th of March at 11AM on Franz Kafka Square (náměstí Franze Kafky) in Prague', *Vodafone: Czech Republic*, March 2010, http://www.vodafone.cz/en/about-vodafone/press-releases/message-detail/the-public-unveiling-of-jiri-davids-key-1/ (Last accessed April 2013).
39 Vodafone, 'Press Release: The Public Unveiling of Jiří David's Key Sculpture'.
40 Quoted in 'About the Museum', *Museum of Communism*, www.muzeumkomunismu.cz/en/about-museum (Last accessed November 2012).
41 Quoted in Kate Connolly, 'Red Revival', *The Guardian*, 7 March 2002, www.guardian.co.uk/world/2002/mar/06/worlddispatch.education (Last accessed November 2012). The following analysis is based on Tony Joel's visit to the museum in November 2011.

42 Winston S. Churchill, 'The Sinews of Peace', *The Churchill Centre and Museum at the Churchill War Rooms*, London, 5 March 1946, www.winstonchurchill.org/learn/biography/in-opposition/qiron-curtainq-fulton-missouri-1946/120-the-sinews-of-peace (Last accessed September 2012).

43 For a succinct overview of the uprising, see Tony Judt, *Postwar: A History of Europe since 1945* (London: Vintage, 2010), pp. 314–23. For a detailed study of its longer-term ramifications, see Rudolf Tökés, *Hungary's Negotiated Revolution: Economic Reform, Social Change and Political Succession, 1957–1990* (Cambridge: Cambridge University Press, 1996).

44 István Zalatnay, 'Meditation on the 1956 Monument in Budapest', *Hungarian Review*, 18 November 2011, www.hungarianreview.com/article/meditation_on_the_monument (Last accessed February 2013). See also David Rennie, 'Hungarians See Red over 1956 Monument', *The Telegraph*, 29 July 2006, www.telegraph.co.uk/news/1525120/Hungarians-see-red-over-1956-monument.html (Last accessed April 2013).

45 For Göncz, see the recent study by Dae Soon Kim, *The Transition to Democracy in Hungary: Árpád Göncz and the Post-Communist Hungarian Presidency* (London: Routledge, 2013). For an online biography of Lugossy, see Galerie Gerhard, 'Mária Lugossy: Biography', *Galerie Gerhard: Bad Berleburg*, www.galerie-gerhard.com/pdf/gg-pdf-lugossy-data-en.pdf (Last accessed December 2012).

46 Up to 1989, in Hungary 'Liberation Day' on 4 April – the day the Red Army had seized control of Budapest – was celebrated as the national remembrance day. The following account of Cold War sites of memory in Budapest is largely based on field research conducted by Tony Joel in November 2011.

47 It states: '25 OCTOBER 1956. IN MEMORY OF THE VICTIMS OF THE MURDEROUS ÁVH' ('*1956 OKTOBER 25. A GYILKOS ÁVH SORTÜZ ÁLDOZATAINAK EMLÉKÉRE*').

48 It is unknown how long this makeshift sign had been erected, but when viewed by Tony Joel in November 2011 it looked quite weathered.

49 According to a UN report dating from the year after the uprising, it was estimated that approximately 2,500–3,000 revolutionaries died across Hungary, of whom some 1,800–2,000 were killed in Budapest. The report estimated a further 13,000 wounded (11,500 in Budapest) received treatment. See 'United Nations Report of the Special Committee on the Problem of Hungary: General Assembly, Official Records, Eleventh Session, Supplement No. 18 (A/3592)', *Magyar Elektronikus Könyvtár (MEK)*, 1957, http://mek.oszk.hu/01200/01274/01274.pdf (Last accessed November 2012), fn. 8, p. 68.

50 It states: '*Az 1956. október 25-i véres csütörtök áldozataira emlékezve, a túlélők.*'

51 Boris Chaliapin, 'Man of the Year: Hungarian Freedom Fighter', *Time* 1957. Front cover image, accessible online at www.time.com/time/magazine/0,9263,7601570 107,00.html (Last accessed December 2012).

52 For a contemporary report, see Henry Kamm, 'Hungarian Who Led '56 Revolt is Buried as a Hero', *The New York Times*, 17 June 1989, www.nytimes.com/1989/06/17/world/hungarian-who-led-56-revolt-is-buried-as-a-hero.html (Last accessed December 2012). See also Judt, *Postwar*, p. 323.

53 UNESCO World Heritage Committee, '11COM VII.A Inscription: Budapest, the Banks of the Danube with the District of Buda Castle (Hungary)', *UNESCO*, http://whc.unesco.org/en/decisions/3728 (Last accessed October 2012).

54 UNESCO, 'Budapest, including the Banks of the Danube, the Buda Castle Quarter and Andrássy Avenue', *UNESCO World Heritage List*, http://whc.unesco.org/en/list/400/ (Last accessed October 2012).

55 Mária Schmidt, ed., *Terror Háza/House of Terror Museum: Catalogue* (Budapest: Public Endowment for Research in Central and East-European History and Society, 2008). p. 5.

56 Ibid.
57 Ibid. p. 21.
58 Ibid. p. 16.
59 Ibid. p. 61.
60 Ibid. p. 67.
61 During a visit in November 2011, staff member Dóra Szkuklik said that, whereas the park initially attracted more Hungarians than foreigners, this trend seems to have reversed over the past decade. Even so, apparently it always has and continues to attract a mixture of visitors.
62 Although apparently born in 1878, once in power Stalin inexplicably changed his birth year to 1879.
63 Erika J. Füstös and Helen Kovács, *In the Shadow of Stalin's Boots: Visitors' Guide to Memento Park* (Budapest: Private Planet Books, 2010). Ákos Réthly, *The Hungarian Revolution, 1956* (Budapest: Private Planet Books, 2006). See also Reuben Fowkes, 'Public Sculpture and Hungarian Revolution of 1956', *Ungarn 1956 – Geschichte und Erinnerung*, www.ungarn1956.de/site/40208667/default.aspx (Last accessed September 2012).
64 Füstös and Kovács, *In the Shadow*, p. 6.
65 Péter László's 1951 limestone Soviet Heroes' Memorial, for instance, features in Hungarian and Russian the inscription: 'In eternal praise of the freedom and independence of the Soviet Union, and in memory of the heroes who fell in the war for the liberation of Hungary'. And Barna Megyeri's 1948 memorial, also of limestone, has in Hungarian and Russian the inscription: 'In gratitude to the Soviet liberators for our freedom'. See ibid. pp. 26–27.
66 Tamás Gyenes' 1957 bronze bust of József Kalamár. István János Nagy's 1968 limestone memorial plaque in honour of János Asztalos. András Nagy Kiss' 1977 bronze memorial plaque in honour of Róbert Kreutz. István Kiss' 1986 bronze memorial to Ferenc Münnich. And Lászlo Marton's 1988 bronze statue of Árpád Szakasits.
67 The seminal work on this topic is Robert Conquest, *The Great Terror: Stalin's Purge in the Thirties* (London: Macmillan, 1968).
68 The former German Democratic Republic (*Deutsche Demokratische Republik*, DDR) was incorporated as part of reunified Germany. For a detailed history of EU membership, see 'The History of the European Union', *European Union*, http://europa.eu/about-eu/eu-history/index_en.htm (Last accessed May 2013).
69 The others were Estonia, Latvia, Lithuania, Slovenia, and Slovakia. Furthermore, Cyprus and Malta also joined on the same day. See ibid.
70 'Milestones: 1953–60. The Warsaw Treaty Organization, 1955', *U.S. Department of State, Office of the Historian*, http://history.state.gov/milestones/1953–60/Warsaw Treaty (Last accessed April 2013).
71 Following Czechoslovakia's peaceful dissolution in 1993, Czechs and Slovakians pursued similar paths but set different paces. Slovakia also eventually joined NATO, but not until March 2004, precisely five years after the Czech Republic. Another former Warsaw Pact member, Romania, also joined NATO at the same time as the Slovakians.
72 For both an audiovisual recording and a full transcript of this speech accessible online, see Ronald Reagan, 'Remarks at the Annual Convention of the National Association of Evangelicals in Orlando, Florida', *The Ronald Reagan Presidential Foundation & Library*, 8 March 1983, www.reaganfoundation.org/bw_detail.aspx? p=LMB4YGHF2& h1 = 0& h2 = 0& sw = & lm = berlinwall&args_a = cms&args_b = 74& argsb = N& tx = 1770 (Last accessed April 2013).
73 Remark based on Tony Joel's observations during a visit to the museum in November 2011, at which time it mostly consisted of a special exhibition of posters. See Tadeusz Skoczek *et al.*, *Museum of Independence in Warsaw from 11th November to 29th February 2012* (Kraków: Drukarnia Kolejowa, 2011).

74 Cities further south such as Wrocław and Warsaw also witnessed lesser demonstrations triggered by the events around Gdansk and in Szczecin. Alex, '1970–71: Uprising in Poland', *Libcom*, 31 October 2008, http://libcom.org/history/1970-71-uprising-poland (Last accessed March 2013).
75 For instance, see Judt, *Postwar*, pp. 585–87.
76 For a promotional website dedicated to the film, see Newt and Callista Gingrich, 'Nine Days that Changed the World: Pope John Paul II. June 2–10, 1979', *Nine Days that Changed the World*, www.ninedaysthatchangedtheworld.com (Last accessed September 2012).
77 Quoted in Robert Forczyk, *Warsaw 1944: Poland's Bid for Freedom* (Oxford: Osprey Publishing, 2009), p. 90. Also Krystyna Wituska, *Inside a Gestapo Prison: The Letters of Krystyna Wituska, 1942–1944* (Detroit: Wayne State University Press, 2006), p. xxii.
78 Standing at over 230 metres, the Palace of Culture and Science remained at the time of writing Poland's tallest building, one of the ten tallest buildings within the EU, and among the twenty tallest skyscrapers in all of Europe. See Emporis, 'Europe's Tallest Buildings – Top 20', *Emporis*, 2013, www.emporis.com/statistics/tallest-buildings-europe (Last accessed January 2013).
79 PKiN, 'History of the Palace of Culture and Science: Not Entirely Spontaneous Present', *PKiN Warszawa*, www.pkin.pl/wp-content/uploads/2012/04/Not-entirely-spontaneous-present.pdf (Last accessed November 2012).
80 The following year, for instance, during his short-lived membership of the ruling communist Polish United Workers' Party (*Polska Zjednoczona Partia Robotnicza*, PZPR) the prolific novelist Jerzy Andrzejewski wrote: 'in the heart of our country, in the heart of Warsaw they have been building … the gigantic Palace of Culture and Science of Józef Stalin. This magnificent gift coming from the Soviet Nation to the Polish Nation symbolizes grandeur of socialistic culture.' See ibid.
81 Andrzej Hrechorowicz, 'Walesa unveils One More for the "Gipper"', *Polskie Radio*, 21 November 2011, www.thenews.pl/1/10/Artykul/58886,Walesa-unveils-one-more-for-the-Gipper (Last accessed February 2013).
82 'Warsaw to Erect Statue to Reagan', *BBC News*, 21 September 2006, http://news.bbc.co.uk/2/hi/europe/5366992.stm (Last accessed February 2013).
83 Ibid.
84 Vanessa Gera, 'Walesa Unveils Statue of Ronald Reagan in Warsaw', *Deseret News*, 21 November 2011, www.deseretnews.com/article/700199832/Walesa-unveils-statue-of-Ronald-Reagan-in-Warsaw.html (Last accessed February 2013).
85 Hrechorowicz, 'Walesa Unveils One More for the "Gipper"'.
86 Ibid.
87 The Telegraph, 'Ronald Reagan Statue Unveiled in Warsaw', *The Telegraph*, 21 November 2011, www.telegraph.co.uk/news/worldnews/europe/poland/8904456/Ronald-Reagan-statue-unveiled-in-Warsaw.html (Last accessed February 2013).
88 Gera, 'Walesa Unveils Statue'.
89 Telegraph, 'Ronald Reagan Statue Unveiled in Warsaw'.
90 Ibid.
91 Hawley, 'Spiegel Interview with Lech Walesa'.
92 'Ronald Reagan Statue to be Unveiled in Hungary', *Huffington Post*, 28 June 2011, www.huffingtonpost.com/2011/06/28/ronald-reagan-statue-hungary-n_885864.html (Last accessed March 2013). Also Pablo Gorondi, 'Ronald Reagan Statue Unveiled in Hungary', *Yahoo! News*, 29 June 2011, http://news.yahoo.com/ronald-reagan-statue-unveiled-hungary-145351000.html (Last accessed March 2013).
93 Ben Birnbaum, 'Statue in Budapest's Liberty Square Credits Reagan for Freedom', *The Washington Times*, 29 June 2011, www.washingtontimes.com/news/2011/jun/29/statue-in-budapests-liberty-square-credits-reagan-/?page=all (Last accessed March 2013).

94 Budai added: 'We loved him not just as a president, but as a man.' Quoted in ibid.
95 Ibid.
96 It meant that Reagan became the fourth former US president to have a Prague street renamed after him, joining George Washington, Woodrow Wilson, and Franklin Delano Roosevelt. See Chris Johnstone, 'Ronald Reagan to be Honoured in Czech Capital', *Czech Position*, 30 June 2011, www.ceskapozice.cz/en/news/society/ronald-reagan-be-honoured-czech-capital (Last accessed March 2013). And also 'Czech Republic Pays Tribute to Ronald Reagan', *Embassy of the United States Prague, Czech Republic* 1 July 2011, http://prague.usembassy.gov/ronald-reagan-street.html (Last accessed March 2013). And for photographs, see 'Ronald Reagan Street in Prague', *flickr*, 1 July 2011, www.flickr.com/photos/usembassy prague/sets/72157627099704332/ (Last accessed March 2013).
97 'Prague Names Street after Ronald Reagan', *Yahoo! News*, 1 July 2011, http://news.yahoo.com/prague-names-street-ronald-reagan-165059516.html (Last accessed March 2013).
98 Embassy of the United States, 'Czech Republic Pays Tribute to Ronald Reagan'. And Prague Security Studies Institute, 'Ronald Reagan: Inspired Freedom. International Conference, Prague, Czech Republic', *Prague Security Studies Institute*, 30 June – 1 July 2011, www.pssi.cz/conferences-and-roundtables/2 (Last accessed March 2013).
99 Analysis of various sites of memory in and around Hanoi is largely based on field research conducted by David Lowe and Tony Joel in February and March 2013. For the museum's website in Vietnamese and English, see *Ho Chi Minh Museum*, www.baotanghochiminh.vn/tabid/528/default.aspx (Last accessed October 2012).
100 For the museum's website in Vietnamese and English, see 'An Introduction of Viet Nam Military History Museum: A Snapshot of its Establishment and Development Process', *Vietnam Military History Museum*, www.btlsqsvn.org.vn/?act=mn_index& lgid = 2 (Last accessed March 2013).
101 Ibid.
102 Our emphasis here is on remembrance that takes place in Hanoi. For an excellent account of the remembering that occurs in a wider sense both across Vietnam and in France, see William Logan and Nguyễn Thanh Bình, 'Victory and Defeat at Điện Biên Phủ: Memory and Memorialization in Vietnam and France', in *The Heritage of War*, eds Martin Gegner and Bart Ziino (Abingdon, Oxon: Routledge).
103 The following account draws on field research Dr Donna-Lee Frieze conducted on behalf of the authors in early 2013.
104 Mr Steve Symms, 'Bill Text, 102nd Congress (1991–92), S.CON.RES.55.IS. To Call for the Construction of an International Memorial to the Victims of Communism (Introduced in Senate – IS)', *The Library of Congress*, 8 July 1991, http://thomas.loc.gov/cgi-bin/query/z?c102:S.CON.RES.55: (Last accessed February 2013). And Mr Dana Rohrabacher, 'Bill Text, 102nd Congress (1991–92), H.CON.RES.228.IH. Concerning an International Memorial to the Victims of Communism. (Introduced in House – IH)', *The Library of Congress*, 30 October 1991, http://thomas.loc.gov/cgi-bin/query/z?c102:H.CON.RES.228: (Last accessed February 2013).
105 The tariff commission relocated in 1988, leaving the building vacant. Dinitia Smith, 'For the Victims of Communism', *The New York Times*, 23 December 1995, www.nytimes.com/1995/12/23/arts/for-the-victims-of-communism.html (Last accessed January 2013).
106 Ibid.
107 Nonetheless, according to the Foundation: 'Donors and ethnic communities throughout the United States reacted favorably. Led by the Vietnamese

Americans in Northern Virginia, the Latvians, Lithuanians, Estonians, Hungarians, and other groups rallied to donate money and effort to the cause.' Victims of Communism Memorial Foundation, 'Victims of Communism Memorial', *Global Museum on Communism*, www.globalmuseumoncommunism.org/content/ victims-communism-memorial (Last accessed January 2013).

108 Ibid.

109 Ibid.

110 Furthermore, replicas of the statue already had been erected in France, the United Kingdom, Nigeria, Taiwan, Canada, and San Francisco's Chinatown, meaning the 'Goddess' already was recognized as a 'global symbol of freedom and democracy'. The sculptor responsible for the San Francisco statue, Thomas Marsh, was approached for the Washington monument. Marsh, who sought accuracy by working with some of the students who had been involved in the Tiananmen Square protests, declined payment for his services. See ibid.

111 For a complete transcript of president Bush's speech as well as a full video recording accessible online, see George W. Bush, 'Victims of Communism Memorial Dedication', *C-Span Video Library*, 12 June 2007, www.c-spanvideo. org/videoLibrary/transcript/transcript.php?programid=176429 (Last accessed February 2013). See also the White House Office of the Press Secretary, 'President Bush Attends Dedication of Victims of Communism Memorial', *The White House: President George W. Bush Archives*, 12 June 2007, http://georgew bush-whitehouse.archives.gov/news/releases/2007/06/20070612-2.html (Last accessed January 2013).

112 Leora Falk, 'Questions rise over Memorials', *Chicago Tribune News*, 13 June 2007, http://articles.chicagotribune.com/2007-06-13/news/0706130254_1_monument-tiananmen-square-communist (Last accessed February 2013).

113 Qin Gang quoted in 'China blasts Bush Tribute to Victims of Communism', *The Epoch Times*, 14 June 2007, www.theepochtimes.com/news/7-6-14/56486.html (Last accessed January 2013).

114 Douglas Birch, 'Putin: Vietnam worse than Stalin Purges', *The Washington Post*, 21 June 2007, www.washingtonpost.com/wp-dyn/content/article/2007/06/21/ AR2007062101885.html (Last accessed January 2013).

115 Here it should be noted that, following the disintegration of the Soviet Union, the Crimean peninsula is an Autonomous Republic but it is officially attached to Ukraine (with Ukrainian the only officially recognized language). Owing to historical factors, however, ethnic Russians make up a strong majority of the peninsula's population (resulting in Russian being the most common language spoken among locals despite its unofficial status).

116 Party leader Leonid Grach was quoted as saying that the museum was 'our response to George Bush, who opened the Victims of Communism Memorial in Washington, and to [pro-Western Ukrainian President] Viktor Yushchenko, who initiated the construction of the Museum of Soviet Occupation in Kiev'. In 'Ukraine's Communists open Museum for U.S. Imperialism Victims', *RIA Novosti*, 21 August 2007, http://en.rian.ru/world/20070821/73004087.html (Last accessed February 2013).

117 Andrei P. Tsygankov, *Russophobia: Anti-Russian Lobby and American Foreign Policy* (New York: Palgrave Macmillan, 2009), p. 55.

118 'Victims of Communism Memorial'.

119 'About the Foundation: International Advisory Council', *Victims of Communism Memorial Foundation*, www.webcitation.org/5yrII6tyj (Last accessed January 2013).

120 'Truman-Reagan Medal of Freedom', *Global Museum on Communism*, www.globalmuseumoncommunism.org/content/truman-reagan-medal-freedom (Last accessed March 2013).

121 'Global Museum on Communism', *Global Museum on Communism*, www.global
museumoncommunism.org (Last accessed March 2013).
122 'Museum Overview', *Global Museum on Communism*, www.globalmuseum
oncommunism.org/museum_overview (Last accessed January 2013).
123 'Museum Mission', *Global Museum on Communism*, www.globalmuseum
oncommunism.org/content/museum-mission (Last accessed January 2013).
124 'Quiz on Communism', *Global Museum on Communism*, www.globalmuseum
oncommunism.org/quiz_communism (Last accessed January 2013). To be fair, it
should be noted that the laughable online quiz is only a minor part of the overall
attempt to educate. The website also features, for instance, an extensive media
archive. And, according to the mission statement, a virtual museum of this kind
'provides an online "meeting place" for scholars, researchers, and activists to
interact and build their educational competence and connects communities
around the world in a common educational mission'. See 'Museum Mission'.
125 'Museum Mission'.
126 'Main Exhibits', *Global Museum on Communism*, www.globalmuseumoncommu-
nism.org/exhibits (Last accessed March 2013).
127 'Museum Mission'.
128 As an indication of how closely the first two phases are connected, the website
features not only numerous photographs of the 'Goddess of Democracy' statue
in Washington but also a special section dedicated to the memorial. Moreover, a
silhouette of the 'Goddess' acts as its official symbol. The message contained on
the information panel adjacent to the Washington memorial, furthermore, is
echoed throughout the virtual museum. For instance: 'The victims were struck
down in an unprecedented imperial communist holocaust through conquests,
revolutions, civil wars, purges, wars by proxy, and other violent means. Totalitarian terror countenanced no challenge, from individuals, institutions, political
parties, or faiths. Instead, it set out the "big lie" that a classless utopian society
with human dignity for all was its goal, then cynically produced exactly the
opposite in nation after nation which succumbed to its armed might, shameless
intrigues, and hypocrisy.' See 'About the Foundation', *Victims of Communism
Memorial Foundation*, www.victimsofcommunism.org/about/ (Last accessed January 2013).
129 'Museum Mission'.
130 James Bamford, *Body of Secrets: Anatomy of the Ultra-Secret National Security
Agency: From the Cold War through the Dawn of a New Century* (New York: First
Anchor Books, 2002), p. 24.
131 Ibid. p. 25.
132 'Vint Hill Farms Station: Current Site Information', *U.S. Environmental Protection
Agency*, May 2010, www.epa.gov/reg3hscd/npl/VA8210020931.htm (Last accessed
February 2013).
133 Our analysis of Vint Hill draws on field research Dr Donna-Lee Frieze
conducted for this project on our behalf in early 2013.
134 Lydia DePillis, 'The Economics of Stephen Fuller: How a Wonky Academic
became a Major Player in the Local Real-Estate Business', *Washington City Paper*,
15 April 2011 (Last accessed January 2013).
135 'Cold War Museum Physical Location – Vint Hill Farm Station', *The Cold War
Museum*, 11 December 2009, www.coldwar.org/museum/physical_location.asp
(Last accessed March 2013).
136 In February 1962, Powers was included as part of an exchange for KGB agent
Vilyam Fisher (a.k.a. Rudolf Abel), who had been imprisoned in the United
States since 1957. The swap took place at the Glienicke Bridge outside of Berlin.
For a short biography of Fisher/Abel, see 'Biography of Vilyam Fisher', *Royal
Air Force Musuem Cosford: National Cold War Exhibition*, www.

nationalcoldwarexhibition.org/explore/biography.cfm?name=Fisher,%20Vilyam (Last accessed December 2012).
137 'Background', *The Cold War Museum*, www.coldwar.org/museum/background. asp (Last accessed December 2012).
138 The exhibit included (in)valuable artefacts such as the helmet Powers wore on his flight and the suitcase he carried over the Glienicke Bridge during his prisoner exchange in 1962. It also featured a lot of photographs and other assorted paraphernalia relating to the U-2 incident.
139 In a 2002 interview, Powers Jr stated that his desire to learn more about his father (who died in 1977, when the son was only twelve years old) ignited his interest in the Cold War. See Andrew DeMillo, 'Atop Old Missile Hold, Cold War Site may Rise: Son of U-2 Pilot Francis Gary Powers envisions a Museum at Lorton', *The Washington Post*, 2 March 2002, www.washingtonpost.com/wp-dyn/articles/A26119–2002Mar1.html (Last accessed January 2013).
140 These included: the Allied Museum, Berlin, Germany; the Atomic Testing Museum, Las Vegas, Nevada; the Central Intelligence Agency (CIA), Langley, Virginia; the Defense Intelligence Agency, Bolling Air Force Base, Washington DC; Experimental Aircraft Association, Oshkosh, Wisconsin; Florida International Museum, St Petersburg, Florida; George C. Marshall Museum, Leesburg, Virginia; George Mason University, Fairfax, Virginia; the National Atomic Museum, Albuquerque, New Mexico; the National Reconnaissance Office, Chantilly, Virginia; the National Security Agency Cryptologic Museum, Fort Meade, Maryland; the National War College, Fort Leslie J. McNair, Washington DC; the Norwegian Aviation Center, Bodø, Norway; Octave Chanute Aerospace Museum, Rantoul, Illinois; PIMA Air and Space Museum, Tucson, Arizona; the Seattle Museum of Flight, Seattle, Washington; the Space and Missile Command Conference, Huntsville, Alabama; Strategic Air Command Museum, Omaha, Nebraska; the Texas Air Museum, Lubbock, Texas; and the United States Air Force Museum, Dayton, Ohio. See 'Background'.
141 For its purpose of raising funds and profile, see ibid.
142 DeMillo, 'Atop Old Missile Hold'.
143 Ibid.
144 Francis Gary Powers Jr, 'The Cold War Museum Moves Closer to a Permanent Residence', *American Institute for History Education (AIHE)*, November 2007, http://americaninstituteforhistory.org/gazette.php?year=2007 (Last accessed January 2013).
145 Fredrick Kunkle, 'Proposed Cold War Museum Falls Short', *The Washington Post*, 15 April 2009, http://articles.washingtonpost.com/2009-04-15/news/36817768_1_cold-war-museum-international-spy-museum-francis-gary-powers (Last accessed January 2013).
146 Francis Gary Powers Jr, 'Spy Tours: The Original Spy Tour of Washington', *Francis Gary Powers, Jr. Expert Public Speaker regarding the Cold War, U-2 Incident and the Need to Preserve Cold War History*, http://garypowers.org/spytours/ (Last accessed March 2013).
147 Museum, 'Cold War Physical Location'.
148 Quotations taken from Vint Hill Economic Development Authority, 'About', *Vint Hill*, www.vinthill.com/about/ (Last accessed April 2013). And Vint Hill Economic Development Authority, 'Real Estate', *Vint Hill*, www.vinthill.com/real-estate/ (Last accessed April 2013).
149 'Cold War Physical Location'.
150 Ibid.
151 Unless indicated otherwise, the following discussion about the Wende Museum is largely informed by the guided tour and semi-structured, open-ended interviews conducted by Dr Donna-Lee Frieze on behalf of the authors in early 2013.

The interviewees were founder and director Justinian Jampol, associate director Donna Stein, manager of collection development Cristina Cuevas-Wolf, and special collections curator John Ahouse.

152 For the museum's website, see Justinian Jampol, 'The Wende Museum', *The Wende Museum*, www.wendemuseum.org (Last accessed May 2013).

153 Justinian Jampol, 'About Us', *The Wende Museum*, www.wendemuseum.org/about-us (Last accessed May 2013).

154 See, for example, Rainer Eckert's comments in Jody K. Biehl, 'East Germany Goes Hollywood: A Cold War Museum in Sunny Climes', *Spiegel Online International*, 22 April 2005, www.spiegel.de/international/east-germany-goes-holly wood-a-cold-war-museum-in-sunny-climes-a-352278.html   (Last   accessed December 2012).

155 'About Arcadia', *Arcadia*, www.arcadiafund.org.uk/about/about-arcadia (Last accessed April 2013).

156 Ibid.

157 Other funding sources include the Getty Foundation and the Institute of Museum and Library Services, while corporate partnerships have been built with Sony, Ziegler Film, Air Berlin, and Lufthansa among others.

158 'Grants (2004): Wende Museum of the Cold War, US', *Arcadia*, www.arcadia-fund.org.uk/grants/endangered-culture/wende-museum-cold-war-us (Last accessed March 2013).

159 'Grants (2012): The Wende Museum', *Arcadia*, www.arcadiafund.org.uk/grants/endangered-culture/wende-museum (Last accessed April 2013).

160 'National Cold War Exhibition', *Royal Air Force Museum Cosford: National Cold War Exhibition*, www.nationalcoldwarexhibition.org/index.cfm (Last accessed May 2013).

161 Jampol, 'About Us'.

162 For a discussion that links the museum to this trend, see David C. Engerman, 'California's Cold War Museum', *Humanities: The Magazine of the National Endowment for the Humanities*, May/June 2011, www.neh.gov/humanities/2011/mayjune/feature/californias-cold-war-museum (Last accessed February 2013).

163 Jampol, 'About Us'.

164 Ibid.

165 Angela Thompson, 'The Wende Museum and Archive of the Cold War', *Angela Thompson's Website*, 2012, http://angela-thompson.com/english/Wende_Museum_English_Version.pdf (Last accessed April 2013), p. 21.

166 See pp. 109–11

4   Defining our times

Some 22 years after the collapse of the Soviet Union it is very easy to meet and engage with consequences and echoes of the Cold War, even with only a hazy idea of what it was all about. There are signs, for instance, that the Cold War is enjoying renewed attention in fiction, documentary, and film. While a comprehensive survey of the genres lies outside the scope of this study, a snapshot is at least suggestive. In the early months of 2013, it is easy to indulge in new offerings such as Ian McEwan's 2012 novel *Sweet Tooth*, whose main characters are spun around MI5 in the 1970s, or the 2011 movie adaptation of John Le Carré's classic novel about MI6, moles, and betrayal, *Tinker, Tailor, Soldier, Spy*. Non-English screen titles include two films from 2012: the Chinese offering *Silent War*, set in the messy intrigues of 1949 Shanghai as the Chinese civil war comes to a climax; and the German film *Shores of Hope*, set in East Germany's port of Rostock amidst dissidence and *Stasi* surveillance in the 1980s. The BBC, furthermore, promises a television season of new works of drama and documentary. Its promotional blurb reads: 'Fifty years after Britain lived in the shadow of the Cold War, BBC Two is set to explore the cultural and political upheaval of a tumultuous period in history that divided the world in half and shaped modern politics.'[1]

In fact, the Cold War is not only around us in ways that are viewed, visited, and contemplated, but also it defines us. At a very basic level of common usage, the idea of a 'post-Cold War era' was a popular idea in western public commentary, although from late 2001 it has been partly usurped by the idea of a 'post-9/11' world. This chapter builds on the two previous chapters 'Nuclear World' and 'Cities and Sites' in attempting to sense the level of new or renewed interest in the idea of the Cold War. We have conceded that trying to gauge public remembering of the Cold War is fraught with problems of both method and selection, but such are the challenges of new and ambitious ventures in research on memory. Taking the exercise further, judging levels of its public recognition in relation to trends taking shape arguably is even more ambitious, but an exercise worth attempting. This chapter suggests that the Cold War – both in its imagined form of the apocalypse that never happened, and its more local manifestations of state-related violence – is growing in public consciousness in differing ways. It continues to thrive on its shadows, the secrecy of espionage and hidden government behaviour inviting curiosity. This trend is nourished by the drip-feed of more information from previously hidden archives or new personal revelations, and it draws on popular culture's habit of reviving and remaking art forms that gripped an earlier imagination. There is energy also in the nexus between heritage, museum, and tourism activity around the Cold War. As an era, it is increasingly embraced in the way that other 'wars' and military histories have entered into cultural heritage and tourism. The Cold War looms large in many modern history textbooks, and history-telling of other forms, sometimes in controversial ways, in different parts of the world. And it is wielded with rhetorical effect by politicians and politically active groups seeking legitimacy, the redress of past wrongs, and strategic positioning in the context of geopolitical change. Together, these broad categories suggest a future for the Cold War in modern public consciousness.

Spies

As the above snapshot of screen and literature suggests, espionage is one of the most enduring dimensions of the struggle between East and West. For historians and educators, intelligence work and the activities of particular spies hold the multiple attractions of immersion in 'top secret' government activity, the drama of spies being pursued and sometimes captured and brought to trial, 'moles' and counter-espionage cat-and-mouse tactics, spies' gadgets and secret ways, and the pervasive, unsettling air of subterfuge that hangs on the practice of spying. Spies were a big part of how the Cold War moved from an imagined threat to a reality within countries in the late-1940s and early-1950s, as the KGB and western intelligence services tried to find ways to peer into each other's secrets. In very brief summary, prominent spies whose activities have been detailed in intelligence gathering and published histories include: US lawyer and government official Alger Hiss, very probably active in passing information to Soviet agents in the mid-1940s and convicted of perjury in 1950;[2] Julius and Ethel Rosenberg, the American couple found guilty of passing atomic bomb secrets to the Soviet Union, tried and sentenced to death in 1951, and executed in 1953; Klaus Fuchs, a British physicist and member of the team building the atomic bomb who passed on details of the project and was convicted of espionage in 1950; another British atomic physicist Allen Nunn-May, convicted of espionage in 1946; and the so-called 'Cambridge Apostles', Guy Burgess, Kim Philby, Donald Maclean, Anthony Blunt, and possibly a fifth agent, all of whom were bright civil servants in the British Foreign Office and intelligence services recruited while at the University of Cambridge in the 1930s. These 'Apostles' passed secrets to Moscow mostly during the 1940s and into the 1950s and, in the case of Burgess, Maclean, and later Philby, defected to the Soviet Union. Blunt did not defect but later confessed his crimes and provided information in return for immunity from prosecution. The trials of Hiss and the Rosenbergs in the United States attracted enormous media coverage. In the same era, highly public defections by Soviet agents to the West, such as Igor Gouzenko (Canada, 1945) and Vladimir Petrov (Australia, 1954), brought home just how active Soviet espionage was at this time. Together, these helped fuel the growth of anti-communism in the West, including a sweeping range of centralized and local measures to identify communist sympathizers and ensure the loyalty of citizens.

Debates over the scale and depth of some of these spies' activities have continued within the academy, the media, and in educational settings. New waves of writing and teaching about spies have been fuelled by recent revelations deriving from: archives released from former communist countries; memoirs and collaborations with former spies;[3] and, especially since 1995, the release of the 'Venona' documents – telegrams sent to the Soviet intelligence agency the NKGB during the 1940s that were decrypted by Anglo-American code-breakers. The Venona cables, for instance, seem to confirm the guilt of Julius Rosenberg but cast some doubt on the guilt of his wife Ethel. Publications drawing on the Venona evidence (a collection which remains partial rather than comprehensive) have drawn conclusions about spies more assertively, but they continue to fuel rather than end debate on the extent to which identified spies leaked information of value, and about the challenges that remain for historians.[4] There persists, however, a keen academic and public appetite for uncovering more of the 'human' in the human intelligence tag by which spying is known, even if post-Soviet revelations might not always tell us a great deal more about the impact of espionage. Venona makes for good lesson plans in the hands of history teachers, inviting the need to understand differences of interpretation among historians, some grasp of the world of secret government activities, a contextual appreciation of the 1940s activities being reported, and a tantalizing glimpse into the world of top secret documents. The Organization of American Historians (OAH) has welcomed teaching plans using the Venona materials along these lines.[5] In Australia, too, new intelligence documents helped rekindle teachers' attraction to the defection of Vladimir Petrov and his wife Evdokia. The Museum of Australian Democracy, located in the nation's capital Canberra where some of the Petrov drama unfolded, provides a historical lesson attuned to schools' curriculum guidelines.[6]

In both of the above examples of espionage in the classroom, students are encouraged to ponder the tension between a democratic state's actions needed to protect national security and its commitment to freedom of speech and thought (and civil rights more broadly). Sweeping anti-communist measures in the United States in the late-1940s and early-1950s have become almost synonymous with the term 'McCarthyism', recalling the US senator who burst on the scene in 1950 with extravagant claims about the numbers of card-carrying members of the Communist Party in the US

State Department. Senator Joseph 'Joe' McCarthy embarked on a four-year mission to rid the United States of communists nested in its public service. He was a consummate media performer – making the most of televised hearings – and adept at tapping angst over the 'loss' of China to Mao Zedong's communists and the deep-rooted counter-subversive tradition in American society: the notion that 'outsiders' have long threatened the nation from within its borders. McCarthy's efforts unfolded alongside Congressional Committees, the pursuits of the Federal Bureau of Investigation (FBI), and a range of administrative and legal measures to catch American communists. Historians such as Ellen Schrecker have provided compelling detail about how McCarthyism 'worked' and ruined the reputations or lives of many who were unjustly accused of subversion and disloyalty.[7] As a term, 'McCarthyism' has grown out of its specific origins – when there were, indeed, a number of Americans who passed information to the Soviet Union and others who were evasive about their loyalties – to become shorthand pejorative for excessive measures to stamp on perceived threats from within, without adequate regard for evidence. Arthur Miller's contemporary play *The Crucible* (1952) used the Salem witchcraft trials as a means of highlighting his dismay at the erosion of civil liberties and warned of the ever-present dangers of the 'witch-hunt', a term that often appears in conjunction with 'McCarthyism'.[8] Since the 1950s, both terms have been deployed with almost predictable regularity, especially by English-speaking journalists and politicians. Such is the extent to which the 'McCarthyist' accusation is thrown about, one American sports journalist had to plead with his colleagues in 2005 not to keep adverting to it in their coverage of Congressional hearings into steroid use in Major League Baseball.[9]

The silver screen and television sets are the best-known spy-catchers, transporting novels such as Ian Fleming's James Bond 007 series into forms watched by millions. While movie buffs and Cold War scholars pore over the best and worst of Hollywood's red-hunting movies of the 1950s and early-1960s, it is the escapist genre of Bond (beginning with *Dr No* in 1962) rather than the moral tale that has grown and thrived beyond the collapse of the Soviet Union. Bond, of course, slipped free of the earlier neat East vs West confrontation in the villainy he thwarted while maintaining the fight against evil masterminds who continue to feed off international rivalries. In the first 007 film of the 1990s, *GoldenEye* (1995), he survives being labelled a 'misogynist dinosaur' and 'relic of the Cold War' by his female boss, M, and overcomes Russian criminals playing havoc with weaponry that survived the dissolution of the Soviet Union. Subsequent Bond movies contain frequent echoes of the Cold War in the form of old scores being settled, nuclear weapons being stolen and deployed, and in the case of *Die Another Day* (2002) the unresolved stand-off between North and South Korea. Beyond 007, other modern spy thriller adaptations including Le Carré's *Tinker, Tailor, Soldier, Spy* and Robert Ludlum's *Bourne* series (2002, 2004, 2007, 2012) testify to the popularity of the genre. The spin-offs, in electronic gaming and merchandising, ensure espionage's place in the leisure pursuits of the consumer classes.

The transition of spying in popular culture from Cold War to post-Cold War thus was made without fuss. Some of the products in the immediate aftermath of rapid changes in Europe and the Soviet Union in the late-1980s carried themes of compromise. Between the fall of the Berlin Wall and the collapse of the Soviet Union, *The Hunt for Red October* (1990), an adaptation of a Tom Clancy novel, depicted a Soviet submarine commander wanting to defect to the United States. *The Quiet American* (2002), based on the Graham Greene novel showing a shallow and self-absorbed CIA agent in Vietnam, was one of the last of the Cold War movies of the immediate post-collapse period because its first screenings occurred on the eve of 9/11.[10] Not surprisingly, subsequent American espionage movies have been interpreted at least partly through the lens of the 'War on Terror'. Elsewhere, successful movies from Germany that enjoyed wide distribution, such as *Goodbye Lenin* (2003) and *The Lives of Others* (2006), introduced a viewing audience to 'Ostalgie', nostalgia for aspects of the old DDR and to the ways of the *Stasi*; and the Korean War is recalled by Korean filmmakers as well as in re-runs of the US television series *M.A.S.H.*[11] Even unhinged from its moorings, a Cold War taxonomy can be wielded with effect. In the 2012 award-winning Hong Kong police thriller called *Cold War*, the title referred to the code name of a rescue operation, and the film made no references whatever to *the* Cold War.

Recalling spying is also popular because it is easily made fun. Even the KGB managed to gain some light-heartedness when put on museum display. The Federal Security Service (successor to the KGB) headquarters in the Lubyanka Building in Moscow opened a small KGB Museum in the mid-1980s, showcasing spy memorabilia for Soviet insiders. In the 1990s it opened to foreigners who booked tours, and showed off a mixture of dusty relics and interesting gadgets, including some proudly captured American spying devices. In recent years it has been closed and its future is not clear; but that does not stop excited journalists from drawing on its celebration of dirty tricks when reporting contemporary stories of espionage.[12] Secret forces (and secrecy more generally) works its way logically into military museum collections. The Imperial War Museum in London, for example, has hosted an exhibition on 'Secret War' – the history and best-known actions of British intelligence forces and special forces – with educational content about the Cold War and invitations to purchase sleuthing handbooks.[13]

The largest museum collection of espionage, the International Spy Museum in Washington DC, makes the fun focus clear in its appeal to kids and kids-at-heart. The only spy museum with a global remit, the museum opened in 2002. Privately run, at a cost of US$ 40 million, it boasts the largest collection of spying artefacts on display anywhere in the world. Backed by an Advisory Board full of former intelligence figures, it aims to educate the public about espionage and its impact on current and historical events.[14] The museum pays homage to early instances of spying, and makes a feature of the continuous terror of Russian secret police from the time of the Bolshevik Revolution when Lenin established the Cheka – the Extraordinary Commission for Combating Counter-Revolution and Sabotage. Elsewhere in the museum, J. Edgar Hoover, head of the FBI and obsessive in his pursuits of suspected communists in the 1950s and 1960s, is not spared in the description of his zealousness – in a way that has stirred commentators to raise question marks over the 'moral equivalence' being suggested between the two internal security forces.[15] The museum also is a space where recollections of the past and works of fiction interact playfully. Amongst the many fascinating secret spy gadgets on display are those that featured in television series such as *The Avengers*, *Mission Impossible*, and *Get Smart*. The gadgets steal the show, too, including an umbrella of the kind the KGB used to inject a poison pellet and kill dissident Georgi Markov in London in 1978, and a KGB lipstick pistol from 1965. While the museum covers spying through the ages, the Cold War, through atomic spies and through the weight of gadgets and popular culture spin-offs made between 1945 and 1991, is the context for most of the exciting items. The museum clearly aims at school groups and provides onsite workshops and fieldtrips on spying and intelligence. There is a series of lesson plans for educators and a book resulting from the museum's travelling exhibition entitled 'The Enemy Within: Terror in America – 1776 to Today'. Inside is a case study of the FBI's investigation of popular actress and comedian Lucille Ball from the early-1950s, including FBI documentation with blacked out material still classified. Reassuringly for students, and perhaps not reflective of the reputations ruined unnecessarily at this time, this was one episode wherein former family connections and malicious gossip did not convince the FBI that Lucy was a threat.[16]

An era for consumption

> The Cold War was – and is – everywhere in America, if one knows where to look for it – underground, behind closed doors, classified, off the map, already crumbling beyond recognition, or right in plain view, it has left an imprint as widespread yet discreet as the tracings of radioactive particles that blew out of the Nevada Test Site in the 1950s.

This was Tom Vanderbilt's assessment of his architecturally-focused tour of US Cold War sites, published in 2002.[17] Since then, the Cold War has stepped more into the sunlight, and not only in the United States. Museums, some of which already have been discussed in the 'Nuclear World' and 'Cities and Sites' chapters, have played important roles in bringing it into view. The level of activity and number of newer ventures suggest strong momentum in this industry.

All museum activity is sensitive to the multiple stakeholders – including financial supporters, politicians, and key interest groups – whose histories are being represented. Museums need to be attuned to the differing profiles of potential visitors. To refer to one previously-mentioned example, the Atomic Heritage Foundation in the United States is doubtless hopeful that, 20 years on from the 'culture war' over the *Enola Gay* at the Smithsonian Institution, the socio-political landscape now provides a strong base for public engagement with the development of the bomb. In fact, the Foundation held a workshop on the controversy, simultaneously acknowledging its impact on museums and establishing daylight between then and now. The Foundation's ambitious oral history project is one example of its determination to capture recollections from the broadest possible range of participants and others affected. It thereby can build something of a social history repository around the bomb.[18] Others are even more bullish about the centrality of the museum in public life. A 2013 posting from the (Nevada) National Atomic Testing Museum's e-bulletin, 'The Blast', contains this from CEO Allan Palmer on the role of museums in 'a chaotic world':

> Finding a straight, honest answer from previously trusted sources is getting more difficult to find. Coupled with a growing public mistrust of big government and academic institutions that seek to mold public policy more through political correctness and self interest than sound public policy, is it any wonder that the average American is distrustful of 'institutions'?
>
> But remove the agendas, political motives, self interest, profit motive and personal benefit from this picture and what emerges is the one remaining public institution left standing: The museum. That's right, museums today generally remain a trusted source of information and history because of public expectations, but more importantly *because* they are created expressly for the purpose of preserving the public trust. A recent study by the American Alliance of Museums found that 87% of people polled saw museums as trustworthy sources of information, ahead of books and television news [emphasis in original].[19]

Putting to one side the self-serving nature of the analysis and the research on which it draws, such a declaration is at least consistent with what we have earlier described as the seemingly insatiable public appetite for communing with the past in a variety of ways – recognizing that communing with the past is not necessarily accompanied by a strong effort to interpret it.

Within this general trend, there are discrete groups who are particularly given to visiting museums bearing Cold War displays. One such group comprises former servicemen who were stationed at military bases in other countries with which they retained some sense of bond: in the case of Western Europe, it might be US soldiers; and, in the case of Eastern Europe, it might Soviet troops. Another group is former national

servicemen who completed their service in the 1950s and much later developed a post-retirement curiosity in what their experience was all about.
Some of the stirrings of Cold War-related museum activity in Northern
Europe are sensitive to the needs of former servicemen and national
servicemen.[20] In Britain, for instance, there are signs of a national service
consciousness in two well-visited military museums. One is the National
Cold War Exhibition at the Royal Air Force Museum in Cosford, Shrop-
shire (discussed in detail further below). Another is the National Army
Museum in London, where the visitor learns: 'You can't understand British
history without understanding the history of the British Army.'[21] A special
exhibition on national service in 2012–13 linked with another display on the
Korean War where some of the servicemen served. British national service
operated from 1949 to 1960, during which time more than 2 million 18–20-
year-old men served eighteen months of compulsory training (extended to
two years during the Korean War years of 1950–53).[22] The National Army
Museum does not give priority to the Cold War in explaining the logic of
national service; it sits alongside the need to manage a far-flung empire and to
re-establish British influence in the postwar world. But, as the Cold War
lends itself easily to 'episodes' such as Korea, the Berlin Crisis of 1961, and
the Cuban Missile Crisis the following year, it helps punctuate the narrative
that ties together displays of national servicemen in service and excerpts of
their later recollections.[23] Similarly, at the National Cold War Exhibition in
Cosford, there is a prominent, multi-display feature on national service.
Those who were visiting the Exhibition on a bleak day in mid-November
2012 included a strong contingent reminiscing about their national service
experience. They made for a contrast with the other main group – a boister-
ous school tour at the opposite end of the age spectrum – and there were few
visitors of in-between age.[24] Both cohorts are important to museums recalling
military preparations and different forms of readiness during the Cold War.

Even if a little off the main tourist beats, the National Cold War Exhibition
(NCWE) testifies to growing confidence in the pull of Cold War tourism. As
its title suggests, it is *the* Cold War museum in Britain, even if it is hosted by
the RAF – something that also colours its exhibits. One of two RAF Museums, Cosford has been an RAF engineering training base since the late-1930s,
and the site of an RAF hospital until 1977. The Cosford RAF museum
opened in 1979, and enjoyed a major upgrade in the mid-1990s. Sponsored
by a number of companies and the injection of funds from the UK Heritage
Lottery Fund, the European Regional Development Fund, and the UK
Ministry of Defence, the NCWE opened on the same site in 2007. It is
housed in a spectacular steel building made of two curvilinear triangles, with
two large exhibition areas divided by a walkway. The exhibition is linked to
an education-friendly website clearly aimed at schools, including a 'national
curriculum' page of key Cold War events and themes.[25] In his welcome
message, patron Air Vice-Marshal (retired) Peter Dye OBE encourages
potential visitors to visit the Cosford site and make extensive use of

web-based material. Reflecting on the Cold War, he points to its enormous reach in human memories, and reminds readers of its unrealized threat:

> ... this exhibition and its special website uses the part played by the Royal Air Force to illuminate and describe that period of history in which our country was no more than 4 minutes away from annihilation ... It was an era so recent that at least half of the World's [sic] current population lived through all or part of it and we believe there was a real risk that, because it never became a full-blown fighting war, it would be consigned quietly to the history books.[26]

The Cold War does not go quietly at Cosford, nor does the RAF's role that, we are reminded, was pre-eminent in maintaining a nuclear deterrent until 1969, when the nuclear baton passed to the Royal Navy's submarines. To a degree that perhaps is logical given its setting, at Cosford the Cold War progressively moves out – according to the logic of exhibits – in concentric circles: from Britain (for a time, with a strong RAF twist); to Western Europe, the Soviet Union and the United States; and then, upon assuming the status of 'global conflict', to other parts of the world such as Asia, Africa, and Latin America. An interactive display enabling visitors to check certain nations for their involvement in the Cold War links to (especially northern) European countries. For visitors, highlights undoubtedly are the many missiles on display and the different aircraft, gleamingly maintained and often suspended from the iron rafters of what are cavernous exhibition rooms. Both the scale and the quality of the textually rich exhibits are equally impressive. There also is an admirable degree of ambition towards comprehensiveness on display. Churchill provides a grand opening, with his comment in March 1946 that an 'Iron Curtain has descended on the Continent' taking up a feature wall. It is followed by excerpts from Truman's speech a year later, including the much-quoted sentence that lay at the heart of what became known as the so-called Truman Doctrine: 'I believe that it must be the policy of the United States to support free peoples who are resisting attempted subjugation by armed minorities or by outside pressures.'[27] Multi-panel display boards feature familiar themes such as MAD from various perspectives, including Britain's development of the bomb, the rise of surveillance, British National Service 1949–60, key identities (including James Bond), and Civil Defence. In addition to detailed presentations on the evolution of missiles (many of which are on display) and the RAF's V-class nuclear strike bombers of the 1950s and 1960s (Valiant, Vulcan, and Victor), there are analyses of the build-up in armed forces of the East and West, and a large display of posters, photographs, and news reports recalling the Greenham Common protestors. The East vs West dual lens plays out on multiple feature boards, complete with encased paraphernalia and news reports, on the themes: Technology; Arts; Sport; Cinema; Literature; Food; Architecture; Lifestyle; and Propaganda.[28]

Figure 4.1 National Cold War Exhibition Building, RAF Museum. Cosford, November 2012.

Wisely, perhaps, museum curators baulk at the suggestion that the Cold War might explain all acts of mass violence in the second half of the twentieth century. Documenting violence more generally requires a focus shift away from the Euro-North American gaze. The Cold War therefore recedes for a time, as a short narrative of 'Violent World' takes over in the later section of the exhibition. On a board of 'Total Casualties', the two world wars are identified (the second being defined in European terms as 1939–45) with corresponding casualty figures, and then the figure of 23.6 million is attributed to '1945–91' (i.e. the span of years is preferred to explicit mention of the Cold War). Europe records the lowest figure in the breakdown of the 23.6 million casualties of this period according to nine geographical regions, with Africa, China, Southeast Asia, and Central and South Asia recording the highest casualty figures in descending order. But displays on the fall of the Berlin Wall and the collapse of the Soviet Union steer visitors back towards a proper 'End'.[29] Like other museums, the NCWE is on the look out for usable anniversaries. It held, for instance, a series of events – including a lecture as well as recreations of civil defence measures and radiation monitoring – to mark the fiftieth anniversary of the Cuban Missile Crisis on 15 October 2012.[30]

The archaeology of the Cold War is a business that has grown fitfully since the early-1990s. According to a 2004 German report: 'The Cold War offers an obscure, intriguing and difficult legacy, in short a great challenge to the conservation field.'[31] In the United States, the Department of Defense assumed responsibility for protection and conservation of Cold War heritage in 1991. A task force set out to 'inventory, protect, and conserve the physical and literary property and relics of the Department of Defense, in the United States and overseas, connected with the origins and the developments of the Cold War'.[32] It follows that the task force's remit is ambitious: in addition to identifying, protecting, and conserving, it seeks to bring together key stakeholders, including archivists, community groups, and historians, who share a commitment 'to understanding the complex meaning of America's rich but harrowing recent past'. As work began on US-based sites, one of the group's first additional ventures was to tour sites formerly and sometimes currently run by the Department in Belgium, England, Germany, Japan, Okinawa (listed separately), and Scotland.[33] Researchers work closely with allies such as the Smithsonian Institution's Air and Space Museum, the US Army's Aberdeen Proving Ground in Maryland, the National Museum of Naval Aircraft in Pensacola, Florida, and the US Air Force Museum in Dayton, Ohio. The Department of Defense's project is ongoing. It has yielded reports (some of which are available, whereas others are withheld) and promises many more. Since June 2010, it has been supplemented by a heritage-driven project to create an inventory of Cold War sites across the United States that might be considered for designation as National Historic Landmarks. There was an urgency about this initiative as most of the sites that might be listed on the National Register of Historic Places are more than 50 years old. Fourteen Cold War sites had been listed on the National Register to that point, including former missile bases, the Oak Ridge nuclear plant, Rocky Flats, radar facilities, and surviving civil defence bunkers. To support future assessments, the project generated a national inventory listing more than 500 separate sites and resources relating to the Cold War.[34]

In the UK, English Heritage, aware of the potential for a Ministry fire sale to preempt heritage considerations, quickly recorded and assessed 150 Cold War sites as recommended for protection in the early-1990s. They have enjoyed success in the form of the transformation of former bunkers for tourism, such as the York Bunker, but also face difficult decisions over other Cold War remains. That Cold War monuments such as concrete boxes are usually stark and ugly does not help.[35] In the corner of a suburban street in Cambridge, England, for example, sits an intimidating grey concrete lump of a building that was built in the 1950s to be regional seat of government in the event of nuclear war.[36] Used for little more than occasional storage in recent years, and the subject of recurrent speculation over its value in heritage, cost, and amenity, its fate remains uncertain. Ongoing work by English Heritage will shape which of the many identified Cold War sites dotting the English countryside might be scheduled. The cruise missile shelters at Greenham Common are on this list already, as is one of the most modern and bomb-proof of all the bunkers built – the so-called 'Magic Mountain' structure completed by the US Air Force in 1989 at the RAF's Alconbury base in Cambridgeshire.[37] Two former missile sites that were on highest alert during the Cuban Missile Crisis, in Rutland and Northamptonshire, were added in 2012 on occasion of the incident's fiftieth anniversary. The National Trust has become owner of other sites such as the Orford Ness Atomic Weapons Research Establishment on the Suffolk coast, where componentry used in the Australian atomic programme was assembled and tested.[38] As with other heritage decisions, a number of factors, not least the funds that might be forthcoming in tight fiscal settings, will determine the extent to which English Heritage's proactivity on legacies of the Cold War will be rewarded.

One of the most striking developments in identifying Cold War heritage on the European continent is driven by the Baltic Initiative and Network. The founder of the network, Johannes Bach Rasmussen, is a Danish landscape architect who was stirred into action in the aftermath of the collapse of communism in Europe by the need to understand a world that had been geographically close during his life yet constantly locked behind closed doors. Subsequent revelations about the extent to which western governments, including the Danish, were absorbed in Cold War defence, alliance, and espionage activities, spurred Rasmussen's efforts to win part- ners to his quest to make the Cold War better known to a broad public through imaginative engagement with its physical legacies. As a consultant with Danish ministries, Rasmussen completed a number of tourism and heritage assessments in former communist countries, and in 2005 he estab- lished the Baltic Initiative and Network (the 'Baltic' defined as those coun- tries with borders on the Baltic Sea). The Network's by-line is 'Protection of Historically valuable Installations and Sites from the Cold War Period', and its main objective is:

> ... to strengthen mutual understanding between countries around the Baltic Sea through an exchange of information on the Cold War period. The idea is that history should be told from the historically valuable sites at which events took place. Relevant sites include, for example: military installations and towns, prisons and prison camps, partisan bunkers, execution sites, secret police offices, sculptures and architecture or simple squares or buildings where memorable events took place.[39]

Membership of the network is broad, consisting of members from govern- ment authorities, institutes, NGOs, museums, or private persons. And a list of contacts takes in groups from Denmark, Estonia, Finland, Germany, Iceland (the exception to the Baltic littoral), Latvia, Lithuania, Norway, Poland, Russia, and Sweden. An Advisory Group includes museum chiefs, the (Polish) president of ICOMOS (the International Council on Monuments and Sites), the International Scientific Committee on

Fortifications and Military Heritage, and senior members of the Russian branch of Memorial (an international history and human rights society).[40] The network is both a central repository of information – about museums, exhibitions, and new eyewitness accounts by victims of the *Stasi* or other forms of oppression – from the countries it covers, and a stimulus for more activity. Recorded testimonies of victims of communist regimes are readily available for educators, and some of the subjects are listed as being available for speaking to school groups. For instance, Albinas Kentra, a former partisan fighter then Gulag prisoner in Lithuania who re-emerged to take the widely-seen video footage of protestors protecting the parliament building and TV Tower in Vilnius, speaks to interested groups about his 'camera as a weapon'.[41] Such information is available on a well-designed website, which also links to one of the main printable outcomes of the Network's activity to date: a *Travel Guide: Traces of the Cold War Period* compiled by Rasmussen. Containing details of 125 relics, sites, and museums in network countries, this 2010 publication was sponsored by the Network and the Archipelago Museum (*Øhavsmuseet*) on Langelands, Denmark. It is a collection of sites that reaches beyond museums and monuments to other structures carrying traces of the communist era, including buildings that used to house KGB headquarters or host party officials on their annual holidays. Those sites on the western side of the former Iron Curtain are predominantly former military installations and museums. As a snapshot from 2010, the guide is an excellent resource and presented in a manner designed to encourage tourists more than it seeks to document sites for their heritage value. It avoids exaggerating the Baltic Initiative and Network's influence through implying significant coordination to the unfolding story of Cold War tourism, but, by definition, marks a step in this direction.[42] In his foreword to the book, Bertel Haarder, Danish Minister for the Interior and Health, outlines a mission to better coordinate the growth of historical consciousness in Northern Europe, and to raise awareness of the legacies of communist regimes among younger generations:

> This guide book has a special objective that I fully support: to use the history of the Cold War period to create historical awareness and greater mutual understanding between the countries around the Baltic Sea. This understanding is a prerequisite to more fruitful international cooperation between people, organizations, companies and international associations.
>
> It is now 20 years since the Berlin Wall fell and the Soviet Union collapsed. This leads me to raise the issue of whether people, and especially the youth of today, for example in the Scandinavian countries, have fully understood what this period meant to world history. Formerly independent nations such as Estonia, Latvia, Lithuania and Poland (all only 1 or 2 hours from Scandinavia by air) spent nearly half a century under Communist dictatorships.

Tens of thousands of families from these countries were deported to remote parts of the Soviet Union with aim of destroying any potential resistance in those countries. Others were executed or sentenced to long periods in prisons or concentration camps simply because their political views were different from those of the rulers. We must not forget what happened to our neighbours, just a few decades ago.[43]

Haarder enthuses about the availability of eyewitness accounts and life stories that are sketched in the book. He is conscious, furthermore, that living memories of the Cold War could begin to recede, and also anxious that the next generation may not recall the crimes of communism. Thus, conservative anxiety joins with heritage tourism to promote shared and common memories of the Cold War. It is early days still for the Baltic Initiative and Network, but in building it Rasmussen has highlighted how these trends can be channelled effectively. Since 2009, he has organized conferences with cultural advisers, heritage experts, tourist authorities, and academics in Gdansk, Berlin, Riga, and Tallinn.

One of the countries covered by the Network hosts a special and controversial collection of Soviet-era memorabilia that is drawing local and international tourists. Around 80 miles west of Vilnius, Lithuania, lies the Soviet sculptures museum Grútas Park (*Grúto parkas*). It is also known as 'Stalin World' for its extensive collection of statues that were torn down in Lithuania during the early-1990s during the popular agitation for restored independence. The park, which opened in 2001, boasts a zoo, children's playground, small art gallery, museum, and café (where diners can choose from local Lithuanian fare or a 'Soviet menu'), but it is the statues that stand out. Near the entrance to Grútas Park is a Soviet train with cattle wagon, as was used in mass deportations to Gulag camps, a memory that also features in some of the museum exhibits. Unlike neighbouring Latvia and Estonia, where most of the torn-down communist statues were destroyed, Lithuanians stored many of them while wondering about their fate. A wealthy entrepreneur Viliumas Malinauskas won the tender called by the Lithuanian government for organizing them as a collection and established an outdoor exhibition based on the 86 statues he gathered (creating a similar site of memory to the Hungarian case of Memento Park in Budapest discussed at length in the previous chapter, though the addition of a zoo and children's playground create a very different atmosphere). Public reaction was mixed at the time of Grútas Park's opening, for at a basic level it appeared to be restoring the fallen idols of former oppressors. And opinion remains mixed, but the park has prospered. Its website's greeting, roughly translated into English, states:

The Grútas Park exposition discloses the negative content of the Soviet ideology and its impact on the value system. The aim ... is to provide an opportunity for Lithuanian people, visitors coming to our country as well as future generations to see the naked Soviet ideology which suppressed and hurt the spirit of our nation for many decades.[44]

The park's statue collection is impressive in scale and presentation, and, according to one newspaper, attracts around 100,000 visitors a year.[45] Some of the larger statues frame the entrance and a circular path takes visitors past the others, and to the gallery, museum, and café. In addition to familiar Russian figures, there are Lithuanian heroes and Lithuanian Communist Party leaders (the party already was strong in the early period of Soviet rule). One of the largest of several Lenin statues is the 20-feet tall statue that a crane wrenched from Vilnius' main square (at that time 'Lenin's Square') in 1991, leaving Lenin's feet behind, attached to the base. The sight of the suspended Lenin was one that made several television news reports and newspaper front pages at the time. Malinauskas revels in the controversy he has stirred and has a long display board full of news reports, many of them international, as the early protests against his park grabbed the attention of news desks far and wide.[46] He, himself, connects directly with some of the dark past Grūtas Park recalls and also with modern-day Lithuania. His uncle died in a Siberian Gulag camp, and his father died soon after returning from one. Malinauskas served in the Soviet army, was a wrestler, and then became a successful exporter of one of Lithuania's speciality foods, mushrooms.

Figure 4.2 Deportation locomotive now on display outside Grūtas Park. Lithuania, November 2012.

Figure 4.3 Evoking the Gulag. Front entrance to Grūtas Park. Lithuania, November 2012.

There is no easy balance to strike between evoking memories of the 'naked Soviet ideology' while emphasizing the appeal of a playground and zoo, or the opportunities for banquets, parties, and family celebrations.[47] There were howls of outrage from Lithuanian nationalists and former freedom fighters at the opening of the park, and although now reputedly the most popular tourist destination in southern Lithuania, the opposition has not died entirely. Even the visitor from abroad might conclude that the park's owners went one Stalinist memory too far with their fence and towers suggestive of a Gulag perimeter fence – and it is probably a blessing that Malinauskas' original plan to transport visitors from Vilnius on cattle trucks used in earlier deportations was deemed too insensitive and failed to go ahead. On the other hand, the organization of the statues amongst trees or on the edge of a children's play area is very different from the public squares and spaces they formerly commanded. The deliberate dislocation and even playful siting of statues formerly invested with the socialist realist mantra of ideological progression under the tutelage of a mentor figure renders them helpless, open to climbing on by children or ogling, as if in a museum of oddities. As one sympathetic cultural reviewer of Grūtas Park mused, it reflects Lithuanians' need to shed 50 years of Soviet permeation into all aspects of public life while simultaneously trying to rebuild a national identity:

> Through a dual process of museumification and commodification, these monuments became separated from the ideology which they represented, as well as society-at-large ... the public has been able to find dialogue, and, most importantly, humor, in the history of the sculptures, by acknowledging their museum and commodity values.[48]

In Eastern Europe, the former Soviet occupation has mostly left scars on the landscape or occasional opportunities for civic projects rather than well-subscribed tourism. More than 1,000 barracks were abandoned in the Visegrad countries (the Czech Republic, Poland, Hungary, and Slovakia). Some became housing projects in Poland and Hungary, and several air bases were converted to civilian use or maintained in their military role, but the majority of former barracks were left to decay. In the words of a Hungarian commentator, these have become 'ghost towns' where the failures of the recent past stare back at onlookers, who do not consider them part of their own history. The exclusion of locals from foreign military activity fostered rumours including secret atomic bomb bunkers, and mysteriously disappearing soldiers and civilians. Today, some niche, off-beat tourism feeds off these myths, inviting treks into the gloomy mysteries of some of the bigger and more intact sites in Poland (Kłomino, Pstraze), the Czech Republic (Milovice, Bzo Dar) and Hungary (Kunmadaras, Szentkirályszbadja). The internet, allowing the uploading of photos, video, music, and personal accounts of visits, provides both opportunity for exchange and an electronic canvas on which to post any communist-era artistry discovered in the remains. The internet also sustains amateur historians who recapture the experience of Soviet occupation through interviews with both Russians and locals and via chat forums.[49]

In Asia, the legacies of the conflict in Vietnam mark tourist trails, as we have discussed in relation to Hanoi. Recently, the Taiwanese islands of Kinmen (formerly Quemoy) and the Matsu Archipelago, located in the northwest Taiwan Strait – only 5 miles from Mainland China in the case of the main Matsu island of Nangan, and less than 2 miles in the case of the Kinmen group – have been increasingly promoted as logical tourist destinations. At the frontline of military jousting between the People's Republic of China (PRC) and Taiwan (then Formosa), the islands existed under a war zone administration that was lifted only in 1994. They became part of Chiang Kai-shek's Republic of China (ROC) when he and some 600,000 of his forces fled the mainland to set up government on Taiwan in 1949. In October that year, Chiang's troops fought off an attempt by Mao to seize

Kinmen. After the Korean War broke out on 25 June 1950, US support for the independent Taiwan firmed immediately. President Truman declared the Straits of Formosa to be neutral and ordered the US Seventh Fleet to patrol them. Taipei militarized both Kinmen and Matsu in ways that presaged a possible offensive against the mainland, as well as in defensive ways, and sent successive waves of national servicemen to bolster the islands' defences. The islands were prominent in world news during 1954–55 and again in 1959, when, in spikes of PRC-ROC tensions following further fortification of the islands, artillery fire from the mainland rained down on the inhabitants. In 1960, policy towards the islands became a recurring argument in the US Presidential debates between candidates Richard Nixon and John F. Kennedy. The coupling of 'Quemoy and Matsu' became something of a Cold War refrain as well as a Cold War flashpoint. From that time, too, relations between ROC troops and the mainland settled into a bizarre ritual of mainland artillery shelling every second day (of shells filled with propaganda rather than high explosives), in return for the US Seventh Fleet maintaining some distance. The shellings stopped in 1979.

In the case of Matsu, the unique underground military tunnels and building architectural features on its main island Nangan were key factors in the Taiwanese government designating it a 'national scenic area' in 1999, and as a potential World Heritage site in 2009. The Bei-Hei granite tunnels, designed to house equipment and protect landing craft linked to hidden outlets, were dug laboriously with simple tools by soldiers, and with considerable loss of life. An iron fort that once housed troops and several machine gun posts is at the other end of the island. One recent optimistic assessment of military and cultural heritage tourism on Matsu drew on a high recommendation from *Lonely Planet* and argued that its 'otherness' – its invitation to recall a vastly different life – leaves it well-placed for further tourist growth.[50]

For Kinmen, the transition from a militarized identity to demilitarization in the 1990s has followed a similar pattern, with regular groups of tourists arriving both from Taiwan's main island and Xiamen province on the Chinese mainland. The economy has undergone the shock of moving from a 'G. I. Joe' focus to catering for tourists, who had been visiting from the mainland in any case in the 1980s under the cover of official visits.[51] The military tunnels of the main island Greater Kinmen also are a tourist drawcard, as is a military museum boasting a jeep in which Chiang Kai-shek toured the island after the invading communists had been seen off in 1949. Kinmen has quickly developed a niche in selling cleavers and knives fashioned out of old artillery shells. Like Matsu, Kinmen's militarized past was the one successfully commodified, and it, too, is seeking World Heritage listing. As the author of a major study on Kinmen's history and remembering puts it:

> If authenticity means faithfulness to an inherited set of practices reproduced in a specific locale for specific purposes unconnected to the

market process, authenticity in Jinmen is distinguished by its link not to the pre-market past but to the geopolitical past.[52]

In making this transition, Kinmen's residents have maintained a narrative of suffering, including some gaining compensation from accidents and appropriations by the ROC government, and a narrative of stoic heroism in the face of constant shelling, as components of their modern identikits.[53] For both island groups, Mainland China (and nearby Xiamen Province in particular) is the major source of envisaged tourist growth. Direct travel has been allowed since 2001, and much of the tourism promotion and development has been aimed in this direction. Matsu has recently voted to introduce gaming. Greater Kinmen and Little Kinmen islands are to be joined by a bridge (over 3 miles long) due for completion in 2016, with 70 per cent of the envisaged traffic being tourists. An extension joining both islands to Xiamen Province has been mooted.[54]

As a source of tourist interest, the Cold War opens up new possibilities, especially where its legacy is marked in the landscape. Morgen Stenak, from the Danish Agency of Culture and responsible for 'Cold War – Hot Heritage' (a project exposing more Danish Cold War heritage to the public in 2012–13), puts it simply:

> Heritage tourism is a growing economy. One of the reasons to designate larger heritage regions is to cater [for] the development of Cold War heritage destinations with a range of interrelated sites that will meet different demands from the tourists.[55]

Texts and textbooks

The Cold War has stamped its contours on understandings of the twentieth century according to how it features in books and other acts of interpretation. In the hands of some, a phenomenon that lasted about 45 years, which was called a 'war' and ostensibly was global in its reach and featured the prospect of ending in cataclysmic nuclear Armageddon, can dominate international histories of the world since 1945. 'Every morning, for nearly half a century, people around the world woke up and wondered if this would be the day the world would end.' So runs the promotional blurb for CNN's 24-part documentary series on the Cold War first screened in 1998–99.[56] It is an exaggerated, perhaps even a sensational claim, but it effectively plays on the constant possibility of nuclear war. The historian Eric Hobsbawm wrote that the Cold War was a 'real' war, according to Hobbes' dictum that war includes a time when the will to do battle is sufficiently known. Indeed, Hobsbawm was even comfortable about describing it as 'a Third World War'.[57]

Unlike Hobsbawm, most historians suggest that the Cold War, while generally described as a global struggle, clearly was different from the two world wars of the first half of the twentieth century. But, in the minds of many, it nonetheless still assumes grand proportions. Whether writing from left or right vantage points, Cold War historians tend to claim that in many countries it shaped policies in relation to politics, cultural affairs, education, science, overseas trade, investment, and aid, as well as the more traditional war-like realms of defence and foreign policy.[58] And, although the proponents of war-by-proxy explanations can overstate the role of the superpowers in initiating 'hot' wars in Africa and Asia, there is strong consensus that Cold War factors accentuated local tensions behind some of the postwar conflicts in these places. These generally shared features stand in contrast to the fierce debates over who was more responsible for 'starting' the Cold War – for enabling US–Soviet relations to deteriorate to the point of such mutual mistrust that normal diplomatic solutions were rendered useless. Until recently, the United States and the Soviet Union tended to dominate in these debates. While American postwar allies such as Britain, West Germany, and France might be allowed some agency, they have tended to play secondary roles in influencing US and Soviet policy direction and mindsets rather than calling the main shots. In brief, according to the orthodox interpretation Stalin was mostly to blame for the origins of the Cold War. He broke wartime promises and was ideologically motivated and relentless in spreading Soviet influence in Eastern Europe after the war, accompanied by an overarching aim of the global spread of communism. Against this mindset, there was little the Americans could have done to avoid a rapid deterioration in relations. Revisionists, on the other hand, find the United States primarily to blame. While the Soviets acted to shore up their influence in Eastern Europe, revisionists suggest that this was defensive action, borne of having been invaded through that region in both world wars (and, stretching back even farther, by Napoleonic France, too). It also was in response to the US expansion of influence in postwar Europe, driven by their economic interests and exaggerated fear of communism. From the 1980s, post-revisionists have built bridges between the two earlier schools of thought, eschewing the apportionment of blame and instead suggesting that, while Stalin's actions in Eastern Europe may have contributed to the rapid breakdown in US–Soviet relations, the Americans did indeed have significant ambitions for extending their view of the postwar world order to Europe, thereby fuelling Stalin's suspicions.[59]

More recent Cold War history has gone in new directions, sometimes with the benefit of new archival material released since the collapse of the Soviet Union. These include greater sensitivity to cultural and technological development, perspectives from the 'periphery', from players other than the major powers, and efforts to 'de-centre' the Cold War, or prevent its overwhelming dominance in efforts to understand change in the second half of the twentieth century. The field remains a thriving and dynamic one as can be seen in the content of journals such as *Diplomatic History* (US), *Cold War History* (UK), and *Journal of Cold War Studies* (US). Herein, the work of other historians such as Anders Stephanson and Geir Lundestad plus the anthropologist Heonik Kwon have stimulated historical debate about relationships between US-defined and otherwise-defined ideas of the Cold War, between centre and periphery or localized conflict, and between geopolitics and social history.[60] In the United States in particular, there is a strong spread of Cold War historians and political scientists across the country in universities and colleges. Leading groups of researchers dedicated to the Cold War include the University of California, Santa Barbara's Center for Cold War Studies, the Harvard Project on Cold War Studies, the George Washington University Cold War Group, and New York University's Center for the United States and the Cold War. These groups foster scholarship, including graduate programmes, and some sustain archival collections. Independent of the academy, but generating voluminous scholarship (particularly that which draws on archival sources opened since the end of the Cold War), is the Cold War International History Project housed in the Woodrow Wilson International Center for Scholars in Washington DC. Several of these groups are producing easily accessible digitized collections of documents that can be readily used by educators around the globe.[61]

An assessment of US universities' and colleges' teaching materials published in 2008 found the subject of the Cold War to be a popular one, generally offered in History and International Relations programmes. It also appeared that the textbooks used were chosen from across the spectrum: orthodox (and neo-orthodox) as articulated by John Lewis Gaddis;[62] revisionist, featuring Walter LaFeber;[63] and, to a lesser extent, post-revisionist interpretations all were in wide use. Another widely-used textbook that combines a de-centring of the Cold War with a post-revisionist sensibility in relation to its beginning and end is David Reynolds' *One World Divisible: A Global History since 1945*. As the title suggests, Reynolds balances the forces of globalization against counter-forces and he finds important agency for the Cold War, but not to the exclusion of developments that owed to multiple phenomena, such as *inter alia* decolonization, urbanization, the communications revolution, second wave feminism, and new social movements.[64]

But the Cold War reaches beyond specialist groups in the academy. In the broader realm of public reading and school-based learning, the Cold War easily has become a dominant narrative framework for historians of the second half of the twentieth century. In other words, several historians have organized their histories of the world since 1945 very much according to the contours of the Cold War, with other themes of change relegated to some sort of secondary status. Journalist-historian Martin Walker, whose time as *Guardian* newspaper correspondent in Moscow gave him participant-observer status, made explicit this approach in the title of his book (of multiple editions) *The Cold War and the Making of the Modern World*.[65] In the hands of some historians, the Cold War simply appropriates the second half of the twentieth century.[66]

As indicated, the same is true for the CNN series *Cold War*. The scale, reach, and success of this documentary series make it stand out as a major bridge between scholarly interpretation and popular understanding of the Cold War. When screened in 1998, it ran in a prime-time slot on Sunday evenings. The US National Council for Social Studies, the peak body for supporting social studies education, soon endorsed the series and it went – in video format and at a nominal price – to US schools with its accompanying book.[67] A linked website, rich with interview material and interactive features (a dream resource for educators), was available until 2009. The series also was an international success. The head of the CNN network Ted Turner lavished money on production and instructed (British) producer Jeremy Isaacs to avoid triumphalism and partisanship in the telling of the story, and to 'do justice to the experience, reasoning, motives and actions of both the protagonist great powers involved'.[68] As the makers proudly boasted, in 'capturing the essence' of the 46-year period, they drew on 'more than 520 interviews, 8,500 film archive stories, 1,500 hours of film reference materials and 1,000 hours of original footage, filmed in 31 countries over a three year period'.[69] The wide list of those involved included Russian filmmakers and historians. In the eyes of many critics, the strategies of even-handedness, recruiting different authorities for episodes, and maximizing the voices and visuals of the times rather than any historian 'talking heads' made for success. Without the authority of guest historians, the selection of materials, the time allocated to certain topics, and the voice-over of narrator Kenneth Branagh all assumed increased importance. Arguably, the most constant thread in what is an essentially thematic format for the series is the arms race. The threat of nuclear apocalypse provides bookends to the series: the opening scenes of the first episode feature a nuclear explosion, and then take the viewer down the corridors, living, and meeting rooms of the Greenbrier Bunker, conjuring the prospect of the US government trying to survive the consequences of full-scale nuclear attack; and the last episode concludes with US president George H.W. Bush's television address of December 1991 declaring the confrontation between the West and communism to be over. Bush said that, for over 40 years, the struggle 'forced all nations to live under the threat of nuclear destruction'.[70]

The *Cold War* series also attracted criticisms, especially from neo-conservatives in the United States, on the grounds of 'moral equivalence': in their efforts towards even-handedness and comparison, the producers had strayed, in the eyes of commentators such as Charles Krauthammer, towards understating the evils of Soviet policy and over-playing the moments of excess in US policy. Krauthammer was particularly incensed by the switch, in one episode, from Stalin's enslavement (and often killing) of millions in labour camps, to the trampling of civil rights in the United States during the anti-communist crusade – or 'McCarthyism' – of the 1950s. Historians of the Cold War and of the Soviet Union engaged in debates that often were predictable according to liberal/conservative lines. The companion book to the series generated almost as much heat as the televised documentary series, and especially enraged conservatives with its finding that it was Gorbachev who called the biggest shots in bringing the Cold War to an end. Historian Robert Conquest, fellow of the conservative Hoover Institution, found many flaws and linked the book's failings to Turner and the liberal media establishment from whence it sprang:

> In a long book supposedly exploring every aspect of the Cold War we may conclude by noting it is strange to find one phenomenon of some significance in covering American attitudes to the Cold War and to the Soviet Union not treated here. That is, the position of the American media. One has only to note that a recent Nexis search of American newspapers in the postwar period reveals the word 'bellicose' applied to Reagan 211 times, to Margaret Thatcher 41 times, and to Brezhnev 5 times – this in a period covering the launch of the Afghan war. This attitude seems to have some application to this book, and of course, to its media sponsor.[71]

Not only were the historical travesties so grave, in the minds of those such as Conquest, but also the stakes were so high: this was a momentous, terrifying, century-defining conflict and the CNN series and its educational embrace meant the potential brain-washing of an entire generation of high school students. As Gabriel Schoenfeld put it, concluding in one of the most detailed public critiques:

> As younger generations that did not live through those terrors come of age, CNN's 24-part *Cold War* series, with its panoply of educational appurtenances, is likely to be the one version of this momentous stretch of the past that most people will see and remember.[72]

Schoenfeld, furthermore, bemoaned the lack of moral difference between the two sides – what she categorizes as 'good' and 'evil' – in the series, and what she regarded as the blurring and erasure of 'the moral and political categories that distinguish a democratic country like the United States from a totalitarian one like the USSR'. Schoenfeld concluded:

> Considering the great lengths to which the Soviet Union went to falsify history, the fact that the Cold War is today being introduced into the standard curriculum of American high schools is a nightmarish irony. It is also an insult to all those who paid a terrible price for risking their own freedom in freedom's name.

The education of young Americans is easily politicized, especially when a broadcaster becomes part of the teachers' toolkits.[73]

    In other places, the lack of knowledge of communism and the consequences of the Cold War is sometimes one of those embarrassing knowledge gaps revealed by surveys of school children that prompts

Western government response.[74] Not surprisingly, it is the American-European Cold War – the most popularly understood version of where the conflict was centred and defined – that is most expected and digested in schools. Finland, for instance, built a core curriculum for upper secondary schools wherein a section on international relations centred on Europe and the United States, taking students from the scramble for empire at the end of the nineteenth century and the First World War, to the interwar years and the Second World War, then the Cold War, and then the 'new period of insecurity' thereafter.[75] In British universities, the Cold War jostles with imperial and other takes on modern history to the extent that it does not enjoy the same programmatic status as in the United States. It does have strong standing in the London School of Economics (currently called its Cold War Studies Programme) and increasingly attracts social history projects aimed at collecting people's memories and connecting them with a formerly militarized British landscape – bunkers, testing grounds, bases where missiles stood ready etc. – and crisis moments such as the Cuban Missiles.[76] The British national curriculum for secondary school history has not made the Cold War a feature recently, although, under the heading of 'European and World History', the content notes list the changing nature of conflict and cooperation between nations and peoples, in addition to both world wars, the Holocaust, and other acts of genocide.[77] The draft curriculum proposed for 2014 onwards is more descriptive and includes references to 'the Cold War and impact of Communism on Europe' as well as 'the end of the Cold War and fall of the Berlin Wall' in relation to Britain in the twentieth century.[78]

These appraisals, of course, relate to educational programmes where the Cold War is present, and it is important to note that this is not the case globally. To provide some perspective, a UNESCO study of the teaching of history in African schools, conducted in 2010, found that:

> ... the most widely quoted themes are prehistory and the history of antiquity; the major empires, the middle ages, Islam; colonization; resistance movements, decolonization; the slave trade; the two world wars; and apartheid as well as socio-economic themes, including underdevelopment and poverty, democracy, etc.[79]

The Indian secondary school curriculum includes a theme on world history in which the late-nineteenth and twentieth centuries, as part of 'Paths to Modernization', feature the East Asian examples of China and Japan. A section on contemporary world politics in the political science field has the 'Cold War Era' as one of nine topics, some of the others including 'US Hegemony in World Politics', 'Alternative Centres of Power', and 'International Organizations'.[80]

The teaching of modern history in Russia has taken a stronger anti-American turn in recent years, as evidenced by two books published in 2007 and a commission ordered by Russian president Dmitry Medvedev in 2009 to counter the rewriting of history in ways prejudicial to Russia. One of the books, by A.V. Filippov, covers the Cold War period and aftermath and seeks to explain why the Soviet Union suddenly collapsed. It does this by finding weaknesses in Soviet leaders (for example, Stalin is brutal and vain, but his obsessive defensiveness also is explicable in the context of recent Soviet history and western hostility) and in the communist system, while maintaining a sympathetic stance towards Russia's entitlement to prominence in international affairs. This includes finding the Americans to have been implacably hostile and deserving of little credit for the end of the Cold War. As one reviewer puts it: 'The book's approach is, at one level, both polemically anti-Western and nationalistic, but without being pro-Soviet'.[81] In pointing to failings of the Soviet system that have been similarly identified by western historians – the inability to deal effectively with different nationalities, the lack of economic incentives and reforms when needed, and the refusal to introduce political reforms – Filippov maintains that Russia did not 'lose' the Cold War, and that *perestroika* triggered the collapse of the Soviet Union. Indeed, Russia offered huge concessions to the United States in the late-1980s but got nothing in return. Vladimir Putin's Russia is treated very sympathetically. A second book, focused on the multi-faceted features of globalization, finds the United States bent on world domination, or maintaining its hegemony, and like Filippov's account, points to modern Russia's need to determine its own affairs without western interference. In both cases, the term 'Cold War' is not deployed often nor with explanatory effect – a reminder that the terminology is very much the product of late-1940s American articulation that then spread through the western world.[82] Previously, in 2003, the Russian Ministry of Education withdrew its approval of a textbook that had highlighted the criminality of Soviet and tsarist regimes, their failures to reform and modernize, and the costs of their repressive state behaviour, especially that of the Soviet Union.[83]

The US–Russian dynamic looms large in these Russian textbooks, but less so in the learning of Russia's neighbours and former socialist republics where Russia is now the 'other', defined in opposition to newly-formed state identities. In general, the history instruction of those parts of the former Soviet Union now functioning as independent states tends to conform to the view that the making of a new nation also requires the destruction of an older one – in this case, a Soviet identity – and the more insistent this process, the more Russia, as the main inheritor of the Soviet identity, is required to respond with its own efforts at refashioning its history. The process is almost dialectical, in a mutual sharpening of different heritage. A 2009 study of almost 200 school history textbooks and teacher guides from the twelve former Soviet republics neighbouring Russia found that, with the exception of Belarus and possibly Armenia, the Russians have become the enemies of those countries.[84] In addition to what might be an expected reaction against decades of Russian/Soviet imperialism, there lies the attraction of detailing past victimization in order to shore up current legitimacy and avenues of possible claims for compensation for past wrongs.

In China, the last two decades have seen a flowering of scholarly activity in relation to the Cold War. In particular, historians in Beijing and Shanghai (including the Center for Cold War International History Studies at East China Normal University, Shanghai) have led the way in drawing on recently opened archives in China and in former communist countries to inject new perspectives into subjects such as the history of the Korean War, of Sino-Soviet relations, and of Sino-US relations. Some of the projects draw on international collaborations, and Cold War studies – with its clear embrace of the 'Cold War' terminology – is beginning to rival other strengths of Chinese historians.[85] In turn, 'world history' is beginning to have a greater presence alongside Chinese content in school textbooks, reflecting, in part, the fruits of these new approaches. But it is harder to argue that these academic initiatives have had great impact at junior and middle levels of education or with a more general public. The Ministry of Education maintains a tight grip on textbooks prescribed for schools; and these tend to couch international relations in the period following the Second World War as deriving from aggressive acts of US imperialism and little more. Television documentary, however, has drawn on some of the new histories in effective, updated renderings of episodes such as the Korean War.[86]

For the Japanese, the Cold War tends to be remembered indirectly, according to the theme of US occupation and strategic consequences of the US alliance. Yet the Cold War's role in the so-called 'memory wars' – where the focus is on representation of Japan's fifteen years of expansion and war between 1931 and 1945 – is significant. Cold War politics is entwined with the long Japanese silence on the violence perpetrated on its northeast Asian neighbours. Japan's isolation from China until the 1980s effectively closed off public debate of atrocities carried out in Manchuria in the 1930s, then in China, and the forced recruitment of Asian women as prostitutes ('comfort women') for the armed forces. The depiction, or absence, of these incidents in Japanese textbooks has been the subject of ongoing debate. The waning of US authority in the post-Cold War era is being felt in Japanese cultural expression, some of which is more muscular than has been the case since the end of the Second World War. And it is reasonable to expect that this waning will impact on future editions of school textbooks, too.[87]

Australian upper level secondary school students draw on a modern world history textbook produced in Britain.[88] In this survey of the twentieth century, the Cold War tells the story of what happened after 1945, although it goes under the heading not of Cold War but 'International Relations'. Those in the United States who railed against the 'moral equivalence' of CNN's *Cold War* probably would react against the even-handedness at work in the book's examination of agency and responsibility in the Cold War. But they might not cavil at the implicit message that, as the Cold War came to dominate international relations in the second half of the twentieth century, so did the United States dominate in its ever greater assumption of power and responsibility for democratic leadership. The Americans' European allies appear to play no significant role. While Korea, Cuba, and Vietnam appear as case studies of Cold War conflicts, it is the transatlantic idea of Cold War that prevails – perhaps unusually so, for an Australian education.[89]

Around the world, cultural institutions play explicit educational roles to varying degrees. While several of the bunkers discussed previously (see Chapter 2) offer special tours and features for school groups, Canada's Diefenbunker makes the strongest connections with school curriculum. The museum engages with the high school subject 'Canadian and World Studies' at two levels, grades 9–10 and grades 11–12. The more junior levels are promised a better understanding of Canada's involvement in the Cold War and understanding of Canada's participation in war, peace, and security exercises. By visiting the museum, furthermore, they will be able to identify some of the main events along a Cold War timeline, and they will understand the main events and main Canadian personalities to have shaped Canadian identity.[90] For Grades 11–12, the museum visit builds advanced understanding. Students will be able to:

- describe the effects of World War I, World War II, the Cold War, and selected regional conflicts on the nations of the world and on international relations over the course of the twentieth century
- demonstrate an understanding of the causes, course, and results of the Cold War (e.g., Stalinism; Cuban missile crisis; Olympic boycotts; destruction of the Berlin Wall)
- demonstrate an understanding of the nature of the world's power structure at the end of the Cold War (e.g., dominance of the United States; economic strength of Europe and Asia; role of religious fundamentalism in the Middle East; Russian assertion of territorial hegemony)
- demonstrate an understanding of how Canada's participation in significant international conflicts (e.g., Cold War; Gulf War) changed the way the country was perceived by the international community
- demonstrate an understanding of the key factors that have led to conflict and war
- demonstrate an understanding of the consequences of war
- describe the key factors that have motivated people to seek peace and to cooperate with others.[91]

The Diefenbunker thus does some heavy lifting in relation to the recent history of Canada in world affairs.

Although in its infancy, one of the most significant coordinated efforts to research, raise awareness, and educate younger generations about the crimes of communism is the European Union's Platform of European Memory and Conscience. It is the product of several streams of activity, including the

EU's declaration on 'European Conscience and Totalitarianism', and the Vilnius event in 2009 calling for the integration of Eastern Europe's experience of totalitarianism into a common European narrative. Since its formation in October 2011, membership of the group has grown rapidly to 37 organizations and institutes by early 2013, most of them being archival and research institutes focused on memory, reconciliation, and victims of totalitarianism or communism. The Platform leadership recognizes the race against time to preserve survivor memories and documentation relating to victims of communism, and has led the way in championing for archival openness and preservation. One of its start-up projects focuses on the totalitarian regimes of the Visegrad region, and aims at a series of meetings and conferences, plus a travelling exhibition on totalitarianism in Europe. Its ambitions in schooling are signalled in a forthcoming 'Reader for Older Secondary School Students'.[92] Historians in the countries of Central Europe appear to be working their way towards the difficult balancing act of drawing on the common experience of Soviet occupation as a basis for shared memories and textbook narratives without losing the sense of national history.[93] This move towards what might be called a pan-European narrative history also is driven by the sense that, having joined the EU, as many eastern European countries have done in the last decade, it was incumbent on them to reassert their Europeanness, and also their separateness from Russia. At the same time, the peoples of Central and Eastern Europe stand as some of the most special victims of a murderous twentieth century if they can tell of multiple acts of violence and oppression without being implicated in any of the crimes described – and deny Russia the status of 'liberator' at the end of the Second World War.[94]

Policy, political speech, and legitimacy

To some extent, the well-studied Cold War has become a casebook – a giant toolkit for those policymakers who make decisions under stress, and for the many observers of these policymakers. Over the 45-year period between the end of the Second World War and the collapse of the Soviet Union, American policymakers had regular recourse to analogies to help them understand Cold War crises and take appropriate actions. In the wake of North Korea's invasion of South Korea on 25 June 1950, for instance, US president Truman invoked memory of the British capitulation to Hitler at the Munich conference in 1938. Munich represented appeasement of a dictator who could not be appeased, but would continue on expansionist paths whenever they sensed weakness. We know that during the tense discussions in the White House in mid-1965 prior to escalating US military involvement in Vietnam, US president Lyndon Johnson and his advisers wondered which analogies best captured the situation they faced: Munich and the dangers of appeasement? The challenge posed at the outbreak of the Korean War in 1950? Or possibly the pivotal battle for the French in Vietnam, at Dien Bien

Phu in 1954? What lessons were drawn, and how influential, helpful, or misleading were the analogies in such cases, remain matters for historical debate.[95]

Since the collapse of communism in Europe, we might logically expect to see greater resort to analogy from an episode in the Cold War, especially with generational change. From the start of the twenty-first century, fewer of the policy-élite and political leaders have personal memories reaching back beyond 1945, and fewer still will have personal recollections in the very near future. Wars, in particular, tend to be remembered, at least in their early stages, according to memories of the last wars in which people were involved. The Cold War, then, to the extent that it was a 'war' or at least harboured 'wars', becomes an easily accessed casebook of analogies. By far the best-known episode for the lessons it suggests to modern policymakers, well after the collapse of the Soviet Union, is the Cuban Missile Crisis. The subject of many books, scholarly articles, opinion pieces, and archival collections, the thirteen days in October 1962 constitute a discrete case study in US executive decision-making under enormous pressure. The 'lesson' can vary considerably, but there is at least popular support for the view that president Kennedy avoided nuclear war through a blend of strength and simplicity in insisting on the speedy removal of the missiles from Cuba while helping his opponent Khrushchev save face in backing away from confrontation by Kennedy's promising not to invade Cuba (and privately promising to remove Jupiter missiles from Turkey). Both of these features grew from his conviction that common ground had to be found if a catastrophe were to be averted. As a lesson, the Cuban Missile Crisis also has featured in commentary on more recent international crises, and in school classrooms.[96] The fiftieth anniversary of the crisis in October 2012 prompted a flurry of renewed musing in Washington, Seoul, and elsewhere, over what JFK might do now, were he alive, in relation to dilemmas such as North Korea's and Iran's nuclear energy programmes and possible weapons manufacture.[97] Or what might George F. Kennan, the former diplomat and policy planner known as the 'father' of the US containment policy, have done?[98] There are limitations to what might be drawn from particular case studies, of course, but in the United States, where most of the case studies and interpretations appear, there remains a strong interest in personality and behaviour in crisis situations.

In the same vein, a half-century of East–West competition in propaganda production, radio and television wars, information services, and publicity campaigns leaves a formidable repository of successes and failures in what is now called 'public diplomacy'. Historian-public diplomacy expert Nicholas Cull has traced the rise and fall of the US Information Agency (set up in 1953 to coordinate a range of information activities, including the Voice of America) as an element of Cold War strategy.[99] Acknowledging that well-tended stories can shape national reputation by leaving lasting impressions, the motto of the US Information Agency was 'Telling America's Story to the World'. Cull has pointed to historical case studies in public diplomacy, lessons of what worked and what did not, and he calls for more so that we end up with a 'Public Diplomacy Playbook' as a next-phase capacity builder.[100] Here, Cold War-era cultural diplomacy can be instructive. In the 1950s, when the Soviet Union effectively was associating international communism with peace, the new US Information Agency took the photographic exhibition 'The Family of Man' on tour. The photographs portrayed all aspects of human life in different cultural contexts and without heavy-handed political messages. It was hugely popular in emphasizing the shared experiences of different peoples, and recaptured some of the humanist ground that Moscow had stolen. In fact, the exhibition even opened in Moscow as part of the American National Exhibition there in 1959. This was the occasion for another celebrated act of unplanned US public diplomacy, the so-called 'kitchen debate' between US vice president Richard Nixon and Soviet premier Khrushchev, inside a model kitchen sponsored by General Electric. Nixon's easy salesmanship for US consumer goods and high living standards, and his good natured but resolved approach to banter with the Soviet leader, again is fondly remembered in the context of modern preoccupations with 'soft power'.[101]

With the possible exception of the Cuban crisis of 1962, Cold War analogies lack the fixedness – the self-evident truths – that stick to Second World War analogies such as 'Munich', 'Yalta', or 'Pearl Harbor'. Yet the tale of bearing up successfully in the struggle against communism nonetheless is a powerful general message with potential for instancing. The Cold War has recurring importance in modern American politics, partly because US politicians are wired to speak about war. In that heady period prior to 2001, for instance, one major study dating from 1997 concluded that the Cold War 'shapes New American Politics'. Having made the term 'liberal' acquire a tinge of pink weakness during the Cold War, the Republicans proved adept at maintaining this connotation through the 1990s and beyond.[102] Strong conservative articulations of domestic and foreign policies drew on a linguistic toolkit that again borrowed from Cold War lessons to frame most of the important debates.[103] Other commentators suggested that rather than worrying about analogies or leaders, it was more important to recognize that the postwar national security state was the main ingredient in 'winning' the Cold War. Its new state–citizen contract and public–private partnerships secured the United States' eventual victory in the long struggle over the Soviet Union: 'America's open society provided domestic institutional arrangements that readily adapted to the Cold War's managerial and technological imperatives'.[104]

As we have seen, the Second World War has a particularly strong hold on the American imagination, as was shown by the repeated references to Pearl Harbor after the 9/11 attack in 2001. Later, in August 2007, president George W. Bush even attempted to draw a historical line between US involvement in the postwar reconstruction of Japan after 1945 and the on-going war in Iraq. Bush likened al-Qaeda's attacks on the United States and its allies to those of Japan in the Second World War, and then reminded his listeners of the opposition that had met the US-led (successful) rebuilding of the Japanese postwar economy, inviting them to view the US occupation of Iraq in the same terms. Bush omitted the Cold War context in which Japan was restored as a bulwark against the Soviet Union and China. His selective efforts were criticized by historians of postwar Japan such as John Dower.[105] And his administration's later references to the Cold War as instructive in the war on al-Qaeda left commentators wondering whether Bush intended to 'contain' America's enemies in Iraq and Afghanistan or engage in 'roll-back'.[106] Elsewhere, several prominent policymakers, including British prime minister Tony Blair, argued that the 9/11 attacks represented the dawn of an era in which there are no guidance markers, a complete break from the past.[107] This stood in stark contrast to political language in the United States. Not only Pearl Harbor, but also the Cold War quickly emerged in subsequent public discussion. From the group often labelled 'neoconservatives' in the United States came a counter-narrative to any notion of a rupture with the past, one of the United States needing to recover its nerve and pursue an aggressive foreign policy underpinned by the spread of values that had prevailed in the struggle against the Soviet Union: freedom, equality, and the spread of democracy – and a responsibility and preparedness to reshape other parts of the world in America's image. A huge literature now explores and critiques the ideas and influence of the 'neocons', some of whom assumed policymaking prominence in the government of George W. Bush. Not all of them drew on historical lessons, and the term neoconservative arguably has been stretched to cover too many varying positions. But, for thinkers such as Richard Perle, Charles Krauthammer, and Michael Leeden, the lessons of the Cold War were hugely important. In the hands of these defence policy commentators, and others involved in think-tanks such as the Project for the New American Century, they also focus on those periods of the Cold War when, in their view, the United States was bold and triumphant. Theirs was an effort to recapture the virtues of Cold War muscularity in US foreign policy, and the moral courage of leaders in particular, rather than one that allowed for all of the messy contours of the 45-year struggle. In other words, détente and 'Carterism' were examples of what not to do, and the resolve and action of presidents Truman, Reagan, and even JFK were models for what might now be emulated in US foreign policy.

Thus, Cold War episodes including the Korean War, the Cuban Missile Crisis, and Reagan's demands that Gorbachev tear down the Berlin Wall enjoyed very public recollection and circulation.[108] Neoconservatives argued for a 'return to history', as they defined it. The American mission to act wherever needed in order to cultivate the growth of 'free' societies, as articulated in key Cold War policy documents such as NSC-68 (1950), was something to be rekindled as a necessary part of national identity. Leading policymakers of the 1950s, such as US secretaries of state, had been right to stress that the struggle against communism was an ideological one in which the American way of life was being challenged – and the attacks of 9/11 represented a new ideological challenge. In Leeden's analysis, radical Islamists in the Middle East had replaced communists. Like communists, in order to survive the radical Islamists apparently needed to carry their revolution to the rest of the world; and in this way the clash between the United States and their new enemy was inevitable. To suggest otherwise was to shirk the responsibility that American forebears had envisaged, and which the likes of Truman and Reagan had courageously shouldered. Such conservative arguments had the added political attraction of making the Truman era the one period of bold internationalism, after which the Democratic Party began to lose its way.[109] Others focused less on analogy or past presidential courage, but drew similar connections between radical Islamism and earlier forms of extremism. In 2004, David Frum and Richard Perle wrote:

> Like communism, this ideology perverts the language of justice and equality to justify oppression and murder. Like Nazism, it exploits the injured pride of once-mighty nations. Like both communism and Nazism, militant Islam is opportunistic – it works willingly with all manner of allies, as the communists and Nazis worked with each other against the democratic West.[110]

The 'War on Terror' thus became the next case of *jus ad bellum* – a successor to twentieth-century conflicts marked by US leadership and success in a just cause.[111]

US president Barack Obama has taken a different line in relation to the Cold War, establishing a strong sense of distance between contemporary world problems and the former era. He angered conservative critics in 2009, when he told students in Moscow that the Cold War came to an end through the actions of many nations, and because the people of Eastern Europe and Russia stood up to bring it to an end. A pivotal role for the United States in bringing down the Soviet empire was missing in Obama's short sketch.[112] Those who look to the Cold War for inspiration, he suggested, need to look forwards instead, and shed old prejudices and suspicions. To the extent that it offers lessons, in Obama's hands, the Cold War demonstrated continuing American virtue and resolve in the preservation of freedom, but it quickly became an immensely dangerous and wasteful contest. It generated a hugely expensive nuclear arms race that has left a dangerous legacy, and requires him and his contemporaries to do more to free the world from nuclear weapons. The United States has a special obligation to provide leadership in this quest, he argued in a speech in 2009, because it remains the only nation to have used it against another country. The Cold War has disappeared, he said, but the nuclear weapons have not.[113]

In June 2013, Obama visited Berlin as the city was beginning a series of events to commemorate the fiftieth anniversary of US president Kennedy's famous visit in 1963, in which he declared solidarity with Europeans in the face of communist hostility. In front of the Schöneberg *Rathaus* in what then was part of West Berlin, JFK declared: '*Ich bin ein Berliner*'. Standing in front of the Brandenburg Gate (where Reagan had delivered his ultimatum to Gorbachev in June 1987), Obama briefly alluded to the collective victory of the West in the Cold War by stating that:

> ... because courageous crowds climbed atop that wall, because corrupt dictatorships gave way to new democracies, because millions across this continent now breathe the fresh air of freedom, we can say, here in Berlin, here in Europe – our values won. Openness won. Tolerance won. And freedom won here in Berlin.[114]

While he spoke of the new challenges shared by Europe and the United States in a way that was vaguely evocative of JFK, pointedly he used the occasion to call for a one-third reduction in US and Russian nuclear arsenals. 'Our work is not yet done,' said Obama, despite the lack of barbed wire and concrete that used to divide Berlin, and he urged leaders not to turn inward.[115] As part of his insistence that we must look forward rather than backward when pursuing peace, furthermore, Obama again reached back to JFK for sage words of advice:

> Chancellor Merkel mentioned that we mark the anniversary of President John F. Kennedy's stirring defense of freedom, embodied in the people of this great city. His pledge of solidarity – 'Ich bin ein Berliner' – [applause] echoes through the ages. But that's not all that he said that day. Less remembered is the challenge that he issued to the crowd before him: 'Let me ask you,' he said to those Berliners, 'let me ask you to lift your eyes beyond the dangers of today' and 'beyond the freedom of merely this city.' Look, he said, 'to the day of peace with justice, beyond yourselves and ourselves to all mankind'.[116]

Post-1991 Russian leaders have engaged with the Soviet past in ways that warrant extended discussion, but some of the main contours can be sketched here. Boris Yeltsin, the first president of the post-Soviet Russian Federation, was surrounded by supporters, nervous, at first about the possibility of a communist restoration, and therefore rejected the Soviet era decisively and loudly. This included street-name changes and the removal of statues and other Soviet symbols; but they also stopped short of comprehensive rejection of sacred sites such as the Lenin Mausoleum on Red Square, or public embrace of the many victims of Stalinism. As his leadership faltered amidst economic shocks and popular unrest in the late-1990s, Yeltsin invoked heroic figures pre-dating 1946 – from Peter the Great to the celebrated general of the Great Patriotic War Marshal Georgy Zhukov – but failed to suppress rising sympathy for the Soviet era or develop strong alternatives, historical touchstones around which identity could be forged.[117] When Vladimir Putin succeeded Yeltsin as president in 2000, he found strengths in different parts of the past – including, most notably, the Soviet era – to create a narrative that arrived at a modern Russia as inheritor of multiple lines of virtue. As we have noted, the Second World War – for Russians the Great Patriotic War – is especially important in this structural history, and therefore Stalin's reputation cannot be sullied completely. Excesses including the purges and the Gulags need to be acknowledged, but they can be explained partly by the gravity of internal and external threats and they can be set against a long list of heroic achievements. When Putin awarded the Order of Merit in 2004 to Soviet Army Marshal Dmitrii Iazov, he honoured an outspoken admirer of Stalin as a military leader and an opponent of historians who said otherwise. In the following year, Putin publicly declared that the collapse of the Soviet Union was the greatest geopolitical catastrophe of the twentieth century. The many Russians who have experienced falling living standards, high unemployment, and other upheavals of an economy in uneven transformation since 1991, could well be expected to agree.[118]

The stirring of European-Baltic memory acts around the story of Soviet occupation of Eastern Europe and the Baltic States from the latter part of the Second World War presents formidable problems for modern-day Moscow. As has been suggested above, Russian leaders have taken very seriously the need to re-craft their history in relation to the Cold War contest with the United States. They also seek to maintain their standing in European history and remain a European power. In declaring this in 2005, Putin exclaimed:

> For three centuries, we – together with the other European nations – passed hand in hand through reforms of Enlightenment, the difficulties of emerging parliamentarianism, municipal and judiciary branches, and the establishment of similar legal systems ... I repeat we did this together, sometimes behind and sometimes ahead of European standards.[119]

The tendency towards a 'common' Eastern European history that emphasizes the dual brown-red totalitarianism of Nazism and Soviet communism erodes this story of continuous Russian enrichment of Europe. Even worse, it diminishes the significance of the Second World War as a discrete event. If the strongest common memory and mechanism that can act towards social cohesion in Russia is the commemoration of the Great Patriotic War, then modern Russian leaders logically insist on it being treated as a unique event in which 'they' (in the guise of the Soviet Union) bore the greatest hardships and contributed the most to Hitler's defeat and the liberation of Europe. As Putin has intended, in this mnemonic event there is continuity between the

Soviet Union and modern Russia, but in other ways the link remains problematic. Russia's legal succession to the Soviet Union is not matched by legal or civic acceptance of the crimes of Stalinism and afterwards. The victims might be commemorated but the crimes have not been squarely faced. Whereas Stalin's excesses often are condemned publicly, he none-theless remains a figure with considerable support in some quarters – with around half the population apparently viewing him as having done more good than harm.[120]

These are some of the more recurring themes in political discourses of countries where the nexus between history and identity draws in the Cold War in insistent ways. They are not the only ones. To recall some obvious examples, in North Korea, Pyongyang has long rehearsed a history of US threats (especially since the stationing of nuclear missiles in South Korea from 1958) as the basis for its need to have its own nuclear weapons. Recent tensions over North Korea's missile testing and nuclear energy programme have triggered recourse to these well-worn themes, albeit with new levels of familiarly bellicose language.[121] In the lead up to the 2008 election in Venezuela, president Hugo Chávez deployed colourful anti-American rhetoric, inviting the electorate to recall US Cold War interventions in Latin America and their attempts to rid themselves of the 'troublesome' Fidel Castro in nearby Cuba.[122] Used strategically, Cold War history retains its capacity to confer legitimacy in political settings.

Voices and ghosts

One of the most significant trends in twentieth-century history is the emergence of new archival information, social histories, fiction, film, and memoirs from various parts of the world. These sources provide stimulation to our knowledge and understanding of recent events in ways that make it increasingly important to move beyond notions of the Cold War as being excluded to the imagined and unrealized threat of apocalyptic war between nuclear powers.

Some of the new sources, such as Soviet documents relating to the Cuban Missile Crisis, or new evidence of cooperation between the KGB and the *Stasi*, inject new life into familiar Cold War episodes and themes.[123] Simi-larly, translations of key documents or, at the more popular level, novels bring fresh material to an English-speaking world that to date has shaped how the Cold War is understood. To take a Vietnamese example, Bao Ninh's 1991 war novel *The Sorrow of War* found its way with a broad read-ership and onto school reading lists. Other material goes to the realities of terror and state violence that thrived in the climate induced by the imagined 'Cold War'. Recent histories of Latin America, for instance, suggest that the Cold War has cast such a long shadow in politics there that we might be unwise to consider it 'over'. If, as historian Greg Grandin argues, the United States legitimized state terror in Latin America since setting the precedent by their sponsored military coup in Guatemala in 1954, they also denied another possibility: the real alternative of Marxism, allied more to progressive ideals and democratic reform than to Moscow. Continuing to deny the alternative is the ongoing work of history in the hands of contemporary leaders and allies.[124]

Acts of remembering are fundamental to some of these histories of terror and violence, especially where there is a strong sense of unresolved tension between different groups and/or between an 'official' narrative and the actual lived experiences and legacies of brutal events. In Indonesia, the counter-coup led by General Suharto that resulted in his supplanting of president Sukarno in 1965–66, also unleashed a wave of violence and killings across the Indonesian archipelago lasting more than five months. More than 500,000 were killed and a further one million were imprisoned. The victims included not only members of the Indonesian Communist Party (*Partai Komunis Indonesia*, PKI), but also those associated or thought to be associated with the PKI (plus, as is the way with both systemic and localized violence, anyone who was in the wrong place at the wrong time). While academics have produced studies based on witness testimonies and subsequent acts of remembering, the lack of state-endorsed truth and reconciliation, and the continued demonization of the PKI, all have made acute the sense of active forgetting. Indonesia's political left was effectively excised, and has not reappeared.[125] Instead, a disturbed landscape invites interpretation through cultural means. As one researcher of the violence on the island of Bali puts it: 'The past soaks into the ground of the present, saturating it with meaning and shifting the landscape with its cultural and emotional weight. It can be buried or even burned, but its ashes change the composition of the soil.'[126] Others have written about the presence of ghosts on lands where mass killings occurred.[127]

The cultural/spectral lens was prominent in a four-day event, held in Jakarta in 2011, which considered 'Indonesia and the World in 1965'. The event, sponsored by the Goethe-Institut, featured dance and puppet theatre as well as academic exchange. Franz-Xaver Augustin, director of the local Goethe-Institut centre, told the *Jakarta Post* that Germany had found a way to deal with the past, and that if a society did not deal with its traumas they would come back to haunt people.[128] Elsewhere, Heonik Kwon has shown how ghosts of those killed in Vietnam play significant cultural roles in modern communities there and provide a means of historical reflection. The extent of building and engineering works undertaken in Vietnam since the 1990s makes the presence of human remains below the surface of life all the more real and has been accompanied by a revival of ancestor worship. If these developments seem too far removed from the idea of remembering the Cold War in Vietnam, then we need to consider the power of social networks resulting in the widespread remembering of ghosts and liberating them from the tragic circumstances of war-related death. In a pointer towards further work on 'spectrally-informed' remembrance of Cold War

violence, Kwon suggests: 'This network of spirits is open to diverse historical identities and mobilizes their individual grievances to an imaginative,
collective drama involving an expanding circle of actors.'[129]

In other parts of Asia, in particular, the Cold War simply is too 'unfinished' to remember in ways that suggest consensus and reconciliation. Even
so, these places are far from devoid of jostling state-centred and socially-
based forms of shared and common memories. Apart from the obvious
example of Koreans enduring ongoing North–South tension, there is an
archipelago of Cold War islands in the East China Sea. Kinmen and Matsu
may embrace tourism and memories of their past valour, but also they
remember the suffering wrought by decades of enforced restrictions and
militarization as they induce tourists to visit military tunnels and purchase
souvenirs such as knives carved out of artillery shells. Upon arrival at the
international airport on the ROC's main island of Taiwan, unsuspecting
visitors may be shocked to discover signs pointing out the way to air-raid
shelters. In the capital Taipei, two museums located within easy walking
distance of each other tell stories that, at best are redolent with tension, and
at worst downright contradictory. The 228 Memorial Museum commemorates the stirring of mass movement towards political reform and
civil liberties in 1947. The museum was built in 1997, exactly 50 years after
the event of 28 February 1947 (from which its name derives), and it faces the
National Taiwan Museum, built in 1908 during the period of Japanese rule
(1895–1945). The protest actions, rejecting the authoritarian government
controls then in place, occurred in the wake of a citizen accidentally killed
by police who were enforcing strict rules about the sale of consumer goods –
in this particular case, contraband cigarettes. The 'event' of 28 February
1947 actually lasted far longer than one day. More than 20,000 were killed in
the weeks that followed, and some of those imprisoned remained locked up
until the early-1980s. Taiwan's leader Chen-Yi enlisted military support from
Chiang Kai-shek (at this time still on Mainland China) to crush the rebels.
According to the 228 Memorial Museum, the crushing of dissent was 'a
Formosan holocaust that left an indelible scar and long-lasting impact on the
minds and souls of the Taiwanese people'.[130] The museum commemorates
those who suffered and locates the event in a narrative of democracy and
concern for human rights stirring in Taiwan – both before the event and in
long-awaited major political changes during the mid-1980s.

A short walk to Taipei's Liberty Square (formerly Memorial Hall Square
but renamed to mark the success of pro-democracy demonstrations held
there in the late-1980s and early-1990s) leads to the grand Chiang Kai-shek
Memorial where the former president's life and spiritual guidance of Taiwan
are celebrated in art, writings, artefacts, and a giant seated statue. An elaborate changing of the guards routine helps give the site prominence on Taipei
tourist itineraries. For a short time, between 2007 and 2009, the hall was
renamed the National Taiwan Democracy Memorial Hall, but Chiang's
plaque was restored after divided opinion, protests, and questions over the

Figures 4.4 and 4.5 Air raid shelter sign at airport. And a memorial to victims in front of the 228 Memorial Museum. Taipei, February 2013.

legality of the change all forced the government's hand. In the hall, Chiang's achievements as Taiwanese president from 1948 to 1975 dominate the exhibits and accompanying narrative. Conveniently, then, there is no attempt to engage with the 228 event of 1947 – or its lingering aftermath. The two museums do not 'meet' at all in their respective acts of remembering and commemoration.[131]

And further north, on the Japanese prefecture island of Okinawa, the sense of popularly remembered grievances resulting from the Cold War is aimed at two centres of power: Tokyo and Washington. The island celebrates its heritage as the centre of the Ryukyu kingdom until it was absorbed into Meiji Japan in 1879. The Okinawan Prefectural Museum traces this period as the source of local cultural pride.[132] Since that time, suggests the museum, Okinawan inhabitants were dragged into Japan's militarism, which led to the island experiencing one of the fiercest battles of the Second World War and (mainland) Japanese military commanders then forcing acts of mass suicide as invading US soldiers approached in 1945. Okinawans then endured American administration for 27 years, until 'Reversion' to Japanese administration in 1972. During that time, the island's strategic significance and usefulness to the United States as a main foothold in the Pacific was underlined by the Korean War and then American intervention in Vietnam. US bases on Okinawa played crucial roles in both conflicts. Since 1972, with Tokyo's agreement, the Americans have maintained around 27,000 military personnel on the islands at several bases, amounting to 75 per cent of all US forces in Japan. While the island's economy has become increasingly dependent on the Americans, its main museum tells of growing calls for independence. Acts of violence have played a role in stirring local antagonism, including, most notably, US servicemen's rape of a twelve-year-old girl in 1995 and another rape case involving two US naval personnel and a local Okinawan woman in 2012.[133] Yet, the vexed issues of what economic alternatives lie ahead for Okinawa, and how Tokyo might change the Cold War script that continues to define Okinawans' identity, await more rigorous decision-making than what has prevailed to date.[134] In contemplating greater independence, as the museum suggests, Okinawans are needing to challenge not just the current policy settings of Tokyo and Washington, but also the two allies' consensus on what is best remembered and what is best ignored or forgotten. The archipelago of Cold War islands is a region from which we should expect increasing numbers of shared and common memories – both in contest and sometimes in joint agitation for change.

Notes

1 As announced at 'BBC Two Announces New Season of Drama and Documentaries to Explore the Cold War', *BBC*, 16 May 2013, www.bbc.co.uk/mediacentre/latestnews/2013/cold-war-season.html (Last accessed May 2013).
2 As with some other cases of espionage, the case against Hiss is not absolutely conclusive but the weight of historical consensus makes it very likely.

3 For example, see Christopher Andrew and Vasili Mitrokhin, *The Sword and the Shield: The Mitrokhin Archive and the Secret History of the KGB* (New York: Basic Books, 2001).

4 For example, see John Earl Haynes, Harvey Klehr, and Alexander Vassiliev, *The Rise and Fall of the KGB in America* (New Haven: Yale University Press, 2006). And the roundtable discussion of this work in Thomas Maddux et al., *H-Diplo Roundtable Review*, vol. XI, no. 9 (14 December 2009). Accessible online at www. h-net.org/~diplo/roundtables/PDF/Roundtable-XI-9.pdf (Last accessed February 2013).

5 Paul Frazier, 'The Venona Project and Cold War Espionage', *Organization of American Historians (OAH) Magazine of History*, October 2010.

6 Museum of Australian Democracy, 'The Petrov Affair', *Museum of Australian Democracy: Red Alert – Spies & Codes – The Affair – Royal Commission – The Split*, http://moadoph.gov.au/exhibitions/online/petrov/ (Last accessed May 2013).

7 Ellen Schrecker, *Many are the Crimes: McCarthyism in America* (Boston: Little, Brown and Company, 1998).

8 Miller's play *The Crucible*, written in 1952, was first performed in January 1953. For his later reflection on what motivated him to write the play, see Arthur Miller, 'Why I Wrote "The Crucible": An Artist's Answer to Politics', *The New Yorker*, 21 October 1996.

9 Thom Loverro, 'A Fraud that is Finally being Exposed', *The Washington Times*, 17 March 2005.

10 Wesley A. Britton, *Onscreen and Undercover: The Ultimate Book of Movie Espionage* (Westport, Connecticut: Praeger, 2006), pp. 98–101.

11 Kang Je-gyu, *Tae Guk Gi: The Brotherhood of War* (South Korea: Samuel Goldwyn Films, 2004).

12 'Cold War Memories are Made of This', *Toronto Star*, 30 June 2010.

13 Visit by David Lowe in November 2012. Also 'Secret War', *Imperial War Museum*, www.iwm.org.uk/exhibitions/iwm-london/secret-war (Last accessed January 2013).

14 'History & Mission', *International Spy Museum*, www.spymuseum.org/about/history-mission/ (Last accessed January 2013). Ronald Radosh, 'Scoping Out the International Spy Museum', *Academic Questions*, vol. 23, no. 3 (2010), p. 287.

15 Radosh, 'Scoping Out the International Spy Museum', pp. 290–91.

16 International Spy Museum, *Educator Guide. The Enemy Within: Terror in America, 1776 to Today* (2004). Accessible online at www.spymuseum.org/files/enemy_edguide.pdf (Last accessed April 2013).

17 Tom Vanderbilt, *Survival City: Adventures among the Ruins of Atomic America* (New York: Princeton Architectural Press, 2002), p. 19.

18 See the high quality oral history website *Voices of the Manhattan Project*, http://manhattanprojectvoices.org (Last accessed March 2013).

19 National Atomic Testing Museum, 'The Blast'.

20 Interview with Mr Morten Stenak, Danish Agency for Culture, in November 2012.

21 Motto used on the website *National Army Museum*, www.nam.ac.uk (Last accessed May 2013).

22 Visit to National Cold War Exhibition by author David Lowe in November 2012.

23 Visit by David Lowe in November 2012. And also 'Special Displays: National Service', *National Army Museum*, September 2011, www.nam.ac.uk/exhibitions/special-displays/national-service (Last accessed May 2013).

24 Visit by David Lowe in November 2012.

25 National Cold War Museum, 'National Curriculum', *Royal Air Force Museum Cosford: National Cold War Exhibition*, www.nationalcoldwarexhibition.org/learn/national-curriculum.cfm (Last accessed October 2012).
26 Air Vice-Marshal (ret'd) Peter Dye OBE, 'About Us', *Royal Air Force Museum Cosford: National Cold War Exhibition*, www.nationalcoldwarexhibition.org/about-us.cfm (Last accessed October 2012).
27 Visit by David Lowe in November 2012.
28 Ibid.
29 Ibid.
30 National Cold War Exhibition, 'Museum Commemorates 50th Anniversary of Cuban Missile Crisis', *Royal Air Force Museum Cosford: National Cold War Exhibition*, 3 October 2012, www.nationalcoldwarexhibition.org/news/article.cfm?news_id=610 (Last accessed November 2012).
31 Hutchings, 'Cold Europe', p. 12.
32 Department of Defense, *Coming in from the Cold: Military Heritage in the Cold War. Report on the Department of Defense Legacy Cold War Project* (Washington DC: US Government Printing Office, 1994), p. 41.
33 Ibid. pp. 3–5.
34 John A. Salmon, *Protecting America: Cold War Defensive Sites. A National Historic Landmark Theme Study* (Washington DC: National Historic Landmarks Program, US Department of Interior, 2011), pp. 97–99, 102.
35 D. Page, 'Protect and Survive', in *Defence Sites: Heritage and Future*, eds C. Clark and C.A. Brebbia (Southampton: WIT Press, 2012).
36 The bunker is in Brooklands Avenue, Cambridge.
37 Wayne Cocroft, 'Archaeological Field Survey and Investigation: Cold War', *English Heritage*, www.english-heritage.org.uk/professional/research/landscapes-and-areas/archaeological-field-survey-and-investigation/cold-war/ (Last accessed March 2013). And Jason Cumming, 'Brits put Cold War Bunker on Preservation List: U.S.-built Fortress left Obsolete by Fall of Berlin Wall becomes Landmark', *NBC News*, 5 November 2009, www.nbcnews.com/id/33506583/ns/world_news-fall_of_the_berlin_wall_20_years_later/t/brits-put-cold-war-bunker-preservation-list/#.UcUyVRyP0QI (Last accessed April 2013).
38 More details of the English Heritage programme are outlined in Cocroft, Thomas, and Barnwell, *Cold War*.
39 'Network', *The Baltic Initiative and Network*, http://coldwarsites.net/network (Last accessed December 2012).
40 Ibid.
41 Ibid.
42 Rasmussen, *Travel Guide*.
43 Ibid. p. 3
44 'About Us', *Grūtas Park*, www.grutoparkas.lt/?lang=gb (Last accessed April 2013).
45 Konstantinas Rečkovas, 'Grutas Park: A Social Realism Museum Attracts 100,000 Visitors a Year', *The Ukrainian Week*, 4 February 2012, http://ukrainianweek.com/History/41349 (Last accessed April 2013).
46 See Craig Nelson, 'Stalin World Opens to Visitors', *The Telegraph*, 1 April 2001, www.telegraph.co.uk/news/worldnews/europe/lithuania/1314998/Stalin-World-opens-to-visitors.html (Last accessed January 2013).
47 Grūtas Park, 'About Us'.
48 Monika Bernotas, 'Grutas Park and the Fate of Soviet Statuary in Lithuania', *Art in Russia*, 7 December 2012, http://artinrussia.org/grutas-park-and-the-fate-of-soviet-statuary-in-lithuania/ (Last accessed January 2013).

49 János Deme, 'Dead Ends of the Socialist Arms Race: Abandoned Soviet Barracks in Central Europe', *Visegrad Revue*, 6 March 2013, http://visegradrevue.eu/?p=1628 (Last accessed April 2013).

50 Chao-Ching Fu, 'From a Military Front to a Cold War Heritage Site: A Study of the Prospect of Matsu Archipelago as Sustainable Tourism Islands', *ICOMOS Open Archive*, 2012, http://openarchive.icomos.org/1258/ (Last accessed May 2013).

51 Michael Szonyi, *Cold War Island: Quemoy on the Front Line* (Cambridge: Cambridge University Press, 2008), p. 209.

52 Ibid. p. 210.

53 Ibid. pp. 236–37.

54 Li Ji-Qiang, 'Construction for Kinmen Bridge Begins and President Ma Hopes it Becomes a New Landmark for Kinmen', *Kinmen County Government*, 13 November 2012, www.kinmen.gov.tw/Layout/main_en/News_NewsContent.aspx?NewsID=103862& path = 5551& LanguageType = 2 (Last accessed May 2013).

55 Morgen Stenak, 'Cold War – Hot Heritage' presentation, 2012, supplied to David Lowe.

56 As appearing on the cases of the videos of the 24-episode series *Cold War* (CNN, 1998).

57 Eric Hobsbawm, *Age of Extremes: The Short Twentieth Century, 1914–1991* (London: Abacus, 1995), p. 226.

58 In addition to discussion below on textbooks, other examples written for a broad readership and sometimes incorporating primary documents and oral histories include Kevin Hillstrom, *The Cold War* (Detroit: Omnigraphics, 2006). Jussi M. Hanhimäki and Odd Arne Westad, eds, *The Cold War: A History in Documents and Eyewitness Accounts* (New York: Oxford University Press, 2003). Robert J. McMahon, *The Cold War: A Very Short Introduction* (London: Oxford University Press, 2003). Katherine A.S. Sibley, *The Cold War* (Westport, Connecticut: Greenwood Press, 1998). James R. Arnold and Roberta Wiener, eds, *Cold War: The Essential Reference Guide* (Santa Barbara: ABC-CLIO, 2012). Jeremy Isaacs and Taylor Downing, *Cold War: An Illustrated History, 1945–1991* (Boston: Little, Brown and Company, 1998).

59 M.F. Hopkins, 'Continuing Debate and New Approaches in Cold War History', *History Journal*, vol. 50, no. 4 (2007). Michael J. Hogan and Thomas G. Paterson, eds, *Explaining the History of American Foreign Relations*, 2nd ed. (Cambridge: Cambridge University Press, 2004). Hope Harrison, 'Teaching and Scholarship on the Cold War in the United States', *Cold War History*, vol. 8, no. 2 (May 2008), pp. 259–64.

60 Geir Lundestad, *The United States and Western Europe since 1945: From 'Empire' by Invitation to Transatlantic Drift* (New York: Oxford University Press, 2003). Anders Stephanson, *Manifest Destiny: American Expansion and the Empire of the Right* (New York: Hill and Wang, 1995). Heonik Kwon, *Ghosts of War in Vietnam* (Cambridge: Cambridge University Press, 2008). Kwon, *The Other Cold War*.

61 Harrison, 'Teaching and Scholarship on the Cold War in the United States', pp. 259–64.

62 John Lewis Gaddis, *We Now Know: Rethinking Cold War History* (New York: Oxford University Press, 1997). And his more recent study *The Cold War: A New History* (New York: Penguin, 2005).

63 Walter LaFeber, *America, Russia and the Cold War, 1945–2002*, 9th ed. (New York: McGraw Hill, 2002). (And a 10th edition, covering 1945–2006, was published in 2008.)

64 Reynolds, *One World Divisible*.

65 Martin Walker, *The Cold War and the Making of the Modern World* (New York: H. Holt, 1995).

66 This tendency is apparent in works such as S.J. Ball, *The Cold War: An International History, 1947–1991* (London: Arnold, 1998). And Wayne C. McWilliams

and Harry Piotrowski, *The World since 1945: A History of International Relations*, 7th ed. (Boulder, Colorado: Lynne Rienner, 2009).

67 Isaacs and Downing, *Cold War*.

68 Quoted in Wiener, *How We Forgot*, p. 263.

69 As appearing on the cases of the videos of the CNN series *Cold War* 1998.

70 Episode 24, 'Conclusions: 1989–91', ibid.

71 Wiener, *How We Forgot*, pp. 264–68. Richard Pipes, Robert Conquest, and John Lewis Gaddis, 'The Cold War over CNN's Cold War', *Hoover Institution: Stanford University*, 1994, www.hoover.org/publications/hoover-digest/article/7459 (Last accessed December 2012).

72 Gabriel Schoenfeld, 'Twenty-Four Lies about the Cold War', *Commentary*, March 1999, www.commentarymagazine.com/article/twenty-four-lies-about-the-cold-war/ (Last accessed December 2012).

73 Since the CNN controversy, the Corporation for Public Broadcasting's education programmes have attracted similar criticisms for their 'emotional' basis of learning.

74 A survey of Swedish children in 2010, for instance, revealed little recognition of 'Gulag' and virtually no recognition of 'Bolshevik', prompting corrective action by the Swedish government. See Norden, 'Swedish School Children's Knowledge of Communist War Crimes is Dire', *Norden: Nordic Council of Ministers' Office in Estonia*, 1 October 2010, www.norden.ee/en/about-us/news/item/7526-swedish-school-childrens-knowledge-of-communist-war-crimes-is-dire (Last accessed January 2013).

75 Finnish Board of Education, *National Core Curriculum for Upper Secondary Schools* (Helsinki: Finnish Board of Education, 2003), p. 183.

76 For example, see the projects 'Cold War Anglia Revealed', *University of East Anglia*, 30 March 2013, www.uea.ac.uk/mac/comm/media/press/2013/March/cold-war-anglia-project (Last accessed April 2013). And Robert Knight, 'Cold War History', *Loughborough University*, www.lboro.ac.uk/departments/phir/research/projects/cold-war-history/ (Last accessed April 2013).

77 UK Qualifications and Curriculum Authority, *History: Programme of Study for Key Stage 3 and Attainment Target (Extract from The National Curriculum 2007)* (Qualifications and Curriculum Authority: Crown Copyright, 2007), p. 116. Accessible online at: http://media.education.gov.uk/assets/files/pdf/h/history%202007%20programme%20of%20study%20for%20key%20stage%203.pdf (Last accessed August 2012).

78 Department for Education, *History: Programmes of Study for Key Stages 1–3* (Crown Copyright, February 2013), p. 9. Accessible online at: https://media.education.gov.uk/assets/files/pdf/h/history%2004-02-13.pdf (Last accessed 3 May 2013).

79 Zakari Dramani-Issifou, *Report on the Current State of History Teaching in Africa* (UNESCO Culture Sector, 2010), p. 9. Accessible online at: www.unesco.org/new/fileadmin/MULTIMEDIA/HQ/CLT/CLT/pdf/General_History_of_Africa/GHA_Evaluation%20Report%20-%20working%20document%203.pdf (Last accessed February 2013).

80 Indian Central Board of Secondary Education, *Senior School Curriculum, 2015*, vol. 1 (New Delhi: Central Board of Secondary Education, 2013). Accessible online at: http://cbseacademic.in/web_material/Curriculum/SrSecondary/2015_Senior_Curriculum_Volume_1.pdf (Last accessed May 2013).

81 David Wedgwood Benn, 'The Teaching of History in Present-Day Russia', *Europe-Asia Studies*, vol. 62, no. 1 (2010). The book referred to is A.V. Filippov, *Noviyshaya istoriya Rossii, 1945–2007. Kniga dlya uchitelya* (Moscow: Prosveshchenie, 2007).

82 Ibid. pp. 176–77.

83 Thomas Sherlock, *Historical Narratives in the Soviet Union and Post-Soviet Russia: Destroying the Settled Past, Creating an Uncertain Future* (New York: Palgrave Macmillan, 2007), pp. 168–73.
84 Torbakov, 'History, Memory and National Identity', p. 213.
85 Zhi Liang, Yafeng Xia, and Ming Chen, 'Recent Trends in the Study of Cold War History in China', *Wilson Center: Cold War International History Project*, 2012, www.wilsoncenter.org/publication/recent-trends-the-study-cold-war-history-china (Last accessed May 2013).
86 Yafeng Xia, 'The Study of Cold War International History: A Review of the Last Twenty Years', *Journal of Cold.War Studies*, vol. 10, no. 1 (2008).
87 For detailed exploration, see Ann Sherif, *Japan's Cold War: Media, Literature, and the Law* (New York: Columbia University Press, 2009).
88 Ben Walsh, *GCSE Modern World History*, 2nd ed. (London: Hodder Education, 2001).
89 Ibid. pp. 318–423.
90 'Your Visit: School Tours – Curriculum Links – Grades 9–10', *Diefenbunker: Canada's Cold War Museum/Musée canadien de la Guerre froide*, http://diefenbunker.ca/pages/school_tours/curriculum_links_grade_9–10.shtml (Last accessed May 2013).
91 'Grades 11–12', ibid.
92 For details, see 'About the Project: Strategic Grant from the International Visegrad Fund', *Platform of European Memory and Conscience*, 17 August 2011, www.memoryandconscience.eu/about-the-platfor/ (Last accessed May 2013).
93 See the discussion between several central European historians in Oldřich Tůma et al., 'Teaching History in Central Europe', *Visegrad Insight*, vol. 1, no. 3 (2013).
94 Torbakov, 'History, Memory and National Identity', pp. 215–16.
95 There also were variations in how these analogies might be applied, according to the 'lessons' advisers took from them. See Yuen Foon Khong, *Analogies at War: Korea, Munich, Dien Bien Phu and the Vietnam Decision of 1965* (Princeton: Princeton University Press, 1992). Jeffrey Record, *Making War, Thinking History: Munich, Vietnam and Presidential Uses of Force from Korea to Kosovo* (Annapolis, Maryland: Naval Institute Press, 2002).
96 Lawrence Freedman, 'Kennedy, Bush and Crisis Management', *Cold War History*, vol. 2, no. 3 (2002). And for a more extended study, see Len Scott, *The Cuban Missile Crisis and the Threat of Nuclear War: Lessons from History* (London: Continuum, 2007). Linda K. Miller and Mary McAuliffe, 'The Cuban Missile Crisis', *OAH Magazine of History*, vol. 8, no. 2 (1994).
97 Graham Allison, 'The Cuban Missile Crisis at 50: Lessons for US Foreign Policy Today', *Foreign Affairs*, vol. 91, no. 4 (July/August 2012). 'Cuban Missile Crisis Offers Lessons Relevant Today', *Korea Times*, 23 October 2012. 'Essence of Decision: The Cuban Missile Crisis Contains Lessons for Nuclear Diplomacy in the 21st Century', *The Times*, 18 October 2012, www.thetimes.co.uk/tto/opinion/leaders/article3571479.ece (Last accessed May 2013).
98 Melvyn P. Leffler, 'Remembering George Kennan: Lessons for Today?', *United States Institute of Peace: Special Report 180* (December 2006).
99 Nicholas Cull, *The Cold War and the United States Information Agency: American Propaganda and Public Diplomacy* (Cambridge: Cambridge University Press, 2008). And Cull's *The Decline and Fall of the United States Information Agency: American Public Diplomacy, 1989–2001* (New York: Palgrave Macmillan, 2012). For British activity, see Richard Aldrich, 'Putting Culture into the Cold War: The Cultural Relations Department (CRD) and British Covert Information Warfare', *Intelligence and National Security*, vol. 18, no. 2 (2003).
100 Nicholas J. Cull, *Public Diplomacy: Lessons from the Past* (Los Angeles: Figueroa Press, 2009). This report is accessible online at: http://uscpublicdiplomacy.org/publications/perspectives/CPDPerspectivesLessons.pdf (Last accessed May 2013).

101 Ibid. pp. 34–36. Also Andrew Wulf, *Moscow '59: The 'Sokolniki Summit' Revisited* (Los Angeles: Figueroa Press, 2010). This report is accessible online at: http://uscpublicdiplomacy.org/publications/perspectives/CPDPerspectivesMoscow59.pdf (Last accessed May 2013).
102 John Kenneth White, *Still Seeing Red: How the Cold War Shapes New American Politics* (Boulder, Colorado: Westview, 1997).
103 See George Lakoff, *Don't Think of an Elephant: Know Your Values and Frame the Debate* (Melbourne: Scribe Publications, 2004).
104 Harvey M. Sapolsky, Eugene Gholz, and Allen Kaufman, 'Security Lessons from the Cold War', *Foreign Affairs*, vol. 78, no. 4 (1999).
105 As reported in the *Boston Review* (Last accessed August 2012) http://bostonreview.net/BR28.1/dower.html.
106 Jan Angstrom, 'Mapping the Competing Historical Analogies of the War on Terrorism: The Bush Presidency', *International Relations*, vol. 25, no. 2 (2011).
107 John Tosh, *Why History Matters* (Houndmills: Palgrave Macmillan, 2008), p. 5
108 David Hoogland Noon, 'Cold War Revival: Neoconservatives and Historical Memory in the War on Terror', *American Studies*, vol. 48, no. 3 (2007).
109 Ibid. Also see David Campbell, *Writing Security: United States Foreign Policy and the Politics of Identity* (Minneapolis: University of Minnesota Press, 1992).
110 Quoted in Noon, 'Cold War Revival', p. 85.
111 Ibid. pp. 75–99.
112 Liz Cheney, 'Obama Rewrites the Cold War', *Wall Street Journal*, vol. 254, no. 10 (13 July 2009).
113 Reported in the *Toronto Star*, 6 April 2009. See Andrew Futter, 'Obama's Nuclear Weapons Policy in a Changing World', *LSE Ideas Series* (2009), p. 14. Accessible online at: www.lse.ac.uk/IDEAS/publications/reports/pdf/SR009/futter.pdf (Last accessed February 2013).
114 For either a full transcript or video of the president's 28-minute speech, see Barack Obama, 'Remarks by President Obama at the Brandenburg Gate, Berlin, Germany', *The White House: President Barack Obama*, 19 June 2013, www.whitehouse.gov/the-press-office/2013/06/19/remarks-president-obama-brandenburg-gate-berlin-germany (Last accessed June 2013).
115 Scott Horsley, 'Obama Evokes Cold War in Speech at Berlin's Brandenburg Gate', *WHQR 91.3fm: Radio with Vision … Listen and See*, 19 June 2013, http://whqr.org/post/obama-evokes-cold-war-speech-berlins-brandenburg-gate (Last accessed June 2013).
116 Obama, 'Remarks by President Obama at the Brandenburg Gate'.
117 Sherlock, *Historical Narratives*, pp. 157–61.
118 Ibid. pp. 162–67.
119 Quoted in Torbakov, 'History, Memory and National Identity', p. 218.
120 Ibid. pp. 221–23. Sherlock, *Historical Narratives*, p. 151.
121 Troy Stangarone, Andrew Kwon, and Peter Taves, 'Has North Korean Rhetoric Changed under Kim Jong-un?', *The Peninsula: Korea Economic Institute (KEI)*, 1 May 2013, http://blog.keia.org/2013/05/has-north-korean-rhetoric-changed-under-kim-jong-un/ (Last accessed May 2013).
122 Juan Forero, 'As Election Looms, Chávez Steps up Rhetoric', *The Washington Post*, 16 October 2008, www.washingtonpost.com/wp-dyn/content/article/2008/10/15/AR2008101503292.html (Last accessed December 2012).
123 These examples result from research promoted by the Wilson Center's Cold War International History Project including Sergo Mikoyan, *The Soviet Cuban Missile Crisis: Castro, Mikoyan, Kennedy, Khrushchev and the Missiles of November* (Stanford, California: Stanford University Press and Woodrow Wilson Center Press, 2012). Walter Süß and Douglas Selvage, 'e-Dossier No. 37 – KGB/Stasi Cooperation', *Wilson Center: Cold War International History Project*, www.

wilsoncenter.org/publication/e-dossier-no-37-kgbstasi-cooperation (Last accessed May 2013).
124 Greg Grandin, *The Last Colonial Massacre: Latin America in the Cold War* (Chicago: University of Chicago Press, 2004).
125 Robert Cribb, 'Unresolved Problems in the Indonesian Killings of 1965–66', *Asian Survey*, vol. 42, no. 4 (2002). And in the same issue of the journal, Mary S. Zurbuchen, 'Memory and the "1965 Incident" in Indonesia'.
126 Quoted in Zurbuchen, 'Memory and the "1965 Incident" in Indonesia', p. 578.
127 Mark Woodward, 'Only Now can We Speak: Remembering Politicide in Yogyakarta', *Sojourn: Journal of Social Sciences in Southeast Asia*, vol. 26, no. 1 (2011), p. 43.
128 Richard Tanter, 'Indonesia's Dangerous Silence', *Inside Story: Current Affairs and Culture from Australia and Beyond*, 28 April 2011, http://inside.org.au/indonesia-dangerous-silence/ (Last accessed May 2013).
129 Kwon, *Ghosts of War in Vietnam*, p. 164 and *passim*.
130 Exhibit Text, Permanent Exhibition of the Taipei 228 Memorial Museum, Taipei, visit by David Lowe and Tony Joel in February 2013.
131 Chiang Kai-shek Memorial Hall, Taipei, visit by David Lowe and Tony Joel in February 2013.
132 Summary from several exhibits at Okinawan Prefectural Museum, Naha, Okinawa, visit by David Lowe and Tony Joel in February 2013.
133 Justin McCurry, 'Two US Sailors Accused of Okinawa Rape', *The Guardian*, 17 October 2012, www.guardian.co.uk/world/2012/oct/17/us-sailors-accused-okinawa-rape (Last accessed February 2013).
134 For more information, see Gavan McCormack and Satoko Oka Norimatsu, *Resistant Islands: Okinawa Confronts Japan and the United States* (Lanham, Maryland: Rowman & Littlefield, 2012). And various chapters in Chalmers Johnson, ed., *Okinawa: Cold War Island* (Cardiff, California: Japan Policy Research Institute, 1999).

5   Endings?

Approaching a quarter-century since the end of eastern European communism and the dissolution of the Soviet Union, several places around the world
still have the Cold War woven into the fabric of their contemporary
identities in such a way that makes it virtually impossible for residents and
visitors alike not to remember this era. As this study has shown, these places
range from small towns and remote settlements such as Vint Hill, Rocky
Flats, Greenham Common, and Semipalatinsk to major cities including
Prague, Budapest, Hanoi, and Hiroshima; and even islands through Asia's
Cold War archipelago stretching from Okinawa to Kinmen. There are further places, too, which have not been covered in this work but nonetheless
boast their own unique ties to the Cold War whether it be due to fleeting
moments or more enduring legacies. Lake Placid, for instance, has been
involved in hosting the Winter Olympics twice (1932 and 1980). It took only
a couple of hours, however, for this small village in the state of New York to
become forever linked to Cold War lore through the so-called 'Miracle on
Ice' hockey match in which Team USA – mostly comprised of college students – defied the odds to somehow defeat the hitherto seemingly invincible
Soviet national team.[1] The enigmatic case of Panmunjom, where the 1953
armistice between North and South Korea was signed, sits at the other end
of the continuum. Dislocated from normalcy and located in the DMZ,
Panmunjom now is an abandoned village that straddles the 'frontline' where
communism and democracy continue to glare at each other six decades after
the ceasefire. It remains to be seen if the future holds anything for Panmunjom other than hosting periodic North–South discussions and daily
busloads of curious tourists. Whereas some of the above places have slipped
comfortably into an 'aftermath period' or 'reflecting phase', for others the
Cold War quite clearly has not yet ended. On the one hand, this may be
due to Cold War tensions remaining unresolved, or, on the other hand, it
can be the result of memory work ensuring that the past stays very much
'alive' in the present. Accordingly, this short concluding chapter eschews the
conventional notion that the Cold War 'ended' abruptly in the early 1990s,
to be consigned to history more or less overnight. Instead, it mounts an
argument for embracing the idea that in many ways the Cold War lingers

on. Given that the fall of the Berlin Wall and the disintegration of the Soviet Union are the conventional touchstones of the 'end of an era' thesis, to illuminate our position that the Cold War past continues to permeate the present there are no two more challenging yet apposite cities to explore than Berlin and Moscow.

Berlin demands special attention in Cold War memory studies. Indeed, the German capital easily could have served as the focal point of Chapter 3 on 'Cities and Sites'. Yet we decided against this obvious approach for two main reasons, both of which relate to the sheer enormity of the case in question. First, if Berlin were to be examined in detail as part of any such chapter then it most likely would result in one of two undesirable outcomes: either a shallow and hopelessly incomplete investigation of this iconic Cold War city if its coverage were kept restricted to the same length as the other places surveyed; or, if explored in a meaningful way, then Berlin inevitably would overshadow all other places explored in the chapter. Second, we did not feel compelled to investigate Berlin in depth because, comparatively speaking, it already has been afforded considerable treatment elsewhere, including full-length memory studies. To cite only one recent example, in 2008 Dirk Verheyen produced *United City, Divided Memories? Cold War Legacies in Contemporary Berlin*, an insightful and highly readable book constructed around the three key themes of Allied occupation, the *Stasi*, and the Wall.[2] The following passages, then, are not primarily concerned with investigating *how* the Cold War is remembered in the German capital in the same way that previous chapters have examined other case studies. Rather, by surveying the diverse *ways* in which the Cold War is confronted, celebrated, commemorated, and commercialized on a mass scale in Berlin, the aim is to show how it perhaps is more accurate to talk of the Cold War lingering in this *sui generis* divided city.[3]

Berlin is universally recognized as the quintessential Cold War city both 'then and now'. From the Berlin Blockade and the subsequent Berlin Airlift in 1948–49, to the construction of the Berlin Wall and resultant Berlin Crisis of 1961, through to the Four Power Agreement on Berlin of 1971 and, some 28 years after its erection, the fall of the Berlin Wall in 1989, no other place on earth comes close to symbolizing the contracted struggle between East and West on the same level as Germany's capital. And nowadays, nowhere else in the world can rival Berlin's quasi-maniacal approach to remembering the Cold War. It is a development that should not be taken for granted, however, because the dynamic and typically volatile nature of Berlin's history means that the Cold War era competes with several other modern epochs on the city's memory landscape. Indeed, layers of contemporary history are borne by Berlin to an extent that is scarcely matched among the world's great cities; it is no exaggeration to say that, on a short walk around the block, one can observe remnants of or memorials to the city's Prussian heritage, Wilhelmine and Weimar periods, the Third Reich, decades of postwar division, and now even its formative post-reunification years. Even so, the Cold War looms large all over the city. As discussed below, it is promoted through a myriad of historical sites, dedicated museums, gift shops, forms of state-centred and socially-based memorialization, and guided tours. For starters, though, it must be acknowledged that on a far more rudimentary level the Cold War's legacy still divides Berlin: after two decades of massive property development projects, the updating (read balancing out) of public utilities and infrastructure across the city, and the increasing gentrification of formerly run-down (and thus far more affordable) boroughs, even for uninitiated tourists visiting Berlin for the first time it remains remarkably easy to identify what parts of the city once belonged to the East or West.[4] In effect, it is an unparalleled case of ubiquitous Cold War vestiges not simply *marking* but rather actually *forming* the entire city. And so long as the 'former' East–West divide remains palpable, it surely is more accurate to speak of the Cold War slowly decomposing in Berlin rather than having ended abruptly with the fall of the Wall and German reunification.

Speaking of the city's division, along with the mushroom cloud the Berlin Wall is *the* iconic image of the Cold War era. Around the city, other extant remnants of the border protection system – or what East Berlin euphemistically called its 'anti-fascist protective rampart' ('*antifaschistischer Schutzwall*') – have been conserved for their cultural significance. These include, for instance, trenches, obstacles at canal openings and in other waterways, perimeter lampposts, command posts and guard watchtowers, patrol tracks, and 'death strips'.[5] Yet it is the actual Wall itself that captivates the popular imagination. Whereas most of it has long since been removed, several sections of the *Mauer* – typically only short, but sometimes considerably longer – still stand. A few examples of the earlier versions have survived, but it is the so-called 'fourth generation' (constructed in 1975) that is best recognized. And, in particular, lengthy sections of this version of the Wall can be found at three prominent locations in Berlin: adjacent to Checkpoint Charlie; in *Bernauer Straße* as part of the Berlin Wall Memorial (*Gedenkstätte Berliner Mauer*), which operates more broadly as the central memorial site of German division;[6] and along the River Spree, located within Friedrichshain-Kreuzberg, a stretch of Wall is now known as the East Side Gallery. At almost a mile long and featuring over 100 murals, it is regarded as perhaps the world's largest open-air art gallery. In a further cultivation of Berlin's iconic Cold War status, segments of the Wall have been exported to virtually every corner of the globe. This trend has occurred in various shapes and sizes and in differing capacities. As mentioned previously in this book, the Wende Museum in California now possesses the longest section of original Wall segments outside of Berlin. And a single segment is erected outside another Cold War museum discussed at length earlier in this work: the House of Terror in Budapest. This particular segment was gifted to Budapest by the Berlin-Hohenschönhausen Memorial (the former *Stasi* remand prison) in 2010 on occasion of the twentieth anniversary of Germany's reunification. Full segments, furthermore, can be found on public display on every continent including, for instance: in the Canadian War Museum in Ottawa; in front of the Harmonie German Club in the Australian capital Canberra; outside the EU parliament in Brussels; in the gardens of the Vatican City; in a Cape Town mall; in parkland in central Seoul; in public gardens in Taipei; at a German school in Mexico City; in the entrance hall of a publishing house in Buenos Aires; and in literally dozens of cities across the United States and throughout Europe.[7] On a far smaller scale according to size but at a much more prolific rate, the mind boggles at how many individual fragments of the Wall must now proliferate around the world given that a souvenir piece of certified *Berliner Mauerstein* has been a seemingly obligatory purchase for anyone who has visited the city since 1990.[8] In summary, the Wall fell spectacularly in 1989 but it did not simply disappear. Instead, it has reappeared all around the globe. Through its paradigmatic Wall, then, Berlin is not merely *remembered* but rather continues to be *recognized* as the quintessential Cold War city. It is hard to imagine it shedding this identity any time soon, not least because of the way in which the city embraces and promotes its Cold War past.

Guided tours dedicated to the Cold War abound in Berlin. Some adopt a subterranean approach and explore the city's 'ghost stations' or the region's nuclear fallout bunkers (discussed below). Other walking tours combine historical sites such as Checkpoint Charlie or sections of the Wall still

Figure 5.1 Murals at the East Side Gallery, Berlin Wall. November 2009.

standing with visits to relevant museums. And a 'Trabi safari', so-named because it involves the no-frills Trabant motorcars that were ubiquitous in the communist bloc, is a novel option for anyone looking for a quicker paced tour of the city with a nostalgic (or *Ostalgie*) twist. Since 2007, tourists looking to further immerse themselves in a faux DDR experience can take a step back in time with accommodation at the Ostel Hostel, where the rooms are furbished with authentic East German furniture and accessories including portraits of former communist leaders Willi Stoph, Walter Ulbricht, and Erich Honecker. At the time of its opening, Tobias Schreiter of *Der Spiegel* described it as a unique case of fabricated retro 'DDR chic'.[9] It is up to the individual to decide whether the Ostel fits neatly within the wider trend of *Ostalgie* or perhaps oversteps the mark to become communist kitsch. In any case, the Ostel features a souvenir shop full of the tacky Cold War memorabilia peddled by countless street vendors across Berlin – Soviet flags, Russian Matryoshka dolls, imitation military clothing and paraphernalia, DDR t-shirts and so on. For any tourists searching for better quality products, Berlin's many gift-shops are heavily stocked with all kinds of Cold War-themed gifts ranging from clothing and coffee mugs through to posters and key rings. Here, one of the most prolific images used is West German photographer Peter Leibing's iconic shot from *Bernauer Straße* on 15 August 1961, when East German border guard Conrad Schumann brazenly defected to the West by jumping over a barbed wire barricade during the initial days of the Berlin Wall's construction. And, in 2011, the city's chain of official souvenir shops even released a new 'Divided City' clothing range based on a stylized map of Berlin divided into four zones of occupation clearly delineated by the Soviet, French, British, and American flags. Far from wanting to divorce itself from the past, then, in a literal sense Berlin now encourages visitors to drape themselves in an image of the city divided along its Cold War lines.

Beyond the prominent examples of Wall remnants, there are Cold War historical sites aplenty in and around Berlin. Underground, there are assorted bunkers constructed in preparation for nuclear warfare, spy tunnels that crossed underneath borders, plus the so-called 'ghost stations' that were closed down so that East Germans could not access the West Berlin transportation network that looped around East Berlin territory courtesy of prewar lines servicing the entire city. Above ground, the (reconstructed) border crossing Checkpoint Charlie reproduces its aura as the portal where East met West, encapsulating the mysterious world of Cold War spies and espionage. Rathaus Schöneberg, which served as West Berlin's town hall during the city's division, was the scene of US president John F. Kennedy's famous '*Ich bin ein Berliner*' speech delivered in June 1963. Within days of his assassination later that year, the square in front of the town hall was renamed *John-F.-Kennedy-Platz*. And, although the Tempelhof Airport closed down in 2008, its crucial role as the main airfield during the Berlin Airlift continues to be commemorated through the adjacent square called the *Platz*

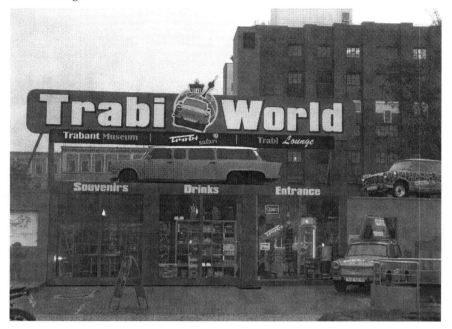

Figure 5.2 Ostalgie or communist kitsch? Trabi World in Berlin. November 2011.

der Luftbrücke. Since 1951, a large memorial has dominated this square. Designed by Eduard Ludwig, it takes the form of an arc with three raised trajectories representing the three air corridors that linked West Germany to West Berlin during the airlift, and its base is inscribed with the names of British and American airmen who lost their lives during operations. Other sites that conjure up darker memories of the Cold War era include the aforementioned *Stasi* reform prison now occupied by the Berlin-Hohenschönhausen Memorial, and in the Lichtenberg district a compound that formerly housed the headquarters of East Berlin's state security now operates as a museum and documentation centre (the *Stasimuseum*).[10] Both of these sites vividly demonstrate how, for victims of *Stasi* crimes in particular, the passing of time does not necessarily heal Cold War wounds in Berlin. In such instances, it is not so much a case of merely remembering but rather continuing to live with the consequences of the Cold War era.

The DDR Museum looks beyond the dominant themes of the Wall and *Stasi* crimes to depict everyday living under the communist dictatorship. With a hands-on approach that requires visitors to engage with the exhibits, it justifiably lays claim to being 'one of the most interactive museums in the world'.[11] Overlooking the River Spree directly behind Berlin's Catholic cathedral (*Berliner Dom*) in the former East German government district in the city's centre, the DDR Museum is in a prime location for tourists. The opposite must be said of the Allied Museum (*Alliiertenmuseum Berlin*)

Figure 5.3 Berlin Airlift Memorial in front of Tempelhof Airport, *Platz der Luftbrücke*. Berlin, November 2011.

perched out on the city's outskirts in the southwestern district of Zehlendorf. There is very good historical reasoning behind the museum's location, however, for Zehlendorf, which belonged to the American sector of divided Berlin, was the onetime epicentre of US military services during the Cold War. In 1949, one of its main thoroughfares was renamed *Clayallee* after US Army General Lucius D. Clay, revered as the 'father' of the Berlin Airlift and consequently made an honorary citizen of the city in 1953. During the Cold War, the Clay Headquarters of the Berlin Brigade was located along *Clayallee*, and so, too, was the Truman Plaza that accommodated for the shopping needs of US personnel and their families stationed at the nearby garrisons or American residential quarter. A short walk further along *Clayallee*, the 750-seat Outpost Theatre was constructed in the 1950s to entertain Berlin Brigade servicemen and their families. Following the Allies' withdrawal from Berlin, in 1998 the landmark theatre was converted into the permanent exhibition hall of the newly founded Allied Museum. The reference to 'allies' in the museum's title is a nod to western alliances during the Cold War as opposed to the earlier wartime partnership that temporarily allied the Western Powers with the Soviets who played such a crucial role in their common fight against Nazism. Indeed, the museum's logo features the Stars and Stripes, the *Tricolore*, and the Union Jack, whereas the Soviets/ Russians are ignored. This standard is replicated again near the museum's main entrance, where the American, French, and British flags are complemented by reunified Germany's *Schwarz-Rot-Gold* flag and the civil flag of the City of Berlin (which served as the flag of West Berlin from 1954 and then was adopted by the reunified city after 1990). And, pointedly, the museum's permanent exhibit inside the Outpost Theatre was created along the theme: 'How Enemies became Friends'. The motto makes it immediately clear that the exhibition focuses on *explicitly* promoting the dual narratives of: first, the Western Powers' protection of West Germans in general and West Berliners in particular; and, second, the swift and successful integration of West Germany into the NATO family to serve as a bulwark against communism. Along the way, the exhibition *implicitly* depicts the erstwhile allies the Soviets as the menacing protagonists – threatening West Berliners' freedom and, by extension, endangering world peace. With very little modification to its displays, in fact, the permanent exhibition could be transformed to fit the inverted motto of 'how friends became enemies'. The museum's western-centric logo, the unmissable five large flags on display at the main entrance, the exhibits, and its periodic publications (plus the accompanying website in English, German, and French) all combine to betray the Allied Museum as the venture of Cold War Warriors still in full flight.[12] Its isolated location far off the beaten track usually trod by tourists ensures that the museum only attracts visitors who plan trips there – presumably ex-service personnel, military history buffs (especially for air war), and anyone with an especially keen interest in the Cold War. The Allied Museum creates an unmistakably binary atmosphere in which the Cold War lingers more than two decades after the fall of the Berlin Wall: communism may have vanished from Europe with the dissolution of the Soviet empire, but those pesky Russians remain the suspicious 'other'.

What, then, is happening in Moscow? The short answer is that there is both remembering and forgetting of the Cold War era.

Despite Moscow's centrality in the Cold War, and the city's attraction to historians as shorthand for 'the Soviet leadership', or 'leaders of the communist bloc', contemporary Moscow seeks to transcend the Cold War both temporally and as a burden that should not be carried. As we noted earlier with reference to the nuclear bunker-cum-party venue, Bunker-42, Moscow invites tourists to revel in iconic engineering and hardware products of the Cold War without worrying overly about a narrative of East vs West or communism vs capitalism to provide substantial contextualization. Bunker-42 appears on some of the lists of popular tourist recommendations;[13] and there are other options for Moscow's tourists to enjoy hands-on Cold War experiences including the aforementioned MIG jet flight and the chance to fire off some rounds with a Kalashnikov AK-47 assault rifle.[14] These occupy the quirky end of the tourist spectrum amidst the many cultural, literary, museum, church, and gallery recommendations. Otherwise, the Cold War's echoes are largely architectural. The central and dominant Red Square and the Kremlin remain the most-frequented of tourist sites, and they partly escape their fourteenth- and fifteenth-centuries' provenance as remembered sites of Soviet power. Red Square bears witness to far more ceremonies and processions from earlier times than have taken place in the twentieth century, and the Kremlin's splendid museums recall earlier Russian history. Yet, the Soviet Union's propaganda and use of media forms such as photographs of Soviet leaders on the Kremlin's ramparts, plus television footage of military parades in Red Square, ensure that these era-distinctive images inform contemporary engagement with these sites of power and culture – at least for the more mature tourist. The so-called Seven Sisters – the huge Stalinist-Gothic buildings constructed between 1947 and 1953 along or near the third ring road of the city approximately five miles from the Kremlin – remain dominant landmarks and features of Moscow's skyline. They were built to meet Stalin's determination that postwar Moscow would boast skyscrapers and impress visitors. The largest of the seven, Moscow

Figure 5.4 One of the Seven Sisters: the Russian Ministry of Foreign Affairs. Moscow, November 2012.

State University, was constructed partly with Gulag labour.[15] Other easily
encountered Soviet-era features are the several excellent examples of socialist
realism artwork found in the Moscow Metro system.

Logically, one of the likely places to find a narrative about Moscow, the
Soviet Union, and the Cold War would be in Moscow's State Central
Museum of Contemporary History of Russia (until 1998, called the
Museum of the Revolution) located near the Garden Ring of the city on
Tverskaya Street. Not surprisingly, given its former title, the balance of
exhibits in this museum is weighted towards the first third of the twentieth
century. But when the display period reaches the end of the Second World
War – or the Great Patriotic War for Russians – the Cold War does not
begin. An exhibit devoted to the early postwar period is entitled 'Restoration of the economy: The history of the USSR in the after-war period,
1946–53'. It includes: material on the successful Soviet development of an
atomic bomb in 1949; the many gifts sent to Stalin that year in celebration
of his 70th birthday and 'the zenith of his personality cult'; the massive
efforts to restore the economy and boost productivity after the devastation
of the Second World War; and evidence of 'a new spiral of repressions'.[16]
Postwar international relations is summed up very briefly in an odd blend
of regret mixed with Soviet-era pride in leading peace movements:

> The leading countries of the anti-Hitler coalition determined the post-
> war world order. The USSR was a founder of the United Nations
> Organization, became a permanent member of the Security Council,
> participated in creating the World Peace Congress and other interna-
> tional democratic organizations.
>
> The emerging thaw in the international climate proved to be not long.
> Former allies passed from the policy of cooperation to the 'cold war', to
> the confrontation of the two world systems.[17]

Elsewhere in the museum's post-1945 depictions of the Soviet Union, the
Cold War remains something of an unremarked constant. The energy
behind change and behind progressive triumph in aviation and nuclear
engineering – in Sputnik's orbit in 1957, and Yuri Gagarin's pioneering
manned spaceflight in April 1961 – comes from the 'super concentration
of material resources and human efforts'.[18] Similarly, the period of *perestroika* – Gorbachev's restructuring reforms from 1985 – is a story of
internally-driven change.[19]

Beyond this museum, there is little attempt in Moscow to hold up the
period of 1945–91 as particularly special, and the strongest memory work
intersecting with the period is marked by an unsettled contest between active
remembering (and rehabilitation) of the victims of Stalinism and active forgetting. Most of the energy in remembering lies with the victims of Stalin,
and centres on the Gulag (an acronym of the Russian *Glavnoye upravleniye
ispravityelno-trudovykh* **lagerey** *i koloniy*, meaning Chief Administration of

Corrective Labor Camps and Colonies). News of the Gulag camps spread first through translations of Aleksandr Solzhenitsyn's *One Day in the Life of Ivan Denisovich* (translated widely in 1962–63), and then his oral history *The Gulag Archipelago* (translated 1973). As Anne Applebaum has written, 'Gulag' has escaped its literal meaning to assume broader standing. It has come to mean not only the administration of labour camps but 'the system of Soviet slave labor itself, in all its forms and varieties: labor camps, punishment camps, criminal and political camps, children's camps, transit camps'. It signifies what prisoners used to call 'the meat-grinder': 'the arrests, the interrogations, the transport in unheated cattle cars, the forced labor, the destruction of families, the years spent in exile, the early and unnecessary deaths'.[20] Between 1929 and 1953 (the period of greatest activity), around 18 million people passed into the Gulag system, and a further six million were sent into exile. How many died or, more commonly, had their lives substantially shortened as a result of passing through the Gulag system, remains hard to guess accurately, but probably more than a million died in the camps, and many more had their lives severely shortened through illness, injury, and deprivation.[21]

The society Memorial plays a major role in remembering victims of repression in Russia. Formed in 1988 in Moscow and St Petersburg under the leadership of radical intellectuals such as Andrei Sakharov and Evgeny Evtushenko, Memorial attracted rising political stars including Boris Yeltsin. Originally wanting to win support for the erection of a monument to the victims of Stalin's Terror of the 1930s, the society went further, supporting political aspirants whose democratic credentials and commitment to civil society and democracy assisted the ongoing process of remembering Stalin's victims, and restoring their standing in some sort of memorial complex. Some of the many provincial Memorial groups had more modest aims and did not embrace the idea of a longer-term mission.[22] But the Moscow centre had this at its core, and became the headquarters of the International Memorial Society founded in 1992. The society's main aims are to:

- promote mature civil society and democracy based on the rule of law and thus to prevent a return to totalitarianism;
- assist formation of public consciousness based on the values of democracy and law, to get rid of totalitarian patterns, and to establish firmly human rights in practical politics and in public life;
- promote the reveal [sic] of truth about the historical past and perpetuate the memory of the victims of political repression exercised by totalitarian regimes.[23]

Memorial's activism on behalf of contemporary victims of acts of repression, including victims in Chechnya, makes it a thorn in the side of recent Russian governments. Its historical work collecting and disseminating details of the deportations to camps in the Gulag system is ongoing, but already has yielded important results. In 1990, the society succeeded in its early quest for a monument to the victims of Stalinism: in the form of a large stone brought from the former prison camps of Solovetskii and placed in Lubyanka Square, in front of the former secret police headquarters. The St Petersburg branch of Memorial is building a virtual museum of the Gulag (which also lists 45 physical museums in countries of the former Soviet Union that focus on, in substantial part at least, victims of Stalin's repression). The emphasis is on recording life stories, artefacts, and other materials from the time of incarcerations, and promoting memorials and other forms of remembering the victims. The work to date is the result of thousands of hours of labour and the volunteering of people from across and beyond Russia. At little more than 2,500 life stories recorded, Memorial still is barely scratching the surface of Gulag legacies. It nonetheless is signalling its dogged determination to continue these painstaking acts of recording and rehabilitation.[24]

Moscow's Memorial headquarters includes an archives centre and formative museum that has begun to host excursions by school children. The society's work and mission is complemented by two separate Moscow museums. The State Museum of Gulag History, on Petrovka Street, is small and averages 20,000 visitors annually. It was established in 2001 by historian and Gulag survivor A.V. Antonov-Ovseenko, and opened its doors in 2004. It focuses on the rise and fall of the Gulag system, drawing on photographs, prisoners' writings, artworks and belongings, documentary movies, and special exhibits that recreate life in the camps. The documentary film by British filmmaker Tom Roberts called *The Death Train* (1998) was screening when the museum was visited in November 2012. Roberts' *The Death Train* recalls the futile attempts by prisoners to build a railway line, under Stalin's orders, linking Eastern and Western Siberia above the Arctic Circle. In 1947, Stalin ordered the building of a section stretching 1,000 miles from Salekhard in Western Siberia eastwards to Igarka. The line was supposed to link up to earlier work westwards of Salekhard that Stalin had commenced but then stopped during the Second World War. Two Gulag camps were built specifically for the railway, and of the roughly 300,000 working on it, upwards of 60,000 died in the process.[25] Photographs of rail tracks twisting and sinking into the tundra feature in Roberts' film, and are some of the more emblematic photographs depicting the Gulag experience. They also appear in the Sakharov Museum (discussed below). More than productive labour such as mining, images of the doomed railway underscore the casualness with which human lives were thrown at labour-intensive enterprises in circumstances likely to result in huge losses of lives and with questionable economic benefit. Party leaders were aware of the economic inefficiency of the Gulag system of labour – even in mining, logging, road building, and the foundation of towns in the Russian Arctic – before Stalin's death. Roberts' film also features harrowing recollections by survivors who tried to build the railway. Some of their strongest memories are of constant hunger – an interminable state of near-starvation – and the climatic extremes of bitter cold in winter and briefly oppressive summers, with the thaw bringing clouds of mosquitoes and other biting insects. The Museum of Gulag History also addresses Stalin's revisions of history at the expense of his enemies. This includes, for instance, before/after photographs of party officials who were seated alongside Stalin and other party leaders but subsequently blacked out (either literally blacked out or made invisible) in adjusted versions of photographs after they had been purged. In the case of artist Alexander Rodchenko, the artist himself was compelled to pour black ink over Uzbek Party leaders whose executions needed to be reflected in a revised version of his 1930s profile of Soviet rule in that state.[26]

The Museum of Gulag History awaits either expansion or being joined to a more formal network of museums remembering the Gulag.[27] Already, there are cross-references between museums and sites recalling the Gulag, underpinned also by the awareness-raising work of the Memorial society. The Andrei Sakharov Museum and Public Centre, overlooking the Yauza River on Moscow's third ring, is devoted to remembering Sakharov's legacy. It aims 'to educate those unfamiliar with past abuses and promote the continued development of intellectual freedom, respect for individuals, and civil and social responsibility in Russia'.[28] The Centre opened in 1996, on the 75th anniversary of Sakharov's birth, and relies primarily on grants and donations for its operation. It attracts a modest 16,000 visitors a year – something that troubled a guide during a visit in November 2012 almost as much as Stalin's popularity troubled her.[29] Logically, the museum and centre celebrate the work and legacies of Andrei Sakharov – the scientist, 'father' of the Soviet hydrogen bomb, and subsequent dissident and human rights activist who died in December 1989 – with a strong emphasis on his civil rights and reform campaigns from the 1960s (for which he and his wife endured exile and several forms of imprisonment during the 1980s). The centre hosts student groups, lectures, and conferences relating to 'the totalitarian past' and human rights. It makes a point of showing how intertwined were the party's communist project and brutality: 'From the beginning, the Soviet attempt to realize its utopian dream was accompanied by the creation of a state system of repression'. Its history of political repression in the Soviet Union cites demographers' estimates that the 'country's population lost about 40,000,000 in population due to repressions during the period from 1917 to 1954'.[30] Its exhibits feature photographs of camps and policy documentation, including certification and orders relating to transportations and, as related by a museum guide, one chilling instruction by Stalin condemning to death 6,000 at one of the camps. The museum also shows clothing, letters, and personal artefacts from those imprisoned. And, consistent with the mission, it demonstrates the fullest possible diversity of Gulag legacies, relating the growing number of memorials scattered throughout the former Soviet Union bearing witness to the horrors of the past.[31]

Outside of Moscow, one of the former 500-odd camps has been transformed into a museum near the town of Perm, at the foot of the Urals some 800 miles east of Moscow. It housed political prisoners until 1988. The Perm-36 Museum has been active in educational programmes and also taking the Gulag story on tour, including a successful trip to the United States in 2006 in collaboration with the US National Park Service.[32] The Gulag, then, is partly-appropriating Russia's Cold War, complicating the idea that the period immediately after the Second World War marks something of a 'start' to the new, Cold War era, by pushing our attention back to the early 1930s when the Gulag camps began their rapid expansion. The rise of the camps and their fall (if not complete dismantling) with Stalin's death in 1953 constitute a mnemonic centre of gravity at the expense of international relations and the imagined threat of nuclear war.

Between Memorial Society, comparable groups working in the Baltic States, and the Sakharov and Gulag museums, there is a loose coalition for justice and history-making from below, through the determined recovery of life stories. The achievements of these groups and organizations might be modest to date, but they show energy and resolve. It is clear from the Visegrad initiatives and Lithuanian school projects discussed earlier, furthermore, that the encouragement of educational reforms may have wider,

Figure 5.5 Gulag Memorial to victims of Stalin, Sculpture Park near Tretiakov Gallery. Moscow, November 2012.

systemic impact. Among the former western Cold War allies, and especially among conservative commentators, the Gulag is a powerful reminder of the good cause that was the Cold War contest. It is more historically tangible than the imagined nuclear war that was avoided, precisely because its victims were so numerous and drawn, geographically, from an 'Evil Empire'. For Applebaum, whose prize-winning book has popularized understanding of the Gulag system and some of its remembering, this was fundamental:

> Already, we are forgetting what it was that mobilized us, what inspired us, what held the civilization of 'the West' together for so long: we are forgetting what it was that we were fighting against. If we do not try harder to remember the history of the other half of the European con-tinent, the history of the other twentieth-century totalitarian regime, in the end it is we in the West who will not understand our past, we who will not know how our world came to be the way it is.[33]

Applebaum further warns of the dangers in forgetting the Gulag and other planned mass-killings and acts of inhumanity: 'Only our ability to debase and destroy and dehumanize our fellow men has been – and will be – repe-ated again and again.'[34]

But, as we have seen in the previous chapter, the same argument causes problems for current Russian leaders. The reasons for forgetting in Russia are many: the legal implications of Russia being a successor to the 'complete' activities of the former Soviet Union have the potential to haunt too many, even before considering the possible financial implications of restitution and acts of compensation for identified victims; the international implications take on similar proportions in relation to the former Socialist Republics that became independent states upon the collapse of the Soviet Union, and potentially undermine the popular desire for Russian pride and strength in the new international order; those who might identify as victims (or whose children might so identify) often accumulated multiple layers of suffering, through war, repression, and as survivors of famines; and such was the scale of state repression that the lines between perpetrators and victims often will be hard to draw. That Moscow's Cold War will resonate publicly also is guaranteed by the government's efforts to control some of the work on remembering discussed in this chapter. Groups such as the Memorial society are NGOs dependent for their funding on overseas funds, and since the middle of 2012 have been caught in the so-called 'foreign agents' legisla-tion: they are required to officially register as 'foreign agents', a term com-monly associated with the Cold War and espionage. There is a familiar ring to Putin's description of the legislation as being necessary in order to avert any outside interference in Russian affairs; and, moreover, the law has the potential to undermine the efforts of non-state agents of remembering. Clearly, Moscow, once a centre of Cold War contest, is likely to remain a centre of contest over memories that at least intersect with the Cold War, even if, like memories recalled elsewhere, their lineage extends to regional and temporal circumstances that the Cold War cannot contain.

This is a theme that flows throughout much of the remembering described in this study. In the many established and stirring activities of remembering we have considered – and we suggest that mnemonic activity relating to the Cold War is growing strongly if not evenly – the Cold War sometimes plays lead roles and sometimes supporting ones. This perhaps is to be expected of a phenomenon that remains pervasive in the hands of historians, but also has explanatory limitations. As the Cold War continues to resist neat definition and temporal boundaries, it harbours memories that draw only partly on its commonly understood form for their articulation. In Berlin, it literally writes itself into the physical shapes of the city; and its physical legacies are scattered in the form of walls, buildings, bunkers and shelters, abandoned and current military bases, and human remains in different parts of the world. In some of these places, such as Taipei, the Cold War, as a concept, sits in the background, its global dimensions secondary to the untangling of histories of occupation and authoritarianism, and ideological contest with Mainland China. In some of the memory work in Central Europe and the Baltic States, too, narratives of occupation and repression take precedence, offering the Cold War a significant support role, rather than the other way around. And in other places it is remembered and shaped according to contemporary politics and economic and political alignments, as well as in specific incidents flavoured with strong nationalist tones. The Cold War as context is seemingly as important, in its remembering, as the Cold War as a unique form of war. As the background to US president Obama's continued push for the elimination of nuclear arsenals, as a special feature of museums, as the backdrop to works of fiction or moving image, or as the narrative spine in history textbooks, the Cold War not only persists but grows in its remembering. In this light, our study anticipates that the field of memory studies will necessarily embrace the Cold War both in its pervasiveness and its slipperiness.

Notes

1 As explained in the introduction, sports-related events or sites have been overlooked in this book because it is anticipated that a future volume in this series will cover this theme as part of a wider study on 'remembering sporting triumphs, tragedies, and rivalries'.
2 Dirk Verheyen, *United City, Divided Memories? Cold War Legacies in Contemporary Berlin* (Lanham, Maryland: Lexington Books, 2008). As a further indicator, see the five-page bibliography of works primarily focusing on Berlin (and its Wall) that is accessible online at: Berlin Wall Memorial/Stiftung Berliner Mauer, 'Material and Books on the Berlin Wall, the German Partition and the GDR', *Berlin Wall Memorial: Bibliography*, 4 March 2010,www.berliner-mauer-gedenkstaette.de/en/bibliography-250.html (Last accessed April 2013).
3 Much of the following analysis is based on multiple trips to Berlin by both authors over several years, from as early as 1990 and as recently as December 2011.

4 For instance, making a short S-Bahn trip from, say, Charlottenburg or Bahnhof Zoo to either the Ostkreuz or Warschauer Straße stations or vice versa is less than a dozen stops, and yet it can make for a most disorientating experience because it is hard to fathom that one has remained within the same city. It is not simply a case of travelling between affluent suburbs and slum neighbourhoods as can be the case in any city, but rather things like architectural styles and streetscapes have a completely different 'historic feel' to them.

5 Klausmeier and Schmidt, *Wall Remnants – Wall Traces.*

6 Berlin Wall Memorial/Stiftung Berliner Mauer, 'Welcome', *Berlin Wall Memorial*, www.berliner-mauer-gedenkstaette.de/en/ (Last accessed December 2012).

7 For an interactive map showing dozens of locations, see 'Where is the Berlin Wall now?' *BBC News*, http://news.bbc.co.uk/2/hi/talking_point/8344662.stm (Last accessed February 2013). For additional discussion, see John Donovan, '20 Years Later, Berlin Wall Fragments Symbolize Freedom and Hope', *ABC News*, 8 November 2009, http://abcnews.go.com/GMA/Weekend/berlin-wall-fragments-scattered-world/story?id=9028105#.Ud1cNBYwaqA (Last accessed December 2012).

8 At last count, between them the two authors own eight pieces of Berlin Wall, purchased on multiple trips to the city between 1990 and 2011. And numerous colleagues and friends who have visited Berlin all own at least one piece, too.

9 Tobias Schreiter, 'DDR Chic: Reliving East Germany in a Berlin Hotel', *Spiegel Online International*, 26 June 2007, www.spiegel.de/international/zeitgeist/ddr-chic-reliving-east-germany-in-a-berlin-hotel-a-490847.html (Last accessed May 2013).

10 For their respective websites, see 'The Memorial', *Gedenkstätte Berlin-Hohenschönhausen*, http://en.stiftung-hsh.de (Last accessed March 2013). And 'House 1 – The Headquarter of the State Security', *StasiMuseum Berlin*, www.stasimuseum.de/en/enindex.htm (Last accessed March 2013).

11 'Welcome to one of the Most Interactive Museums in the World!', *DDR Museum*, www.ddr-museum.de/en/museum/ (Last accessed November 2012).

12 For the museum's website, see *Allied Museum/Alliiertenmuseum Berlin*, www.alliiertenmuseum.de/en (Last accessed November 2012). For examples from its long-running (but intermittent) series of publications that feature text in German, English, and French, see Helmut Trotnow, ed., *Ein Alliierten-Museum für Berlin/An Allied Museum for Berlin/Un Musée des Alliés à Berlin* (Berlin: Ruksaldruck, Summer 1995). And Allied Museum/Alliiertenmuseum Berlin, *2 + 4 = 1. Die internationale Regelung der deutschen Einheit/ 2 + 4 = 1. The International Agreement on German Unity: Special Exhibtion, 23 September 2000 to 14 January 2001/ 2 + 4 = 1. Le règlement international de l'unité allemande* (Berlin: Allied Museum, 2000).

13 Bunker-42 is recommended by popular tourist websites including 'Bunker-42 on Taganka (Cold War Museum)', *TripAdvisor: The World's Largest Travel Site*, www.tripadvisor.com.au/Attraction_Review-g298484-d2141443-Reviews-Bunker_42_-on_Taganka_Cold_War_Museum-Moscow_Central_Russia.html (Last accessed November 2012). And 'Bunker-42 on Taganka', *Expedia*, www.expedia.co.in/Bunker-On-Taganka-Moscow.d6156062.Attraction (Last accessed November 2012).

14 As suggested by 'Moscow Shooting Experience: Shoot an AK-47 at the Central Shooting Club', *Lonely Planet*, www.lonelyplanet.com/russia/moscow/activities/private-tours/moscow-shooting-experience (Last accessed January 2013).

15 The seven buildings are the Ministry of Foreign Affairs, the Red Gates Administration, the Hotel Ukraine, Moscow State University, the Kotelnicheskaya Embankment Apartments, the Kudrinskaya Square Building, and the Hotel Leningradskaya.

16 Visit by David Lowe in November 2012. See also 'Restoration of Economy. The History of the USSR in the After-War Period, 1946–53', *The State Central*

Museum of Contemporary History of Russia, http://eng.sovr.ru/expo/e11/ (Last accessed April 2013).

17 Visit by David Lowe in November 2012.

18 Ibid.

19 Ibid.

20 Anne Applebaum, *Gulag: A History* (New York: Anchor, 2004), pp. xv–xvi.

21 Ibid., p. xvii. See also Michael Ellman, 'Soviet Repression Statistics: Some Comments', *Europe-Asia Studies*, vol. 54, no. 7 (2002).

22 Anne White, 'The Memorial Society in the Russian Provinces', *Europe-Asia Studies*, vol. 47, no. 8 (1995).

23 'The Charter of the International Volunteer Public Organization: "Memorial" Historical, Educational, Human Rights and Charitable Society', *Memorial*, 19 April 1992 (Revised version adopted 18 December 1998), www.memo.ru/eng/about/charter.htm (Last accessed May 2013).

24 Gulag Museum, 'Virtual Museum of the Gulag: Collections', *Gulag Museum*, www.gulagmuseum.org/start.do?&language=2 (Last accessed May 2013).

25 This figure is taken from Tom Roberts, *The Death Train* (1998). Like much of the statistical measuring in relation to the Gulag system, it is difficult to be confident beyond estimates.

26 Visit by David Lowe to the State Museum of Gulag History in November 2012.

27 Sophia Kishkovsky, 'Moscow to get Major Gulag Museum', *The Art Newspaper*, 12 April 2013, www.theartnewspaper.com/articles/Moscow+to+get+major+Gulag +museum/29311 (Last accessed May 2013).

28 As described by 'About Center', *Andrey Sakharov Museum and Public Center*, www.prison.org/english/ngoand.htm (Last accessed May 2013).

29 Visit by David Lowe to the Andrei Sakharov Museum and Public Center in November 2012. See also 'The Andrei Sakharov Museum and Public Center: "Peace, Progress, Human Rights"', *Russian Museums*, www.russianmuseums.info/ M1623 (Last accessed May 2013).

30 Visit by David Lowe to the Andrei Sakharov Museum and Public Center in November 2012.

31 Ibid.

32 Martin Blatt, 'Remembering Repression: The GULAG as an NPS Exhibit', *Perspectives on History*, vol. 46, no. 8 (2008).

33 Applebaum, *Gulag: A History*, p. 576.

34 Ibid.

Bibliography

1983: The Brink of Apocalypse. 75 mins: Channel 4, 2007.

Aldrich, Richard. 'Putting Culture into the Cold War: The Cultural Relations Department (CRD) and British Covert Information Warfare.' *Intelligence and National Security*, vol. 18, no. 2 (2003): pp. 109–33.

Alex. '1970–71: Uprising in Poland.' *Libcom*, 31 October 2008, http://libcom.org/history/1970-71-uprising-poland (Last accessed March 2013).

Allied Museum/Alliiertenmuseum Berlin. *2 + 4 = 1. Die internationale Regelung der deutschen Einheit/ 2 + 4 = 1. The International Agreement on German Unity: Special Exhibition, 23 September 2000 to 14 January 2001/ 2 + 4 = 1. Le règlement international de l'unité allemande*. Berlin: Allied Museum, 2000.

——. 'Allied Museum.' *Allied Museum/Alliiertenmuseum Berlin*, www.alliiertenmuseum.de/en (Last accessed November 2012).

Allison, Graham. 'The Cuban Missile Crisis at 50: Lessons for US Foreign Policy Today.' *Foreign Affairs*, vol. 91, no. 4 (July/August 2012): pp. 11–18.

Alperovitz, Gar. *The Decision to Use the Atomic Bomb and the Architecture of an American Myth*. New York: Alfred A. Knopf, 1995.

Alpventures. 'UFO Tours – From Roswell to Area 51 and Beyond: Southwest UFO Discovery Tour.' *Alpventures*, www.alpventures.com/topsecret/TS_southwest_ufo_discovery_tour_PART1.html (Last accessed March 2013).

Amanat, Abbas, and Magnus T. Bernhardsson, eds. *Imagining the End: Visions of Apocalypse from the Ancient Middle East to Modern America*. London: I.B.Tauris, 2001.

AMSE. *American Museum of Science & Energy (AMSE)*, http://amse.org/sponsorship/amse-foundation/ (Last accessed March 2013).

Anderson, Benedict. *Imagined Communities*. London: Verso, 1983.

The Andrei Sakharov Museum and Public Center. 'The Andrei Sakharov Museum and Public Center: "Peace, Progress, Human Rights".' *Russian Museums*, www.russianmuseums.info/M1623 (Last accessed May 2013).

——. 'About Center.' *Andrey Sakharov Museum and Public Center*, www.prison.org/english/ngoand.htm (Last accessed May 2013).

Andrew, Christopher, and Vasili Mitrokhin. *The Sword and the Shield: The Mitrokhin Archive and the Secret History of the KGB*. New York: Basic Books, 2001.

Angstrom, Jan. 'Mapping the Competing Historical Analogies of the War on Terrorism: The Bush Presidency.' *International Relations*, vol. 25, no. 2 (2011): pp. 224–42.

Applebaum, Anne. *Gulag: A History*. New York: Anchor, 2004.

Arcadia. 'About Arcadia.' *Arcadia*, www.arcadiafund.org.uk/about/about-arcadia (Last accessed April 2013).

——. 'Grants (2004): Wende Museum of the Cold War, US.' *Arcadia*, www.arcadia-fund.org.uk/grants/endangered-culture/wende-museum-cold-war-us (Last accessed March 2013).

——. 'Grants (2012): The Wende Museum.' *Arcadia*, www.arcadiafund.org.uk/grants/endangered-culture/wende-museum (Last accessed April 2013).

Arnold, James R., and Roberta Wiener, eds. *Cold War: The Essential Reference Guide*. Santa Barbara: ABC-CLIO, 2012.

Ash, Timothy Garton. 'Václav Havel: Director of a Play that Changed History.' *The Guardian*, 19 December 2011, www.guardian.co.uk/commentisfree/2011/dec/18/vaclav-havel-changed-history1 (Last accessed October 2012).

Ashplant, T.G., Graham Dawson, and Michael Roper, eds. *The Politics of War Memory and Commemoration*. London: Routledge, 2000.

——. 'The Politics of War Memory and Commemoration: Contexts, Structures and Dynamics.' In *The Politics of War Memory and Commemoration*, edited by T.G. Ashplant, Graham Dawson, and Michael Roper. London: Routledge, 2000: pp. 3–85.

Assmann, Aleida. 'Europe: A Community of Memory? (Twentieth Annual Lecture of the GHI, 16 November 2006).' *GHI Bulletin*, no. 40 (Spring 2007): pp. 11–25.

——. 'On the (In)compatibility of Guilt and Suffering in German Memory.' *German Life and Letters*, vol. 59 (April 2006): pp. 187–200.

——. 'Re-Framing Memory. Between Individual and Collective Forms of Constructing the Past.' In *Performing the Past: Memory, History, and Identity in Modern Europe*, edited by Karin Tilmans, Frank Van Vree, Jay M. Winter. Amsterdam: Amsterdam University Press, 2010: pp. 35–50.

Assmann, Aleida, and Sebastian Conrad, eds. *Memory in a Global Age: Discourses, Practices and Trajectories*. Basingstoke, Hampshire: Palgrave Macmillan, 2010.

'Atomic Bomb Site Open to Tourists.' *China Journeys*, 16 October 2012, http://china-journeys.com/travel-updates/atomic-bomb-site-open-to-tourists.html (Last accessed April 2013).

Atomic Heritage Foundation. 'Our Mission.' *Atomic Heritage Foundation*, www.atomicheritage.org/index.php/about/about-us.html (Last accessed March 2013).

Ball, S.J. *The Cold War: An International History, 1947–1991*. London: Arnold, 1998.

The Baltic Initiative and Network. 'The Ejby Bunker, Copenhagen.' *The Baltic Initiative and Network*, http://coldwarsites.net/country/denmark/the-ejby-bunker-copenhagen (Last accessed March 2013).

——. 'Network.' *The Baltic Initiative and Network*, http://coldwarsites.net/network (Last accessed December 2012).

——. 'Secret Nuclear Bunker, Ligatne.' *The Baltic Initiative and Network*, http://coldwarsites.net/country/latvia/secret-nuclear-bunker-ligatne (Last accessed April 2013).

Bamford, James. *Body of Secrets: Anatomy of the Ultra-Secret National Security Agency: From the Cold War through the Dawn of a New Century*. New York: First Anchor Books, 2002.

BBC. 'BBC Two Announces New Season of Drama and Documentaries to Explore the Cold War.' *BBC*, 16 May 2013, www.bbc.co.uk/mediacentre/latestnews/2013/cold-war-season.html (Last accessed May 2013).

BBC News. 'BBC News: Secret Underground City For Sale.' *YouTube*, www.youtube.com/watch?v=V-bYGlijhIU (Last accessed November 2012).

——. 'Warsaw to Erect Statue to Reagan.' *BBC News*, 21 September 2006, http://news.bbc.co.uk/2/hi/europe/5366992.stm (Last accessed February 2013).

——. 'Where is the Berlin Wall Now?' *BBC News*, http://news.bbc.co.uk/2/hi/talking_point/8344662.stm (Last accessed February 2013).

Beazley, Olwen. 'A Paradox of Peace: The Hiroshima Peace Memorial (Genbaku Dome) as World Heritage.' In *Fearsome Heritage: Diverse Legacies of the Cold War*, edited by A.J. Schofield and Wayne Cocroft. Walnut Creek: Left Coast Press, 2009: pp. 33–50.

Benn, David Wedgwood. 'The Teaching of History in Present-Day Russia.' *Europe-Asia Studies*, vol. 62, no. 1 (2010): pp. 173–77.

Berlin Wall Memorial/Stiftung Berliner Mauer. 'Material and Books on the Berlin Wall, the German Partition and the GDR.' *Berlin Wall Memorial: Bibliography*, 4 March 2010, www.berliner-mauer-gedenkstaette.de/en/bibliography-250.html (Last accessed April 2013).

———. 'Welcome.' *Berlin Wall Memorial*, www.berliner-mauer-gedenkstaette.de/en/ (Last accessed December 2012).

Bernotas, Monika. 'Grutas Park and the Fate of Soviet Statuary in Lithuania.' *Art in Russia*, 7 December 2012, http://artinrussia.org/grutas-park-and-the-fate-of-soviet-statuary-in-lithuania/ (Last accessed January 2013).

Biehl, Jody K. 'East Germany Goes Hollywood: A Cold War Museum in Sunny Climes.' *Spiegel Online International*, 22 April 2005, www.spiegel.de/international/east-germany-goes-hollywood-a-cold-war-museum-in-sunny-climes-a-352278.html (Last accessed December 2012).

Birch, Douglas. 'Putin: Vietnam Worse than Stalin Purges.' *The Washington Post*, 21 June 2007, www.washingtonpost.com/wp-dyn/content/article/2007/06/21/AR2007062101885.html (Last accessed January 2013).

Birnbaum, Ben. 'Statue in Budapest's Liberty Square Credits Reagan for Freedom.' *The Washington Times*, 29 June 2011, www.washingtontimes.com/news/2011/jun/29/statue-in-budapests-liberty-square-credits-reagan-/?page=all (Last accessed March 2013).

Bix, Herbert. *Hirohito and the Making of Modern Japan*. New York: HarperCollins, 2000.

Black, Toban. 'Glimpsing a History of Anti-Nuclear Activism.' *Waging NonViolence: People-Powered News & Analysis*, 13 September 2009, http://wagingnonviolence.org/feature/glimpsing-a-history-of-anti-nuclear-activism/ (Last accessed December 2012).

Blatt, Martin. 'Remembering Repression: The GULAG as an NPS Exhibit.' *Perspectives on History*, vol. 46, no. 8 (2008): pp. 30–32.

Blažek, Petr. 'Memorial Places.' *Jan Palach: Charles University Multimedia Project*, www.janpalach.cz/en/default/mista-pameti (Last accessed January 2013).

Boulder Public Library. 'Maria Rogers Oral History Program.' *Boulder Public Library*, http://oralhistory.boulderlibrary.org (Last accessed January 2013).

Briggs, Raymond. *When the Wind Blows*. London: Hamish Hamilton, 1982.

'British Buyers Snap Up Bunkers.' *Toronto Star*, 12 July 2003.

Britton, Wesley A. *Onscreen and Undercover: The Ultimate Book of Movie Espionage*. Westport, Connecticut: Praeger, 2006.

Brokaw, Tom. *The Greatest Generation*. New York: Random House, 1998.

Brown, Kate. *Plutopia: Nuclear Families, Atomic Cities, and the Great Soviet and American Plutonium Disasters*. New York: Oxford University Press, 2013.

Bunker-42. 'Bunker-42 on Taganka.' *Bunker-42*, http://bunker42.nichost.ru (Last accessed April 2013).

Bush, George W. 'Victims of Communism Memorial Dedication.' *C-Span Video Library*, 12 June 2007, www.c-spanvideo.org/videoLibrary/transcript/transcript.php?programid=176429 (Last accessed February 2013).

Cameron, Rob. 'Prague Monument to Communist Victims Damaged in Explosion.' *Radio Praha*, 11 November 2003, www.radio.cz/en/section/curraffrs/prague-monument-to-communist-victims-damaged-in-explosion (Last accessed October 2012).

Campbell, David. *Writing Security: United States Foreign Policy and the Politics of Identity.* Minneapolis: University of Minnesota Press, 1992.

Carbonell, Bettina Messias, ed. *Museum Studies: An Anthology of Contexts.* Oxford: Blackwell Publishing, 2004.

Carroll, Sam. '"I was Arrested at Greenham in 1962": Investigating the Oral Narratives of Women in the Committee of 100.' *Oral History*, vol. 32, no. 1 (2004): pp. 35–48.

Catford, Nick. *Subterranean Britain: Cold War Bunkers.* London: Folly Books, 2010.

Central Office of Information (for the Home Office). *Protect and Survive.* London: Her Majesty's Stationery Office, 1976. (Reprinted 1980.)

Chaliapin, Boris. 'Man of the Year: Hungarian Freedom Fighter.' *Time*, 1957, Front cover.

Cheney, Liz. 'Obama Rewrites the Cold War.' *Wall Street Journal*, vol. 254, no. 10 (13 July 2009): pp. A13.

Churchill, Winston S. 'The Sinews of Peace.' *The Churchill Centre and Museum at the Churchill War Rooms, London*, 5 March 1946, www.winstonchurchill.org/learn/biography/in-opposition/qiron-curtainq-fulton-missouri-1946/120-the-sinews-of-peace (Last accessed September 2012).

City of Rijswijk Public Information Department. *Rijswijk Travel Planner.* Rijswijk: September 2009.

Cocroft, Wayne. 'Archaeological Field Survey and Investigation: Cold War.' *English Heritage*, www.english-heritage.org.uk/professional/research/landscapes-and-areas/archaeological-field-survey-and-investigation/cold-war/ (Last accessed March 2013).

Cocroft, Wayne, Roger Thomas, and P. Barnwell. *Cold War: Building for Nuclear Confrontation 1946–1989.* English Heritage, 2005.

Coffey, Liz. 'Titan Missile Museum: Authenticate!' *Conelrad*, December 2003, www.conelrad.com/groundzero/index.php?zero=01 (Last accessed March 2013).

Cold War. 24 episodes: CNN, 1998.

'Cold War Memories are Made of This.' *Toronto Star*, 30 June 2010.

The Cold War Museum. 'Background.' *The Cold War Museum*, www.coldwar.org/museum/background.asp (Last accessed December 2012).

——. 'Cold War Museum Physical Location – Vint Hill Farm Station.' *The Cold War Museum*, 11 December 2009, www.coldwar.org/museum/physical_location.asp (Last accessed March 2013).

Conelrad, http://conelrad.com/index.php (Last accessed November 2012).

Coney, George. 'Protect and Survive: An Archive of UK Civil Defence Material.' *Atomica*, 2002, www.atomica.co.uk (Last accessed January 2013).

Confino, Alon, and Peter Fritzsche. 'Introduction: Noises of the Past.' In *The Work of Memory: New Directions in the Study of German Society and Culture*, edited by Alon Confino and Peter Fritzsche. Urbana; Chicago: University of Illinois Press, 2002: 1–21.

——, eds. *The Work of Memory: New Directions in the Study of German Society and Culture.* Urbana; Chicago: University of Illinois Press, 2002.

Connolly, Kate. 'Red Revival.' *The Guardian*, 7 March 2002, www.guardian.co.uk/world/2002/mar/06/worlddispatch.education (Last accessed November 2012).

Conquest, Robert. *The Great Terror: Stalin's Purge in the Thirties.* London: Macmillan, 1968.

Cordonnery, Laurence. 'The Legacy of French Nuclear Testing in the Pacific.' In *The Oceans in the Nuclear Age: Legacies and Risks*, edited by David D. Caron and Harry N. Scheiber. Leiden: Martinus Nijhoff, 2010: pp. 69–78.

Cribb, Robert. 'Unresolved Problems in the Indonesian Killings of 1965–66.' *Asian Survey*, vol. 42, no. 4 (2002): pp. 550–63.

'Cuban Missile Crisis offers Lessons relevant Today.' *Korea Times*, 23 October 2012.

Cull, Nicholas. *The Cold War and the United States Information Agency: American Propaganda and Public Diplomacy*. Cambridge: Cambridge University Press, 2008.

——. *The Decline and Fall of the United States Information Agency: American Public Diplomacy, 1989–2001*. New York: Palgrave Macmillan, 2012.

Cull, Nicholas J. *Public Diplomacy: Lessons from the Past*. Los Angeles: Figueroa Press, 2009.

Cumming, Jason. 'Brits Put Cold War Bunker on Preservation List: U.S.-built Fortress Left Obsolete by Fall of Berlin Wall Becomes Landmark.' *NBC News*, 5 November 2009, www.nbcnews.com/id/33506583/ns/world_news-fall_of_the_berlin_wall_20_years_later/t/brits-put-cold-war-bunker-preservation-list/ –.UcUyV RyP0QI (Last accessed April 2013).

Danish Agency for Culture. 'Danish Cold War Hot Spots Open to the Public.' *Danish Agency for Culture*, 28 February 2013, www.kulturstyrelsen.dk/english/news/danish-cold-war-hot-spots-open-to-the-public/ –.UdfxrxYwaqC (Last accessed May 2013).

Danish Institute for International Studies. 'Denmark During the Cold War: Highlights of the DIIS Report, National Security Policy and the International Environment 1945–91.' 30 June 2005.

Dapkus, Liudas. 'Lithuanian Archive Releases KGB Collaborator Names.' *The Seattle Times*, 22 February 2012, http://seattletimes.com/html/nationworld/2017567459_apeulithuaniakgb.html (Last accessed January 2013).

David, Jiří. *Klíčová socha*, http://www.klicovasocha.cz (Last accessed April 2013).

Davoliūtė, Violeta. 'The Prague Declaration of 2008 and its Repercussions in Lithuania: Historical Justice and Reconciliation.' *Lituanus: Lithuanian Quarterly Journal of Arts and Sciences*, vol. 57, no. 3 (2011): pp. 49–62.

DDR Museum. 'Welcome to one of the Most Interactive Museums in the World!' *DDR Museum*, www.ddr-museum.de/en/museum/ (Last accessed November 2012).

Deme, János. 'Dead Ends of the Socialist Arms Race: Abandoned Soviet Barracks in Central Europe.' *Visegrad Revue*, 6 March 2013, http://visegradrevue.eu/?p=1628 (Last accessed April 2013).

DeMillo, Andrew. 'Atop Old Missile Hold, Cold War Site may Rise: Son of U-2 Pilot Francis Gary Powers Envisions a Museum at Lorton.' *The Washington Post*, 2 March 2002, www.washingtonpost.com/wp-dyn/articles/A26119–2002Mar1.html (Last accessed January 2013).

Department for Education (UK). *History: Programmes of Study for Key Stages 1–3*. Crown Copyright, February 2013.

Department of Defense. *Coming in from the Cold: Military Heritage in the Cold War. Report on the Department of Defense Legacy Cold War Project*. Washington DC: US Government Printing Office, 1994.

DePillis, Lydia. 'The Economics of Stephen Fuller: How a Wonky Academic Became a Major Player in the Local Real-Estate Business.' *Washington City Paper*, 15 April 2011, www.washingtoncitypaper.com/articles/40709/the-economics-of-stephen-fuller/full/ (Last accessed January 2013).

Diefenbunker. *Diefenbunker: Canada's Cold War Museum/Musée canadien de la Guerre froide*, www.diefenbunker.ca/en_index.shtml (Last accessed May 2013).

———. 'Your Visit: School Tours – Curriculum Links – Grades 9–10.' *Diefenbunker: Canada's Cold War Museum/Musée canadien de la Guerre froide*, http://diefenbunker. ca/pages/school_tours/curriculum_links_grade_9–10.shtml (Last accessed May 2013).

Donovan, John. '20 Years Later, Berlin Wall Fragments Symbolize Freedom and Hope.' *ABC News*, 8 November 2009, http://abcnews.go.com/GMA/Weekend/ berlin-wall-fragments-scattered-world/story?id=9028105 –.Ud1cNBYwaqA (Last accessed December 2012).

Dower, John W. *Ways of Forgetting, Ways of Remembering: Japan in the Modern World*. New York: The New Press, 2012.

Dramani-Issifou, Zakari. *Report on the Current State of History Teaching in Africa*. UNESCO Culture Sector, 2010.

Dubin, Steven C. *Displays of Power: Controversy in the American Museum from the Enola Gay to Sensation*. New York: University Press, 1999.

Dülffer, Jost. 'Erinnerungspolitik und Erinnerungskultur – Kein Ende der Geschichte.' In *Eine Ausstellung und ihre Folgen: Zur Rezeption der Ausstellung 'Vernichtungskrieg. Verbrechen der Wehrmacht 1941 bis 1944'*, edited by Hamburger Institut für Sozialforschung. Hamburg: HIS Verlagsges.mbH, 1999: pp. 289–312.

Dye, Air Vice-Marshal (ret'd) Peter. 'About Us.' *Royal Air Force Museum Cosford: National Cold War Exhibition*, www.nationalcoldwarexhibition.org/about-us.cfm (Last accessed October 2012).

Ellman, Michael. 'Soviet Repression Statistics: Some Comments.' *Europe-Asia Studies*, vol. 54, no. 7 (2002): pp. 1151–72.

Eltringham, Nigel, and Pam Maclean, eds. *Remembering Genocide*. (Series editors David Lowe and Tony Joel, Remembering the Modern World.) Abingdon, Oxon: Routledge, 2014 (scheduled).

Embassy of the United States, Prague. 'Czech Republic Pays Tribute to Ronald Reagan.' *Embassy of the United States Prague, Czech Republic* 1 July 2011, http:// prague.usembassy.gov/ronald-reagan-street.html (Last accessed March 2013).

Emporis. 'Europe's Tallest Buildings – Top 20.' *Emporis*, 2013, www.emporis.com/ statistics/tallest-buildings-europe (Last accessed January 2013).

Engerman, David C. 'California's Cold War Museum.' *Humanities: The Magazine of the National Endowment for the Humanities*, May/June 2011, www.neh.gov/huma-nities/2011/mayjune/feature/californias-cold-war-museum (Last accessed February 2013).

'Essence of Decision: The Cuban Missile Crisis contains Lessons for Nuclear Diplo-macy in the 21st Century.' *The Times*, 18 October 2012, www.thetimes.co.uk/tto/ opinion/leaders/article3571479.ece (Last accessed May 2013).

Euro Information. 'Slovenská republika: 2 Euro Commemorative Design 2009.' *The Euro Information Website*, www.ibiblio.org/theeuro/InformationWebsite.htm?http:// www.ibiblio.org/theeuro/forum/viewtopic.php?f=81&t=535& p = 1977 (Last accessed November 2012).

European Union. 'The History of the European Union.' *European Union*, http:// europa.eu/about-eu/eu-history/index_en.htm (Last accessed May 2013).

Expedia. 'Bunker-42 on Taganka.' *Expedia*, www.expedia.co.in/Bunker-On-Taganka-Moscow.d6156062.Attraction (Last accessed November 2012).

Falk, Leora. 'Questions Rise over Memorials.' *Chicago Tribune News*, 13 June 2007, http://articles.chicagotribune.com/2007-06-13/news/0706130254_1_monument-tiananmen-square-communist (Last accessed February 2013).

Finkelstein, Norman. *The Holocaust Industry: Reflections on the Exploitation of Jewish Suffering*. London: Verso, 2000.

Finney, Patrick. *Remembering the Road to World War Two: International History, National Identity, Collective Memory*. Abingdon, Oxon: Routledge, 2011.

Finnish Board of Education. *National Core Curriculum for Upper Secondary Schools*. Helsinki: Finnish Board of Education, 2003.

flickr. 'Ronald Reagan Street in Prague.' *flickr*, 1 July 2011, www.flickr.com/photos/usembassyprague/sets/72157627099704332/ (Last accessed March 2013).

Forczyk, Robert. *Warsaw 1944: Poland's Bid for Freedom*. Oxford: Osprey Publishing, 2009.

Forero, Juan. 'As Election Looms, Chávez Steps up Rhetoric.' *The Washington Post*, 16 October 2008, www.washingtonpost.com/wp-dyn/content/article/2008/10/15/AR2008101503292.html (Last accessed December 2012).

Fowkes, Reuben. 'Public Sculpture and Hungarian Revolution of 1956.' *Ungarn 1956 – Geschichte und Erinnerung*, www.ungarn1956.de/site/40208667/default.aspx (Last accessed September 2012).

Frank, Richard B. *Downfall: The End of the Imperial Japanese Empire*. New York: Penguin, 1999.

Frazier, Paul. 'The Venona Project and Cold War Espionage.' *Organization of American Historians (OAH) Magazine of History*, October 2010, pp. 35–39.

Freedman, Lawrence. 'Kennedy, Bush and Crisis Management.' *Cold War History*, vol. 2, no. 3 (2002): pp. 1–14.

Freeman, Lindsey A. 'Happy Memories under the Mushroom Cloud: Utopia and Memory in Oak Ridge, Tennessee.' In *Memory and the Future: Transnational Politics, Ethics and Society*, edited by Yifat Gutman, Adam D. Brown, and Amy Sodao. London: Palgrave Macmillan, 2010: pp. 158–75.

Frei, Norbert. *Adenauer's Germany and the Nazi Past: The Politics of Amnesty and Integration*. Translated by Joel Golb. New York: Columbia University Press, 2002.

Fu, Chao-Ching. 'From a Military Front to a Cold War Heritage Site: A Study of the Prospect of Matsu Archipelago as Sustainable Tourism Islands.' *ICOMOS Open Archive*, 2012: pp. 631–38. http://openarchive.icomos.org/1258/ (Last accessed May 2013).

Fukuyama, Francis. *The End of History and the Last Man*. London: Penguin Books, 1992.

Fussell, Paul. 'Thank God for the Atom Bomb.' *The Guardian*, 5 February 1989, pp. 9–11.

Füstös, Erika J., and Helen Kovács. *In the Shadow of Stalin's Boots: Visitors' Guide to Memento Park*. Budapest: Private Planet Books, 2010.

Futter, Andrew. 'Obama's Nuclear Weapons Policy in a Changing World.' *LSE Ideas Series*. (2009): pp. 13–17.

Gable, Eric, and Richard Handler. 'Forget Culture, Remember Memory? (Keynote Address).' Paper presented at the Annual Meeting of the Southern Anthropological Society, Staunton, Virginia, 2008: pp. 23–44.

Gaddis, John Lewis. *The Cold War: A New History*. New York: Penguin, 2005.

——. *We Now Know: Rethinking Cold War History*. New York: Oxford University Press, 1997.

Gedenkstätte Berlin-Hohenschönhausen. 'The Memorial.' *Gedenkstätte Berlin-Hohenschönhausen*, http://en.stiftung-hsh.de (Last accessed March 2013).

Gegner, Martin. 'War Monuments in East and West Berlin: Cold War Symbols or Different Forms of Memorial?' In *The Heritage of War*, edited by Martin Gegner and Bart Ziino. Abingdon, Oxon: Routledge, 2012: pp. 64–87.

Gegner, Martin, and Bart Ziino, eds. *The Heritage of War*. (Series editors William Logan and Laurajane Smith, Key Issues in Cultural Heritage.) Abingdon, Oxon: Routledge, 2012.

Genocide and Resistance Research Centre of Lithuania. 'The Memorial Complex of the Tuskulėnai Peace Park.' *Genocide and Resistance Research Centre of Lithuania*, www.genocid.lt/tuskulenai/en/ (Last accessed March 2013).

——. *The Museum of Genocide Victims: A Guide to the Exhibitions*. Vilnius, 2006.

——. 'An Outline of the History of the Genocide and Resistance Research Centre of Lithuania.' *Genocide and Resistance Research Centre of Lithuania*, www.genocid.lt/centras/en/ (Last accessed December 2012).

——. *The Secrets of Tuskulėnai Manor (Guide Pamphlet)*. Vilnius.

Gera, Vanessa. 'Walesa Unveils Statue of Ronald Reagan in Warsaw.' *Deseret News*, 21 November 2011, www.deseretnews.com/article/700199832/Walesa-unveils-statue-of-Ronald-Reagan-in-Warsaw.html (Last accessed February 2013).

Gerhard, Galerie. 'Mária Lugossy: Biography.' *Galerie Gerhard: Bad Berleburg*, www.galerie-gerhard.com/pdf/gg-pdf-lugossy-data-en.pdf (Last accessed December 2012).

Gillis, John, ed. *Commemorations: The Politics of National Identity*. Princeton: University Press, 1994.

Gingrich, Newt and Callista. 'Nine Days that Changed the World: Pope John Paul II. June 2–10, 1979.' *Nine Days that Changed the World*, www.ninedaysthatchanged theworld.com (Last accessed September 2012).

Gorondi, Pablo. 'Ronald Reagan Statue Unveiled in Hungary.' *Yahoo! News*, 29 June 2011, http://news.yahoo.com/ronald-reagan-statue-unveiled-hungary-145351000.html (Last accessed March 2013).

Gough, Paul. 'The Greater London Council: Selected Peace Sites.' *Vortex*, www.vortex.uwe.ac.uk/places_of_peace/sites.htm (Last accessed November 2012).

Grandin, Greg. *The Last Colonial Massacre: Latin America in the Cold War*. Chicago: University of Chicago Press, 2004.

Gray, Peter, and Kendrick Oliver, eds. *The Memory of Catastrophe*. Manchester: Manchester University Press, 2004.

Green, Eric. 'Civil Defense Museum.' *Civil Defense Museum*, www.civildefensemuseum.com/index.html (Last accessed April 2013).

Green, Jim. 'Dumping on Traditional Owners: The Ugly Face of Australian Racism.' *ABC: The Drum*, 29 March 2012, www.abc.net.au/unleashed/3919296.html (Last accessed February 2013).

The Greenbrier. 'Bunker History.' *The Greenbrier: America's Resort*, www.greenbrier.com/Activities/The-Bunker/Bunker-History.aspx (Last accessed February 2013).

Grūtas Park. 'About Us.' *Grūtas Park*, www.grutoparkas.lt/?lang=gb (Last accessed April 2013).

Gudgin, Sarah (Interviewer), and Sue Sanders (Interviewee). 'Extract from Interview with Sue Sanders.' *Museum of London*, 2009, www.museumoflondon.org.uk/Collections-Research/Collections-online/object.aspx?objectID=object-800279& start = 5& rows = 1 (Last accessed March 2013).

Gulag Museum. 'Virtual Museum of the Gulag: Collections.' *Gulag Museum*, www. gulagmuseum.org/start.do?&language=2 (Last accessed May 2013).

Hachiya, Michihiko. *Hiroshima Diary: The Journal of a Japanese Physician, August 6 – September 30, 1945*. Translated by Warner Wells. Chapel Hill: University of North Carolina Press, 1995.

Halbwachs, Maurice. *On Collective Memory*. Translated by Lewis A. Coser. Chicago and London: The University of Chicago Press, 1992 [1925].

Hall, Allan. 'World Leaders Gather to see the Berlin Wall Topple Again, 20 Years On.' *Daily Mail Online*, 10 November 2009, www.dailymail.co.uk/news/article-1226507/20-years-Berlin-Wall-topples-again.html (Last accessed November 2012).

Hanhimäki, Jussi M., and Odd Arne Westad, eds. *The Cold War: A History in Documents and Eyewitness Accounts*. New York: Oxford University Press, 2003.

Harrison, Hope. 'Teaching and Scholarship on the Cold War in the United States.' *Cold War History*, vol. 8, no. 2 (May 2008): pp. 259–84.

Hasegawa, Tsuyoshi. *Racing the Enemy: Stalin, Truman and the Surrender of Japan*. Cambridge, Massachusetts: The Belknap Press of Harvard University Press, 2006.

Hass, Matthias. *Gestaltetes Gedenken: Yad Vashem, das U.S. Holocaust Memorial Museum und die Stiftung Topographie des Terrors*. Frankfurt/New York: Campus, 2002.

Hawley, Charles. 'Spiegel Online Interview with Lech Walesa: "It's Good that Gorbachev was a Weak Politician."' *Spiegel Online International*, 6 November 2009, www.spiegel.de/international/europe/spiegel-online-interview-with-lech-walesa-it-s-good-that-gorbachev-was-a-weak-politician-a-659752.html (Last accessed November 2012).

Haynes, John Earl, Harvey Klehr, and Alexander Vassiliev. *The Rise and Fall of the KGB in America*. New Haven: Yale University Press, 2006.

Hebbeln, Toke Constantin. *Shores of Hope*. 116 mins. Germany, 2012.

Heinemann, Winfried, Axel Klausmeier, Michael Kubina, Anke Kuhrmann, Jochen Maurer, Leo Schmidt, and Manfred Wilke. *Die Berliner Mauer—Vom Sperrwall zum Denkmal*, edited by Deutsches Nationalkomitee für Denkmalschutz. Vol. 76/1, Bühl: KONKORDIA GmbH, 2009.

Herf, Jeffrey. *Divided Memory: The Nazi Past in the Two Germanys*. Cambridge, Massachusetts: Harvard University Press, 1997.

Hersey, John. *Hiroshima*. Harmondsworth, Middlesex: Penguin, 1946.

Hibakusha: Survivors of Hiroshima and Nagasaki. Translated by Gaynor Sekimori. Tokyo: Kôsei Publishing Company, 1986.

Hillstrom, Kevin. *The Cold War*. Detroit: Omnigraphics, 2006.

Hipperson, Sarah. 'Greenham Common Women's Peace Camp, 1981–2000.' *Greenham Common Women's Peace Camp*, www.greenhamwpc.org.uk (Last accessed December 2012).

'Hiroshima Peace Memorial (Genbaku Dome).' *UNESCO World Heritage List*, http://whc.unesco.org/en/list/775 (Last accessed December 2012).

'Hiroshima Peace Memorial Museum: Exhibit Text.' (February 2013).

Ho Chi Minh Museum, www.baotanghochiminh.vn/tabid/528/default.aspx (Last accessed October 2012).

Hobsbawm, Eric. *The Age of Empire: 1875–1914*. London: Abacus, 1994.

——. *Age of Extremes: The Short Twentieth Century, 1914–1991*. London: Abacus, 1995.

Hobsbawm, Eric, and Terence Ranger, eds. *The Invention of Tradition*. New York: Cambridge University Press, 1983.

Hogan, Michael J. 'The Enola Gay Controversy: History, Memory, and the Politics of Presentation.' In *Hiroshima in History and Memory*, edited by Michael J. Hogan. New York: Cambridge University Press, 1999: pp. 200–32.

Hogan, Michael J., and Thomas G. Paterson, eds. *Explaining the History of American Foreign Relations*. 2nd ed. Cambridge: Cambridge University Press, 2004.

Hopkins, M.F. 'Continuing Debate and New Approaches in Cold War History.' *History Journal*, vol. 50, no. 4 (2007): pp. 913–34.

Horsley, Scott. 'Obama Evokes Cold War in Speech at Berlin's Brandenburg Gate.' *WHQR 91.3fm: Radio with Vision … Listen and See*, 19 June 2013, http://whqr.org/post/obama-evokes-cold-war-speech-berlins-brandenburg-gate (Last accessed June 2013).

Hrechorowicz, Andrzej. 'Walesa Unveils One More for the "Gipper."' *Polskie Radio*, 21 November 2011, www.thenews.pl/1/10/Artykul/58886,Walesa-unveils-one-more-for-the-Gipper (Last accessed February 2013).

Hudson, Kate. 'Remembering Greenham Common.' *The New Statesman*, 10 December 2007, www.newstatesman.com/archive/2013/04/remembering-greenham-common (Last accessed April 2013).

Hutchings, Fleur. 'Cold Europe: Discovering, Researching and Preserving European Cold War Heritage.' Cottbus: Department of Architectural Conservation at the Brandenburg University of Technology, February 2004.

Imperial War Museum. 'Greenham Common: The Women's Peace Camp 1981–2000.' *Imperial War Museum*, http://archive.iwm.org.uk/upload/package/22/greenham/index.htm (Last accessed January 2013).

Indian Central Board of Secondary Education. *Senior School Curriculum, 2015*. Vol. 1, New Delhi: Central Board of Secondary Education, 2013.

The Institute for the Study of Totalitarian Regimes. 'Personnel File of Lt. Ludvík Zifčák: Career of the "Dead Student."' *The Institute for the Study of Totalitarian Regimes (Ústav pro studium totalitních režimů)*, www.ustrcr.cz/en/personnel-file-ludvik-zifcak (Last accessed October 2012).

Institute of Medicine, and National Research Council. 'Exposure of the American People to Iodine-131 from Nevada Nuclear-Bomb Tests: Review of the National Cancer Institute Report and Public Health Implications.' *National Center for Biotechnology Information (NCBI)*, 1999, www.ncbi.nlm.nih.gov/books/NBK100842/ (Last accessed April 2013).

International Spy Museum. *Educator Guide. The Enemy Within: Terror in America, 1776 to Today*. 2004.

——. 'History & Mission.' *International Spy Museum*, www.spymuseum.org/about/history-mission/ (Last accessed January 2013).

Isaacs, Jeremy, and Taylor Downing. *Cold War: An Illustrated History, 1945–1991*. Boston: Little, Brown and Company, 1998.

Iversen, Kristen. *Full Body Burden: Growing Up in the Nuclear Shadow of Rocky Flats*. New York: Crown Publishing, 2012.

IWM. 'Secret War.' *Imperial War Museum*, www.iwm.org.uk/exhibitions/iwm-london/secret-war (Last accessed January 2013).

Jacobs, Robert A. *The Dragon's Tail: Americans Face the Atomic Age*. Amherst: University of Massachusetts Press, 2010.

Jampol, Justinian. 'About Us.' *The Wende Museum*, www.wendemuseum.org/about-us (Last accessed May 2013).

——. 'The Wende Museum.' *The Wende Museum*, www.wendemuseum.org (Last accessed May 2013).

Je-gyu, Kang. *Tae Guk Gi: The Brotherhood of War*. 148 minutes. South Korea: Samuel Goldwyn Films, 2004.

Ji-Qiang, Li. 'Construction for Kinmen Bridge Begins and President Ma Hopes it Becomes a New Landmark for Kinmen.' *Kinmen County Government*, 13 November 2012, www.kinmen.gov.tw/Layout/main_en/News_NewsContent.aspx?NewsID= 103862& path = 5551& LanguageType = 2 (Last accessed May 2013).

Joel, Tony. *The Dresden Firebombing: Memory and the Politics of Commemorating Destruction*. London: I.B.Tauris, 2013 (in press).

Johnson, Chalmers, ed. *Okinawa: Cold War Island*. Cardiff, California: Japan Policy Research Institute, 1999.

Johnstone, Chris. 'Ronald Reagan to be Honoured in Czech Capital.' *Czech Position*, 30 June 2011, www.ceskapozice.cz/en/news/society/ronald-reagan-be-honoured-czech-capital (Last accessed March 2013).

Judt, Tony. *Postwar: A History of Europe since 1945*. London: Vintage, 2010.

Kacvinský, Martin. 'Brno – Key Sculpture – Jiri David (CZ), 2010.' *360 Cities*, www.360cities.net/image/key-sculpture-revoluce – 12.65,0.00,110.0 (Last accessed April 2013).

Kamm, Henry. 'Hungarian Who Led '56 Revolt is Buried as a Hero.' *The New York Times*, 17 June 1989, www.nytimes.com/1989/06/17/world/hungarian-who-led-56-revolt-is-buried-as-a-hero.html (Last accessed December 2012).

Kansteiner, Wulf. 'Finding Meaning in Memory: A Methodological Critique of Collective Memory Studies.' *History and Theory*, no. 41 (May 2002): pp. 179–97.

Karacs, Sarah. 'The Velvet Revolution: Czech Students Look Back at What Their Forebears Started.' *Spiegel Online International*, 20 November 2009, www.spiegel.de/international/spiegel/the-velvet-revolution-czech-students-look-back-at-what-their-forebears-started-a-661999.html (Last accessed January 2013).

Kattago, Siobhan. *Ambiguous Memory: The Nazi Past and German National Identity*. Westport, Connecticut: Praeger, 2001.

Kelly, Cynthia, ed. *Remembering the Manhattan Project: Perspectives on the Making of the Atomic Bomb and its Legacy*. River Edge, New Jersey: World Scientific Publishing, 2005.

Khong, Yuen Foon. *Analogies at War: Korea, Munich, Dien Bien Phu and the Vietnam Decision of 1965*. Princeton: Princeton University Press, 1992.

Kidd, William, and Brian Murdoch, eds. *Memory and Memorials: the Commemorative Century*. Aldershot: Ashgate, 2004.

Kim, Dae Soon. *The Transition to Democracy in Hungary: Árpád Göncz and the Post-Communist Hungarian Presidency*. London: Routledge, 2013.

Kimball, Daryl, and Tom Collina. 'Nuclear Weapons: Who Has What at a Glance.' *Arms Control Association*, April 2013, www.armscontrol.org/factsheets/Nuclearweaponswhohaswhat (Last accessed May 2013).

King, Michael. *Death of the Rainbow Warrior*. Harmondsworth: Penguin, 1986.

Kishkovsky, Sophia. 'Moscow to get Major Gulag Museum.' *The Art Newspaper*, 12 April 2013, www.theartnewspaper.com/articles/Moscow+to+get+major+Gulag+museum/29311 (Last accessed May 2013).

Klausmeier, Alex, and Leo Schmidt. *Wall Remnants – Wall Traces: The Comprehensive Guide to the Berlin Wall*. Berlin: Westkreuz-Verlag, 2004.

Knight, Robert. 'Cold War History.' Loughborough University, www.lboro.ac.uk/departments/phir/research/projects/cold-war-history/ (Last accessed April 2013).

Kohn, Richard H. 'History and Culture Wars: The Case of the Smithsonian Institution's Enola Gay Exhibition.' *Journal of American History*, vol. 82, no. 3 (December 1995): pp. 1036–63.

Koshar, Rudy. *From Monuments to Traces: Artifacts of German Memory, 1870–1990*. Berkeley: University of California Press, 2000.

Kunkle, Fredrick. 'Proposed Cold War Museum Falls Short.' *The Washington Post*, 15 April 2009, http://articles.washingtonpost.com/2009-04-15/news/ 36817768_1_cold-war-museum-international-spy-museum-francis-gary-powers (Last accessed January 2013).

Kwon, Heonik. *Ghosts of War in Vietnam*. Cambridge: Cambridge University Press, 2008.

———. *The Other Cold War*. New York: Columbia University Press, 2010.

LaFeber, Walter. *America, Russia and the Cold War, 1945–2002*. 9th ed. New York: McGraw Hill, 2002.

Lakoff, George. *Don't Think of an Elephant: Know Your Values and Frame the Debate*. Melbourne: Scribe Publications, 2004.

Leffler, Melvyn P. 'Remembering George Kennan: Lessons for Today?' *United States Institute of Peace: Special Report 180*. (December 2006).

Levy, Alexandra. 'The Manhattan Project: Interpreting Controversial History.' *National Trust for Historic Preservation: Preservation Leadership Forum*, 15 May 2013, http://blog.preservationleadershipforum.org/2013/05/15/manhattan-project-inter-preting/ –.UZP5D7Xvtys (Last accessed May 2013).

Levy, Daniel, and Natan Sznaider. *The Holocaust and Memory in the Global Age*. Translated by Assenka Oksiloff. Philadelphia: Temple University Press, 2006.

Liang, Zhi, Yafeng Xia, and Ming Chen. 'Recent Trends in the Study of Cold War History in China.' *Wilson Center: Cold War International History Project*, 2012, www. wilsoncenter.org/publication/recent-trends-the-study-cold-war-history-china (Last accessed May 2013).

Linenthal, Edward Tabor. *Sacred Ground: Americans and their Battlefields*. Urbana: University of Illinois Press, 1993.

Logan, William, and Nguyn Thanh Bình. 'Victory and Defeat at Điện Biên Phủ: Memory and Memorialization in Vietnam and France.' In *The Heritage of War*, edited by Martin Gegner and Bart Ziino. Abingdon, Oxon: Routledge, 2012: pp. 41–63.

Loverro, Thom. 'A Fraud that is Finally Being Exposed.' *The Washington Times*, 17 March 2005.

Lundestad, Geir. *The United States and Western Europe since 1945: From 'Empire' by Invitation to Transatlantic Drift*. New York: Oxford University Press, 2003.

Lunn, Kenneth, and Martin Evans. *War and Memory in the Twentieth Century*. Oxford, UK: Berg, 1997.

Maclellan, Nic. 'The Nuclear Age in the Pacific Islands.' *The Contemporary Pacific*, vol. 17, no. 2 (2005): pp. 363–72.

Maddux, Thomas, John Ehrman, Benjamen B. Fischer, Richard Gid Powers, Ellen Schrecker, John Earl Haynes, and Harvey Klehr. 'H-Diplo Roundtable Review,' *H-Diplo Roundtable Review*, vol. XI, no. 9 (14 December 2009).

Maier, Charles S. 'A Surfeit of Memory? Reflections on History, Melancholy and Denial.' *History and Memory*, vol. 5, no. 2 (1993): pp. 136–52.

———. *The Unmasterable Past: History, Holocaust, and German National Identity*. Cambridge, Mass.: Harvard University Press, 1988.

Manchanda, Arnav. 'When Truth is Stranger than Fiction: The Able Archer Incident.' *Cold War History*, vol. 9, no. 1 (2009): pp. 111–33.

Mastny, Vojtech. 'How Able was "Able Archer"? Nuclear Trigger and Intelligence in Perspective.' *Journal of Cold War Studies*, vol. 11, no. 1 (2009): pp. 108–23.

Matsui, Kazumi. 'Hiroshima Peace Declaration.' 6 August 2012.

Matthews Jr., Melvin E. *Duck and Cover: Civil Defense Images in Film and Television from the Cold War to 9/11*. Jefferson, North Virginia: McFarland and Co., 2012.

McCamley, Nick. *Cold War Secret Nuclear Bunkers: The Passive Defence of the Western World*. London: Pen & Sword, 2007.

McCormack, Gavan, and Satoko Oka Norimatsu. *Resistant Islands: Okinawa confronts Japan and the United States*. Lanham, Maryland: Rowman & Littlefield, 2012.

McCurry, Justin. 'Two US Sailors Accused of Okinawa Rape.' *The Guardian*, 17 October 2012, www.guardian.co.uk/world/2012/oct/17/us-sailors-accused-okinawa-rape (Last accessed February 2013).

McKeati, J. 'Remember the Rainbow Warrior and the Marshall Islands.' *Greenpeace*, 9 July 2010, www.greenpeace.org/international/en/news/Blogs/nuclear-reaction/remember-the-rainbow-warrior-and-the-marshall/blog/12910/ (Last accessed October 2012).

McMahon, Robert J. *The Cold War: A Very Short Introduction*. London: Oxford University Press, 2003.

McWilliams, Wayne C., and Harry Piotrowski. *The World Since 1945: A History of International Relations*. 7th ed. Boulder, Colorado: Lynne Rienner, 2009.

Mead & Hunt Inc., Christina Slattery, Mary Ebeling, Erin Pogany, and Amy R. Squitieri. 'The Missile Plains: Frontline of America's Cold War (Historic Resource Study of Minuteman Missile National Historic Site, South Dakota, Prepared for United States Department of the Interior, National Park Service, Midwest Regional Office).' *National Park Service*, 2003, www.nps.gov/mimi/historyculture/upload/MIMI HRS 2006.pdf (Last accessed March 2013).

Memorial. 'The Charter of the International Volunteer Public Organization: "Memorial" Historical, Educational, Human Rights and Charitable Society.' *Memorial*, 19 April 1992 (Revised version adopted 18 December 1998), www.memo.ru/eng/about/charter.htm (Last accessed May 2013).

Merali, Zeeya. 'Did China's Nuclear Tests Kill Thousands and Doom Future Generations?' *Scientific American*, 8 July 2009, www.scientificamerican.com/article.cfm?id=did-chinas-nuclear-tests (Last accessed November 2012).

Mikailienė, Živilė. 'Soviet Vilnius: Ideology and the Formation of Identity.' *Lithuanian Historical Studies*, vol. 15 (2010): pp. 171–89.

Mikoyan, Sergo. *The Soviet Cuban Missile Crisis: Castro, Mikoyan, Kennedy, Khrushchev and the Missiles of November*. Stanford, California: Stanford University Press and Woodrow Wilson Center Press, 2012.

Miller, Arthur. 'Why I Wrote "The Crucible": An Artist's Answer to Politics.' *The New Yorker*, 21 October 1996, pp. 158–64.

Miller, Linda K., and Mary McAuliffe. 'The Cuban Missile Crisis.' *OAH Magazine of History*, vol. 8, no. 2 (1994): pp. 24–41.

Moeller, Robert G. *War Stories: The Search for a Usable Past in the Federal Republic of Germany*. Berkeley/Los Angeles: University of California Press, 2001.

Molella, Arthur. 'Exhibiting Atomic Culture: The View from Oak Ridge.' *History and Technology*, vol. 19, no. 3 (2003): pp. 211–26.

Müller, Jan-Werner. 'Introduction.' In *Memory and Power in Post-War Europe: Studies in the Presence of the Past*, edited by Jan-Werner Müller. Cambridge: Cambridge University Press, 2002: pp. 1–35.

Museum of Australian Democracy. 'The Petrov Affair.' *Museum of Australian Democracy: Red Alert – Spies & Codes – The Affair – Royal Commission – The Split*, http://moadoph.gov.au/exhibitions/online/petrov/ (Last accessed May 2013).

Museum of Communism. 'About the Museum.' *Museum of Communism*, www.muzeumkomunismu.cz/en/about-museum (Last accessed November 2012).

National Army Museum. *National Army Museum*, www.nam.ac.uk (Last accessed May 2013).

——. 'Special Displays: National Service.' *National Army Museum*, September 2011, www.nam.ac.uk/exhibitions/special-displays/national-service (Last accessed May 2013).

National Atomic Testing Museum. *National Atomic Testing Museum*, www.nationalatomictestingmuseum.org/exhibit-featured.aspx (Last accessed August 2012).

——. 'Exhibit – Area 51.' *National Atomic Testing Museum*, www.nationalatomictestingmuseum.org/exhibit-area51.aspx (Last accessed October 2012).

National Cold War Exhibition. 'Biography of Vilyam Fisher.' *Royal Air Force Museum Cosford: National Cold War Exhibition*, www.nationalcoldwarexhibition.org/explore/biography.cfm?name=Fisher, Vilyam (Last accessed December 2012).

——. 'Greenham Common.' *RAF Museum Cosford: National Cold War Exhibition*, www.nationalcoldwarexhibition.org/learn/social-economic-issues/greenham-common.cfm (Last accessed November 2012).

——. 'Museum commemorates 50th Anniversary of Cuban Missile Crisis.' *Royal Air Force Museum Cosford: National Cold War Exhibition*, 3 October 2012, www.nationalcoldwarexhibition.org/news/article.cfm?news_id=610 (Last accessed November 2012).

——. 'National Cold War Exhibition.' *Royal Air Force Museum Cosford: National Cold War Exhibition*, www.nationalcoldwarexhibition.org/index.cfm (Last accessed May 2013).

——. 'National Curriculum.' *Royal Air Force Museum Cosford: National Cold War Exhibition*, www.nationalcoldwarexhibition.org/learn/national-curriculum.cfm (Last accessed October 2012).

National Park Service. 'Nike Missile Site.' *National Park Service: Golden Gate National Recreation Area*, www.nps.gov/goga/nike-missile-site.htm (Last accessed March 2013).

Nelson, Craig. 'Stalin World Opens to Visitors.' *The Telegraph*, 1 April 2001, www.telegraph.co.uk/news/worldnews/europe/lithuania/1314998/Stalin-World-opens-to-visitors.html (Last accessed January 2013).

Neumann, Klaus. *Shifting Memories: The Nazi Past in the New Germany*. Ann Arbor: University of Michigan Press, 2003.

The Nike Historical Society. *NikeMissile.org*, http://nikemissile.org (Last accessed March 2013).

Niven, Bill, ed. *Germans as Victims*. New York: Palgrave Macmillan, 2006.

Noon, David Hoogland. 'Cold War Revival: Neoconservatives and Historical Memory in the War on Terror.' *American Studies*, vol. 48, no. 3 (2007): pp. 75–99.

Nora, Pierre. 'Between Memory and History: Les Lieux de Mémoire.' *Representations*, no. 26 (1989): pp. 7–25.

Norden. 'Swedish School Children's Knowledge of Communist War Crimes is Dire.' *Norden: Nordic Council of Ministers' Office in Estonia*, 1 October 2010, www.norden.

ee/en/about-us/news/item/7526-swedish-school-childrens-knowledge-of-communist-war-crimes-is-dire (Last accessed January 2013).

Novick, Peter. *The Holocaust in American Life.* Boston: Houghton Mifflin, 1999.

NTDTV. 'European Parliament Assessing the Impact of Nuclear Testing in Xinjiang.' *YouTube*, www.youtube.com/watch?v=uPGcpXLydYk (Last accessed January 2013).

Nuclear Claims Tribunal: Republic of the Marshall Islands. 'Welcome to the Marshall Islands Nuclear Claims Tribunal.' *Nuclear Claims Tribunal*, http://nuclearclaimstribunal.com (Last accessed March 2013).

Nunn, Judy. *Maralinga.* Sydney: William Heinemann, 2009.

Obama, Barack. 'Remarks by President Obama at the Brandenburg Gate, Berlin, Germany.' *The White House: President Barack Obama*, 19 June 2013, www.whitehouse.gov/the-press-office/2013/06/19/remarks-president-obama-brandenburg-gate-berlin-germany (Last accessed June 2013).

Office of the Press Secretary, The White House. 'President Bush Attends Dedication of Victims of Communism Memorial.' *The White House: President George W. Bush Archives*, 12 June 2007, http://georgewbush-whitehouse.archives.gov/news/releases/2007/06/20070612–2.html (Last accessed January 2013).

Ohnie. 'Nuclear Free Independent Pacific.' *Moana Nui*, 19 February 2013, http://mnaa-ca.org/nuclear-free-independent-pacific/ (Last accessed March 2013).

Okney, Philip A. 'Legacies and Perils from the Perspective of the Republic of the Marshall Islands Nuclear Claims Tribunal.' In *The Oceans in the Nuclear Age: Legacies and Risks*, edited by David D. Caron and Harry N. Scheiber. Leiden: Martinus Nijhoff, 2010: pp. 49–67.

The Organising Bureau of European School Student Unions (OBESSU) and The European Students' Union (ESU). '17 November: International Day of Students.' *17 NOV: International Day of Students*, http://17thofnovember-internationaldayofstudents.webstarts.com (Last accessed October 2012).

Page, D. 'Protect and Survive.' In *Defence Sites: Heritage and Future*, edited by C. Clark and C.A. Brebbia. Southamption: WIT Press, 2012: pp. 93–103.

Parfrey, Adam, ed. *Apocalypse Culture II.* Los Angeles: Feral House, 2000.

Parrish, J.A. 'The Kelvedon Hatch Secret Nuclear Bunker: The Biggest and Deepest Cold War Bunker Open to the Public in Southeast England.' *The Kelvedon Hatch Secret Nuclear Bunker*, www.secretnuclearbunker.com (Last accessed January 2013).

Peitsch, Helmut, Charles Burdett, Claire Gorrara, ed. *European Memories of the Second World War.* New York/London: Berghahn Books, 1999.

Peterson, Christian. *Ronald Reagan and Antinuclear Movements in the United States and Western Europe.* Lewiston, New York: Edwin Mellen Press, 2003.

Pipes, Richard, Robert Conquest, and John Lewis Gaddis. 'The Cold War Over CNN's Cold War.' *Hoover Institution: Stanford University*, 1994, www.hoover.org/publications/hoover-digest/article/7459 (Last accessed December 2012).

PKiN. 'History of the Palace of Culture and Science: Not Entirely Spontaneous Present.' *PKiN Warszawa*, www.pkin.pl/wp-content/uploads/2012/04/Not-entirely-spontaneous-present.pdf (Last accessed November 2012).

Planet, Lonely. 'Moscow Shooting Experience: Shoot an AK-47 at the Central Shooting Club.' *Lonely Planet*, www.lonelyplanet.com/russia/moscow/activities/private-tours/moscow-shooting-experience (Last accessed January 2013).

Platform of European Memory and Conscience. 'About the Project: Strategic Grant from the International Visegrad Fund.' *Platform of European Memory and Conscience*, 17 August 2011, www.memoryandconscience.eu/about-the-platfor/ (Last accessed May 2013).

Polskie Radio. 'Agnieszka Holland's Czech "Human Torch" Movie to Premiere in Prague.' *Polskie Radio*, 22 January 2013, www.thenews.pl/1/11/Artykul/124864, Agnieszka-Hollands-Czech-human-torch-movie-to-premiere-in-Prague (Last accessed January 2013).

Powers Jr., Francis Gary. 'The Cold War Museum moves closer to a Permanent Residence.' *American Institute for History Education (AIHE)*, November 2007, http://americaninstituteforhistory.org/gazette.php?year=2007 (Last accessed January 2013).

———. 'Spy Tours: The Original Spy Tour of Washington.' *Francis Gary Powers, Jr. Expert Public Speaker regarding the Cold War, U-2 Incident and the Need to Preserve Cold War History*, http://garypowers.org/spytours/ (Last accessed March 2013).

Prague Information Service. 'About Prague.' *PragueWelcome: Prague's Official Tourist Portal*, www.praguewelcome.cz/en/visit/ (Last accessed January 2013).

Prague Security Studies Institute. 'Ronald Reagan: Inspired Freedom. International Conference, Prague, Czech Republic.' *Prague Security Studies Institute*, 30 June – 1 July 2011, www.pssi.cz/conferences-and-roundtables/2 (Last accessed March 2013).

presseurop. 'Giving the Velvet Revolution the Finger.' *presseurop*, 23 November 2009, www.presseurop.eu/en/content/news-brief/142411-giving-velvet-revolution-finger (Last accessed February 2013).

Radio Prague. 'The "Velvet Revolution."' *Radio Prague's 'History Online' Virtual Exhibit*, http://archiv.radio.cz/history/history15.html (Last accessed October 2012).

Radosh, Ronald. 'Scoping Out the International Spy Museum.' *Academic Questions*, vol. 23, no. 3 (2010): pp. 287–97.

Rasmussen, Johannes Bach. *Travel Guide: Traces of the Cold War Period. The Countries around the Baltic Sea*. Copenhagen: Norden, 2010.

Reagan, Ronald. 'Remarks at the Annual Convention of the National Association of Evangelicals in Orlando, Florida.' *The Ronald Reagan Presidential Foundation & Library*, 8 March 1983, www.reaganfoundation.org/bw_detail.aspx?p=LMB4YGHF2& h1 = 0& h2 = 0& sw = & lm = berlinwall&args_a = cms&args_b = 74& argsb = N& tx = 1770 (Last accessed April 2013).

Reardon, Sarah. 'Manhattan Project National Park Plan Raises Questions.' *New Scientist*, 9 August 2012, www.newscientist.com/article/dn22157-manhattan-project-national-park-plan-raises-questions.html?page=1-.UdZHLxYwaqA (Last accessed March 2013).

Rečkovas, Konstantinas. 'Grutas Park: A Social Realism Museum Attracts 100,000 Visitors a Year.' *The Ukrainian Week*, 4 February 2012, http://ukrainianweek.com/History/41349 (Last accessed April 2013).

Record, Jeffrey. *Making War, Thinking History: Munich, Vietnam and Presidential Uses of Force from Korea to Kosovo*. Annapolis, Maryland: Naval Institute Press, 2002.

Renan, Ernest. '"What is a Nation?" (Lecture delivered at the Sorbonne on 11 March 1882).' Translated by Martin Thom. In *Becoming National: A Reader*, edited by Geoff Eley and Ronald Grigor Suny. New York: Oxford University Press, 1996, 42–56.

Rennie, David. 'Hungarians See Red over 1956 Monument.' *The Telegraph*, 29 July 2006, www.telegraph.co.uk/news/1525120/Hungarians-see-red-over-1956-monument.html (Last accessed April 2013).

Réthly, Ákos. *The Hungarian Revolution, 1956*. Budapest: Private Planet Books, 2006.

Reuters. 'Czechs Protest against Austerity Plans.' *Reuters*, 17 November 2011, www.reuters.com/article/2011/11/17/czech-protests-idUSL5E7MH3A620111117 (Last accessed February 2013).

Reynolds, David. *One World Divisible: A Global History since 1945*. London: Penguin Books, 2000.

Reynolds, Wayne. *Australia's Bid for the Bomb*. Melbourne: Melbourne University Press, 2000.

RIA Novosti. 'Ukraine's Communists Open Museum for U.S. Imperialism Victims.' *RIA Novosti*, 21 August 2007, http://en.rian.ru/world/20070821/73004087.html (Last accessed February 2013).

Richter, Jan. 'Národni třída: Prominent Prague Boulevard that has Witnessed History.' *Radio Praha*, 17 November 2010, www.radio.cz/en/section/special/narodni-trida-prominent-prague-boulevard-that-has-witnessed-history (Last accessed October 2012).

Roberts, Tom. *The Death Train*. 1998.

Robie, Dave. *Eyes of Fire: The Last Voyage of the Rainbow Warrior*. Auckland: Lindon, 1986.

The Rocky Flats Cold War Museum. 'Mission Statement.' *The Rocky Flats Cold War Museum*, www.rockyflatscoldwarmuseum.org/mission.html (Last accessed March 2013).

Rocky Flats Virtual Museum. '1969 Fire Exhibit.' *Rocky Flats Virtual Museum*, www.colorado.edu/journalism/cej/exhibit/index.html (Last accessed February 2013).

Rohrabacher, Mr Dana. 'Bill Text, 102nd Congress (1991–92), H.CON.RES.228.IH. Concerning an International Memorial to the Victims of Communism. (Introduced in House – IH).' *The Library of Congress*, 30 October 1991, http://thomas.loc.gov/cgi-bin/query/z?c102:H.CON.RES.228: (Last accessed February 2013).

Romaniec, Rosalia. 'From Antagonists to Friends: 20 Years of the German-Polish Treaty.' *Deutsche Welle (DW)*, 17 June 2011, www.dw.de/from-antagonists-to-friends-20-years-of-the-german-polish-treaty/a-15164723 (Last accessed June 2012).

'Ronald Reagan Statue to be unveiled in Hungary.' *Huffington Post*, 28 June 2011, www.huffingtonpost.com/2011/06/28/ronald-reagan-statue-hungary – n_885864.html (Last accessed March 2013).

Rosenberg, Emily. *A Date Which Will Live: Pearl Harbor in American Memory*. Durham & London: Duke University Press, 2003.

Royal Commission into British Nuclear Tests in Australia. 'The Report of the Royal Commission into British Nuclear Tests in Australia, Volume I.' Australian Government, Department of Resources, Energy and Tourism, 1985, www.ret.gov.au/resources/radioactive_waste/documents/royal commission into british nuclear tests in australia vol 1.pdf (Last accessed November 2012).

Sagatova, Dinara. 'Semipalatinsk Polygon: A Nuclear Test Site.' *Semipalatinsk Polygon*, www.dinarasagatova.com/polygon/ (Last accessed January 2013).

Salmon, John A. *Protecting America: Cold War Defensive Sites. A National Historic Landmark Theme Study*. Washington DC: National Historic Landmarks Program, US Department of Interior, 2011.

Sapolsky, Harvey M., Eugene Gholz, and Allen Kaufman. 'Security Lessons from the Cold War.' *Foreign Affairs*, vol. 78, no. 4 (1999): pp. 77–89.

'Sarov's Museum of Nuclear Weapons.' *RIA Novosti*, http://en.rian.ru/photolents/20130131/179143978_1/Sarovs-Museum-of-Nuclear-Weapons.html (Last accessed March 2013).

Schabas, William A. 'Convention on the Prevention and Punishment of the Crime of Genocide: Introduction, Procedural History, Documents, and Status.' *United Nations: Audiovisual Library of International Law*, http://untreaty.un.org/cod/avl/ha/cppcg/cppcg.html (Last accessed December 2012).

Schäfer, Stephanie. 'The Hiroshima Peace Memorial Museum and its Exhibition.' In *The Power of Memory in Modern Japan*, edited by Wolfgang Schwentker and Sven Saaler. Folkestone: Global Oriental, 2008: pp. 155–70.

Schell, Jonathan. 'The Spirit of June 12.' *The Nation*, 14 June 2007, www.thenation. com/article/spirit-june-12 – axzz2YFIGyR1t (Last accessed October 2012).

Schmid, Sonja D. 'Celebrating Tomorrow Today: The Peaceful Atom on Display in the Soviet Union.' *Social Studies of Science*, vol. 36, no. 3 (June 2006): pp. 331–65.

Schmidt, Mária, ed. *Terror Háza/House of Terror Museum: Catalogue*. Budapest: Public Endowment for Research in Central and East-European History and Society, 2008.

Schoenfeld, Gabriel. 'Twenty-Four Lies about the Cold War.' *Commentary*, March 1999, www.commentarymagazine.com/article/twenty-four-lies-about-the-cold-war/ (Last accessed December 2012).

Schrecker, Ellen. *Many are the Crimes: McCarthyism in America*. Boston: Little, Brown and Company, 1998.

Schreiter, Tobias. 'DDR Chic: Reliving East Germany in a Berlin Hotel.' *Spiegel Online International*, 26 June 2007, www.spiegel.de/international/zeitgeist/ddr-chic-reliving-east-germany-in-a-berlin-hotel-a-490847.html (Last accessed May 2013).

Scott, Len. *The Cuban Missile Crisis and the Threat of Nuclear War: Lessons from History*. London: Continuum, 2007.

Seltz, Daniel. 'Remembering the War and the Atomic Bombs: New Museums, New Approaches.' *Radical History Review*, vol. 72 (1999): pp. 92–108.

Sherif, Ann. *Japan's Cold War: Media, Literature, and the Law*. New York: Columbia University Press, 2009.

Sherlock, Thomas. *Historical Narratives in the Soviet Union and Post-Soviet Russia: Destroying the Settled Past, Creating an Uncertain Future*. New York: Palgrave Macmillan, 2007.

Shine, Greg. 'Presenting History at SF-88: An Exploration and Critical Analysis of the Role of Memory in Cold War Historical Interpretation at the Golden Gate National Recreation Area's Nike Missile Site SF-88.' *NikeMissile.org*, 1998, http://nikemissile.org/ColdWar/GregShine/shine.shtml (Last accessed December 2012).

Sibley, Katherine A.S. *The Cold War*. Westport, Connecticut: Greenwood Press, 1998.

Skoczek, Tadeusz, Krzysztof Mordyński, Stefan Artymowski, Paweł Bezak, and Sylwia Szczotka. *Museum of Independence in Warsaw from 11th November to 29th February 2012*. Kraków: Drukarnia Kolejowa, 2011.

Škodová, Alena. 'Memorial to the Victims of Communism Unveiled in Prague.' *Radio Praha*, 23 May 2002, www.radio.cz/en/section/curraffrs/memorial-to-the-victims-of-communism-unveiled-in-prague (Last accessed October 2012).

Skultāns, Vieda. *The Testimony of Lives: Narrative and Memory in Post-Soviet Latvia*. London: Routledge, 1998.

Smith, Anita. 'Colonialism and the Bomb in the Pacific.' In *Fearsome Heritage: Diverse Legacies of the Cold War*, edited by John Schofield and Wayne Cocroft. Walnut Creek, California: Left Coat Press, 2009: pp. 51–71.

Smith, Dinitia. 'For the Victims of Communism.' *The New York Times*, 23 December 1995, www.nytimes.com/1995/12/23/arts/for-the-victims-of-communism.html (Last accessed January 2013).

Smith, Jennifer, ed. *The Antinuclear Movement*. San Diego: Greenhaven Press, 2002.

Smith, Roy H. *The Nuclear Free and Independent Pacific Movement after Muroroa*. London: I.B.Tauris, 1997.

Snyder, Timothy. *Bloodlands: Europe between Hitler and Stalin.* New York: Basic Books, 2010.

Sontag, Susan. *Regarding the Pain of Others.* New York: Farrar, Straus and Giroux, 2003.

Stangarone, Troy, Andrew Kwon, and Peter Taves. 'Has North Korean Rhetoric Changed under Kim Jong-un?' *The Peninsula: Korea Economic Institute (KEI)*, 1 May 2013, http://blog.keia.org/2013/05/has-north-korean-rhetoric-changed-under-kim-jong-un/ (Last accessed May 2013).

StasiMuseum Berlin. 'House 1 – The Headquarter of the State Security.' *StasiMuseum Berlin*, www.stasimuseum.de/en/enindex.htm (Last accessed March 2013).

The State Atomic Energy Corporation (ROSATOM). 'About Nuclear Industry.' *ROSATOM*, www.rosatom.ru/en/about/nuclear_industry/ (Last accessed March 2013).

The State Central Museum of Contemporary History of Russia. 'Restoration of Economy. The History of the USSR in the After-War Period, 1946–53.' *The State Central Museum of Contemporary History of Russia*, http://eng.sovr.ru/expo/e11/ (Last accessed April 2013).

Statistics Lithuania. 'Census 2011 (Data from Population and Housing).' *Statistics Lithuania: Official Statistics Portal*, 2011, http://osp.stat.gov.lt/en/2011-m.-surasymas (Last accessed December 2012).

Steinberg, Marc. 'Anytime, Anywhere: Tetsuwan Atomu Stickers and the Emergence of Character Merchandizing.' *Theory, Culture & Society*, vol. 26, no. 2–3 (March/ May 2009): pp. 113–38.

Stephanson, Anders. *Manifest Destiny: American Expansion and the Empire of the Right.* New York: Hill and Wang, 1995.

Stern, Sheldon M. *The Cuban Missile Crisis in American Memory: Myths versus Reality.* Stanford, California: Stanford University Press, 2012.

———. *The Week the World Stood Still: Inside the Secret Cuban Missile Crisis.* Stanford, California: Stanford University Press, 2005.

Subterranea Britannica, http://www.subbrit.org.uk (Last accessed October 2012).

Süß, Walter, and Douglas Selvage. 'e-Dossier No. 37 – KGB/Stasi Cooperation.' *Wilson Center: Cold War International History Project*, www.wilsoncenter.org/ publication/e-dossier-no-37-kgbstasi-cooperation (Last accessed May 2013).

Swerdlow, Amy. *Women Strike for Peace: Traditional Motherhood and Radical Politics in the 1960s.* Chicago: University of Chicago Press, 1993.

Symms, Mr Steve. 'Bill Text, 102nd Congress (1991–92), S.CON.RES.55.IS. To Call for the Construction of an International Memorial to the Victims of Communism (Introduced in Senate – IS).' *The Library of Congress*, 8 July 1991, http://thomas.loc.gov/cgi-bin/query/z?c102:S.CON.RES.55: (Last accessed February 2013).

Szasz, Ferenc M., and Issei Takechi. 'Atomic Heroes and Atomic Monsters: American and Japanese Cartoonists Confront the Onset of the Nuclear Age, 1945–80.' *The Historian*, vol. 69, no. 4 (Winter 2007): pp. 728–52.

Szonyi, Michael. *Cold War Island: Quemoy on the Front Line.* Cambridge: Cambridge University Press, 2008.

Takada, Jun. *Chinese Nuclear Tests.* Tokyo: Iryo Kagakusha, 2009.

Tanter, Richard. 'Indonesia's Dangerous Silence.' *Inside Story: Current Affairs and Culture from Australia and Beyond*, 28 April 2011, http://inside.org.au/indonesia-dangerous-silence/ (Last accessed May 2013).

Taylor, Bryan C. 'Revis(it)ing Nuclear History: Narrative Conflict at the Bradbury Science Museum.' *Studies in Cultures, Organizations and Societies*, vol. 3, no. 1 (1997): pp. 119–45.

Taylor, Jerome. 'The World's Worst Radiation Hotspot.' *The Independent*, 10 September 2009, www.independent.co.uk/news/world/europe/the-worlds-worst-radiation-hotspot-1784502.html (Last accessed November 2012).

Telegraph, The. 'Ronald Reagan Statue Unveiled in Warsaw.' *The Telegraph*, 21 November 2011, www.telegraph.co.uk/news/worldnews/europe/poland/8904456/Ronald-Reagan-statue-unveiled-in-Warsaw.html (Last accessed February 2013).

Thompson, Angela. 'The Wende Museum and Archive of the Cold War.' *Angela Thompson's Website*, 2012, http://angela-thompson.com/english/Wende_Museum_English_Version.pdf (Last accessed April 2013).

Times, The Epoch. 'China Blasts Bush Tribute to Victims of Communism.' *The Epoch Times*, 14 June 2007, www.theepochtimes.com/news/7-6-14/56486.html (Last accessed January 2013).

Titan Missile Museum. 'Welcome to the Titan Missile Museum: A Rare Journey into Cold War History.' *Titan Missile Museum*, www.titanmissilemuseum.org (Last accessed April 2013).

Tökés, Rudolf. *Hungary's Negotiated Revolution: Economic Reform, Social Change and Political Succession, 1957–1990*. Cambridge: Cambridge University Press, 1996.

'Toppling of Dominoes marks Fall of Berlin Wall.' *CBC News*, 9 November 2009, www.cbc.ca/news/world/story/2009/11/09/berlin-wall-celebrations.html (Last accessed June 2012).

Torbakov, Igor. 'History, Memory and National Identity: Understanding the Politics of History and Memory Wars in Post-Soviet Lands.' *Demokratizatsiya: The Journal of Post-Soviet Democratization*, vol. 19, no. 3 (2011), 209–32.

Tosh, John. *Why History Matters*. Houndmills: Palgrave Macmillan, 2008.

TripAdvisor. 'Bunker-42 on Taganka (Cold War Museum).' *TripAdvisor: The World's largest Travel Site*, www.tripadvisor.com.au/Attraction_Review-g298484-d2141443-Reviews-Bunker_42_on_Taganka_Cold_War_Museum-Moscow_Central_Russia.html (Last accessed November 2012).

Trotnow, Helmut, ed. *Ein Alliierten-Museum für Berlin/An Allied Museum for Berlin/Un Musée des Alliés à Berlin*. Berlin: Ruksaldruck, Summer 1995.

Tsutsui, William M., and Machiko Ito, eds. *In Godzilla's Footsteps: Japanese Pop Culture Icons on the Global Stage*. New York: Palgrave Macmillan, 2006.

Tsygankov, Andrei P. *Russophobia: Anti-Russian Lobby and American Foreign Policy*. New York: Palgrave Macmillan, 2009.

Tuchner, Michael. *The Sinking of the Rainbow Warrior*. 93 mins. 1993.

Tůma, Oldřich, Mária Schmidt, Juraj Marušiak, Gábor Gyáni, and Paweł Ukielski. 'Teaching History in Central Europe.' *Visegrad Insight*, vol. 1, no. 3 (2013): pp. 6–11.

Tweedie, Neil. '1961: Codeword to Enter Secret Bunker at the End of the World.' *The Telegraph*, 30 December 2011, www.telegraph.co.uk/news/uknews/defence/8978410/1961-files-codeword-to-enter-secret-bunker-at-the-end-of-the-world.html (Last accessed March 2013).

Týc, Roman. 'Galerie.' *romantyc*, http://romantyc.info/galerie/ (Last accessed February 2013).

UK Qualifications and Curriculum Authority. *History: Programme of Study for Key Stage 3 and Attainment Target (Extract from The National Curriculum 2007)*. Qualifications and Curriculum Authority: Crown Copyright, 2007.

UNESCO. 'Budapest, including the Banks of the Danube, the Buda Castle Quarter and Andrássy Avenue.' *UNESCO World Heritage List*, whc.unesco.org/en/list/400/ (Last accessed October 2012).

UNESCO World Heritage Committee. '11COM VII.A Inscription: Budapest, the Banks of the Danube with the District of Buda Castle (Hungary).' *UNESCO*, whc. unesco.org/en/decisions/3728 (Last accessed October 2012).

United Nations. 'Convention on the Prevention and Punishment of the Crime of Genocide.' *United Nations*, 9 December 1948, www.un.org/millennium/law/iv-1.htm (Last accessed December 2012).

United Nations Special Committee on the Problem of Hungary. 'United Nations Report of the Special Committee on the Problem of Hungary: General Assembly, Official Records, Eleventh Session, Supplement No. 18 (A/3592).' *Magyar Elektronikus Könyvtár (MEK)*, 1957, http://mek.oszk.hu/01200/01274/01274.pdf (Last accessed November 2012).

University of East Anglia. 'Cold War Anglia Revealed.' *University of East Anglia*, 30 March 2013, www.uea.ac.uk/mac/comm/media/press/2013/March/cold-war-anglia-project (Last accessed April 2013).

U.S. Department of State. 'Milestones: 1953–60. The Warsaw Treaty Organization, 1955.' *U.S. Department of State, Office of the Historian*, http://history.state.gov/milestones/1953–60/WarsawTreaty (Last accessed April 2013).

U.S. Environmental Protection Agency. 'Vint Hill Farms Station: Current Site Information.' *U.S. Environmental Protection Agency*, May 2010, www.epa.gov/reg3hscd/npl/VA8210020931.htm (Last accessed February 2013).

Vanderbilt, Tom. *Survival City: Adventures among the Ruins of Atomic America*. New York: Princeton Architectural Press, 2002.

Vaughan, David. 'The Revolution Begins.' *Radio Praha*, 11 August 2012, www.radio.cz/en/section/archives/the-revolution-begins-1 (Last accessed October 2012).

Veitch, James. 'A Sordid Act: The Rainbow Warrior Incident.' *New Zealand International Review*, vol. 35, no. 4 (July 2010): pp. 6–9.

Verheyen, Dirk. *United City, Divided Memories? Cold War Legacies in Contemporary Berlin*. Lanham, Maryland: Lexington Books, 2008.

Victims of Communism Memorial Foundation. 'About the Foundation.' *Victims of Communism Memorial Foundation*, www.victimsofcommunism.org/about/ (Last accessed January 2013).

——. 'About the Foundation: International Advisory Council.' *Victims of Communism Memorial Foundation*, www.webcitation.org/5yrIl6tyj (Last accessed January 2013).

——. 'Global Museum on Terrorism.' *Global Museum on Terrorism*, www.globalmuseumoncommunism.org (Last accessed March 2013).

——. 'Main Exhibits.' *Global Museum on Communism*, www.globalmuseumoncommunism.org/exhibits (Last accessed March 2013).

——. 'Museum Mission.' *Global Museum on Communism*, www.globalmuseumoncommunism.org/content/museum-mission (Last accessed January 2013).

——. 'Museum Overview.' *Global Museum on Communism*, www.globalmuseumoncommunism.org/museum_overview (Last accessed January 2013).

——. 'Quiz on Communism.' *Global Museum on Communism*, www.globalmuseumoncommunism.org/quiz_communism (Last accessed January 2013).

——. 'Truman-Reagan Medal of Freedom.' *Global Museum on Communism*, www.globalmuseumoncommunism.org/content/truman-reagan-medal-freedom (Last accessed March 2013).

——. 'Victims of Communism Memorial.' *Global Museum on Communism*, www. globalmuseumoncommunism.org/content/victims-communism-memorial   (Last accessed January 2013).

Vietnam Military History Museum. 'An Introduction of Viet Nam Military History Museum: A Snapshot of its Establishment and Development Process.' *Vietnam Military History Museum*, www.btlsqsvn.org.vn/?act=mn_index& lgid = 2 (Last accessed March 2013).

VilNews. 'Napoleon Named Vilnius "Jerusalem of the North."' *VilNews: The Voice of International Lithuania*, 9 January 2011, http://vilnews.com/2011–01-napoleon-named-vilnius-'jerusalem-of-the-north' (Last accessed January 2013).

Vint Hill Economic Development Authority. 'About.' *Vint Hill*, www.vinthill.com/about/ (Last accessed April 2013).

——. 'Real Estate.' *Vint Hill*, www.vinthill.com/real-estate/ (Last accessed April 2013).

Vodafone. 'Press Release: People Responded to Vodafone's Appeal by Collecting over 85 Thousand Keys.' *Vodafone: Czech Republic*, December 2009, www.vodafone.cz/en/about-vodafone/press-releases/message-detail/people-responded-to-vodafones-appeal-by-1/ (Last accessed April 2013).

——. 'Press Release: The Public Unveiling of Jiří David's Key Sculpture will Take Place on the 9th of March at 11AM on Franz Kafka Square (náměstí Franze Kafky) in Prague.' *Vodafone: Czech Republic*, March 2010, www.vodafone.cz/en/about-vodafone/press-releases/message-detail/the-public-unveiling-of-jiri-davids-key-1/ (Last accessed April 2013).

Voices of the Manhattan Project, http://manhattanprojectvoices.org (Last accessed March 2013).

Vulliamy, Ed. 'David Cameron's Rightwing "Allies" March in Riga to Commemorate the SS: Row over SS Veterans' Parade in Latvia Puts the Spotlight on Tory Links to Eastern Europe's Far Right Nazi Sympathisers.' *The Guardian*, 14 March 2010, www.guardian.co.uk/world/2010/mar/14/latvia-divided-communists-nazis   (Last accessed March 2013).

Walker, J. Samuel. 'Recent Literature on Truman's Atomic Bomb Decision: The Search for Middle Ground.' *Diplomatic History*, vol. 29, no. 2 (2005): pp. 311–34.

Walker, Martin. *The Cold War and the Making of the Modern World.* New York: H. Holt, 1995.

Walsh, Ben. *GCSE Modern World History.* 2nd ed. London: Hodder Education, 2001.

Waterfield, Doug. 'The Doomtown Series.' *DougWaterfield.com*, http://dougwaterfield.com/portfolio/doomtown (Last accessed March 2013).

Weeks, Theodore R. 'Remembering and Forgetting: Creating a Soviet Lithuanian Capital, Vilnius 1944–49.' *Journal of Baltic Studies*, vol. 39, no. 4 (2008): pp. 517–33.

Welzer, Harald, Sabine Moller, and Karoline Tschuggnall. *'Opa war kein Nazi': Nationalsozialismus und Holocaust im Familiengedächtnis.* Frankfurt-am-Main: Fischer Verlag, 2002.

White, Anne. 'The Memorial Society in the Russian Provinces.' *Europe-Asia Studies*, vol. 47, no. 8 (1995): pp. 1343–66.

White, John Kenneth. *Still Seeing Red: How the Cold War Shapes New American Politics.* Boulder, Colorado: Westview, 1997.

Whitehair, Jennifer. 'Flashback Friday: When the Atom was King.' *Vegas.com*, 7 August 2009, http://blog.vegas.com/more-las-vegas-news/flashback-friday-when-the-atom-was-king-2633/ (Last accessed April 2013).

Wiener, Jon. *How We Forgot the Cold War: A Historical Journey across America.* Berkeley: University of California Press, 2012.

Winter, Jay. *Remembering War: The Great War between Memory and History in the Twentieth Century.* New Haven: Yale University Press, 2006.

——. *Sites of Memory, Sites of Mourning: The Great War in European Cultural History.* Cambridge: University Press, 1996.

Winter, Jay, and Emmanuel Sivan. 'Setting the Framework.' In *War and Remembrance in the Twentieth Century*, edited by Jay Winter and Emmanuel Sivan. Cambridge: Cambridge University Press, 1999: pp. 6–39.

Wittner, Lawrence S. *The Struggle against the Bomb.* 3 vols. Vol. 1. *One World or None: A History of the World Nuclear Disarmament Movement through 1953*, Stanford: Stanford University Press, 1993.

——. *The Struggle against the Bomb.* 3 vols. Vol. 2. *Resisting the Bomb: A History of the World Nuclear Disarmament Movement, 1954–70*, Stanford: Stanford University Press, 1997.

——. *The Struggle against the Bomb.* 3 vols. Vol. 3. *Toward Nuclear Abolition: A History of the World Nuclear Disarmament Movement, 1971 to the Present*, Stanford: Stanford University Press, 2003.

——. *Working for Peace and Justice: Memoirs of an Activist Intellectual.* Knoxville: University of Tennessee Press, 2012.

Wituska, Krystyna. *Inside a Gestapo Prison: The Letters of Krystyna Wituska, 1942–1944.* Detroit: Wayne State University Press, 2006.

Wohlmuth, Radek. 'Památník 17. listopadu na Národní třídě hajluje a fuckuje.' *Týden*, 22 November 2009, www.tyden.cz/rubriky/kultura/vytvarne-umeni/pamatnik-17-listopadu-na-narodni-tride-hajluje-a-fuckuje_149002.html (Last accessed February 2013).

Woodward, Mark. 'Only Now can We Speak: Remembering Politicide in Yogyakarta.' *Sojourn: Journal of Social Sciences in Southeast Asia*, vol. 26, no. 1 (2011): pp. 36–57.

World Health Organization (WHO). 'Ionizing Radiation: Health Effects of the Chernobyl Accident.' *World Health Organization*, April 2011, www.who.int/ionizing_radiation/chernobyl/en/ (Last accessed November 2012).

World Heritage Committee. 'UNESCO World Heritage Convention concerning the Protection of the World Cultural and Natural Heritage, World Heritage Committe Report, Twentieth Session, Merida, Mexico, 2–7 December 1996, Annex V: Statements by China and the United States of America during the Inscription of the Hiroshima Peace Memorial (Genbaku Dome).' *UNESCO*, 1996, whc.unesco.org/archive/repco96x.htm – annex5 (Last accessed February 2012).

Wulf, Andrew. *Moscow '59: The 'Sokolniki Summit' Revisited.* Los Angeles: Figueroa Press, 2010.

Xia, Yafeng. 'The Study of Cold War International History: A Review of the Last Twenty Years.' *Journal of Cold War Studies*, vol. 10, no. 1 (2008): pp. 81–115.

Xiangrui, Liu, and Huang Zhiling. 'City Bases Smart Success on Legacy.' *China Daily*, 1 March 2012, www.chinadaily.com.cn/bizchina/innovative/2012–03/01/content_14740592.htm (Last accessed April 2013).

Yahoo! News. 'Prague names Street after Ronald Reagan.' *Yahoo! News*, 1 July 2011, http://news.yahoo.com/prague-names-street-ronald-reagan-165059516.html (Last accessed March 2013).

Young, James E. 'Holocaust Museums in Germany, Poland, Israel, and the United States.' In *Contemporary Responses to the Holocaust*, edited by Konrad Kwiet and Jürgen Matthäus. Westport: Praeger, 2004: pp. 249–74.

——. *The Texture of Memory: Holocaust Memorials and Meaning.* New Haven: Yale University Press, 1993.

Zalatnay, István. 'Meditation on the 1956 Monument in Budapest.' *Hungarian Review*, 18 November 2011, www.hungarianreview.com/article/meditation_on_the_monument (Last accessed February 2013).

Zertal, Idith. *Israel's Holocaust and the Politics of Nationhood.* Cambridge: Cambridge University Press, 2005.

Ziino, Bart, ed. *Remembering the Great War.* (Series editors David Lowe and Tony Joel, Remembering the Modern World.) Abingdon, Oxon: Routledge, 2014 (scheduled).

Zurbuchen, Mary S. 'Memory and the "1965 Incident" in Indonesia.' *Asian Survey*, vol. 42, no. 4 (2002): pp. 564–81.

Index

Note: page numbers in **bold** refer to illustrations.